M

REPRESENTATIVE ONE-ACT PLAYS BY AMERICAN AUTHORS

SELECTED, WITH BIOGRAPHICAL NOTES

BY

MARGARET GARDNER MAYORGA, M.A.

BOSTON

LITTLE, BROWN, AND COMPANY

1925

DEDICATED

TO MY MOTHER

PREFACE

THIS collection contains twenty-four of the most significant one-act plays of the Little Theatre movement in America. Some of them have not been previously printed; others have been out of print for some time or are inaccessible. I have made the collection in the hope that by bringing them together in one volume they will not be immediately lost. Although the war has for a moment scattered many of the Little Theatres and stunted the growth of the new play form, it is because the art is now at a pause that it may be more easily surveyed.

While there are many who believe that one-act plays are more or less frivolous and ought to be enjoyed rather than analyzed, I have taken the liberty, in this collection, of being serious. Too often the frothy one-act play has been exploited and the sincere effort overlooked, but it is indeed true that beneath the movement as a whole there exists a purpose worthy of serious consideration.

During the last few years, both here and abroad, there has been discussion of the one-act play which has been feeling toward the establishment of the one-act form as a new and distinct type. The few who have written about it are agreed that the one-act play is properly analogous to the short-story, that it is quite as rigid a form, and that it is as different a type from the longer play as the short-story is from the novel. It cannot, if a good one-act play, be either expanded into three acts or condensed from the longer play without a loss. Because of this integrity, the one-act play is an art form, tending toward a perfect whole, and therein lies its contrast to the playlet of vaudeville and to the curtain raiser. The one-act

play is not the familiar vaudeville sketch; upon this point
the vaudeville managers are quite as insistent as are the
managers of the Little Theatres. The vaudeville managers
have been extremely wary of the intrusion of the new
type. In return, the managers of the Little Theatres have
had small desire to produce the vaudeville playlets.

But to understand the new play one must know something
of the theatres which have cultivated it: the so-called "Little
Theatres." To the uninitiated the term is vague, and even
those who are acquainted with it use it more or less loosely.
Speaking generally, the Little Theatre may be said to be an
organization of earnest workers interested more in the future
of the drama than in their own pecuniary gains. The size
of the theatre is of no vital consideration, although it happens
that the type of drama which is now prevalent can be most
successfully presented in a small playhouse. Specifically,
the Little Theatres are those small playhouses which are
dotting the land from coast to coast, termed variously:
amateur, social, community, but more often "Little",
and in which some local company produces at regular inter-
vals and with a sincere purpose its repertory of plays. There
are the private clubs, such as the Plays and Players of
Philadelphia; private theatres, such as the Bramhall Playhouse of New York; high school organizations, such as Our
Little Theatre of South Bend, Indiana; college workshops,
as at Harvard; theatre societies (without a box office), such
as the Provincetown Players; theatre workshops, such as
the New York organization of that name; Little Theatres
nominally and little theatres in size. Since the first venture
of 1906 there have arisen some eighty of them.[1] More often
than not these companies produce the one-act play, both
because it is more easily sustained than a longer play of
corresponding aim, and because it is an experiment on a
smaller scale. In spite of the fact that many of the plays

[1] For a list of these, see Appendix of Constance D'Arcy Mackay: "Little
Theatres in the United States", and Appendix of Thomas H. Dickinson:
"The Insurgent Theatre."

have been handicapped by crude scenery and cruder acting, some have emerged full of promise for the one-act form.

In making the selection for this volume, I have made no attempt to include only the best one-act plays; such a collection would need to exclude many which, in aim if not in execution, are exceedingly significant. For in a new movement we are interested far more in the potentiality of growth than in the first offspring, however perfect some of the first may be.

But in tracing the veins of development, I encountered the necessity of inventing in some places a new terminology. Although connotations will immediately present themselves to many, some further definition may not be amiss. The term "dramatic episode" has hitherto been variously used, but never to designate a distinct type; the term "impressionistic episode" has not been previously employed.

I have used "dramatic episode" to designate the play which presents a single and complete static situation, as opposed to the tragedy or the comedy which presents a series of situations or the developing situation. *In the Zone* is an example of the type. It presents one complete episode in the passage of a tramp steamer through the war zone. The play opens upon a group of sailors assembled in the forecastle and closes upon the same group. Although each man has added another experience to his life during the progress of the play, he is essentially the same person when the curtain falls as he was when it arose. There has been no development of character. Similarly, the action of the group is no farther advanced at the end of the play than it was at the beginning. It is conceivable that the entire episode might recur. The play is not one of development, but of exposition.

In the same manner the "impressionistic episode" is a play of exposition, but it differs from the "dramatic episode" in that it is subjective where the "dramatic episode" is objective. It is the play of mood; it is the "dramatic episode" shown to us through the personality of the author. The other terms are familiarly employed and need no explanation, although it might prove wise to mention that I have used "fantasy" rigidly for the play which tends to the dominance of fancy, and "poetic drama", whether in verse or prose, for the play of imagination.

The classification represents every type of play which has been produced in the Little Theatres, and the space devoted to each type in the volume is approximate to its importance in Little Theatre history. The arrangement of grouping was necessitated by the aim to represent types rather than theatres or sections of the country, and has no reason in its arrangement other than that it seemed to be psychological. The plays have all been produced by Little Theatres in this country, some many times; and probably there is no Little Theatre audience which will not immediately recognize at least one of its own plays.

It is to be hoped that the selection may in some way give satisfaction to the generous friends who have so kindly helped in its compilation. Authors have willingly sent plays for my perusal; managers and producers have everywhere helped me to find the authors. But particularly am I indebted to those whose plays are here included. I have to thank the New York centre of the Drama League, among others, for the opportunity it gave me of reading rare and scattered publications. Special acknowledgment must be made to the publishers, and especially to Mr. Roland Holt, for their permissions to reprint — without which the book would not have been possible. For valuable suggestions I am indebted to Mr. Clayton Hamilton and Mr. D. L. Clark of Columbia University, Dr. Edgar A. Hall and Mr. Emory Holloway of Adelphi College, Miss Rica Brenner and Miss Gertrude A. Smith. My personal gratitude must further extend to all those whose single acts have brought this work to its completion.

M. G. M.

June, 1919.

CONTENTS

xi

CONTENTS

THE ONE–ACT PLAY

AFTER the manner of the short-story, the one-act play may be spelled with the hyphen, for the form has developed certain compact qualities during the last twenty-five years which make it seem to parallel the short-story form.

The one-act play, however, is not new. Short plays, like tales, have always existed, although the short humorous play shows a continuous development which the short serious play lacks. Indeed, it is possible to trace back the one-act farce as far as the Commédia dell' arte, and probably, although the intervening history may involve more or less conjecture, even to the "satyric" play of the Greeks. In the Commédia dell' arte, at least, the skits and pranks of Harlequin, Punchinello, and their companions were presented in a short farcical form. In fact, the Commédia dell' arte consisted almost entirely of one-act farces. From Italy the farce passed to Spain and France, from France to Germany and to England, and thence, finally, to America. Among the one-act plays of the Little Theatre to-day is found the direct descendant of the form.

From the one-act farce the short comedy arose. It may have developed because of the fact that Molière could not write a farce without basing it upon life, and that he occasionally wrote plays of one act. However that may be, the one-act plays of Molière are the first to show the comedy spirit. Among his contemporaries was Noël Hauteroche, whose one-act plays, which were truly more comic than farcical, were among the earliest to be generally recognized and used in the Comédie (1672). His work, although it shows the strong influence of the old farce, is based primarily upon French life. After Hauteroche, La Fontaine further developed the one-act comedy, and after him there follows a long line — Dancourt, Dufresny, Le Grand, Le Sage, Lafont, Destouches, Boissy, and others, to the present time — all of whom have used the one-act form as a comic type.

England, too, has had a definite one-act humorous play, beginning probably with Haywood's Interludes and extending through Robert Cox's Drolleries to Lacy's British Drama and the curtain raisers of the present day. In Germany also, and in Spain particularly, there has been a correspondingly continuous development of the short humorous form.

The serious play of one act, however, fails to show such continuous development. Its appearance, until the latter part of the nineteenth century, has been sporadic. The reason for this may be found in the fact that formerly the shorter form was not held in such high repute as the longer, but was considered well enough for buffoonery which would tire were it extended, or for humorous dialogue which contained little action and of which the dramatic possibilities were soon exhausted. In its early form it might be likened to the conversational sketch with sometimes incidental horse play between two people of our vaudeville stage. In proportion as the short form had come to be associated with the slap-stick drama, it was considered not a serious form, nor the most worthy.

Although there did develop a short religious drama, this arose from the people, and was looked upon rather as a form of religion than of art. This drama included the mysteries, miracle plays, moralities, and passion plays which grew up from the primitive soil of all nations. These plays constituted, moreover, a growth and a death in themselves, and show no extraneous development. There were also the short and serious school plays of England and of Holland, but neither did these foster a continuous one-act drama. Although throughout the nineteenth century there were sporadic appearances in England of a one-act play which was not comic — a romantic drama, a historic drama, a dramatic sketch — present records show that scarcely one a year was produced during the century. Should future research bring to light even several times that many, it could not be said that the serious one-act play was a developed type. The mass of curtain raisers were farce, comedy, travesty, extravaganza, burlesque, burletta, comic opera, operetta, and comedietta. Nor was the serious one-act play which did exist known outside of England; it could not have influenced France and Germany in the recent development. In Germany, Hans Sachs employed the short play, but his influence was popular, not literary, and it did not institute a genre. The more or less continuous serious play of Spain has also not been known outside of the country. Nor have any of these nineteenth-century plays in any country aspired to a literary art.

Yet with the twentieth century, there has appeared almost simultaneously in Germany, England, France, and in America, a serious and literary one-act form. It has not been caused by the American vaudeville melodrama, for where this is either a patched and pasty cardboard production or the result of condensing a full-length play into a playlet, the new one-act play is sufficient unto itself, and has for its purpose, in addition to dramatic appeal, perfection of form.

Where, then, was the inception of the literary one-act play, a form which Maeterlinck, Sudermann, Barrie, Shaw, Hauptmann, and many others considered worthy of their pens? It seems that some definite force must have entered the theatre at the end of the nineteenth century to cause a simultaneous and prolific growth of such plays from many nations, where, previously, the one-act form had not been thought the highest type of drama. In the short farcical conversations, humor alone had been relied upon to hold the attention of the audience, for drama, such as that of Euripides, Shakespeare, Racine, Goethe, could not develop itself within the compass of one act. But Ibsen brought the dramatic idea. An idea, such a one as is the theme of an act of Hauptmann's "Weavers" or of Barker's "Madras House", can present a dramatic development or a series of dramatic developments within a short space of time, and furthermore, can do it as effectively in one act as in several. Accordingly, if the one-act play embodies an "idea", it gains dramatic possibilities. By just such a substitution of idea for mere humor the one-act play has been lifted above the realm of farce and buffoonery. It is improbable that any writer or writers set about deliberately to dignify the one-act form; it so happens, however, that whereas what had formerly been considered the best drama could not present itself effectively in one act, the newer drama can. The fact that Great Britain has taken the lead both in the drama of ideas and in the serious one-act play makes it seem possible that the impulse which produced the one may be responsible for both fields of endeavor.

But in any survey of the one-act play, the free theatre must also be considered. It is true that the free theatre was created in order to produce the plays of Ibsen and his followers, and probable that the new one-act drama has been created in order to sustain the free theatre. Otherwise the fact that the "dramatic idea" had made the one-act form usable might not alone account for its universal use. Given an art theatre, the production of a good short play is always preferable to that of a poor long one. With the high ideals of the free theatres and the small number of plays of the Ibsen rank, the one-act play seems the inevitable consequence.

But there is yet another cause for its general use. By the end of the nineteenth century the short-story had come to be a developed type. However differently it was applied by the people of the various nations, it everywhere fostered the belief in a short form with a singleness of impression for its purpose. People had become accustomed to the small unit, and had learned to admire it. Its application in the field of drama was only a step. On investigation, one finds that many of the writers of one-act plays are also writers of short stories.

Local conditions, it is true, have had a great deal to do with the development of the one-act form in each country, for although the impulse was everywhere the same, the results have differed. In England, for instance, during the nineteenth century, the two-act play had been more generally used than in other countries; therefore the step to the one-act play was correspondingly short. In Ireland, the presence of a National Theatre and the lack, at that time, of a national playwright, called forth directly a body of one-act literature. Germany was friendly to the one-act form because her naturalistic turn of mind at this time rendered even her longer drama episodic.

It is from the universal acceptance of the serious one-act play as a new form that the desire to regard the humorous play in the same manner has arisen. The effect of this desire has been a remolding of all the short plays, whether they have been comedy, farce, or melodrama, to conform with the new ideals, so that, in spite of their heredity, many of these plays are now developing toward the art type.

Because the development of the type is still transitional, its history can hardly yet be written. Any selection of one-act plays at the present time must include many which are directly descended from the old farce and are not really exponents of the new play. But there must be enough of the new, also, to prove that it exists, and in America, which has shown itself so able to excel in the short-story, the development of the one-act play is significant.

REPRESENTATIVE ONE-ACT PLAYS

SAM AVERAGE

PERCY MACKAYE

MR. PERCY MACKAYE is so well known that little need
be said of him here. He was born in New York on March
16, 1875, of a family which had already won laurels for
itself in drama. His father, Steele MacKaye, wrote some
twenty-five plays in about the same number of years, and
the son, Percy, has written more than twenty-five in four-
teen years.

Mr. MacKaye was educated at Harvard University, and
later studied at the University of Leipzig. Dartmouth
College conferred upon him the honorary degree of Master
of Arts in 1914. He has traveled extensively in Europe,
residing a different times at Rome, Brunnen (Switzerland),
Leipzig, and London. From 1900 to 1904 he taught in a
private school in New York. But since that time he has
been engaged entirely in dramatic art. He is a member
of the National Institute of Arts and Letters.

Mr. MacKaye's efforts in the dramatic field have been
varied. He has to his credit masques, pageants, operas,
as well as plays; and he is, in addition, an able lecturer and
contributor to magazines. His works are: "A Garland
to Sylvia", "The Canterbury Pilgrims", "The Scarecrow",
"Fenris the Wolf", "Jeanne D'Arc", "Sappho and Phaon",
"Mater", "Anti-Matrimony", "Tomorrow", "Yankee Fantasies" (five one-act plays), "A Thousand Years Ago",
"Saint-Gaudens Masque, Prologue", Gloucester Pageant,
Pittsburgh Pageant, "Sanctuary" (a Bird Masque), Saint

Louis Masque, "The New Citizenship", "Caliban", "Sinbad, The Sailor", "The Immigrants", "The Canterbury Pilgrims", "Washington, the Man Who Made Us."

Of his "Yankee Fantasies", "Sam Average" is perhaps the most popular.

SAM AVERAGE

A SILHOUETTE

***

By PERCY MACKAYE

"Sam Average" was originally produced at the Toy Theatre, Boston, on February 26, 1912.

Original Cast

ANDREW . . . . Mr. Freedley
JOEL . . . . Mr. Bunker
ELLEN . . . . Miss Lingard
SAM AVERAGE . . . . Mr. Menard

SAM AVERAGE

SCENE. *An intrenchment in Canada, near Niagara Falls, in the year 1814. Night, shortly before dawn.*

On the right, the dull glow of a smouldering wood-fire ruddies the earthen embankment, the low-stretched outline of which forms, with darkness, the scenic background.

Near the centre, left, against the dark, a flag with stars floats from its standard.

Beside the fire, ANDREW, *reclined, gazes at a small frame in his hand; near him is a knapsack, with contents emptied beside it.*

On the embankment, JOEL, *with a gun, paces back and forth, a blanket thrown about his shoulders.*

JOEL (*with a singing call*). Four o'clock! — All 's well!

[*Jumping down from the embankment, he approaches the fire.*

ANDREW. By God, Joel, it 's bitter.

JOEL (*rubbing his hands over the coals*). A mite sharpish.

ANDREW (*looks up eagerly*). What?

JOEL. Cuts sharp, for Thanksgivin'.

ANDREW (*sinks back, gloomily*). Oh! (*A pause*) I wondered you should agree with me. You meant the weather. I meant —

[*A pause again.*

JOEL. Well, Andy : what 'd you mean?

ANDREW. Life.

JOEL. Shucks!

ANDREW (*to himself*). Living!

JOEL (*sauntering over left, listens*). Hear a rooster crow?

ANDREW. No. What are you doing?

JOEL. Tiltin' the flag over crooked in the dirt. That 's our signal.

ANDREW. Nothing could be more appropriate, unless we buried it — buried it in the dirt!

JOEL. She 's to find us where the flag 's turned down. I fixed that with the sergeant all right. The rooster crowin' 's *her* watch-word for us.

ANDREW. An eagle screaming, Joel: that would have been better. (*Rising*) — Ah!
[*He laughs painfully.*

JOEL. Hush up, Andy! The nearest men ain't two rods away. You 'll wake 'em. Pitch it low.

ANDREW. Don't be alarmed. I 'm coward enough.

JOEL. 'Course, though, there ain't much danger. I 'm sentinel this end, and the sergeant has the tip at t'other. Besides, you may call it the reg'lar thing. There 's been two thousand deserters already in this tuppenny-ha'penny war, and none on 'em the worse off. When a man don't get his pay for nine months — well, he ups and takes his vacation: why not? When Nell joins us, we 'll hike up the Niagara, cross over to Tonawanda and take our breakfast in Buffalo. By that time, the boys here will be marchin' away toward Lundy's Lane.

ANDREW (*walks back and forth, shivering*). I 'm afraid.

JOEL. 'Fraid? Bosh!

ANDREW. I 'm afraid to face —

JOEL. Face what? — We won't get caught.

ANDREW. Your sister — my wife.

JOEL. Nell! — Why, ain't she comin' here just a-purpose to get you? Ain't there reason enough, Lord knows? Ain't you made up your mind to light out home anyhow?

ANDREW. Yes; that 's just what she 'll never forgive me for. In her heart she 'll never think of me the same. For she knows as well as I what pledge I 'll be breaking — what sacred pledge.

JOEL. What you mean?

ANDREW. No matter, no matter: this is gush.
[*He returns to the fire and begins to fumble over the contents of his knapsack. Joel watches him idly.*

JOEL. One of *her* curls?

ANDREW (*looking at a lock of hair, in the firelight*). No; the baby's, little Andy's. Some day they'll tell him how his father —

[*He winces, and puts the lock away.*

JOEL (*going toward the embankment*). Listen!

ANDREW (*ties up the package, muttering*). Son of a traitor!

JOEL (*tiptoeing back*). It's crowed. — That's her.

[*Leaping to his feet, Andrew stares toward the embankment where the flag is dipped; then turns his back to it, closing his eyes and gripping his hands.*

After a pause, silently the figure of a YOUNG WOMAN *emerges from the dark and stands on the embankment. She is bare-headed and ill-clad.*

Joel touches Andrew, who turns and looks toward her.

Silently, she steals down to him and they embrace.

ANDREW. My Nell!

ELLEN. Nearly a year —

ANDREW. Now, at last!

ELLEN. Hold me close, Andy.

ANDREW. You're better?

ELLEN. Let's forget — just for now.

ANDREW. Is he grown much?

ELLEN. Grown? — You should see him! But so ill: What could I do? You see —

ANDREW. I know, I know.

ELLEN. The money was all gone. They turned me out at the old place, and then —

ANDREW. I know, dear.

ELLEN. I got sewing, but when the smallpox —

ANDREW. I have all your letters, Nell. Come, help me to pack.

ELLEN. What! You're really decided —

JOEL (*approaching*). Hello, Sis!

ELLEN (*absently*). Ah, Joel: that you?

(*Eagerly, following Andrew to the knapsack*)

But my dear —

ANDREW. Just these few things, and we 're off.

ELLEN (*agitated*). Wait; wait! You don't know yet why I 've come — instead of writing.

ANDREW. I can guess.

ELLEN. But you can't: that 's — what 's so hard. I have to tell you something, and then — (*Slowly*) I must know from your own eyes, from yourself, that you wish to do this, Andrew: that you think it is *right*.

ANDREW (*gently*). I guessed that.

ELLEN. This is what I must tell you. — It 's not just the sickness, it 's not only the baby, not the money gone — and all that; it 's — it 's —

ANDREW (*murmurs*). My God!

ELLEN. It 's what all that brings — the helplessness: I 've been insulted. Andy —
(*Her voice breaks*)
— I want a protector.

ANDREW (*taking her in his arms, where she sobs*). There, dear!

ELLEN (*with a low moan*). You know.

ANDREW. I know. — Come, now: we 'll go.

ELLEN (*her face lighting up*). Oh! — and you *dare*? It 's *right*?

ANDREW (*moving from her, with a hoarse laugh*). *Dare*? Dare I be damned by God and all His angels? Ha! — Come, we 're slow.

JOEL. Time enough.

ELLEN (*sinking upon Joel's knapsack as a seat, leans her head on her hands, and looks strangely at Andrew*). I 'd better have written, I 'm afraid.

ANDREW (*controlling his emotion*). Now don't take it that way. I 've considered it all.

ELLEN (*with deep quiet*). Blasphemously?

ANDREW. Reasonably, my brave wife. When I enlisted, I did so in a dream. I dreamed I was called to love and serve our country. But that dream is shattered. This sordid war, this political murder, has not one single prin-

ciple of humanity to excuse its bloody sacrilege. It does-
n't deserve my loyalty — our loyalty.

ELLEN. Are you saying this — for my sake? What of
"God and His angels"?

ANDREW (*not looking at her*). If we had a just cause — a
cause of liberty like that in Seventy-six; if to serve one's
country meant to serve God and His angels — then, yes:
a man might put away wife and child. He might say:
"I will not be a husband, a father; I will be a patriot."
But now — like this — tangled in a web of spiders — caught
in a grab-net of politicians — and you, you and our baby-
boy, like this — hell let in on our home — no, Country
be cursed!

ELLEN (*slowly*). So, then, when little Andy grows up —

ANDREW (*groaning*). I say that the only thing —

ELLEN. I am to tell him —

ANDREW (*defiantly*). Tell him his father deserted his country, and thanked God for the chance.

(*Looking about him passionately*)

Here!

(*He tears a part of the flag from its standard, and reaches it
toward her*)

You're cold; put this round you.

[*As he is putting the strip of colored silk about her shoulders,
there rises, faint yet close by, a sound of fifes and flutes, playing the merry march-strains of "Yankee Doodle."*

*At the same time, there enters along the embankment, dimly,
enveloped in a great cloak, a tall* FIGURE, *which pauses beside
the standard of the torn flag, silhouetted against the first pale
streaks of the dawn.*

ELLEN (*gazing at Andrew*). What's the matter?

ANDREW (*listening*). Who are they? Where is it?

JOEL (*starts, alertly*). He hears something.

ANDREW. Why should they play before daybreak?

ELLEN. Andy —

JOEL (*whispers*). Ssh! Look out: we're spied on.

[*He points to the embankment. Andrew and Ellen draw back.*

THE FIGURE (*straightening the flag-standard, and leaning on it*). Desartin'?

ANDREW (*puts Ellen behind him*). Who's there? The watchword!

THE FIGURE. God save the smart folks!

JOEL (*to Andrew*). He's on to us. Pickle him quiet, or it's court-martial!
(*Showing a long knife*)
Shall I give him this?

ANDREW (*taking it from him*). No; *I* will.

ELLEN (*seizing his arm*). Andrew!

ANDREW. Let go.
(*The Figure, descending into the entrenchment, approaches with face muffled. Joel draws Ellen away. Andrew moves toward the Figure slowly. They meet and pause*)
You 're a spy!
[*With a quick flash, Andrew raises the knife to strike, but pauses, staring. The Figure, throwing up one arm toward the blow, reveals — through the parted cloak — a glint of stars in the firelight.*[1]

THE FIGURE. Steady boys: I'm one of ye. The sergeant told me to drop round.

JOEL. Oh, the sergeant! That's all right, then.

ANDREW (*dropping the knife*). Who are you?

THE FIGURE. Who be *I*? My name, ye mean? — My name's Average: Sam Average: Univarsal Sam, some o' my prophetic friends calls me.

ANDREW. What are you doing here — now?

THE FIGURE. Oh, tendin' to business.

JOEL. Tendin' to *other* folks' business, eh?

THE FIGURE (*with a touch of weariness*). Ye-es; reckon that *is* my business. Some other folks is me.

JOEL (*grimacing to Ellen*). Cracked!

---

[1] The head and face of the Figure are partly hidden by a beak-shaped cowl. Momentarily, however, when his head is turned toward the fire, enough of the face is discernible to reveal his narrow iron-gray beard, shaven upper lip, aquiline nose, and eyes that twinkle in the dimness.

THE FIGURE (*to Andrew*). You're a mite back'ard in wages, ain't ye?

ANDREW. Nine months. What of that?

THE FIGURE. That's what I dropped round for. Seems like when a man's endoored and fit, like you have, for his country, and calc'lates he'll quit, he ought to be takin' a little suthin' hom' for Thanksgivin'. So I fetched round your pay.

ANDREW. My pay! You?

THE FIGURE. Yes; I'm the paymaster.

ELLEN (*coming forward, eagerly*). Andy! The money, is it?

THE FIGURE (*bows with a grave, old-fashioned stateliness*). Your sarvent, Ma'am!

ANDREW (*speaking low*). Keep back, Nell.

(*To the Figure*)

You — you were saying —

THE FIGURE. I were about to say how gold bein' scarce down to the Treasury, I fetched ye some s'curities instead: some national I.O.U's, as ye might say.

(*He takes out an old powder horn, and rattles it quietly*)

That's them.

(*Pouring from the horn into his palm some glistening, golden grains*)

Here they be.

ELLEN (*peering, with Joel*). Gold, Andy!

JOEL (*with a snigger*). Gold — nothin'! That's corn — just Injun corn: ha!

THE FIGURE (*bowing gravely*). It's the quality, Ma'am, what counts, as ye might say.

JOEL (*behind his hand*). His top-loft leaks!

THE FIGURE. These here karnels, now, were give' me down Plymouth way, in Massachusetts, the fust Thanksgivin' seems like I can remember. 'T wa'n't long after the famine we had thar. Me bein' some hungry, the red folks fetched a hull-lot o' this round, with the compliments of their capting — what were his name now? —

Massasoit. This here 's the last handful on 't left. Thought ye might like some, bein' Thanksgivin'.

JOEL (*in a low voice to Ellen*). His screws are droppin' out. Come and pack. We 've got to mark time and skip.

THE FIGURE (*without looking at Joel*). Eight or ten minutes still to spare, boys. The sergeant said — wait till ye hear his jew's-harp playin' of that new war tune: *The Star Spangled Banner.* Then ye 'll know the coast 's clear.

JOEL. Gad, that 's right. I remember now.

[*He draws Ellen away to the knapsack, which they begin to pack. Andrew has never removed his eyes from the tall form in the cloak.*

Now, as the Figure pours back the yellow grains from his palm into the powder horn, he speaks, hesitatingly.

ANDREW. I think — I 'd like some.

THE FIGURE. Some o' what?

ANDREW. Those — my pay.

THE FIGURE (*cheerfully*). So; would ye?

(*Handing him the horn*)

Reckon that 's enough?

ANDREW (*not taking it*). That 's what I want to make sure of — first.

THE FIGURE. Oh! So ye 're hesitatin'!

ANDREW. Yes; but I want you to help me decide. Pardon me, Sir; you 're a stranger; yet somehow I feel I may ask your help. You 've come just in time.

THE FIGURE. Queer I should a-dropped round jest now, wa'n't it? S'posin' we take a turn.

[*Together they walk toward the embankment.*

By the knapsack, Ellen finds the little frame.

ELLEN (*to herself*). My picture!

[*She looks toward Andrew affectionately.*

Joel, lifting the knapsack, beckons to her.

JOEL. There 's more stuff over here.

[*He goes off, right; Ellen follows him.*

ANDREW (*to the Figure*). I should like the judgment of your experience, Sir. I can't quite see your face, yet you appear to be one who has had a great deal of experience.

THE FIGURE. Why, consid'able some.

ANDREW. Did you — happen to fight in the late war for independence?

THE FIGURE. Happen to?

(*Laughing quietly*)

N-no, not fight: ye see — I was paymaster.

ANDREW. But you went through the war?

THE FIGURE. Ye-es, oh yes; I went through it. I took out my fust reg'lar papers down to Philadelphie, in '76, seems like 't was the fourth day o' July. But I was paymaster afore that.

ANDREW. Tell me: I 've heard it said there were deserters even in those days, even from the roll-call of Washington. Is it true?

THE FIGURE. True, boy? — Have ye ever watched a prairie fire rollin' towards ye, billowin' with flame and smoke, and seed all the midget cowerin' prairie-dogs scootin' for their holes? Wall, that 's the way I watched Howe's army sweepin' crosst the Jarsey marshes, and seed the desartin' little patriots, with their chins over their shoulders skedaddlin' home'ards.

ANDREW. What — the Americans!

THE FIGURE. All but a handful on 'em — them as weren't canines, ye might say, but men. *They* set a back-fire goin' at Valley Forge. Most on 'em burnt their toes and fingers off, lightin' on 't thar in the white frost, but they stuck it through and saved — wall, the prairie-dogs.

ANDREW. But they — those others: What reason did they give to God and their own souls for deserting?

THE FIGURE. To who?

ANDREW. To their consciences: What was their reason? It must have been a noble one in Seventy-six. *Their* reason *then:* don't you see, I must have it. I must know what reason real heroes gave for their acts. You were there. You can tell me.

THE FIGURE. *Real* heroes, eh? Look around ye, then:
To-day 's the heroic age, and the true brand o' hero is
al'ays in the market. Look around ye!

ANDREW. What, here — in this war of jobsters, this petty
campaign of monstrous boodle?

THE FIGURE. Thar we be!

ANDREW. Why, here are only a lot of cowardly half-men,
like me — lovers of their own folks — their wives and
babies at home. They 'll make sacrifices for them. But
real men like our fathers in Seventy-six: they looked in
the beautiful face of Liberty, and sacrificed to *her!*

THE FIGURE. Our fathers, my boy, was jest as fond o'
poetry as you be. They talked about the beautiful face
o' Liberty same 's you; but when the hom'-made eyes and
cheeks of their sweethearts and young uns took to cryin ',
they desarted their beautiful goddess and skun out hom'.

ANDREW. But there were some —

THE FIGURE. Thar was some as didn't — yes; and thar 's
some as don't to-day. Those be the folks on my pay-roll.
Why, look a-here: I calc'late I wouldn't fetch much on
the beauty counter. My talk ain't rhyme stuff, nor the
Muse o' Grammar wa'n't my schoolma'am. Th' ain't
painter nor clay-sculptor would pictur' me jest like I
stand. For the axe has hewed me, and the plough has
furrered; and the arnin' of gold by my own elbow-grease
has give' me the shrewd eye at a bargain. I manure my
crops this side o'Jordan, and as for t'other shore, I'd ruther
swap jokes with the Lord than listen to his sarmons. And
yet for the likes o' me, jest for to arn my wages — ha, the
many, many boys and gals that 's gone to their grave-beds,
and when I a-closed their eyes, the love-light was shinin'
thar.

ANDREW (*who has listened, with awe*). What *are* you? What
are you?

THE FIGURE. Me? I'm the pay-master.

ANDREW. I want to serve you — like those others.

THE FIGURE. Slow, slow, boy! Nobody sarves *me*.

ANDREW. But they died for you — the others.

THE FIGURE. No, 't wa'n't for me: 't was for him as pays the wages: the one as works through me — the one higher up. I'm only the pay-master: kind of a needful make-shift — his obedient sarvent.

ANDREW (*with increasing curiosity, seeks to peer in the Figure's face*). But the one up higher — who is he?

THE FIGURE (*turning his head away*). Would ye sarve him, think, if ye heerd his voice?

ANDREW (*ardently, drawing closer*). And saw his face!

[*Drawing his cowl lower and taking Andrew's arm, the Figure leads him up on the embankment, where they stand together.*

THE FIGURE. Hark a-yonder!

ANDREW (*listening*). Is it thunder?

THE FIGURE. Have ye forgot?

ANDREW. The voice! I remember now: — Niagara!

[*With awe, Andrew looks toward the Figure, who stands shrouded and still, facing the dawn. From far off comes a sound as of falling waters, and with that — a deep, murmurous voice, which seems to issue from the Figure's cowl.*

THE VOICE. I am the Voice that was heard of your fathers, and your fathers' fathers. Mightier — mightier, I shall be heard of your sons. I am the Million in whom the one is lost, and I am the One in whom the millions are saved. Their ears shall be shut to my thunders, their eyes to my blinding stars. In shallow streams they shall tap my life-blood for gold. With dregs of coal and of copper they shall pollute me. In the mystery of my mountains they shall assail me; in the majesty of my forests, strike me down; with engine and derrick and mill-stone, bind me their slave. Some for a lust, some for a love, shall desert me. One and one, for his own, shall fall away. Yet one and one and one shall return to me for life; the deserter and the destroyer shall re-create me. Primeval, their life-blood is mine. My pouring waters are passion, my lightnings are laughter of man. I am the One in whom

the millions are saved, and I am the Million in whom the
one is lost.

ANDREW (*yearningly, to the Figure*).   Your face!

(*The Figure turns majestically away.   Andrew clings to
him*)

Your face!

[*In the shadow of the flag, the Figure unmuffles for an instant.
Peering, dazzled, Andrew staggers back, with a low cry, and,
covering his eyes, falls upon the embankment.*

*From away, left, the thrumming of a jew's-harp is heard,
playing " The Star Spangled Banner."*

From the right, enter Joel and Ellen.

Descending from the embankment, the Figure stands apart.

JOEL.   Well, Colonel Average, time 's up.

ELLEN (*seeing Andrew's prostrate form, hastens to him*).   Andy!
What 's happened?

ANDREW (*rising slowly*).   Come here.   I 'll whisper it.

[*He leads her beside the embankment, beyond which the dawn
is beginning to redden.*

JOEL.   Yonder 's the sergeant's jew's-harp.   That 's our signal, Nell.   So long, Colonel.

THE FIGURE (*nodding*).   So long, sonny.

ANDREW (*holding Ellen's hands, passionately*).   You understand?   You *do?*

ELLEN (*looking in his eyes*).   I understand, dear.

[*They kiss each other.*

JOEL (*calls low*).   Come, you married turtles.   The road 's
clear.   Follow me now.   Sneak.

[*Carrying his knapsack, Joel climbs over the embankment,
and disappears.*

The thrumming of the jew's-harp continues.

*Ellen, taking the strip of silk flag from her shoulders, ties it
to the standard.*

ANDREW (*faintly*).   God bless you!

ELLEN (*as they part hands*).   Good-bye!

[*The Figure has remounted the embankment, where — in the
distincter glow of the red dawn — the grey folds of his cloak,*

hanging from his shoulders, resemble the half-closed wings of an eagle, the beaked cowl falling, as a kind of visor, before his face, concealing it.

THE FIGURE. Come, little gal.

(Ellen goes to him, and hides her face in the great cloak. As she does so, he draws from it a paper, writes on it, and hands it to Andrew, with the powder horn)

By the bye, Andy, here 's that s'curity. Them here 's my initials : they 're all what 's needful. Jest file this in the right pigeonhole, and you 'll draw your pay. — Keep your upper lip, boy. I 'll meet ye later, mebbe, at Lundy's Lane.

ANDREW *(wistfully)*. You 'll take her home?

THE FIGURE. Yes : reckon she 'll housekeep for your uncle, till you get back; won't ye, Nellie? Come, don't cry, little gal. We 'll soon git 'quainted. 'T aint the fust time sweethearts has called me *Uncle.*

[Flinging back his great cloak, he throws one wing of it, with his arm, about her shoulders, thus with half its reverse side draping her with shining stripes and stars. By the same action, his own figure is made partly visible — the legs clad in the tight, instep-strapped trousers [blue and white] of the Napoleonic era. Holding the girl gently to him — while her face turns back toward Andrew — he leads her, silhouetted against the sunrise, along the embankment, and disappears. Meantime the thrumming twang of the jew's-harp grows sweeter, mellower, modulated with harmonies that, filling now the air with elusive strains of the American war-hymn, mingle with the faint dawn-twitterings of birds.

Andrew stares silently after the departed forms; then, slowly coming down into the entrenchment, lifts from the ground his gun and ramrod, leans on the gun, and — reading the paper in his hand by the growing light — mutters it aloud:

U. S. A.

Smiling sternly, he crumples the paper in his fist, makes a wad of it, and rams it into his gun-barrel.

CURTAIN

SIX WHO PASS WHILE THE LENTILS BOIL

STUART WALKER

MR. STUART WALKER was born in Augusta, Kentucky. In 1890 he moved to Cincinnati where he entered the University and received his degree. Some time later he came to New York and completed a course at the American Academy of Dramatic Arts. He then secured a position with Belasco, and quickly rose to be General Director. In 1914, he organized and established his own Portmanteau Company, which has been very significant in Little Theatre history. The Portmanteau stage is complete theatrically and can be packed up and carried, in its entire form, from one city to another. For this reason it is probably better known nationally than any other Little Theatre.

Mr. Walker has produced in this theatre : "The Moon Lady", which he wrote in 1908; "Six Who Pass While the Lentils Boil", written in 1915 (and which it might be interesting to note was completed in a single day); "The Trimplet", 1915; "The Seven Gifts of Pantomime", 1915; "Nevertheless", 1915; "The Lady of the Weeping Willow Tree", 1916; "The Birthday of the Infanta", 1916; "The Very Naked Boy", 1916; and "The Medicine Show", 1916.

In addition to the plays which he has given with the Portmanteau Company, Mr. Walker has produced a dramatization of Booth Tarkington's "Seventeen", and "Jonathan Makes a Wish." His Portmanteau plays have been published under the title "Portmanteau Plays."

SIX WHO PASS WHILE THE LENTILS BOIL

BOIL

BY STUART WALKER

"Six Who Pass While the Lentils Boil" was originally produced at an invitation performance at Christodora House, New York City, July 14, 1915. The first public performance was at Jordan Hall, Boston, February 14, 1916. Both performances were given under the auspices of the Portmanteau Theatre.

Original Cast

	1915	1916
THE PROLOGUE	Henry Kiefer	Lew Medbury
THE DEVICE-BEARER	Edmond Crenshaw	Edmond Crenshaw
BOY	James W. Morrison	Gregory Kelly
QUEEN	Judith Lowry	Judith Lowry
MIME	William Farrell	Wilmot Heitland
MILKMAID	Nancy Winston	Nancy Winston
BLINDMAN	Joseph Graham	Edgar Stehli
BALLAD SINGER	Tom Powers	Stuart Walker
HEADSMAN	McKay Morris	McKay Morris

SIX WHO PASS WHILE THE LENTILS BOIL

THE SCENE *is a kitchen.*

THE PERIOD *is when you will.*

Before the opening of the curtains the Prologue enters upon the forestage and summons the Device-Bearer who carries a large copper pot.

PROLOGUE. This is a copper pot. (*The Device-Bearer shows it to the audience carefully*) It is filled with boiling water. (*The Device-Bearer makes the sound of bubbling water*) It is on the fire. See the flames. (*The Device-Bearer sets the pot in the center of the forestage and blows under it with a pair of bellows*) And see the water boiling over. (*The Device-Bearer again makes the sound of bubbling water and then withdraws to where he can see the play from the side of the forestage*) We are looking into the kitchen of the Boy whose mother left him alone. I do not know where she has gone but I do know that he is gathering lentils now.

YOU. What are lentils?

PROLOGUE. A lentil? Why a lentil, don't you see, is not a bean nor yet a pea; but it is kin to both . . . You must imagine that the boy has built the fire and set the water boiling. He is very industrious but you need not feel sorry for him. His mother is very good to him and he is safe. Are you ready now? . . . Very well. Be quiet.

[*The Prologue claps his hands twice.*

The curtains open and a kitchen is disclosed. There are a bench, a stool and a cupboard. A great door at the back opens into a corridor. There are also two windows — one higher than the other — looking upon the corridor. At the right a door opens into the bedroom of the Boy's mother. A great pewter spoon lies upon the shelf in the cupboard.

A large Butterfly comes in through the doorway, flits about and looks off stage.

The song of the Boy is heard from the garden.

The Butterfly goes to the door, poises a moment, then alights on the cupboard.

The Boy enters with a great bowl filled with lentils.

The Butterfly flies to the bowl and satisfied returns to the cupboard.

The Boy smiles at the Butterfly but he does not touch him. Then he empties the lentils into the pot and water splashes on his careless hand.

A moan is heard in the distance.   The Boy and the Butterfly go to the door.

The Queen's voice is heard calling:

Butterfly, Butterfly, where shall I hide?

[*Enter the Queen.*

QUEEN.   Boy, Boy — oh, I am distraught!

YOU.   What is distraught?

PROLOGUE.   Distraught means distracted, perplexed, beset with doubt, worried by some fear.

BOY (*pityingly*).   Why are you distraught?

QUEEN.   Oh — Oh — Oh — They are going to behead me!

BOY.   When?

QUEEN.   Before mid-day.

BOY.   Why are they going to behead you?   Is it a story? Tell it to me.

QUEEN.   I was guilty of a breach of etiquette.

BOY.   What is that?

QUEEN.   I did something that was considered bad manners and the law says the punishment is decapitation.

YOU.   What is decapitation?

PROLOGUE.   Decapitation is beheading; cutting off one's head.

BOY.   Why, only kings and queens can be decapitated.

QUEEN.   Oh, I know — I know —

BOY (*disappointed*).   Are you a queen?

QUEEN.   Yes.

BOY. I thought all queens were big. My mother says **they** are always regal. And my mother knows.

QUEEN. Oh, I *am* the queen. *I am* the queen; but I **am** so unhappy.

BOY. My mother told me kings and queens knew no fear? Why, you're afraid.

QUEEN. Oh, Boy, Boy, I *am* your queen and I *am* afraid and unhappy. And queens are just like other people when they are afraid and unhappy.

BOY (*disappointed*). Aren't they always regal?

QUEEN. No — no. Oh, little boy, hide me, hide me from the Dreadful Headsman!

BOY. I haven't any place to hide you. You couldn't get under the bench and you couldn't get into the cupboard.

QUEEN. Little boy, can't you see that I shall lose my head if I am found?

BOY. You might have hidden in the pot if I hadn't put it on the fire.

QUEEN. Oh — Oh — Oh —

BOY. I'm sorry.

QUEEN. I am distraught.

BOY. Well, I'll hide you, because you are distraught; but — I am not sure you are a queen. . . . Where's your crown? You can't be a queen without a crown!
[*She reaches up to her head.*

QUEEN. Oh, I was running so fast that it must have slipped from my head. (*Sees the Butterfly*) Butterfly, tell him I am your Queen.
[*The Butterfly flies to her head and lights on her disheveled locks like a diadem.*

BOY. Oh, I have talked to the Queen! . . . You can hide in my mother's bedroom in there; but first please tell me a story.

QUEEN. They will find me here. I'll tell you a story afterward.

BOY. I want you to tell me now.

QUEEN. Well, you watch at the door and warn me when

you see some one coming. (*The Butterfly brushes her ear*)
But stay, the Butterfly says he'll watch.

[*The Butterfly goes to the door.*

BOY. Will he know?

QUEEN. Oh, yes. He is a wonderful butterfly — wise beyond his years.

BOY. Sit down and tell me your story.

[*He places a black pillow for the Queen on the step and an orange pillow for himself.*

QUEEN. Last night we celebrated the second year of peace with the neighboring kingdom. We were dancing the minuet just after the banquet, when I stepped on the ring-toe of my husband the King's great aunt.

BOY. Didn't you say excuse me?

QUEEN. It was useless. The law says that if a queen steps on the ring-toe of the King's great aunt or any member of her family the Queen must be beheaded while the King's four clocks are striking twelve at mid-day.

BOY. Oh, that means to-day?

QUEEN. Yes.

BOY. Why, it's almost mid-day now. See, I've just set the lentils boiling.

QUEEN. If you can hide me until after the King's four clocks strike twelve I shall be safe.

BOY. Why are there four clocks?

QUEEN. Because the law allows only one clock for each tower in the castle.

BOY. Then I hear all the King's clocks every day! There's a big clock, and two clocks not so big, and a tiny little clock.

QUEEN. Yes, those are the four.

BOY. Why will you be safe *after* the four clocks strike twelve?

QUEEN. Because that is the law.

BOY. Aren't laws funny?

QUEEN. Funny? This one is very sad, I think.

BOY. Mightn't it be twelve any mid-day?

QUEEN. No; the Prime Minister of my grandfather who passed the law decided that it meant only the following mid-day.

BOY (*rising and rushing to the door*). They'll find you here.

QUEEN (*rising calmly*). Oh, no, this is the short cut to the beheading block. Through that corridor.

BOY. Why didn't you run the other way?

QUEEN. Because they always search for escaped people in that direction. So I ran through your garden and into this room. They'll never search for me so close to the castle.

BOY. How did you escape?

QUEEN. I —

[*The Butterfly seems agitated.*

BOY. You —

QUEEN. Some one is coming. Hide me!

BOY. In here — in my mother's room. 'Sh! 'Sh!

[*The Queen goes out.*
Enter the Mime.
He pokes his head in the lower window and peeps around the door.
The boy turns.

BOY (*weakly*). Are you the Dreadful Headsman?

MIME. *What?*

BOY. Are you the Dreadful Headsman?

MIME. Do I look like a headsman?

BOY. I don't know; I've never seen one.

MIME. Well, suppose I am.

BOY. Are you?

MIME. Maybe I am.

BOY. Oh!

MIME. Booh!

BOY. I'm — I'm — not afraid.

MIME. Bah!

BOY. And my mother isn't here.

MIME. Br — r — r — r!

[*The Boy reaches for his knife.*

MIME. Bing!

BOY. I wasn't going to hurt you!

MIME. 'Sh . . . 'Sh! . . . 'Sh! . . .

BOY. I'll give you my knife if you'll go 'way.

MIME. Ah, — ha!

BOY. It's nearly mid-day and you'd better go.

MIME. Well, give me the knife.

BOY. Promise me to go.

MIME (*laughs, turning away*). Aren't you going to the beheading?

BOY. No. I have to boil the lentils for our mid-day meal.

MIME. May I come back and eat some?

BOY. You'll have to ask my mother.

MIME. Where is she?

BOY. She's over that way. She went to the market to buy a bobbin.

YOU. What is a bobbin?

PROLOGUE. A bobbin is a spool upon which thread is wound, and it is sharp at one end so that it can be easily passed backward and forward, to and fro, through the other threads in making lace.

MIME (*starting off*). Well, I'll be back to eat some lentils.

BOY (*too eagerly*). You'd better hurry.

MIME. You seem to want to get rid of me.

BOY (*allaying suspicion*). Well, I think you'd better go or you'll be late — and it's very wrong to be late.

MIME (*going toward the door*). I think I'll (*changing his mind*) sit down.

BOY (*disappointed*). Oh!

MIME. What would you say if I wasn't the Headsman?

BOY. But you said you were.

MIME. I said *maybe* I was.

BOY. Aren't you?

MIME. Maybe I'm not.

BOY. Honest?

MIME. Um, hum.

BOY (*relieved*). Oh! . . .

MIME. You *were* afraid.

BOY. No . . . I wasn't.

MIME. Would you fight?

BOY. You bet I would.

MIME. It wouldn't take me a minute to lick you.

BOY. Maybe it wouldn't, but I wouldn't give up right away. That would be cowardly. . . . Who are you?

MIME. I'm a mime —

BOY. What's a mime?

MIME. A mime's a mime.

BOY. Go on and tell me.

MIME. A mime's a mountebank.

BOY. What's a mountebank?

MIME. A mountebank's a strolling player.

BOY. Are you going to perform for me?

MIME. Not to-day — I'm on my way to the decapitation.

BOY. Do you want to see the decapitation?

MIME. Well, yes. But most of all I want to pick up a few coins.

BOY. How?

MIME. Why, I'll perform after the Queen has lost her head.

BOY. Won't you be too sorry?

MIME. No. You see, I'll be thinking mostly about what I'm going to do. I have to do my best because it is hard to be more interesting than a decapitation. And after it's all over the crowd will begin to talk and to move about: and I'll have to rush up to the front of them and cry out at the top of my lungs, "Stop — Ho, for Jack the Juggler! Would you miss him? In London where the king of kings lives, all the knights and ladies of the Court would leave a crowning to watch Jack the Juggler toss three golden balls with one hand or balance a weathervane upon his nose." Then a silence will come upon the crowd and they will all turn to me. Some one will say, "Where is this Jack the Juggler?" And I shall answer, "Jack the Juggler, the greatest of the great, the pet of kings, entertainer to the Pope and the joy of Cathay stands before you." And

I'll throw back my cloak and stand revealed. So! Some one will then shout, "Let us have it, Jack." So I'll draw my three golden balls from my pouch — like this — and then begin.

[*The Boy is watching breathlessly and the Butterfly is interested too. Their disappointment is keen when Jack does nothing.*

BOY. Aren't you going to show me?

MIME. No, I must be off.

BOY. Aren't you ever coming back?

MIME. Maybe, yes; perhaps, no.

BOY. I'll give you some lentils if you'll juggle the balls for me.

MIME (*sniffs the pot*). They aren't cooked yet.

BOY. Let me hold your golden balls.

MIME (*takes a gold ball from his pouch and lets the Boy hold it*). Here's one.

BOY. And do they pay you well?

MIME (*taking the ball from the Boy*). Ay, that they do. If I am as interesting as the beheading I'll get perhaps fifteen farthings in money and other things that I can exchange for food and raiment.

BOY. I'm going to be a mime and buy a castle and a sword.

MIME. Maybe so and maybe not. Who knows? . . . Good-by.

[*He goes out.*

BOY (*to the Butterfly*). If he had been the Dreadful Headsman I would have slain him. So! . . . "Ah, wicked headsman, you shall not behead the Queen! . . . Cross not that threshold or I'll run you through."

[*Throughout this the Butterfly shows great interest and enters into the spirit of it, being absorbed at times and frightened at others.*

Enter the Milkmaid at door.

MILKMAID. Pst! . . . Pst!

BOY (*startled*). Oh!

MILKMAID. Are you going to the decapitation?

BOY. No. Are you?

MILKMAID. That I am.

BOY. Will your mother let you go?

MILKMAID. She doesn't know.

BOY. Did you run away?

MILKMAID. No. I went out to milk the cow.

BOY. And did you do it?

MILKMAID. Yes.

BOY. Why didn't you wait until you came back?

MILKMAID. My mother was looking and I had to let her see me doing something.

BOY. How did you get away when you took the milk pails into the house?

MILKMAID. I didn't take them in. As soon as my mother turned her back I hid the pails and I ran through here to take a short cut.

BOY. Where did you hide the milk?

MILKMAID. In the hollow tree.

BOY. Won't it sour?

MILKMAID. Maybe.

BOY. Won't your mother scold you?

MILKMAID. Yes, of course, but I couldn't miss the beheading.

BOY. Will you take the sour milk home?

MILKMAID. Yes, and after my mother scolds me I'll make it into nice cheese and sell it to the King's Cook and then mother will forgive me.

BOY (*sniffing the pot*). You'd better hurry. It's nearly midday. Don't you smell the lentils?

MILKMAID. The headsman hasn't started yet

BOY (*giggling*). He'd better hurry.

MILKMAID. They can't find the Queen.

BOY (*so innocently*). Did she escape?

MILKMAID. Yes.

BOY. Are they hunting for her?

MILKMAID. Yes, and they've offered a big reward to the person who finds her.

BOY. How much?

MILKMAID. A pail of gold and a pair of finger rings.

BOY. That's a good deal . . . with a pail of gold I could buy my mother a velvet dress and a silken kerchief and a bonnet made of cloth of gold — and I could buy myself a milk-white palfrey.

MILKMAID. And you'd never have to work again.

BOY. But she's such a gentle queen. Where are they hunting her?

MILKMAID. Everywhere.

BOY. Everywhere! . . . Maybe she's waiting at the be-heading block.

MILKMAID. Silly goose! She wouldn't try to escape this way. She'd go in the opposite direction.

BOY. Do people always run in the opposite direction?

MILKMAID. Of course, everybody knows that.

BOY. I wish I could go.

MILKMAID. Come on.

BOY. Um — uh. The lentils might burn.

MILKMAID. Pour some cold water on them.

BOY. Um — uh. I promised I wouldn't leave the house.

MILKMAID. Oh, it will be wonderful!

BOY. The Mime will be there.

MILKMAID. The one with the long cloak and the golden balls?

BOY. Um — uh.

MILKMAID. Ooh!

BOY. How did you know?

MILKMAID. I saw him on the way to the market one day — and when my mother wasn't looking at me I gave him a farthing.

BOY. Is he a good juggler?

MILKMAID. He's magic! Why, he can throw three golden balls in the air and catch them with one hand and then keep them floating in the air in a circle.

BOY. And can he balance a weathervane on his nose while it's turning?

MILKMAID.   Yes, and he can balance an egg on the end of a long stick that is balanced on his chin!

BOY.   Oh — I wish I could see him.

[*Looks at the pot to see if the lentils are done.*

MILKMAID.   Come on!

BOY.   Well —

[*Begins to weaken and just as he is about to start, the Butterfly flits past him into the Queen's room.*

MILKMAID.   Oh — what a lovely butterfly!

BOY.   No — No — I can't go.   But you had better hurry.

MILKMAID.   Well, I'll try to catch the butterfly first.

BOY.   Oh, no, you mustn't touch that butterfly.

MILKMAID.   Why?

BOY.   Because — because he's my friend.

MILKMAID.   Silly!

BOY.   He *is* a good friend and he's the wisest butterfly in the world.

MILKMAID.   What can he do?

BOY.   He can almost talk.

MILKMAID.   Almost? . . .   Oh, I know.   I'm a goose.   You want to play a trick on me so I'll miss the beheading.

BOY.   You'd better hurry.

MILKMAID.   I wish you'd come.

BOY (*sadly*).   I can't.   I've a duty to perform.

MILKMAID.   Aren't duties always hard?   [*Both sigh.*

She takes up her milk pail.

BOY.   What are you going to do with that pail?

MILKMAID.   I'm going to stand on it. . . .   Good-by.

[*She goes out.*

BOY.   Good-by.   (*He watches for a moment, then goes to the pot and tries the lentils; then whispers through door to the Queen*)   The lentils are getting soft.

[*There is a fumbling in the passage and a voice is heard,* "Help the blind.   Help the blind."

[*The Butterfly returns to the top of the cupboard.*

The Blind man appears at the door.

PROLOGUE. He's blind, but he'll show you how the blind can see.

BLIND MAN (*sniffing*). Cooking lentils?

BOY. Yes.

BLIND MAN. Cook, which way to the beheading?

BOY. Keep straight ahead — the way you are going, old man.

BLIND MAN. Don't you want to take me with you?

BOY. I'm not going.

BLIND MAN. Not going to the beheading?

BOY. No, I have to cook the lentils.

BLIND MAN. Come on and go with me and maybe I'll give you a farthing.

BOY. I can't.

BLIND MAN. Yes, you can. Who else is here?

BOY (*swallowing: it's hard to fib*). No one.

BLIND MAN. Can't you run away? Your mother won't know you've gone.

BOY. It's my duty to stay here.

BLIND MAN. It's your duty to help a poor blind man, little boy.

BOY. Are you stone blind?

BLIND MAN. Yes.

BOY. Then how did you know I was a *little* boy?

BLIND MAN. Because you *sound* like a little boy.

BOY. Well, if you're stone blind why do you want to go to the beheading?

BLIND MAN. I can see with my ears.

BOY. Aw —

BLIND MAN. Didn't I know you were a little boy?

BOY. Yes, but you had to guess twice. First you thought I was a cook.

BLIND MAN. Well, aren't you cooking lentils?

BOY. Yes; but you can smell them.

BLIND MAN. Well, I see with my nose, too.

BOY. Aw — how can you see with your nose?

BLIND MAN. If you give me some bread I'll show you.

BOY. I can't give you any bread, but I'll give you some raw lentils.

BLIND MAN. All right. Give me lentils.

BOY. . . . I'll put them by the pot — Ready.

BLIND MAN. All right. (*Sniffs. Walks to the pot and gets lentils and puts them in an old pouch*) Isn't that seeing with my nose?

BOY. H'm! (*In wonder*) Now see with your ears and I'll give you some more lentils.

BLIND MAN. All right. Speak.

[*The Boy gets behind the stool and speaks.*
The Blind man goes toward him. The Boy moves around stealthily.

BLIND MAN. You're cheating. You've moved.

BOY (*jumping up on the bench*). Well, where am I?

BLIND MAN. You're standing on something.

BOY. How did you guess it?

BLIND MAN. I didn't guess it. I know it.

BOY. Why can't I do that?

BLIND MAN. You can if you try; but it takes practice.

BOY. Can you see the door now?

BLIND MAN. No. I've turned around too many times. Besides there is more than one door.

BOY. Oh — m-m. . . You aren't really blind!

BLIND MAN. Blind people learn to use what they have. Once I too could see with my eyes.

BOY. Just like me?

BLIND MAN. Yes. And then I didn't take the trouble to see with my ears and my nose and my fingers — after I became blind I had to learn . . . Why, I can tell whether a man who passes me at the palace gate is a poor man or a noble or a merchant.

BOY. How can you do that?

BLIND MAN. By sound of the step

BOY. Aw — how can you do that?

BLIND MAN. Shut your eyes and try it.

BOY. Well, I know what you are. That would be easy.

BLIND MAN. I'll pretend I'm somebody else.

[Feels with his stick; touches bench. Feels around again.

BOY. Why are you doing that?

BLIND MAN. To see how far I can walk without bumping into something.

BOY. Um —

BLIND MAN. Ready.

BOY (*hides face in hands*). Yes.

BLIND MAN. Don't peep.

[The Boy tries hard not to.

BOY. I won't.

BLIND MAN. All ready. (*Shuffles like a commoner*) Who was it?

BOY. A poor man.

BLIND MAN. See how easy?

BOY. I could see him as plain as if I had my eyes open. . . . Now try me again.

BLIND MAN. Ready.

BOY. All right.

[The Blind Man seems to grow in height. His face is filled with a rare brightness. He steadies himself a moment and then walks magnificently down the room.

BOY (*in beautiful wonder*). A noble! I could see him.

BLIND MAN. All you have to do is try.

BOY. I always thought it was terrible to be blind.

BLIND MAN. Sometimes it is.

BOY. But I thought everything was black.

BLIND MAN. It used to be until I taught myself how to see.

BOY. Why is it terrible sometimes?

BLIND MAN. Because I cannot help the poor who need help. If I had money I could feed the hungry and clothe the poor little beggar children in winter!

BOY. Would a pail of gold and a pair of finger rings help you feed the hungry and clothe the poor little beggar children in winter?

BLIND MAN. A pail of gold! I have dreamed of what I might do with so much wealth!

BOY.   I can get a pail of gold if I break a promise.

BLIND MAN.   Would *you* break a promise?

BOY   . . . No — but — No!

BLIND MAN.   Of course you wouldn't.

BOY.   I couldn't break a promise for *two* pails of gold.

BLIND MAN.   Nor twenty-two, little boy.

BOY.   When you walked like a noble I saw a beautiful man behind my eyes with a crown of gold.

BLIND MAN.   If you broke a promise for a pail of gold and two finger rings you would never see a beautiful noble with a crown of gold when you closed your eyes . . .

BOY.   Can blind men see beautiful things even when it's rainy?

BLIND MAN.   Blind men can always see beautiful things if they try.   Clouds and rain are beautiful to me — and when I get wet I think of the sunshine.   I saw sunshine with my eyes when I was a little boy.   Now I see it with my whole body when it warms me.   I saw rain with my eyes when I was a little boy.   Now I see it with my hands when it falls on them — drop — drop — drop — dropity — dropity — and I love it because it makes the lentils grow.

BOY.   I never thought of that.   Rain makes me stay indoors and I never like it except in June.

BLIND MAN.   You don't have to stay in for long.

BOY.   Can blind men see beautiful things in a beheading?

BLIND MAN.   No.   But I must be there with the crowd.   I shall tell stories to the people and perhaps they will give me food or money.

BOY.   Can't you stay and tell me stories?

BLIND MAN.   No.   I must be on my way . . .   If I do not see the beheading I cannot tell about it when I meet some one who was not there.   Oh, I shall make a thrilling tale of it.

BOY.   Tell it to me when you come back.

BLIND MAN.   If you give me some cooked lentils.

BOY.   I'll save you some.

BLIND MAN. Are the lentils nearly done?

BOY. Half.

BLIND MAN. I must be on my way then. . . . Good-by.
[*Starting to go in the wrong direction.*

BOY. Here's the door.

BLIND MAN. Thank you, little boy. . . . Don't forget to
see with your ears and nose and fingers.
[*The Blind Man goes out.*

BOY. I won't.

BLIND MAN. Good-by.

BOY. Good-by. (*The Boy covers his eyes and tries to see
with his ears and his nose*) It's easier with the ears.
[*Singing is heard.*
Enter the Ballad-Singer.

SINGER. Hello!

BOY. Hello!

SINGER. How are you?

BOY. I'm very well.

SINGER. That's good.

BOY. Thank you.

SINGER. Cooking?

BOY. Yes.

SINGER (*coming into the room*). Something good?

BOY. Lentils.

SINGER. Give me some?

BOY. They aren't done.

SINGER. Nearly. I can smell them.

BOY. Do you like them?

SINGER. When I'm hungry.

BOY. Are you hungry now?

SINGER. I'm always hungry.
[*They laugh.*

BOY. Were you singing?

SINGER. Yes.

BOY. Do you like to sing?

SINGER. When I get something for my ballads.

BOY. Are you a ballad-singer?

SINGER. Yes.

BOY. Sing one for me?

SINGER. Give me some lentils?

BOY. I'll give you some raw lentils.

SINGER. I want some of the cooked ones.

BOY. They aren't done.

SINGER. Are they nearly done?

BOY. More than half.

SINGER. I like them that way.

BOY. All right. Sing me a ballad.

SINGER. Well, give me the lentils first.

BOY. Oh, no, sing the ballad first.

SINGER. No, sir, give me the lentils first.

BOY. That isn't fair.

SINGER. Why not? After I sing to you maybe you won't pay me.

BOY. Yes, I will.

SINGER. Then why not pay me first?

BOY. You might not sing.

SINGER (*laughing*). Yes, I will.

BOY (*laughing*). Well, I'll give you some lentils at the end of each verse.

SINGER. That's a bargain.

BOY. Sing.

SINGER (*sings one line*).

Six stalwart sons the miller had —
Give me the lentils.

BOY. Finish that verse.

SINGER. I did finish it.

BOY. Now that's not fair. You only sang a line.

SINGER. Well, a line's a verse.

BOY (*with a gesture that indicates how long a verse ought to be*). I meant a whole verse.

SINGER (*mimicking the gesture*). A line's a whole verse.

BOY. Oh, now, be fair, I mean a *whole*, whole verse.

SINGER. You mean a *stanza*.

BOY. I always heard it called a verse.

SINGER. Well, keep the bargain. I sang a verse. Give me some lentils.

BOY (*rising and taking a very few lentils on his spoon*). Next time I mean a stanza. . . . Here are some lentils.

[*The Ballad-Singer eyes the meager portion, cools it and eats.*

SINGER. Stingy.

BOY. Isn't that *some* lentils?

SINGER (*laughs*). Well —

BOY. Now begin again.

SINGER. At the end of every stanza a spoonful of lentils.

BOY. I didn't say a spoonful.

SINGER (*starts to go*). Very well, I won't sing a ballad.

BOY. All right. I'll give you a spoonful at the end of each — stanza.

[*He sits on the floor by the pot of lentils.*

SINGER (*sings*).

The Ballad of the Miller and His Six Sons

Six stalwart sons the miller had
All brave and fair to see —
He taught them each a worthy trade —
And they grew gallantly.
Tara — da — da — da-da-da — da-da-da
Tara — da — da — da-de — da-dee.

Give me some lentils.

BOY. Here . . . Hurry up.

SINGER (*sings*).

The first was John of the dimpled chin
And a fist of iron had he —
He learned to wield the broadsword well
And turned to soldiery.
Tara — da — da, etc.

BOY. Please! Please don't stop.

SINGER. Keep to the bargain.

BOY. Here, take two spoonfuls and finish without stopping.

SINGER (*sings rest of ballad*).

> The second son was christened Hugh
> And curly locks had he —
> He learned to use the tabor and lute
> And turned to minstrelsy.
> Tara — da — da, etc.
>
> The third was James of the gentle ways
> And speech of gold had he —
> He learned his psalms and learned his creed
> And turned to simony.
> Tara — da — da, etc.
>
> The fourth was Dick of the hazel eye,
> And a steady hand had he —
> With a hammer and saw and a chest of tools
> He turned to carpentry.
> Tara — da — da, etc.
>
> The fifth was Ned of the velvet tread
> And feather fingers had he.
> He used his gifts in a naughty way
> And turned to burglary.
> Tara — da — da, etc.
>
> The sixth was Robin, surnamed the Rare,
> For always young was he —
> He learned the joy of this sunny world
> And turned to poetry.
> Tara — da — da, etc.
>
> The Miller approached three score and ten,
> A happy man was he,
> His five good sons and the one who was bad
> All turned to gallantry.
> Tara — da — da, etc.

BOY.   Sing me another.

SINGER.   A spoonful at the end of every stanza.

BOY. Don't stop after you begin.
SINGER. Pay me in advance.
BOY. I suppose I'll have to.
[*He feeds the Ballad-Singer.*
SINGER (*sings second ballad*).

The Ballad of the Three Little Pigs

Two little pigs were pink — pink — pink —
And one little pig was black — black —
The three little pigs were very good friends,
But one little pig was black — black.

Three little pigs would play — play — play —
But one little pig was black — black —
And three little pigs would have a jolly time
Though one little pig was black — black.

Three little pigs soon grew — grew — grew —
And one little pig was black — black.
The three little pigs became fat hogs —
And one fat hog was black — black.

The two fat hogs were pink — pink — pink —
And one fat hog was black — black.
The three fat hogs all made good ham,
Though one fat hog was black — black.

BOY. Sing me another.
SINGER. I can't. I'm tired.
BOY. Are you going to sing those at the beheading?
SINGER. What beheading?
BOY. At the Queen's beheading.
SINGER. Where?
BOY. Over there.
SINGER. When?
BOY. To-day.
SINGER. I must be going. Certainly I'll sing there and I'll take up a collection.

BOY.   It's going to be before the King's four clocks strike
twelve.

SINGER.   It's nearly time now.   If I can collect a piece of gold
I can buy a vermilion robe and sing at the King's court.

BOY.   I could collect a pail of gold and two finger rings and
sit at the feet of the King if I'd break a promise.

SINGER.   Perhaps you will.

BOY.   Would you?

SINGER.   I'd rather sing along the highway all my life.   It
is better to dream of a vermilion robe than to have one that
is not honestly got.

BOY.   The Blind Man said something like that.

SINGER.   Who said what?

BOY.   The Blind Man said if I broke a promise I'd never
again see a beautiful noble with a golden crown when I
closed my eyes.

SINGER.   He was right.

BOY.   When you get your vermilion robe will you let me
see it?

SINGER.   That I will. . . .   Good-by.

BOY.   Good-by.

[*Singer goes out.*

BOY (*hums a snatch of the ballads*).

[*The Headsman steps into the door and plants his axe beside
him for an impressive picture.   The Boy turns and starts
in terror.*

HEADSMAN.   Have you seen the Queen?

BOY.   Sir?

HEADSMAN.   Have you seen the Queen?

BOY.   How should I, sir?   I've been cooking the lentils.

HEADSMAN.   She is here!

BOY.   How — could — she — be — here, sir?

HEADSMAN.   Well, if she isn't here, where is she?

BOY (*relieved*).   I don't know where she is if she isn't here, sir.

HEADSMAN.   She has too much sense to hide so near the castle
and on the short cut to the headsman's block . . . Do
you know who I am?

BOY. I think so — sir.

HEADSMAN. Think? Don't you *know?*

BOY. Yes, sir.

HEADSMAN. Who am I then?

BOY. You're the Dreadful Headsman.

HEADSMAN. I am the winder of the king's four clocks *and* when I am needed I am the best headsman in three kingdoms. And *this* is my axe.

BOY. Is it sharp?

HEADSMAN. It will split a hair in two.

[*Runs finger near blade meaningly.*

BOY. Oh!

HEADSMAN. A hair in two!

BOY. Would you really cut off the Queen's head?

HEADSMAN. That's my business: to cut off heads and the nobler the head the better my business.

BOY. She's such a nice queen.

HEADSMAN. Have you seen her?

BOY. Y — es, sir.

HEADSMAN. When?

BOY. One day — when I was boiling some lentils.

HEADSMAN. Did you see her neck?

BOY. Yes, sir.

HEADSMAN. Not much bigger than a hair.

BOY (*desperately friendly*). Have you seen my knife?

HEADSMAN (*sharply*). *I'm* talking about the Queen and I'm going to talk about myself until I hear the King's trumpeter calling me to the beheading.

BOY. Yes, sir.

[*Edging between the bench and door of the room where the Queen is hidden.*

HEADSMAN. Sit down.

BOY. I'd rather stand, sir.

HEADSMAN. *Sit down!* And I'll tell you how I'm going to behead the Queen.

BOY. You can't behead her after the King's four clocks have struck twelve.

HEADSMAN.   How did you know that?

BOY (*realizing his blunder*).   Well —

HEADSMAN.   Nobody knows that except the royal family and people of the court.

BOY.   A little — bird told — me.

HEADSMAN.   Where is the little bird that I may cut its head off?

BOY.   Don't hurt the little bird, but tell me how you are going to behead the Queen.

HEADSMAN.   Well — (*At the stool*) This is the block. There's the Queen behind the iron gate. We'll say that door is the gate.

(*The Boy starts*)

And out there is the crowd. Now, I appear like this and walk up the steps. The crowd cheers, so I bow and show myself and my axe. Then I walk over to the gate —

BOY.   Don't go in there. That's my mother's room and you might frighten *her*.

HEADSMAN.   Who's in your mother's room?

BOY.   *She* is.

HEADSMAN.   Well, if she's in there, maybe she'd like to hear my story.

BOY.   She's in bed.

HEADSMAN.   Sick? (*The Boy nods vigorously*) All right. . . . Well, I've bowed to the crowd and I start for the Queen. — If you won't open the door, you pretend you're the Queen.

BOY.   I don't want to be the Queen.

HEADSMAN.   Come on and pretend. I walk up to the gate — so, and open it and then I say "Your Majesty, I'm going to cut off you head" and she bows — *bow* — (*The Boy bows*) And then I say "Are you ready?" and she says, "I am ready." Then I blindfold her —

BOY.   Now, don't blindfold me, sir!

HEADSMAN.   I'm showing you how it's done.

BOY.   But if you blindfold me I can't see when you do it.

HEADSMAN (*admitting the point*). All right. . . . Then I blindfold her and I lead her to the block and I say, "Have you made your peace with Heaven?" and she says, "Yes." . . .

BOY. If you won't tell me any more I'll give you my knife.

HEADSMAN. Aren't you interested?

BOY. Yes, but your axe is so sharp and it might slip.

HEADSMAN. Sharp? It will cut a hair in two, but I know how to handle it. . . . Come on . . . (*The Boy reluctantly falls into the picture again*) And then . . . (*Raising his axe*) And then . . . (*Headsman sees the Butterfly*) And then . . . How-d'-ye-do, Butterfly?

[*The Boy runs to the pot unnoticed by the Headsman.*

BOY. Lentils, lentils, boil the time away
That my good queen may live to-day.

[*The Headsman and the Butterfly are having quite a game. Suddenly the great clock begins to strike and the two next larger follow slowly.*

The Headsman rushes to the back door with his axe.

HEADSMAN. Why doesn't the trumpeter blow his call!

[*The Boy counts the strokes of the clock and as the third clock strikes twelve he rushes to the door of the bedroom.*

BOY. Queen! Queen! It's mid-day.

HEADSMAN. Queen — queen — (*He strides to the bedroom and drags the Queen out*) The little clock hasn't struck yet! (*He pulls the Queen toward the rear door and shouts*) Here! Here! don't let the little clock strike! I've won the pail of gold!

[*The Boy has set the bench in the doorway so that the Headsman stumbles. The Butterfly keeps flying against the Headsman's nose, which makes him sneeze.*

BOY. No one heard you!

QUEEN. Let me go! Let me go!

HEADSMAN (*sneezing as only a headsman can*). The Queen! The Queen!
(*The little clock begins to strike.*
The Boy counts eagerly, one, two, three, etc.

Between strokes the Headsman sneezes and shouts) The
Queen! The Queen!
[*At the fifth stroke the Headsman falls on his knees. The
Queen becomes regal, her foot on his neck.
The Boy kneels at her side.*

QUEEN. Base villain! According to the law I am saved!
But you are doomed. As Winder of the King's four clocks
the law commands that you be decapitated because the
four clocks did not strike together. Do you know that
law?

HEADSMAN. Oh, Lady, I do, but I did but do my duty. I
was sharpening my axe this morning and I couldn't wind
the clocks. Intercede for me.

QUEEN. It is useless.

BOY. Is there any other headsman?

QUEEN. The law says the Chief Headsman must behead
the Chief Winder of the King's four clocks.

BOY. Can the Dreadful Headsman behead himself?

QUEEN. Aye, there's the difficulty.

HEADSMAN. Oh, your Majesty, pardon me!

BOY. Yes, pardon him.

QUEEN. On one condition: He is to give his axe to the
museum and devote all his old age to the care of the King's
four clocks. . . . For myself, I shall pass a law requiring
the ladies of the court to wear no jewels. So, if the King's
aunt can wear no rings, she assuredly cannot have a ring-
toe, and hereafter I may step where I please. . . . Sir
Headsman, lead the way. . . . And now, my little boy,
to you I grant every Friday afternoon an hour's sport with
the Mime, a spotted cow for the little Milkmaid, a cushion
and a canopy at the palace gate for the Blind Man, a vermilion cloak for the Ballad-Singer, a velvet gown, a silken
kerchief and a cloth-of-gold bonnet for your mother, and
for yourself a milk-white palfrey, two pails of gold, two
finger rings, a castle and a sword. . . . Arise, Sir Little
Boy. . . . Your arm.

BOY. May I take my knife, your Majesty?

QUEEN. That you may. (*He gets the knife and returns to her. She lays her hand on his arm*) Sir Headsman, announce our coming.

HEADSMAN. Make way — make way — for her Majesty the Queen.

QUEEN (*correcting*). *And* Sir Little Boy.

HEADSMAN. What's his other name, your Majesty?

BOY (*whispering with the wonder of it all*). Davie.

QUEEN (*to the Headsman*). Davie.

HEADSMAN. Make way — make way for her Majesty the Queen and Sir Davie Little Boy.

[*They go out.*

Immediately the Boy returns and gets the pot of lentils and runs after the Queen as

The Curtains Close.

" VOICES "

HORTENSE FLEXNER

Miss Hortense Flexner is a resident of Louisville, Kentucky, where she was born on April 10, 1885. In 1903 she entered Bryn Mawr, but remained there only for the Freshman year, completing her academic education at the University of Michigan. There she received the degree of A.B. in 1907 and the degree of A.M. in 1910.

In addition to "Voices", which was printed originally in *The Seven Arts*, Miss Flexner is the author of a number of poems which have been printed in various magazines.

Stuart Walker has produced "Voices" with his Portmanteau Company and has in his repertory for future production Miss Flexner's "Three Wise Men of Gotham" and "The Road." Her "The Broken God" was produced by the Little Theatre Society of Indiana at Indianapolis in January, 1916.

"VOICES"

By HORTENSE FLEXNER

"Voices" was originally produced under the direction of Stuart Walker and the Portmanteau Company, New York, 1916.

Original Cast

YVONNE . . . . Judith Lowry
THE OTHER . . . . Florence Wollersen

Printed originally in *Seven Arts*.

Application for the right of performing "Voices", must be made to Miss Hortense Flexner, 948 South Second Street, Louisville, Kentucky, or to Mr. Stuart Walker, 304 Carnegie Hall, New York City.

" VOICES "

SCENE. *The main street of Domremy, in front of the shattered church sacred to Jeanne D'Arc. Roofless houses and broken buildings stand huddled in ruins. The place is deserted and silent. From the right comes a peasant girl, Yvonne, finely made and young. She wears a coarse, wool skirt and a gray shawl loosely folded about her shoulders. Taking her way down the sunken street, she pauses before the door of the church and kneels. As she does so, another peasant girl, slight and erect, comes silently from the church. The time is late afternoon in May. The south wind is stirring. Yvonne stands.*

YVONNE.   I heard a voice that called across the wind.

THE OTHER.   A voice? My thoughts were prayers.
What vision I have seen, no words have said.

YVONNE.   The dead! Their souls are strange upon the air,
And cannot find the way to Paradise.
Perhaps they spoke.

THE OTHER.   Or cannon far away.

YVONNE (*covering her ears*).   O, no —

THE OTHER.   Alas — and did you live in **Domremy**?

YVONNE.   Before they came. But now
The great shells have not left a house — not one.
Even the Church,
Jeanne's church in which she heard the angels speak,
Is broken to the ground —

THE OTHER.   Jeanne dwelt once in a **prison far from home**;
There was a day — ah well —
She can forego the church.

YVONNE (*with energy*).   But no! We will rebuild it stone by
    stone,
  There is no villager shall rest
  Till it is whole.

THE OTHER.   There's better work to do for Jeanne
  Than build a church.

YVONNE.   And let her think we have forgot again?
  Or that we are afraid?

THE OTHER.   It was so long ago — and now —

YVONNE.   But Jeanne is Domremy!
  We think of her, as if she had not died.
  In early Spring
  We make a pageant — every Spring for Jeanne,
  To show her as a girl, here where she lived,
  And heard the voices first — a shepherd girl,
  In clothes like these, like yours.
  I was the Maid last May!

THE OTHER.   You Jeanne?   And rode a charger too?
  In armor like a man's.   And were you mocked,
  Until you crowned the King that day at Rheims,
  Thrown in a cell — and burned — all in the play?

YVONNE.   You saw it then?   Perhaps you lived near by?

THE OTHER.   Near by.

YVONNE.   And are you coming now to find the things
  The soldiers have not battered to a ruin?

THE OTHER.   Not I — no — no —

YVONNE (*with defiance*).   Nor I!

THE OTHER.   What then?   A hidden relic in the church?

YVONNE.   I should not seek for that in Domremy.
  The one I wore so many years for luck,
  About my throat, I gave the lad who played
  Jeanne's lover in the fête.   (*Stolidly*)
  Relic and lad are buried in a ditch
  Beyond Arras — how should I know?

THE OTHER.   And so you came?

YVONNE.   I came to pray Jeanne D'Arc.

THE OTHER.   Trudged all the way through blood and mire —

YVONNE. To pray her come again. They say she hears,
When May is young, and that her spirit flies
Close — close to Domremy when leaves are new,
And tender things are born.
THE OTHER. You'd have her come? Is there not strife
  enough?
France has good friends, and all the kings are crowned.
YVONNE. Jeanne D'Arc would make an end of war.
She'd stop the guns!
When she was just a girl — alone and mocked,
She took a sword and flashed it through the land,
Until she pressed the foe upon the sea.
And would she not to-day?
Shall one love France the less for being safe
In Paradise?
THE OTHER. Poor Jeanne.
YVONNE (remembering). It was a miracle —
THE OTHER. I do not know.
YVONNE. She was so young, so slight — but all her soul
Burned as a torch.
A spirit lies in Jeanne to wake the dead.
If she should come, we could not wait and wait,
Gain here, lose there, hide in the trenches, wait,
And drag the war to years.
O, she would show the way!
No girl, this time, but saint she'd draw her sword —
THE OTHER (sharply). No — no —
YVONNE (mocking). Jeanne D'Arc without a sword!
THE OTHER. Without a sword!
YVONNE. It was her strength. She saw it in a dream —
THE OTHER. Jeanne had her soul before she had the sword.
YVONNE (scornfully). A soul against the guns!
THE OTHER. It is the only thing they may not break.
YVONNE. But who would know Jeanne D'Arc without her
  sword?
THE OTHER. Hush! She will weep in Paradise for that.
YVONNE (frightened). I love her —

THE OTHER. She hates her sword!

YVONNE. You dare! She carried it the day
They crowned the King.

THE OTHER. The day she failed! Poor Jeanne! She did
not know
A peasant girl must never crown a king,
Nor fight his foes. If she had known —
If she had only known —

YVONNE (*more and more amazed*). But Jeanne did know. A
spirit showed the way.

THE OTHER (*continuing*). She would have struck the King —
there as he knelt,
And killed him with her sword. It was her sin
She did not kill the King. He was the foe
Of France — all kings are foes of all the men
They rule. How else should they send men to death
For little things? What that a King can fear
Is worth the death of one — one peasant lad,
Who loves the sky?
Jeanne was no saint — she was a shepherd girl,
Who did not know how things would come to pass.

YVONNE. The voices spoke —

THE OTHER. O yes — the voices. Better had she heard
Her pitying heart —

YVONNE. Jeanne was a soldier maid. Her pitying heart
Was but the girl —

THE OTHER. It was herself — the most of her — the flame!
And it shall lead when she shall come again.

YVONNE. A pitying heart the leader of a host?

THE OTHER (*gladly*). Yes — yes. A pitying heart!

YVONNE (*as if humoring one a little mad*). And what host
then?

THE OTHER. A host of pitying hearts, which kings shall fear,
More than defeat and death.

YVONNE (*making ready to go*). It is a dream — as mine — a
dream.

THE OTHER. The voices were not more.

YVONNE.   If that were true, Jeanne would be here to-day,
   And my prayer heard.
THE OTHER (*continuing in exaltation*). An army kings shall fear,
   A silent host,
   Scattered — bereft —
   Mourning at broken hearthstones in all lands,
   Hating one thing — a hate that makes them kin,
   Stronger than blood and bone — the hate of death.
   Which is their love of life.
   These Jeanne shall lead, the brooding ones who give
   In grief and tears, knowing so well the end,
   The raw earth mound that's left, where kings have passed.
   These Jeanne shall find —
YVONNE (*stirred*).   Women — women of France.
THE OTHER.   Women of all the earth shall be Jeanne's
      strength.
   And she shall go to them,
   In peasant clothes — a maid !
   And where she finds a woman at her toil,
   She'll stop and say,
   "Would you have back your dead ? "
   And by their answer they shall follow Jeanne,
   Until her army, swelling like a flood,
   Pours down the earth undammed.
   What can the kings build up against this tide,
   The woe and rage, impatience and despair
   Of all the withheld women of all years,
   Borne down on them at last ?
   What can they do, if men no longer mad,
   But grim with agony and blood and death,
   Leap from the trenches, break the mighty guns,
   And with the women turn their faces home ?
   O, in that hour the puny kings shall see
   As some great mountain blotting out the sun,
   The shadow of our wrath,
   And know defeat — all kings alike —
   But people shall be free !

YVONNE (*rapt*).   Jeanne and the women — when?

THE OTHER.   She was a peasant girl —

YVONNE (*looking down at her wooden shoes*).   A peasant girl!
  (*As she lifts her eyes, she is alone.   With terror*)   Voices!
  It was the Maid herself.
  I am afraid.
  [*She kneels upon the stone step of the church, in the crack of
  which, strangely, a lily is growing.*

CURTAIN

THE MERRY MERRY CUCKOO

JEANNETTE MARKS

Miss Jeannette Marks was born in 1875 in Chattanooga, Tennessee, but spent her early life in Philadelphia. Her father, the late William Dennis Marks, was Professor of Dynamics at the University of Pennsylvania and President of the Edison Electric Light Company, besides being the author of several scientific books. Miss Marks attended school at Dresden and in this country before entering Wellesley College, where she was graduated in 1900. After a year of graduate work at Wellesley, she became instructress in the department of English Literature at Mt. Holyoke College, where she is now teaching Nineteenth Century Poetry and Play Writing. There she has instituted the Poetry Shop Talks, where poets and writers speak to the students on the authors of the day.

Miss Marks' interest in Wales was the result of several summers spent among the Northern Welsh mountains, where she walked over the hills and through the valleys, knapsack on back, and became intimately acquainted with Welsh peasant life.

The result of her intimate observation is to be found in her books and in her many short stories published in magazines.

Several years ago, on a homeward voyage from England, Edward Knobloch discussed with the author the dramatic possibilities of some of her short stories. "Three Welsh Plays" is the result. Two of these were entered by an acquaintance, without the author's knowledge, in the competition for Lord Howard DeWalden's prize for the best Welsh play in 1911, and were awarded first place by the Welsh National Theatre, although the prize had been planned for a three-act play.

Her published works are: "The Cheerful Cricket", 1907; "The English Pastoral", 1908; "Through Welsh Doorways", 1909; "The End of a Song", 1911; "A Girl's School Days and After", 1911; "Gallant Little Wales", 1912; "Vacation Camping for Girls", 1913; "Leviathan", 1913; "Early English Hero Tales", 1915; "The Sun Chaser", in *Best Short Stories* for 1916; "Three Welsh Plays", 1917; "Madame France" and "Courage", 1919.

THE MERRY MERRY CUCKOO

By JEANNETTE MARKS

"The Merry Merry Cuckoo" was originally produced at the Toy Theatre, Boston, in 1911.

Original Cast

DAVID	Mr. Mac Gregor Jenkins
ANNIE	Ruth B. Delano
PASTOR MORRIS	Mr. Pettis
LOWRY PRICHARD	Mary Kellogg
GUTO PRICHARD	Mr. Clarke

THE MERRY MERRY CUCKOO

SCENE. *A garden. Cottage at back running from right to center. A group of three windows in the shape of a bay, showing a bed inside and an old man lying on it. A door leads into cottage. A gate in fence on the right side leads to the road and village beyond. All of the left side of stage a garden and orchard, with a path through it to a gate in wall at back; garden wall to left, at back over it village chapel from which the church music comes.*

A thatched cottage with whitewashed walls. Ivy is growing about the doorway, and hanging from the thatch above the door; fuchsia bushes on either side of door; trees to the left in garden, including holly and yew; green grass; mountains beyond cottage and garden and chapel. In the foreground, to right by cottage door, is a washtub.

It is about six o'clock, the first Monday in April. Towards end of act the sun sets.

At rise of curtain, windows of the cottage closed, and Annie, old, very plump, with sparse gray hair escaping from under her white cap and damp on her forehead from work, and wearing a short skirt, apron, fichu over shoulders, clogs on her feet, is washing. Church music off left continues a minute after rise of curtain. David calls out. Annie leaves the tub and hurries to the windows to open them from the outside. David, a very old man, with white hair and thin face, is seen lying in bed.

DAVID (*calling*). Annie, Annie!

ANNIE (*opening windows*). Aye, lad dear, I was listenin' for ye; yiss, yiss, an' expectin' ye to call.

DAVID (*sleepily*). I was dreamin' an' — dear, dear, what a dream! It seemed like fifty years ago when we were married, an', you remember, we stood out there in the garden that first night. Are there any violets bloomin' yet?

ANNIE.   Not yet, Davy lad.

DAVID.   An' the marsh marigolds?

ANNIE.   I'm thinkin' they're sure to be out.

DAVID.   An' that same night, Annie, do ye remember we heard the cuckoo singin'?

ANNIE.   Aye, lad darlin', fifty years ago this comin' week, an' a cuckoo singin' to us every spring since then. (*Annie takes a tumbler from the sill and gives him a spoonful of medicine*) Take this, dear; there, 'twill be makin' ye better.

DAVID (*taking medicine*).   An' well?

ANNIE.   Yiss, yiss, better.

DAVID.   But the cuckoo, will the cuckoo be singin' soon?

ANNIE (*words inconclusive*).   Lad, dear, no more, or ye'll be havin' an attack an' — Dear people, chapel is out, an' I hear them on the road!

DAVID (*plaintively*).   The Monday meetin'. Why have ye not been?

ANNIE.   Work is keepin' me home, lad.

DAVID.   But, Annie, ye've not said a word of the cuckoo.

ANNIE (*sending her voice up as cheerfully as she can*).   Aye, the cuckoo; yiss, the cuckoo —

DAVID (*clasping and unclasping his hands*).   Has it come? Did ye hear it?

ANNIE (*gulping*).   David, dear, if ye'd but listen to what I was a-goin' to say. I was a-goin' to say that I've not heard the cuckoo yet, but that everthin's over-early this spring in Wales, an' I'm expectin' to hear one any time now. 'Tis so warm there might be one singin' at dusk to-day — there might be!

DAVID (*brightening*).   Might there be, Annie?

ANNIE (*smoothing his head with her hand*).   Aye, lad. Hush, lad, they're singin' in the chapel!

[*She stands there with one hand resting on his forehead, listen-*

*ing to the singing of Penlan, a hymn by David Jenkins.
When the music stops, she moves away.*

DAVID. 'Tis over-early, an', Annie —

ANNIE. Davy dear, be still! Pastor Morris says — Tut,
tut, I'll close the window, for there comes that Lowry
Prichard and her man.

[*Annie closes windows hastily and goes back to her washing.
Enter from right Lowry and her husband Guto, coming from
the Monday prayer meeting and carrying hymnals. Lowry
dressed in Welsh costume, clogs, short full skirt, striped apron,
white sleeves from elbow to wrist, tight bodice, shawl over her
shoulders, white cap, and tall, Welsh beaver hat. Guto, Welsh
beaver hat on like his wife's, striped vest, brass buttons on lapels
of black cloth coat, long, somewhat tight trousers. At sight
of washtub and Annie busy over it, Lowry and Guto make
gestures of shocked dismay to each other.*

LOWRY. Good evenin', Annie Dalben.

ANNIE (*wiping her wet hand on her apron*). Good evenin',
Lowry Prichard, an' to you, Guto.

GUTO. Good evenin', mum.

LOWRY. How is your man?

ANNIE. He's no better.

LOWRY. Is he worse?

ANNIE. Nay.

LOWRY. We missed ye, Annie Dalben.

GUTO. Aye, we did. Why were ye not at meetin'?

ANNIE. I've my man to mind these days.

LOWRY (*triumphantly*). But ye said he was no worse, ye
did.

ANNIE. Aye, I did, but I cannot leave him alone.

GUTO. But ye're neglectin' chapel an' forgettin' the Lord
Annie Dalben. Ye'll go quite on the downfall, like
this.

LOWRY. Aye, ye've not been to meetin's, an' 'tis bad when
he's dyin' for ye to forget your Lord. Is he in there?

ANNIE (*moving protectingly nearer the closed window*). Yiss.

LOWRY. Why were ye washin'?

ANNIE. Ye've no cause to ask that — ye know. Except I did the washin', what would there be for me to care for David with — now that he needs me?

GUTO. Yiss, but ye could do it on some other day.

ANNIE. Nay, for the ladies are waitin' now for what they've given me to do — an' they so kind.

LOWRY. I see Pastor Morris comin' in.

ANNIE. Aye, he's comin' every day an' some days bringin' me the food from his own table for my man.

[*Enter Pastor Morris, young, earnest and rather severe because of his youth.*

LOWRY (*the inquisitional look on her face deepening, and her voice growing more shrill, pointing to Annie*). Ye see, sir, what Annie Dalben's been doin' while we were in meetin'. She's needin' a sermon, aye, that she is.

GUTO. She's goin' quite on the downfall, sir.

ANNIE. Lowry Prichard, ye've no cause to speak so about me. When was I ever absent when my man was well? But now, sir, (*turning to Morris*) as ye know, he's ill an' needin' me an' all the s'illin's I can earn. I cannot go away from him.

LOWRY (*speaking to Pastor Morris*). She's needin' your advice, sir. 'Tis that she is needin' whatever. Warn her well.

GUTO. Yiss, an' rebuke her.

LOWRY. Ye're young, sir, but ye're the instrument of the Lord whatever. 'Tis your duty to bring her back to her conscience.

GUTO. Amen.

[*Lowry and Guto go off very self-righteous and looking triumphantly at Annie, who, quiet, her face pale and weary, turns to her washing and rubs and rinses diligently, while the minister is talking.*

MORRIS (*gently*). I've been troubled, for I knew that it would come to this, Annie. I should have spoken with you before about going to chapel. Some one could be found to stay with David while you were at meeting. You have not been to chapel for a month, Annie.

ANNIE (*continuing her work, but in her voice the attitude of the older woman towards the young man*). Ye're very kind, sir, to take the interest, but I'm thinkin' ye cannot understand. There's been no occasion, sir, for ye to understand through what I've been goin' these days.

[*She rubs her sleeve across her tear-filled eyes and continues washing sturdily.*

MORRIS. Yes, but, Annie, what is David thinking? Does he want you to stay away from the meetings where you have always been together?

ANNIE. Nay, sir.

MORRIS. Has he spoken of your staying away?

ANNIE (*reluctantly*). Aye, sir, he asked this evenin' why I was not in meetin'.

MORRIS (*reflectively*). He did. Well, I am thinking that —

ANNIE (*dropping her work and speaking as if worried*). Nay, sir, I've no cause to excuse myself to ye — ye're naught but a lad. 'Tis past your knowledge how my man is everythin' to me — everythin', he is. He's been such a husband as no one but myself can know, thinkin' of me all the time, livin' for me, as gentle an' tender to me as if I had been a child, an' now, sir, he's ill — he may be dyin', an' I can think of nothin' but doin' everythin' for — (*David taps on window and Annie turns to open it*) Aye, lad dear. 'Tis the Pastor comin' to see ye again.

DAVID (*smiling and holding out one weak old hand*). Good evenin', sir, such a grand day, with spring everywhere. We've been expectin' the cuckoo, sir — the wife and I. Have ye heard the cuckoo, yet, Annie?

MORRIS (*starting to speak*). 'Twill be a fortnight be —

ANNIE (*interrupting hurriedly*). Nay, lad dear, I've been busy, but I'm thinkin' I'm likely to hear it now any moment — aye, any moment.

MORRIS. But, Annie, the cuckoo doesn't —

ANNIE. Tut, sir, I could almost promise the cuckoo would be singin' at sundown whatever — aye, indeed, lad darlin'. Now I'll —

DAVID (*interrupting*).   Annie, ye mind that baby cuckoo we
saw the sky-lark a-feedin' that first spring in Blaen Cwm?
It all comes back so clear now an' clearer every moment.
I'd not once thought of it, sir, since then.

MORRIS.   But, David, the —

ANNIE (*speaking to David and closing the windows*).   Lie down,
lad darlin', an' be quiet.   I'll call ye, if the cuckoo sings.
[*In the distance the choir can be heard practising Cariad, a
revival hymn, in the chapel.   Continues until Annie is alone
and talking to herself.*

MORRIS (*severely*).   But, Annie, you know the cuckoo will
not sing at least for another fortnight.   It is mid-April
before the cuckoo sings.

ANNIE (*wearily*).   Aye, sir.

MORRIS.   Why did you say that to David?

ANNIE.   He's achin', sir, to hear the cuckoo sing, an' I'm
wantin' to comfort him.

MORRIS.   But, Annie, it is a lie to say what you did to
him.

ANNIE (*vigorously*).   Aye, sir, but I'm not carin' whatever.

MORRIS (*severely*).   Not caring about telling a lie?

ANNIE.   Nay, sir, I'm not carin' about anythin' but makin'
him happy.

MORRIS (*rebukingly*).   Annie!   (*Annie continues washing and
does not reply*)   Annie!   Well, indeed, Annie, if there is
nothing I can do for you, and you will not listen to me, I
must be going to choir practice.   I promised to be there
this evening.

ANNIE (*without turning from the tub*).   Aye, sir.   (*Pastor
Morris off through garden path to choir practice.   Goes to
left.   Annie continues washing until he is well out of sight.
She stands up straight and looks about the garden*)   He's
wantin' to hear the cuckoo more nor anythin' else, dear,
dear!   Everywhere 'tis green now, an' the lilies will be
here before long — but lad, lad, the cuckoo, will it come?
(*She goes to left into garden, the wet clothes in a basket under
her arm and stands there, looking about*)   'Twas over there

it laid its egg in the robin's nest this year ago in May —
aye, an' one poor little bird pushed the other out, an' ye
picked it up, lad dear, an' were so tender with it. An'
they're not wantin' ye, Davy, my old lad darlin', to think
the cuckoo will be singin' soon. Dear God, is there to be
no cuckoo singin' for the lad again? Just once more,
dear God, to sing to him and comfort him? Aye! just
the one song? No cuckoo? Aye, there will be a cuckoo
singin', there shall be a cuckoo singin'! (*She looks towards
the closed windows behind which David lies, and puts down
her basket of clothes*) He's asleep! Hush, I'll be the
cuckoo! He'll wake an' think the spring has really come.
Here by this tree. They're in the chapel, an' they'll never
know. (*Throughout this scene, until Lowry speaks, a cuckoo
song is being played very softly. And it is into a few notes
of this, several times repeated, that Annie swings when she
actually sings her cuckoo song. She opens her mouth to begin, a look of appealing misery on her face*) 'Twas somethin' like this: *Coo-o. Coo-o!* Tut, that sounds like a
hen. I know, it goes over an' over again, sing-song,
sing-song, like this: *cu-cu, cu-cu.* Aye, that's better.
(*She rocks herself backwards and forwards practising it and
repeating cu-cu, cu-cu*) 'Tis growin' better, but lad, lad,
I'm plannin' to deceive ye whatever! (*Brushes tears away
impatiently and begins song again*) *Cucu-cu, cucu-cu,
cucucu-cu, cu!* Aye, that's fair; aye, 'tis fine! He'll not
know me from a real cuckoo. I'll try it loud now, for
ye've no long, dearie.
[*She holds eagerly on to tree beside her, so lost in the cuckoo
music that she is not aware of a head popping up behind the
garden wall and down again. She draws a long breath and
begins, softly, slowly, the song sounding as if it came from a
distance. She waits a moment, — the heads are well above the
wall now in amazement, — and then sings more loudly,
making the song sound as if it came from the garden where she
is standing.*

DAVID (*calling*). Annie!

ANNIE (*hurrying to open his windows*). Aye, lad dear, I'm comin'.

DAVID (*ecstatically*). Annie, Annie, dear, I heard the cuckoo singin'; I was dreamin' again, an' all at once I heard the cuckoo singin' in the garden, loud and clear. It sang three times; first, it sounded like somethin' else, 'twas so breathless; then it sang quiet an' sweet like a cuckoo; an' the third time it seemed comin' from the old mill wheel.

ANNIE. But, lad darlin', ye've heard it. an' I'm that glad! Three times; yiss, yiss, 'tis a real fine cuckoo. Now ye're happy, darlin', an' ye'll sleep well upon it.

DAVID (*disappointedly*). Did ye no hear it?

ANNIE. I'm thinkin' I did an' thinkin' I didn't.

DAVID. Where were ye?

ANNIE. Out in the garden, hangin' out the clothes.

DAVID (*still more disappointedly*). An' ye didn't hear it?

ANNIE. I'm no certain, darlin'; I heard somethin' — I did, indeed.

DAVID (*proudly*). 'Twas the cuckoo, Annie dear; I'm hearin' it first every year; ye must be growin' deaf.

ANNIE. Yiss, yiss. Now go to sleep, an' I'll call ye if I hear the cuckoo sing.

DAVID. Will it sing again?

ANNIE. Aye, darlin', if ye heard it once, 'tis sure to sing again.

DAVID. I'll be gettin' well, Annie, is it not so?

ANNIE (*turning away suddenly*). Indeed, lad dear, ye'll be about among the heather 'fore long.

DAVID (*speaking quietly, almost to himself*). To think the cuckoo's singin' — singin' for me!

ANNIE. Aye, aye; now go to sleep.

[*He lies back and closes his eyes obediently. Annie, drying her eyes on her apron, goes to left towards her basket of clothes. She stands by the tree where she had sung the cuckoo song for David, unconscious that two people are head and shoulders above the garden wall, looking at her.*

LOWRY (*in a loud voice*). So ye've come back, Annie Dalben, to sing the cuckoo again.

GUTO. Aye, we heard ye singin' the cuckoo.

LOWRY. Pooh, 'tis a pretty cuckoo ye make, an old woman like you, an' a pretty song!

ANNIE. Lowry Prichard, have a care!

GUTO. 'Tis over-early for the cuckoo, is it not?

ANNIE. Yiss.

GUTO. An' what are ye singin' in your garden for, an' David dyin'?

[*Annie does not reply but stoops to her basket of clothes and begins to hang them out.*

LOWRY. So ye'll give no answer? Well, indeed, maybe ye'll answer Pastor Morris. Aye, Guto, go fetch the Pastor.

[*Guto goes off to left, through garden gate in garden wall.*

LOWRY (*going towards the windows behind which David lies*). 'Tis a godly song ye've sung, Annie, an' a tale for the chapel, eh?

ANNIE (*following and stepping in front of Lowry*). Ye may go out of this garden, an' that this minute!

LOWRY (*making her way nearer and nearer the window*). Nay, nay, I'm a-goin' to speak with David an' tell him he's a cuckoo for a wife. Tut, ye look fair crazy, Annie, crazy with wrath! Your hair is all rumpled, an' your smock is dirty. David, bein' a cuckoo is —

[*But the taunt is left unfinished, for at that moment young Morris comes in hastily, Guto following.*

MORRIS (*authoritatively*). Annie! Lowry! Annie, is this I hear true? Have you been imitating the cuckoo?

ANNIE. Aye, sir.

MORRIS (*turning to Lowry and Guto*). You may go. Leave this to me.

[*Guto and Lowry go off right, through front gate, staring in at David as they pass.*

MORRIS (*sternly*). So, Annie, you have been acting the cuckoo — acting a lie. With this lie upon you, how will it be with salvation?

ANNIE (*hotly*). Salvation, sir? I've no mind to your salvation; no, nor to heaven's, if the Lord makes this singin' a lie! I'm thinkin' of David as I've thought of him these fifty years, years before ye were born, sir, an' if a lie will make him happy when he's dyin', then I'm willin' to lie, an' do it every minute of the day.

MORRIS. That means you are willing to sin?

ANNIE. Aye, sir, to sin. I'm a willin' sinner!

MORRIS (*more gently*). You are overwrought, Annie.

ANNIE (*wearily*). Ye're all against me, sir.

MORRIS. Nay, nay, but wouldn't it be better if I were to tell David about the cuckoo?

ANNIE (*sobbing*). Oh, no, no, no, sir! Not that!

MORRIS (*stretching out his hand to comfort her*). Annie, there, there, you mustn't cry so.

ANNIE. 'Tis all the happiness he's got, an' he's goin'. Oh, my lad, my lad!

MORRIS. There, there, Annie!

ANNIE. We've been married fifty years this spring, an' every spring we've listened for the cuckoo an' not one missed. An' now he's a-dyin' an' a-wantin' to hear it so, an' 'twas over-early, an' then I thought of bein' the cuckoo myself. Oh, Davy, Davy darlin'!

MORRIS (*altogether forgetting his pastoral severity*). There, Annie, there, dear, tell me about it! We'll see, Annie.

ANNIE. There's no more. Only he kept askin' about the spring, the violets an' marsh marigolds, an' I knew all the time he was thinkin' of the cuckoo an' not askin' because he was goin' an' mightn't hear it. An' then he did. An' I said I thought he'd hear one this evenin', that everythin' was over-early whatever. After that he seemed happier than I'd seen him, an' I closed his windows an' went off into the garden to practise it. I worked at it till I could do it fair. Oh, Davy, Davy lad!

MORRIS. Now, Annie dear, don't cry, just tell me more.

ANNIE. Then, sir, I sang the song here by this tree, an' when he called me to him, there was such a look of joy on his face as has not been there this long time. 'Tis the last happiness I can give him, sir.

DAVID (*calling*). Annie, Annie!

ANNIE. He's callin'. Aye, lad dear, I'm comin'.

[*She goes into cottage and, after opening all the windows, stands by the foot of David's bed.*

DAVID. Have ye heard the cuckoo singin'?

ANNIE. No, not yet. It must be singin' again soon.

DAVID (*anxiously*). Ye're sure 'tis *goin'* to sing?

ANNIE (*gathering him up and turning his pillow*). Indeed, yiss, an' with the windows all open, ye'll be hearin' it fine an' clear, ye will. I'll go back up into the garden to see is the cuckoo there.

DAVID. Will it be singin' over an' over again, the way it did that first time?

ANNIE. Aye, I'm thinkin' so, lad darlin'. Ye must listen quietly.

DAVID. 'Twas so beautiful singin'. I'd like hearin' it with ye here beside me.

ANNIE (*kissing him*). I'll come back, lad.

DAVID. Aye, I'll be waitin' for ye.

[*Annie goes out of the cottage door and back into garden where Pastor Morris is standing, his hat off, while Annie and David are talking together. He can see them both, but David cannot see him. Annie and Morris converse in whispers. The cuckoo song begins to be played softly.*

MORRIS. Is he worse?

ANNIE (*looking at Morris beseechingly*). I cannot tell, sir, but he's longin' to hear the cuckoo sing again.

MORRIS. I see, and you are wishing to do it again?

ANNIE. Yiss, an' with the lad dyin', can ye tell me not to do what Davy is askin' for? Each time might be his last, sir.

MORRIS (*after a moment's hesitation*). Nay, go sing for him. I will stand guard for you, and no one shall disturb you.

ANNIE (*a deep sigh of relief*). Oh, sir, thank you! 'Tis sure to be a comfort. But ye're harmin' your conscience for me, sir, are ye?

MORRIS (*humbly*).   I'm not saying, Annie; I'm over-young to have a conscience in some things.

ANNIE (*taking his hand to kiss it*).   May God bless ye, sir, for bein' kind to an old woman!

[*The sun has set behind the chapel, and it is rapidly growing dark as the music grows louder.   Morris steps back to the garden gate to keep watch.   Annie stands by the tree and, dropping her hands by her side, lifting her head, and swaying her old body to and fro, sings the cuckoo song over and over again three times.   David has risen in bed, an expression of rapturous delight upon his face as he leans against the casement listening.   The lights are being lighted in the chapel, and the chapel bell begins to ring.*

DAVID (*calling faintly*).   Annie, Annie darlin', come quickly, the cuckoo's singin'!

ANNIE (*hastening towards him*).   Yiss, lad, I'm comin'.

DAVID (*stretching out his hands towards her*).   Annie, sweetheart, did ye *hear* the cuckoo singin'?

ANNIE.   Yiss, dearie, loud and clear.

DAVID (*trying to imitate its song while his voice grows fainter*).   It sang over an' over like this —

ANNIE (*within the cottage and beside David*).   Yiss, dear, I see.

DAVID (*sinking back into her arms*).   An' — it — was — quiet — but — Annie —

ANNIE (*holding him to her and crying out*).   Lad, lad dear. Davy, can ye not speak to me?

[*The bell for chapel stops ringing.   The organ playing "Jesus, Lover of my Soul" is heard.   Morris is standing by the gate, facing towards the old people, his hat off, his head bowed.*

CURTAIN

SINTRAM OF SKAGERRAK

SADA COWAN

Miss Sada Cowan (in private life, Mrs. Fredrick James Pitt) was educated at a private boarding school near Boston. At the age of fifteen she went to Germany to study music. She found, however, that this work did not entirely satisfy her and so she began a series of travels which extended over a number of years.

"Sintram of Skagerrak" was written in Frankfort, Germany, late one evening, as the result of the inspiration which Frederick Lamond aroused through his piano recital of Chopin. The play itself was written in less than two hours and has never been altered by the addition or the elimination of a word.

Miss Cowan has published "In the Morgue", "The State Forbids", and "Investigation." In addition to these, she has produced "Playing the Game", "Pomp", "The Wonder of the Age", "The Moonlit Way", "Abdul the Azra", "The Honor of America", and "I Wish I Knew."

SINTRAM OF SKAGERRAK

By SADA COWAN

"Sintram of Skagerrak" was originally produced by the Brooklyn Repertory Theatre, April 27, 1917.

Original Cast

SINTRAM	Harmon Cheshire
GUNHILDE	Ethel Rosemon

SINTRAM OF SKAGERRAK

SCENE. *A high, bare cliff, situated on the edge of the shore, in a bleak, barren country. Against this cliff the breakers dash unceasingly, splitting with a roar and thud; tossing their spray high into the air.*

It is a moonlight night in summer.

On the peak of the cliff, and looking out upon the ocean, stands Sintram, an emaciated, frail, sickly lad of about twenty. As the curtains part, he stretches his arms out impetuously towards the sea, uttering a prolonged "Ah . . . h . . . h!" then lets them fall languidly to his side and hangs his head, as though weary of his whole existence. He continues to stand, apathetic and listless, for several moments, gazing spellbound upon the ocean. Unobserved by him across the rocks, Gunhilde enters: a vivacious girl of eighteen, plainly dressed as befits her lowly station. She looks about and behind her as if afraid of being followed, then, a rock hiding Sintram from her view, calls softly.

GUNHILDE. Sintram . . . ! Sintram . . . ! (*Sintram, lost in his morose brooding, does not hear her, but continues to stand staring at the ocean*) Sintram . . . ! Sintram . . . ! Ah, there you are. I hoped that I should find you.

[*Sintram turns slowly and descends the cliff with tired, dragging step; she runs eagerly towards him.*

SINTRAM (*angrily*). What are you doing here, Gunhilde, at this hour?

GUNHILDE. Sh . . . h . . . h . . . ! Not so loud! Some one will hear you.

SINTRAM. What are you doing here! Have I not forbidden your creeping out of your house, like a thief in the night, to look for me!

GUNHILDE. Be kind . . . be gentle, Sintram.

SINTRAM (*sternly*). Your Father thinks you at home. Why do you deceive him? Go home! (*She does not move. Kindly*) Go, little friend, little playmate! You know it is for your good I would have you go . . . go home!

GUNHILDE. No.

SINTRAM. We have said all that we had to say to each other. Why have you come back again?

GUNHILDE. I had to see you once more Sintram before . . . (*her voice breaks*) . . . before they take you away. I shall be at work in the morning when they come for you. [*She covers her face with her hands and begins to sob.*

SINTRAM (*furiously*). Stop that senseless crying! Leave me alone. Do you think that my soul is not racked enough? (*Sadly*) All night I have sat on the edge of the cliff saying "Good-by" to the sea. We understand each other, the mad, wild, restless ocean and I. And all night she has wept for me . . . wept in her anguish. (*Pushing Gunhilde aside*) I have no need of woman's tears.

GUNHILDE (*awed*). Often it seems to me, Sintram, as though there were something uncanny about you. As though you lived on this earth among us, without really being one of us. When you have taken me in your arms and have kissed me tenderly . . . (*bitterly*) just as if I were a little child, I have felt that worlds and worlds lay between us. What is it, Sintram? Have you a secret which you have kept from me? (*He gives no answer, but dumbly nods his head in assent*) I thought so. Will you not tell it to me before you go?

SINTRAM (*hastily*). No . . . no . . . you could not understand.

GUNHILDE. Let me try . . . come . . . tell me! (*She leads him to a rock where they sit beside each other, she still holding his hand. He shivers nervously and coughs*) You ought not to be here in the night air.

SINTRAM. I am not cold (*shivers again*) but . . . . I feel — afraid. Gunhilde, come closer . . .

GUNHILDE (*moves nearer to him*). Why, you are shivering! Here, let me fasten your coat, you poor boy.

SINTRAM (*shaking her off and turning on her with sudden, unexpected fury*). Bah! Do you begin too? Can I not have just this one night in peace? Is it not time enough for me to begin my life as a puppet . . . to-morrow?

GUNHILDE (*hurt*). Why, Sintram!

SINTRAM. I mean what I say, every word of it and I know what I'm saying. (*She attempts to touch him*) Leave me alone! Do you hear? Do not touch me. To-night is mine . . . MINE! And if the night air kills me . . . let it kill. But just this once I am going to forget that I am nothing but the shadow of a man, sick and miserable, cheated by nature of all that a man should have; blind-folded and handicapped in Life's race . . . even before I entered it. Beaten before the first step was taken! But to-night I am a man! To-morrow I will be the half-dead invalid dragged, against my will, to warmer climes, where my soul will sicken . . . (*harshly*) that my body may live.

GUNHILDE (*gently*). How bitterly you speak. It is not for long that you are going.

SINTRAM. You know that it is forever. (*Takes a deep breath, then coughs*) That this air . . . cool and sharp . . . this air I love is as so much poison to me. And you know just as well as I do that I will never come back.

GUNHILDE (*hiding her tears and trying to cheer him*). But it must be wonderful in the warm sunshine, among eternal flowers. Oh, I should love it — I wish that I too might go. This land is hateful to me. 'Tis so cold and bleak, and nothing green ever grows. Nothing but seaweed and nasty slimy things from the sea. I asked your guardian to-day to tell me about the place to which he was taking you and he said that it was like fairyland . . . like Paradise; full of roses and palms and . . . Why, it must be glorious, Sintram!

SINTRAM. Things to please a soft woman . . . not for a man. (*A moment's pause, them to himself*) And I must

go away and leave her. (*Covers his eyes with his hands and
rocks to and fro with emotion*) Oh, God, that is beyond
my strength!

GUNHILDE. Her? Whom do you mean . . . me?

SINTRAM. That is my secret, Gunhilde.

GUNHILDE (*passionately*). Tell me . . . you must tell
me.

SINTRAM. No . . . no . . . you would not understand. I
am afraid that you would think me mad.

GUNHILDE. Tell me.

SINTRAM. I have kept it to myself these three years. I will
keep it to the end.

GUNHILDE. But you can have no secrets from me. You
should have none. 'Tis breaking your oath.

SINTRAM (*perplexed*). My oath? My oath?

GUNHILDE. Why, do you not recall the day we stood here on
the cliff and drank the red wine together from your little
silver cup?

SINTRAM. Yes.

GUNHILDE. And you said, as you held the cup up . . . so (*she
raises one arm above her head, laughing, and looks towards
the sea*) "I swear to you, little comrade, that as long as I
live I shall never withhold one thought, keep back one
single feeling, or shut out my soul for one single instant
from . . . her whom I love! And then you threw the
cup far out into the sea. Do you not remember, Sintram?

SINTRAM. Yes . . . yes . . . I remember.

GUNHILDE. So you must trust me and if you have kept anything hidden from me you must tell it to me now.

SINTRAM. I will tell it to you Gunhilde . . . I will. (*He
looks at her a moment sympathetically as though he would like
to spare her the pain of that which he is about to say*) You
love me . . . do you not?

GUNHILDE. I adore you.

SINTRAM. You have been a dear little friend, a loyal comrade these two years; I shall miss you.

GUNHILDE.   Oh, Sintram . . . !   (*With a voice too old for her years*)   I wish that I could have been more to you than I have been.

SINTRAM.   What do you mean?

GUNHILDE.   Nothing . . . nothing!   (*Hastily trying to hide her emotion*)   I have no wish to burden you with my secret. Let me hear yours.

SINTRAM.   Presently.   First I want you to tell me something.   You are sorry that I have to leave you . . . are you not?

GUNHILDE.   How can you ask?   You know it.

SINTRAM.   But you hope some day to see me again, or to hear from me at least, do you not?

GUNHILDE.   Yes, soon.

SINTRAM.   Then listen and see if you can possibly feel as I feel, for even as you love me, and more . . . much more, I too love.   (*Gunhilde tightens her hold upon his hand and smiles happily, thinking that he is alluding to her. Sadly and slowly*)   No . . . not you, little playmate, little friend; but a wild, beautiful woman who sometimes mocks me and torments me, and sometimes caresses and quiets me.   Her moods are my moods.   Her feelings are mine. When she is angry, my soul responds and is filled with a vague restlessness; when she is calm, her peace rests on me; when she is powerful, my poor, sickly body feels her strength; and when she is vindictive, I too cry for human life . . . and blood!   [*During his entire speech Gunhilde has sat dumbfounded, now she breaks forth passionately.*

GUNHILDE.   You love some one else!   You have deceived me, telling me that you had no mistress; you love a cruel, bad woman . . . Who is she?

SINTRAM.   Be quiet, Gunhilde, and I will tell you everything. Only be quiet . . . you will not be jealous when you have heard all.

GUNHILDE (*dreamily*).   And I thought that you cared because you were leaving me.

SINTRAM. I do care . . . but listen. I want you to understand. (*Calmly*) I have always lived here, as you know,
little comrade. In that old house, just the other side of
the cliff, I was born; weighed down with riches and an
untarnished name. My people had intermarried closely:
(*bitterly*) no strong, vital peasants' blood ran in my veins.
(*Quietly*) My Mother's bed-room faced the ocean, so the
first sound which reached my ears when I came to the world
was . . . the moan of the sea. My Mother died when I
was born, so the sea became my Mother and sang her
lullabys to me until I fell asleep, stilled by her soft crooning.
(*Scornfully*) Then I grew up . . . weak . . . delicate
. . . sick . . . ! The boys used to ridicule me because I was
not able to spring from one rock to another, laughing and
shouting as they did. They made fun of me and then
went away, leaving me sitting (*points*) just there. Hour
after hour I would stay there with tears in my eyes gazing
out at the sea. And then, ah . . . how grateful I was . . .
she would dance and prance and splash and roar . . . all
to please and amuse me; calling softly to me not to be
sad! And she would weave her most beautiful fairy tales
for me in the loom of the waves. In the ever-changing
whitecaps I saw all the heroes of my boyhood fancy pass
before me. So, as the sea had once taken the place of my
Mother, she became, in turn, my playmate. Are you
tired listening, Gunhilde?

GUNHILDE. No, dear, no. Go on . . . !

SINTRAM. Then my boyhood vanished and I grew to be a
man: a weak, puny man, able to dream dreams in the
moonlight, to write sad verse, to kiss your soft lips — and
there my strength ended. Often when you had left me
in the evening, my soul afire from the moonbeams and the
light on the waves; when my body . . . (*Breaks off suddenly, remembering that she is little more than a child*)
What am I saying to you? I forgot, little girl, forgive me.
I am so used to talking to myself, forgive me . . . Gunhilde.

GUNHILDE.   What happened to you, Sintram, when you stayed alone in the moonlight after I had gone? Tell me. I will understand. I am not such a child as you think.

SINTRAM (*reflects, then almost spontaneously*). I used to sit on the edge of the peak, just where you found me to-night, and listen to the same soft voice calling to me not to be sad. Then I would close my eyes and lie on the very edge of the rock so that the spray might dash into my face. (*Rapturously*) It felt like woman's tears upon my eyes and lips, and I used to wonder why the ocean wept. But now I know. To all my longings, thoughts, and desires the ocean responded; so, in turn, she became . . . my mistress . . . and I love her! There you have my secret (*Laughs loudly and harshly*) "Sintram the Scatter-brained" in love with the sea!

GUNHILDE.   There is nothing so strange about that, Sintram; you have lived here always and the ocean has become a part of your life. If you had been strong and poor you could have been a sailor. Why, look at all the boys who have run away from home to become sailors. Many men love the sea . . . that is not strange.

SINTRAM (*interrupting passionately*).   They never loved her as I love her. (*Takes her hand violently and speaks rapidly*) To me she is not a thing of water and foam, as she is to you, Gunhilde, but she is a woman! A moody, beautiful woman, with a wonderful body and golden hair, and her soul . . . . Ah! how shall I tell you of her soul or of her soft voice when she loves me and takes me in her arms? But she is capricious . . . as capricious as she is beautiful.

GUNHILDE.   What do you mean? Is this some poem that you have written?

SINTRAM (*oblivious to her, and talking to himself, staring all the while before him*).   How many nights have I lain awake in my bed and have listened to her murmur and sing and call me. Then, in an uncontrollable frenzy, when I have rushed bare-footed to answer her bidding, she has mocked me and scoffed me; she has risen up in stormy anger, cut-

ting my face with her lashes of spray and has laughed and
laughed at me, until I have covered my face with my hands
and gone sobbing back to my bed.

GUNHILDE. I cannot understand you, Sintram.

SINTRAM. No, dear, no . . . I did not think you would. I
hardly understand myself; only this I know, Gunhilde,
that to go away from here and never to look upon her
again is like tearing my heart out of my body. (*A pause
in which he listens to the crash of the breakers on the rocks
below*) Here . . . ! Listen how angry she is, and how
she hates me to-night.

GUNHILDE. What foolishness! It is going to storm, that is
all.

SINTRAM. Oh, you have not learned her language as I have.
Listen! see if her voice carries no meaning to you. (*They
both listen silently for several moments, in which a dull roar
and thud is heard; then Sintram begins to chant, strongly
accenting every other syllable*) Sintram . . . ! Sintram
. . . going . . . away . . . ! Away . . . ! To new
loves . . . ! He is false . . . ! False . . . ! Ugh . . . !
Did you hear her shriek then . . . ?

GUNHILDE. No, I heard nothing; not even the wind.

SINTRAM. She hates me, Gunhilde . . . my Beloved hates
me! [*He shudders.*

GUNHILDE (*tenderly and sadly*). Would that your voice
were so when you talk of me; your eyes never looked for
me as they look when you speak of her. I love you,
Sintram.

SINTRAM (*indifferently*). Yes . . . yes . . . I know.

GUNHILDE. No . . . you do not know; not as you think.
You have treated me always as a child . . . a little child.

SINTRAM. But you are a child!

GUNHILDE. I am a woman . . . a woman . . . and I love you.
(*He looks at her surprised, almost startled. She lays her hand
on his*) Forget your foolish fancy, for it is only a fancy,
and let me be your love; take me away with you to-morrow and I will love you forever. Take me . . . do! You

little know how I have suffered since I have cared for you,
how my passion for you has nearly killed me. All that gave
me strength and courage was to feel that you loved no one
else, and now . . . ! But soon you will be well and strong
again, and then you will look back upon all this as on some
wild, strange dream. [*While speaking, she has been drawing closer to him and has been caressing him. Now she sits
with one arm about his neck, her cheek pressed to his.*

SINTRAM. Oh . . . how warm you are . . . how warm! [*He
shivers.*

GUNHILDE. Kiss me . . . Sintram!

SINTRAM (*opening his eyes, looking into space and talking to
himself*). If I take her with me perhaps I would grow
well and strong; perhaps I would no longer be lonely . . .
and I might forget. . . .

GUNHILDE (*whispering*). Kiss me, Sintram . . . I love you!
[*He looks at her a moment, then takes hold of her, and crushing
her with all his strength to him, he gives her a long kiss. Suddenly he jumps up, startling her, and looks about excitedly.*

SINTRAM. What was that?

GUNHILDE (*dazed from the suddenness of the interruption*).
What, Sintram . . . ? What is it . . . ?

SINTRAM. I heard a dull thud . . . and a moan from the sea.

GUNHILDE (*drawing him back to the rock*). You are fanciful
and nervous to-night. There was no noise. (*Sintram
sits for a moment beside her, but he is restless and a strained
tension is visible in his every motion. Finally he springs up
and runs to and fro on the cliff, peering on every side; seeing
nothing, he comes back to Gunhilde. Rising*) How strange
you are! I never saw you so before. Is it because you
are going away to-morrow? Look at me. . . . AT me
. . . not into space! (*Awed*) There is a distant, far-away
. . . something . . . in your eyes which I have never seen
in the eyes of any man. . . . It frightens me! [*She
draws away from him.*

SINTRAM (*stands as though listening to a far-away voice, then
breaks out suddenly*). There . . . ! Did you not hear it

then? (*This time he dashes to the top of the cliff, where he had originally been standing; she follows him. He stares silently out at the ocean, moving nervously and excitedly the while; finally he takes Gunhilde's hand*) Look . . . Gunhilde . . . look!

GUNHILDE (*looking in the direction in which he is pointing*). Where? What?

SINTRAM (*straining his eyes*). Far out beyond those jagged rocks, far . . . far out!

GUNHILDE. I see nothing! (*Horrified*) At what are you staring so, Sintram?

SINTRAM. There is something white floating on the waves . . . it is coming nearer and nearer. (*Pause*) I think it is . . . a corpse!

GUNHILDE (*utters a long drawn out*) "Oh . . . h . . . h . . . h . . . !" (*She lies down and leans way over the cliff. Then she rises*) But I see . . . nothing!

SINTRAM (*pointing*). Not below us! There . . . there! Can you not see? It is a woman with open, glassy eyes and golden hair, entwined like a fisherman's net about her white body.

GUNHILDE. All I see is a shimmer of gold from the moon.

SINTRAM. She is floating nearer . . . nearer . . . ! Look, she is not dead! She moves! She breathes . . . ! Her breast heaves slowly!

GUNHILDE (*puzzled*). I see nothing but the waves rising and falling in the moonbeams.

SINTRAM (*leaning over the cliff*). Now she lies at the very foot of the cliff . . . see . . . see . . . (*Pause*) She is rising . . . she is standing upon the water. (*Surprised*) Gunhilde . . . ! She is looking at us! She is calling me! Can you not hear her?

GUNHILDE (*laying her hand on his arm restrainingly*). Are you mad . . . Sintram . . . !

SINTRAM (*happily*). She is jealous of you, Gunhilde . . . my ocean love is jealous. (*He laughs loudly. Then he is suddenly very still and peers tensely below him, in happy as-*

tonishment) She is beckoning to me . . . she holds out
her arms to me! (*In ecstasy*) Oh, Beloved . . . At last
. . . ! [*He extends his arms to the imaginary woman and
plunges headlong over the cliff.*
GUNHILDE (*shrieks*). Sintram . . . ! Sintram . . . !

(*As the curtains close*).

WILL O' THE WISP

DORIS F. HALMAN

Miss Doris F. Halman was born in Ellsworth, Maine, October 28, 1895. She was educated in Boston, and graduated from Radcliffe in 1916.

She has published "The Land Where Lost Things Go", which received a prize from the Drama League, and "It Behooves Us", plays written in the interest of war sentiment.

Her "Will O' the Wisp" was produced by Professor George P. Baker in his "47 Workshop" at Cambridge, Massachusetts, in 1916, and her "Rusted Stock" by the same company in 1917. In addition, "Will O' the Wisp" has been given by "The Players' Workshop" of Chicago, The Theatre Arts Club of Detroit, and by amateurs in New York City and in Ellsworth, Maine.

WILL O' THE WISP

By DORIS F. HALMAN

"Will O' the Wisp" was originally produced under the direction of Professor George P. Baker in his "47 Workshop" at Cambridge, Massachusetts, on December 8, 1916.

Original Cast

THE WHITE-FACED GIRL . . .	Miss Vianna Knowlton
THE COUNTRYWOMAN	Miss Eleanor Hinkley
THE POET'S WIFE	Miss Frederica Gilbert
THE SERVING-MAID	Miss Mary Ellis

WILL O' THE WISP

SCENE. *Interior of a farmhouse at the end of things. A plain, gray room, with black furniture and a smoke-blackened fireplace. Door to outside, left back. Door to stairs, right. Fireplace in upper right-hand corner; armchair in lower right-hand corner. Below the door, left, a square table with a chair at either side. The whole center of the wall, back, is taken up by a huge window, through which one can glimpse the black spaces of a moor, rising in the distance to a sharp cliff-head silhouetted against the intense blue of an early evening sky. With the passage of the action, this blue fades into a starless night. There are two candles burning in the room, one on the table, the other on a shelf above the armchair.*

When the curtain rises, the countrywoman, an old and withered dame, is lighting the candle on the table. Crouching by the fireplace at the other side of the room, is the ragged figure of a girl with a white face and big wistful eyes, a strange little figure wearing a tight-fitting gray cap which covers all her hair, a silent figure, never speaking. Until she lifts her head, she is little more than a dim gray heap in the shadows.

THE COUNTRYWOMAN. So I don't know what's to become of me any more, with my one boarder gone. A poet he was, to be sure, but a good one; and he paid me enough every summer to keep my soul and body together through the rest of the long year. Seven summers he came that way, and now the time's gone by, and I hear never no word. How I'm to keep myself alive, I don't know; and since I've took you in, bless you, there's the two of us. It may be you'll have to go again, the way you came, out of the night, though you're a great comfort bein' here to talk to, and a help to me in my work. Not but what there'd be more comfort yet, if your poor tongue weren't cursed with dumbness! (*She turns away, sighing, and a queer smile flickers over the stray's face*)

Dear sake, yes, I'm growin' used to you. But a stray who comes to the land's end is as welcome as any other. Nor are those likely to reach here at all, who aren't vagabonds — or poets. By which I think that my poet is gone for good, and you must follow after, and then I'll be left to dwell for the rest of my days alone with the spirits of the moor and of the sea beyond. Oh, alack! (*She sits down, wiping her eyes*)

I'll not forget the night you came. A month ago it was; the second of June; and the day before was the time the poet always come, himself. When I see your white face peerin' through the window there, I thought 'twas him, late, and lookin' in for the joke of it, to see if I'd given him up. Then in another minute you was standin' in the door, poor white creature that you were. And behind you was the wind sweepin' over the moor, and the waves sighin' up the cliffhead from the sea. God knows where you come from, and you couldn't tell. But you're not troublesome. (*The creature smiles at her, as the old woman goes over to her, and pats her shoulder*)

No, you're not. Neither was he. Off all the time he was, with the will-o'-the-wisps of the field and the mermaids of the deep, learnin' their sweet songs. No trouble at all, either of you, — only, *he* paid. (*A knock at the door. The old woman starts and cries out joyfully. As she hurries to open, she does not notice that the girl's face grows illumined as she stretches forth her thin arms in a gesture of infinite grace*)

He's come! After four weeks, at last! He'll pay again! [*The door, opened by her, reveals a woman in her thirty-fifth year, dressed in the extreme of style. She enters, followed by a black-clad maid, who carries a traveling bag. Disappointed, but amazed, the old woman falls back before her. By this time, the figure near the fireplace is crouching expressionless as before.*

THE STYLISH LADY. Is this the farmhouse at the land's end?

THE COUNTRYWOMAN. Yes, so please you.

[*She curtsies as well as her bent back will permit. The stray's eyes have gone from the lady to the maid, and are fixed on the servant when the lady speaks.*]

THE LADY. Ah! — You may set down the bag, Nora.

THE MAID (*with a soft brogue*). Yes, ma'am.

[*She gazes nervously about the dusky room.*]

THE LADY (*to the countrywoman*). My husband sent me to you.

[*Quick as a flash, the stray's big eyes are fastened on the lady. They never waver till the end of the scene.*]

THE COUNTRYWOMAN. Your husband? How? There are no husbands at the land's end. Nobody but me.

THE LADY. My husband has been here. He used to board with you, in the summer time.

THE COUNTRYWOMAN. Oh! The poet?

THE LADY. Yes. I am the poet's wife.

THE COUNTRYWOMAN. But —

THE LADY. We've not been married very long. (*She hastens to add, with a forced sigh*) Of course, it pained me to leave him! But I was so wearied from social pleasures that he *wanted* me to rest; and what was I to do? I was even growing bored, not being as fresh as he to such fulness of life. But you can know nothing of that, here at the end of things. You've never seen the world?

THE COUNTRYWOMAN (*glancing through the window*). I've seen how big it is, and how — queer.

[*Her voice grows hushed with awe. Follows a slight pause. The serving-maid becomes aware of the crouching stray, and moves farther away, crossing herself. The lady's stare at the old woman ends in a burst of laughter.*]

THE LADY. Oh, how amusing! I think I shall enjoy my stay with you. Will you take me in for a while?

THE COUNTRYWOMAN (*cackling with pleasure*). Now, by all the clouds in the sky to-night, I will!

THE LADY. I shall require a room for myself and another for my maid.

THE COUNTRYWOMAN. And your husband, good ma'am? Doesn't he come?

THE LADY. No. I thought better not. . . . There seemed to be some influence here that was not good for him.

THE COUNTRYWOMAN. Here, ma'am? At the land's end he loved so much?

THE LADY (*laughing unpleasantly*). Oh, I don't deny he found his inspiration in this neighborhood. Summer brought his best work, every one knows that. . . . Tell me, how did he use to spend his time?

THE COUNTRYWOMAN. Why, most of it, out there.
[*She waves her hand toward the darkening scene beyond the windows.*

THE LADY (*sitting at the right of the table*). Ah? You see, he never told me about it in detail, for fear I — couldn't understand. But you think I can understand, don't you?

THE COUNTRYWOMAN. Good ma'am, are you acquainted with the spirits?

THE LADY. Certainly not! What spirits?

THE COUNTRYWOMAN. Those he knew.

THE LADY. Oh! So he did have other friends — beside yourself?

THE COUNTRYWOMAN. They was all his friends, good ma'am. He's the only person I ever knew could walk on the moor by night, without the will-o'-the-wisp should dance him over the cliff. Instead o' that, it taught him the tune it dances to, and he made a song out of it. My own man ventured into the darkness years ago, and never came back more. But the poet and It was friends.

THE LADY. A will-o'-the-wisp, what is that?

THE COUNTRYWOMAN (*in a voice of awe*). It's what keeps you in the house o' nights. It's a wavin' light that beckons you to follow it. And when you've been for miles and miles,

always behind, why, then it leaves you; and the morning
finds you dead in a ravine, or floatin' under the cliff-head
in the sea.

THE LADY (*laughing*). Oh, really! What a pleasant com-
panion for my husband! (*The crouching figure creeps forward a bit from its place by the fireside. Again the maid,
flattened against the wall, crosses herself*) But pray tell
me, whom else did he know?

THE COUNTRYWOMAN. Poor Will, a goblin who cries through
the land's end, under the curse of an old, old sin. And
the mermaids with green hair, that sing when a ship goes
down.

THE LADY. Did my husband tell you all this?

THE COUNTRYWOMAN. Yes, good ma'am, and more; whenever for hunger he come home, he had a tale for me.

THE LADY. And you believed it?

THE COUNTRYWOMAN. He was a dear young man, I'm not
even blamin' the spirits, that they loved him.

THE LADY (*laughing*). But, I mean, do you believe in *spirits?*

THE COUNTRYWOMAN. How could I choose? I see them, I
hear them. The night your husband should have come —
that was the first of June — I saw the will-o'-the-wisp out
yonder on the moor, as plain as I see my candles. Not
dancin' it was, but goin' quite slow and steady-like, with
its lantern lit, as if it was seekin' him. And I'm not
wonderin' if, sooner or later, it didn't come peepin' and
lookin' through this very window into my house, to find
the friend it missed.

THE LADY. Oh, what nonsense! What utter, silly bosh!
[*The serving-maid comes down to the left of the table, speaking
in a worried whisper.*

THE MAID. I'd not be sayin' the like, ma'am, if I was you.
It's offering the goblins temptation.

THE LADY (*turning, astonished*). What You, too, Nora?
I thought you had more sense!

THE MAID. In the old country, ma'am, it's the way with us
all, to believe.

THE LADY. Oh, dear me! Well, I can't grow superstitious, Nora, just to oblige you. That will do.

THE MAID. Yes, ma'am. . . . But I think I'll be leaving you.

THE LADY. What?

THE MAID. Oh, it's afraid I am, what with the old woman's talk, and the look of the moor outside. We'd better be going, ma'am, the both of us. There's no good waits for us here.

THE LADY. You may go when you please. For myself, I prefer to stay and meet — some of my husband's friends. I shall certainly not be frightened away by the tales my husband — left behind for me.

[*She laughs again unpleasantly; and the creeping figure comes very near her chair. Across the table, the maid bursts into tears, and sinks down in the chair opposite.*

THE MAID (*sobbing*). How shall I take me way back, alone? Oh, the Lord pity me!

THE COUNTRYWOMAN. There, there, good soul, the spirits wish you no harm, they'll not hurt you.

THE LADY (*impatiently*). Oh, both of you, be still!

THE COUNTRYWOMAN. Now, you see, your husband should have come.

THE LADY. My good woman, I told you, I preferred not; he is so contented where he is — among *my* friends.

THE COUNTRYWOMAN. Alack! Is he then never to come again?

THE LADY. Don't expect him.

THE COUNTRYWOMAN. But the songs? The tunes he made, and paid for with his heart?

THE LADY. Fortunately, it's no longer a question of that.

[*The stray's white face peers round at her. Its eyes seem to burn the woman in the chair.*

THE COUNTRYWOMAN. Good ma'am, pretty ma'am, you don't mean he's give up — singin'?

THE LADY. Oh, yes. Poets usually do, you know, when they marry rich women. Weak, the lot of them.

[*The crouching figure half starts up; its teeth are bared; then it sinks back again. The countrywoman, covering her head with her apron, begins to sway in her chair.*]

THE COUNTRYWOMAN. Alack! Alack the day! Alack the winter time!

THE LADY. Indeed? I didn't know people like you cared for poetry.

THE COUNTRYWOMAN. He'll sing no more, he'll pay no more. The land's end will be poor and still.

THE LADY. Ah, now I understand you. You have a point of view; well, so have the wives of poets. Just as he gave you comfort in return for his inspiration, we give them ease in which to love us. Why shouldn't we? Why should they play at their little toy battle with life, when we can put all existence into their very hands? That is our mission; and it makes them very comfortable, I assure you.

[*The stray springs up with clawing hands behind the lady. The countrywoman sees her.*

THE COUNTRYWOMAN. Here, girl, here!

[*At the cry, the stray sinks back on the floor. But her eyes never cease to burn the woman's face. The poet's wife, looking down, has now become aware of her. Her silly suspicion seems assured.*

THE LADY (*sharply*). Who is this?

THE COUNTRYWOMAN (*moving the stray back*). A poor waif, ma'am. A harmless, dumb waif, who helps me in the house.

THE LADY. Oho! Did you mention her among my husband's friends?

THE COUNTRYWOMAN. Why, no. He never saw her. Been here only a month, she has, the poor creature.

THE LADY. Where did she come from?

THE COUNTRYWOMAN. The good Lord knows! Not I.

THE LADY. Ah. Well, from the looks of her, I should say it didn't matter, how long she was with you. . . . Come here, girl.

THE COUNTRYWOMAN. Mind what the lady bids you.

[*The figure on the floor lifts a face, now expressionless, to the poet's wife. For the third time, the maid crosses herself.*

THE LADY. Hm! The total effect of you is not — dangerous. (*She takes the stray's face between her hands. A violent shudder shakes the latter from head to foot, as she shrinks back with a gliding motion; but this does not discourage the poet's wife*) Don't be afraid of me, silly thing! (*She turns to the countrywoman*) Funny how fashion impresses them, isn't it? This girl turned clammy cold.

THE COUNTRYWOMAN (*nodding*). It's the feel of her.

[*The poet's wife returns to her scrutiny of the girl's face.*

THE LADY. Yet, you know, your features aren't so bad. If you only had a little color. . . . You should never wear gray with that white face of yours. (*She addresses the room in general, and the maid in particular*) Country people invariably have no idea how to dress. Eh, Nora?

THE MAID. Ma'am, for the love of God, be careful! I'm not liking the eyes of herself!

THE LADY (*laughing lightly*). Oh, her eyes are so much better than her clothes! But I forgot; you're not fit to talk to to-night, are you? Well, that will do. (*She turns back to the countrywoman*) Why do you let your servant wear that awful cap? Doesn't she ever take it off?

THE COUNTRYWOMAN. Many's the time I've spoke of it; but it's a stubborn habit with her. So I lets her have her way, for peace.

THE LADY (*to the stray*). But, my poor girl, that cap is awful! If only your hair showed, you'd be so much better looking. What makes you wear it?

[*For answer, the stray, rising, shuffles past the poet's wife to the table. It is the first time during the scene that she has looked away from her. As she nears the table, the maid on the other side shrinks back. Once there, the stray turns on the woman, and, watching her instead of what she herself does, she reaches for the candle. She lifts the metal extinguisher from the candlestick, holds it out so that the poet's wife may see it, then with a*

*quick motion places it over the flame.   The candle goes out,
leaving the room dim with one light.   In her nervousness, the
serving-maid sobs once aloud.*

THE COUNTRYWOMAN.   What would this be?

THE LADY.   Do you know what she meant?

THE COUNTRYWOMAN.   I don't see — I don't see. . . .

THE LADY.   She's probably mad, poor soul.

THE MAID.   Oh, Mother of God! Mother of God! The
magic!

THE LADY.   I fail to find any magic in a candle going out,
when I've just watched the process.   Really, I prefer bed
to such gloomy companionship.   (*She rises, and speaks to
the countrywoman*) Will you light us upstairs, please.   I'm
quite sorry I came.

THE COUNTRYWOMAN (*re-lighting the second candle*).   There,
there, good ma'am.   It'll all be more cheerful in the
morning.

THE LADY.   I feel as if morning would never come, with this
whole night dragging at me.

[*The countrywoman gives the candle to Nora, who has picked
up her mistress' bag.   Then the old dame crosses toward the
candle on the shelf.*

THE COUNTRYWOMAN.   Now, if you and your woman will
follow me. . . .   The poet's room was ready for him. . . .
[*This mention of the poet brings another convulsive motion
from the stray.   The lady's attention is thereby arrested.*

THE LADY.   Where does that creature sleep?

THE COUNTRYWOMAN.   Oh, down here, on a mat by the fireside.   She'll not trouble you more, good ma'am.   She'll
not trouble you more.

[*She opens the door to the stairs.*

THE LADY (*after a brief hesitation*).   Come, Nora.
[*She goes out.   The countrywoman pauses to speak to the
stray.*

THE COUNTRYWOMAN.   Good night, girl.   Go to sleep
quietly.   (*She disappears, and we hear her voice*) Now,
good ma'am.   Now, so please you. . . .

[The room, lighted only by Nora's candle, is dim again. Outside, the night is very black. The serving-maid crosses the room silently. In its center, she passes close to the stray, who has crept there to look after the poet's wife. The maid, making a quick detour, gasps with terror. When she reaches the fireplace, she rushes for the stairs with a little scream that puts her candle out; we hear the door bang behind her. The room is completely black.

A silence. Then the motion of some one springing upright; and the place is suffused with a dim glow of orange light. The light shines from the orange-red hair of the white-faced girl, a burning mass of quivering, gleaming strands. And the girl herself stands revealed, a spirit-creature, red and white and clad in fluttering gray, her body slim and swaying with infinite grace. Not even the poet's wife could question the beauty of her wild white face, lit into a fierce exaltation by the glow of that tumbling hair. In her fingers is the ugly cap, held mockingly toward the door; and then she drops it.

Now a faint music sounds from somewhere, a langorous melody; and the spirit begins to sway to it. Not quite a dance, yet nothing else, this moving through the room.

The door to the stairs opens, and the poet's wife appears, trailing a white room-robe about her. The white-faced girl smiles at her, smiles quite close to her, with a demon behind her smile.

THE LADY. Who are you? — Why do you smile at me, — unless — you're *glad* that I came down? — You knew I would answer to that music — *he* used to sing me a song to it, when he courted me. — Was it out of his love for you, he made that song? — Oh, it might well have been, you with your long white arms and your strange white face! — But he sang it to me, do you hear? To me, to me, to me, it is my song!

You smile. — You are so sure it isn't mine. — But you aren't singing it now, any more than I am! — Where does that music come from? — What *are* you?

Oh, I knew there was something here that held him.— I

had all the right to him. — I took his life, and made of it what I would, — but I couldn't reach his soul. It was bound up to something else, his soul. — I wanted to see. — I see now. — But I don't understand!

What are you? Can you talk? You can, you can, you devil! You called me down to tell your story, didn't you? Well, triumph over me, — triumph! — only *speak!* (*The white-faced girl, in her dance, is moving toward the outer door, ever eluding the poet's wife, who takes a few steps after her*)

No, you're not going away without it, you and your magic hair! (*She reaches desperately for the waving hand, which glides from under her grasp*)

You burned him with that hair — you burned the soul out of him. — But now I've come in his place, and you can't burn me, and I *will* learn why you smile! (*Again the reach, and the white hand slips away*)

Do you mean you can't talk? — Or do you want me alone? (*The white-faced girl, near the door, has raised a beckoning hand. There is now a teasing invitation in her smile*) Oh, I'm not afraid to go with you, out there! — Wait! Wait!

[*For the white-faced girl has opened the door. As the poet's wife crosses the room, the countrywoman comes, drawn by the talk, down the stairs. She gives a sudden shriek.*

THE COUNTRYWOMAN. Oh, God!

THE LADY (*briefly turning, annoyed*). What, you?

THE COUNTRYWOMAN. I heard. I came. (*The poet's wife takes another step*)

Don't follow, don't follow, for the love of Heaven! It's the Will-O'-The-Wisp!

[*In the doorway, the white-faced girl stoops, and smiles her smile, and beckons.*

THE LADY (*with authority*). Let be! — I am going after her! — I am going to learn the truth!

[*She nears the door, just as the serving-maid appears at the foot of the stairs. With a scream, Nora rushes to the poet's wife, and clings to her.*

THE MAID. Stay back! Stay back! It's to your death you go!

THE LADY (*pushing her to the floor*). Take your hands off me. — There are no such things as spirits! — It's a trick they made for me! — my husband and her! WAIT! —
[*For the white-faced girl has passed outside. Only the glow of her hair, quite near, shines in through the open door.*

THE COUNTRYWOMAN. The Will-O'-The-Wisp! — It's her! — It's her!

THE MAID (*crying out at the same time*). Stop, I tell ye! — Stop, stop, stop!
[*The poet's wife is on the threshold. The orange light recedes, and the room darkens.*

THE LADY (*almost majestic*). Wait! — I'm not afraid! — WAIT FOR ME! —
[*She, too, passes outside the door. The serving-maid breaks into a torrent of sobs. After a moment, in which the countrywoman reaches the window, the room is black again. And the music has died away.*

THE COUNTRYWOMAN. Hush! — (*The sobs of the serving-maid die down to a low moan*) Come here by me at the window. Ah, see!

THE MAID (*whispering*). What is it?
[*Now through door and window, there can be seen in the distance a moving light, growing smaller and smaller, making straight for where one saw the cliff-head over the sea.*

THE COUNTRYWOMAN. The light! The Will-O'-The-Wisp! And something white behind it.

THE MAID (*whispering*). Is it — me mistress?

THE COUNTRYWOMAN (*turning away*). Yes. God have mercy upon her.
[*The maid has dragged herself over to the window, and kneels on the floor, looking out.*

THE MAID. A shadow in the dark, lit up by that thing ahead! Oh, it is! It is!

THE COUNTRYWOMAN (*nerving herself for the sight*). Ah, the spirit! — it's *out beyond* the cliff-head! And the cold sea lies beneath! Woe to one who follows the Will-O'-The-Wisp! Woe!

[*Then a slight pause, in which the light no longer moves.*

THE MAID (*crying out*). Look, where the light is after standing still! And not a sign of *her!* — Oh, she's gone over! Gone, she is! And she'll never come back! —

[*She starts to keen — three long ochones — as the curtain falls.*

"BEYOND"

ALICE GERSTENBERG

Miss Alice Gerstenberg was born in Chicago and was educated there and at Bryn Mawr College. Her first novel, "Unquenched Fire", was published in 1912 and republished in England the following year. Miss Gerstenberg's other publications are a novel, "The Conscience of Sarah Platt", "A Little World", a book of four short plays for girls; "Overtones", a one-act play; and "Alice in Wonderland", a three-act dramatization of Lewis Carroll's "Alice in Wonderland" and "Through the Looking-Glass."

"Overtones" was produced with great success by the Washington Square Players during their first season, and later by vaudeville companies in which Helene Lackaye and Lily Langtry starred. "Alice in Wonderland" was produced at the Fine Arts Theatre, Chicago, and at the Booth Theatre, New York City. The music for the dramatization was written by Eric De Lamarter. Under Miss Gerstenberg's own supervision, the Players' Workshop of Chicago produced her "Beyond", and "The Pot Boiler." "The Pot Boiler", in addition, has been played in the Theatre Workshop of New York, by the Arthur Maitland Players, San Francisco, in the trenches in France, and in vaudeville. Other one-act productions of Miss Gerstenberg are: "The Unseen", "The Buffer", "Attuned", "Hearts", "He Said and She Said", and "The War Game" (written in collaboration).

Miss Gerstenberg has not confined her activities in behalf of the drama to the writing of plays, however. She is Secretary of the Society of Midland Authors, a member of the Drama League Board in Chicago, Chairman of a Drama Committee at the Chicago Arts Club, and President of the Chicago Bryn Mawr College Club.

"BEYOND"

By ALICE GERSTENBERG

"Beyond" was originally produced by the Players' Workshop of Chicago, April 23, 1917.

Original Cast

A WOMAN . . . . Gertrude Hemken

Stage setting designed and executed by J. Blanding Sloan.

"BEYOND"

SCENE.   *The curtain rises in darkness.   The stage lights up slowly.*

The scene suggests limitless space and mist and is played behind a curtain of gauze.   The floor rises from right to left as if misty clouds had made irregular stepping stones to heights off left.   The wraith of a woman enters, looking misty in blue, lavender, and flesh colored chiffon, but one is less conscious of body than of the embodiment of spirit.   She enters timidly, in awe, not sure of a welcome.   She has died and is now passing upward to meet and to be judged by the All Powerful whom she cannot see but whom she supposes is high up off left.   She speaks in that direction and moves slowly from right to left as if drawn by a magnet.

WRAITH.   Is this the way I should go? You send no answer. Yet I am drawn this way, and it leads upward. Are You drawing me to Your Throne for judgment?   I see nothing, my eyes are still blind to God, and yet I have died; that other part of me lies white and cold, unwarmed by the burning candles, the petals of pink roses, and the kisses of the one who weeps for me. Does his desire for me halt the progress of my soul, does his great love for me still keep me thinking of him? And because I think of him — do You keep me blind to You? *That* would be strange! For when I lived, my love for him seemed to bring me nearer to You. Does it follow then that to know You in life one must love — and to know You in death one must forget? But I do not want to forget him! (*Pauses anxiously*) Are You angry? You do not answer. All is silent. I am alone, terribly alone. (*Takes timid step forward left*)

I seem to have come a very long way. I seem to have the form of myself; yet I left it solidly back there. This which I am is not solid — as if able at any moment to melt into mist — but if I become mist where does that "I" of "me" go that can think? I do not want to lose the "I" of "me" that thinks. Must I lose it? (*Pauses*)

Perhaps You are jealous of Your Power and will not take me in until I let You merge my "I" in You! But I do not want to obliterate myself! I am *I!* Yet, if You say that You are You, the weaker of us must give in! That means — Oh, You are terribly strong and make me afraid! (*Retreats a step*) They teach us to be afraid of You. They quote Your threats from the Book. They say You have promised punishments beyond the imagination of human minds for limitless agony, but I do not believe it! (*Softly*) If You are without pity, You are not God! (*Pauses*) You might have struck me because I am rebellious and critical of You, but nothing has happened.

(*Steps forward left*) I am daring to come a little nearer to You. If it is Your decree that I walk this way, as millions have walked before me and millions will after me, You ought to take care of me.

They tell and believe a lot of things about You, but no man really knows. Will You tell me Your secret? Or must I wander eternally? If You have nothing more than this to offer, it would be better to go back to him. He is calling. (*Puts hands to her ears*) I would rush back if I could but I do not seem able, nor can I go forward very fast. Why is it? What do You want me to do? (*Pauses*) Can You not understand my language? or do You refuse to hear? Are You going to forget me? Is this terrible silence to be my punishment? Have You turned away from me? Answer! Answer!!

Is there no one else about? No one else in trouble like mine? No company for me? But others have died. Where are they? Has each one had to go through this alone? Is this to be the experience of every one? Or have You singled me out for the torture of eternal solitude? Have I offended You so deeply that You will not even listen? Have I transgressed beyond forgiveness? Is it possible You cannot read my soul and are judging my life from the surface as the world saw it, that You are not omniscient enough to go below the surface and know me as I really am? Silence! Silence!!

(*Hysterically*) What do You want of me? Does it amuse You to see me suffer? Or are You jealous of my will? Do You demand abject submission? Must I give in and bend the knee to You? Must I humiliate myself and implore the mercy You should extend unasked if You are as they say You are, powerful enough to be everywhere and see everything always? Even though You may know my life like an open page, does it amuse You to have me suffer it again in the telling? Is my life history a story to You? Does it give You pleasure to discipline me? Must I throw myself before You in despair to give You the chance to appear noble and raise me in mercy? Or are You angry because I question You! Answer! Just one word!! I am Your slave!!! (*Throws herself upon her knees*)

I yield, conquered! Beaten!

It is true, I sinned! The unpardonable — for a woman — The world condemned, made me endure its averted gaze. My husband would not give me legal freedom; I could not, would not renounce my lover. My crime was infidelity. A certain kind of punishment must be listed for that. I plead guilty and await punishment. (*Pauses*) Still You do not answer!! Are You not satisfied to see me willing to accept Your punishment? — What more do You want? (*Pauses*)

Would you have me say I am sorry I loved him? Say I am sorry? (*Gives way to tremendous emotion*) Do not ask it of me! I cannot say it!! It would only be a lie!

I am *not* sorry! Oh, God, punish me, but do not expect me to regret! Hear me; and understand!

My father was good, but it often seemed as if You were against him! In despair he killed himself! I hope You were kind to him when he passed this way. What did You do to him? (*Pauses*) Mother had too many children. The last one killed her. I hope You rewarded her here for all her hardship there. I was the eldest, had to support them — came home — so tired — spent the night helping them make flowers they sold. Their little thin faces, their patient little hands, the tears that came and the laughter that never did — Oh, God, why do You rob children of their childhood? I could not bear it! I had a chance to marry for money. I sacrificed myself for them! Do You not praise us for sacrificing ourselves for others? The world called the marriage legal; it was hallowed by Your church! But if You think it made me honorable and good, I know in my soul You are wrong! My greatest sin was *then* when I was not true to myself!! (*Pauses*) I hated him! He was old, hard, chose me because I was poor and in his power. Every penny he gave had to be earned in service. I conscientiously kept the bargain, even though my heart was black with ever-increasing hatred toward the world and him and You! Yes, my hatred for him made me doubt You — all Your handiwork! And I counted up against You all I had to endure, and then — my lover came.

I fled to the arms of him who sits now by the white, cold shell of me, weeping. He weeps because he thinks he has lost me; perhaps, because he feels I am in anguish here — but he need not weep for loss of love; my love will never cease! My love for him is part of You — and *You* are *eternal!!* (*Moves left almost imperceptibly*)

Through him I lost the blackness of my heart and saw the wonder of Your purple mountains, blue-green seas, and even the beauty of Your mighty storms, sweeping rains, and icy frosts — and I loved because of him all the crea-

tures You have made and all Your trees and all Your
flowers and even all the weeds. Although the world pointed
a finger at me, I bore with dignity and without complaint,
knowing that my heart was whiter because of love.

My Love and I, walking hand in hand, heard the birds in
Your forest and through them the voice of You. We
stood on hill crests, awed by the beauty of Your landscapes,
and, moved by the marvelous colors, worshiped the artist
in You. We saw the mists of evening hover over mountain peaks and fancied they were veils hiding You. But
WE KNEW YOU WERE THERE! And our love rose
as one love to YOU! ! !

Is a love that brings consciousness of You a sin? Was my
love for him a sin? Was not rather that other relation-
ship, the real sin against You because through it I lost You?
Will *You* judge as the world judges? Is Your silence and
this solitude a place for my soul to battle for itself?

Still—You do not answer and see—how far I've come!
I did not know I was moving nearer to You—but I have!
How much farther must I come? *Then* will You answer
me?

(*With triumphant conviction and faith*) You cannot deny me!
In *my* idea of God there is Justice!! To plead for mercy
and to implore forgiveness is to confess a God that can be
swayed! *My* God needs no finite aid in judgment! If
You are at all, You are supreme! (*By this time she has
reached the height at left*) Punish! If you think You must
—but I come to You with love and expectant of Justice!!
[*As she goes off left a glow of light illumines her face.*

CURTAIN

A GOOD WOMAN

GEORGE MIDDLETON

Mr. George Middleton was born in Paterson, New Jersey, on October 27, 1880. He received his Bachelor's degree at Columbia University in 1902. Since 1912 he has been literary editor of *LaFollette's Weekly* and, in addition, has been a frequent contributor to magazines and reviews on dramatic and literary subjects.

He has published three collections of one-act plays, "Embers" (which includes "The Failures", "The Gargoyle", "In His House", "Madonna", and "The Man Masterful"); "Tradition" (which includes "On Bail", "Their Wife", "Waiting", "The Cheat of Pity", and "Mothers"); and "Possession" (which includes "The Groove", "A Good Woman", "The Black Tie", "Circles", "The Unborn"). Several of his one-act plays have appeared in single form: "Criminals", a play about marriage, "Back of the Ballot", a woman suffrage farce, and "The Reason", which appeared in a magazine. His longer published plays are "Nowadays" and "The Road Together."

"Embers" was one of the first collections of one-act plays to be written and published by an American. In fact, Mr. Middleton has been a pioneer in advocating the serious consideration of the printed play. He has lectured widely on "The One-Act Play in America and Abroad" before many colleges, Little Theatres, and clubs, and has written several interesting magazine articles on the subject. Perhaps the most notable is "The Neglected One-Act Play", which was published in *The New York Dramatic Mirror* in 1912.

Mr. Middleton is not a closet dramatist, however. His acted plays are even more numerous than those which have been published. He has written, in collaboration, "The Cavalier", "The Sinner", "Hit the Trail Holliday", "Polly with a Past", "Through the Ages", and is the sole author of "The Wife's Strategy", "The House of a Thousand Candles", "Rosalind at Red-gate", "The Enemy", "Adam and Eva", "Back to Nature", "The Cave Lady", and "The Prodigal Judge", all of which have been produced professionally throughout the United States.

A GOOD WOMAN

By GEORGE MIDDLETON

"A Good Woman" was originally produced by the Northampton Municipal Theatre Company at the private theatre
in the home of Mr. George B. McCallum, Northampton,
Massachusetts, January 6, 1916.

Original Cast

CORA WARREN . . . . Gertrude Workman
HAL MERRILL . . . . William H. Powell

Reprinted from "Possession and Other One-Act Plays" by permission of and by
special arrangement with Mr. George Middleton and Henry Holt and Company.
Application for the right of performing "A Good Woman" must be made to Samuel French and Company, 28–30 West 38th Street, New York City.

A GOOD WOMAN

SCENE: *At Cora Warren's flat. A large city in New York State. Late one winter evening.*

A small room in what is a modest but comfortable flat, up several flights of stairs. In back, a door opens on the landing. A snow-lined window may be seen at the right through the pretty lace curtains. Opposite this a door leads off into the other rooms. The furnishings are simple but adequate; wicker chairs, a couch, a small table, carefully selected pictures, some bookshelves, and a large warm rug upon the hardwood floor are conspicuous. A house telephone is on the left wall near the door. There is something seclusive, personal, and intimate about the little room, softly lighted by several shaded wicker-lamps which blend in color with the one-toned patternless wall-paper.

Outside the wind is heard howling as it drives the snow and sleet against the window. After some moments, a bell is heard. Cora Warren enters quickly and opens the outer door, admitting Hal Merrill. She closes the door and kisses him.

Cora Warren is a woman of thirty, full of rich feeling, sensitive, impulsive, yet withal clear-visioned and courageous. There is every mark of refinement, culture, and distinction in speech, with nothing exotic or abnormal in her manner. She is in a pretty negligée.

Hal Merrill is older, beginning to settle, in fact, but full of mental and physical vigor, in spite of features which, when relaxed, betray a certain careworn expression. He, too, is evidently well-born, and has had, no doubt, many advantages. His heavy overcoat, rubbers, and soft felt hat are wet with the snow.

CORA. I'm so glad you've come. Why, you're all wet.

HAL (*taking off his overcoat*). I walked uptown.

CORA (*playfully admonishing him throughout*).   In this storm?
And you knew I was waiting?

HAL.   You are always waiting.

CORA.   You'll get your death, dear.   Give me the coat.
I'll hang it over a chair before the gas stove.   And your
feet — my — my!   Soaked?

HAL.   No, rubbers.

CORA.   So you *did* mind me and wear them.

HAL.   Yes.

[*Kicking them off.*

CORA.   You must take more care of yourself.   What would
I do if you were ill?   You should have ridden.

HAL.   It clears your thoughts to walk with the snow beating in your face.

CORA (*detecting a hidden meaning*).   Hal?

HAL.   It's good to be here with you again, Cora.

CORA (*cheerfully again*).   Yes : it's been so long since yesterday.   (*They laugh*)   Now sit down and rest.   I've a hot
toddy all ready for you.

HAL.   Just what I wanted.

CORA.   Here's your pipe — old and strong as ever.   Did you
forget the tobacco?

HAL.   No.   (*Taking the pipe*)   You always make it seem
like home, dearest.

CORA (*hurt*).   "Seem?"

HAL (*holding her hand during a slight pause*).   You know
what I mean.

CORA (*as she strikes a match and lights the pipe which he has
filled*).   How worn and tired you are, dear.   I'll be glad
when this lawsuit is over.   Just relax.   Let go.   (*She kisses
him*)   Dearest.   (*Cora takes up the coat and rubbers, going
out quickly in back.   Hal stops smoking, the smile disappears, and his head lowers, as he seems overcome with the
mood he has been trying to fight back.   Cora comes in unobserved with the toddy.   She looks at him, shakes her head and
then comes, placing her hand on his arm.   He starts up from
his reverie*)   What is it, Hal?

HAL.   Nothing.

CORA (*not believing him*).   Take this, dear.

HAL.   Thanks. (*He sips it*) Um! it's hot, Cora. Just
the right amount of sugar, too. (*Cora watches him questioningly as he sips it slowly. She picks up a couple of sofa
cushions and comes over to him, placing them by him, on the
floor. She sits on them, waiting for him to speak*) That
tastes good.

CORA.   You're sure you didn't get chilled?

HAL.   I walked rapidly.

CORA.   Did anything go wrong with the case?

HAL (*patting her*).   What makes you think that?

CORA.   Something's worrying you.

HAL.   Something did: but it's all settled now.

CORA.   So that's why you walked in the storm?

HAL.   Yes.

CORA.   I'm glad it's settled; only I should like to have
helped settle it.

HAL.   Cora?

CORA (*she turns and looks up into his face*).   Yes?

HAL.   I wonder how great a test your love for me would stand?

CORA.   Could I have given more?

HAL.   There *is* something more I must ask.

CORA (*puzzled*).   Something more? Tell me, Hal.

HAL (*holding her head between his hands*).   Is your love strong
enough to accept a silence?

CORA.   Aren't there silent places in every love?

HAL (*with some slight hesitation*).   I mean if — if I should *do*
something which I thought best not to explain.

CORA (*simply*).   I should accept everything so long as you
were honest with me. Only —

HAL.   Only what, dear?

CORA (*thoughtfully*).   Silence itself is not always honest.

HAL.   In this particular matter will you let me be the judge
of that?

CORA.   A woman in my position must accept.

HAL.   Cora!

CORA (*quickly*). Oh, I didn't mean that, Hal; *that* was unworthy of me.

HAL You know how I love you.

CORA. Yes, yes, dear. Of course I know. I am ashamed of nothing. I'm proud of all we have here in the quiet. But the snow beating against the window has been reminding me all day of the world outside.

HAL. The snow is so free!

CORA. Yes; and you and I are bound by secrecy. That's what hurts; the secrecy.

HAL (*stroking her hair*). If you could only be my wife.

CORA (*smiling*). Just for the freedom it would give me to share everything in the open with you. That's all. Just for the freedom we can't have now.

HAL. But, Cora, even in marriage itself only the happy are free.

CORA (*intimating a hidden thought*). I suppose the most difficult thing for some people is to *give* freedom. (*He nods in understanding*) Poor Hal! How you have suffered, too, with this tangle we are in. (*The 'phone rings. They are surprised*) Who could that be?

HAL (*nervously*). No one knows your number?

CORA. No.

[*The ring is repeated.*

HAL (*dismissing it*). Central's made a mistake. Don't answer it.

CORA. Everything startles me so these days. (*Dismissing it too*) Have another toddy?

HAL. Not now.

CORA. Tell me about the case. Is "Boss" McQuinn still going to take his libel suit into court?

HAL. It's called for to-morrow at ten.

CORA (*pleased*). To-morrow! It's come at last, then, after all your months of work. To-morrow. (*With a sigh*) And I can't be there in court to hear you when you testify, or to follow, in the open, each step we've talked over here. That's where my position hurts.

HAL (*with apparent difficulty throughout*). Perhaps I sha'n't take the stand against McQuinn, after all.

CORA. You mean it won't be necessary?

HAL. Not exactly that.

CORA. But what you wrote about McQuinn in the Monthly ——?

HAL. Every word of my exposure was true.

CORA. But you've said so often the whole defense of the magazine in McQuinn's libel suit against it rests on *your* testimony alone.

HAL. Yes, yes.

CORA (*disappointed*). I see. You mean the Monthly has decided to retract?

HAL. No.

CORA (*not quite grasping the significance*). Is this why you walked with the snow beating in your face?

HAL (*with feeling*). This is the silent place! I'm not going to testify in this suit, after all. Please don't question me about it, dear.

CORA (*startled*). Not going to testify?

HAL (*earnestly*). Just trust me, Cora; and let me be silent as to the reason.

CORA (*restraining her instinctive impulse to question and placing her hands on his shoulders*). Whatever is the reason, I know you must have suffered. It is not like you to give up. (*He lowers his eyes*) You've never asked anything greater of me than this silence.

HAL (*deeply moved*). Perhaps I've never given anything greater, Cora.

[*The 'phone rings again : they look toward it.*

CORA (*slowly*). Did you give our number to any one?

HAL (*nervously*). No.

[*It rings again.*

CORA. Nobody ever rings here but you. (*She goes apprehensively to the 'phone in spite of his movement to restrain her*) Yes, this is Cora Warren. . . . Who? . . . Mr. McQuinn! (*They look at each other. She quickly controls herself and speaks casually*) Mr. Merrill? . . . You're mistaken — why should *he* be here? . . . There's no need of ringing me up later. (*She hangs up the receiver*) He laughed, Hal. He *laughed!* (*She goes to him*) He has found out about you and me!!

HAL. No, no.

CORA (*shaken*). That's what it is. It was the *way* he laughed !

HAL (*confused*). Nonsense.

CORA (*slowly grasping the situation*). For months you've told me McQuinn has been fighting for his political life, desperate over your exposures. He's been doing everything to "get" your witnesses — to "get" something on you. Why, he offered you money — enough to make you independent for life. You refused all that; but, *now*, you're going to do what he wants.

HAL. I'm doing what I want, I tell you; what *I* want.

CORA. That's not so. This investigation has been your absorbing passion for months. You've seen what it means to the hundreds of women and children who have suffered by his exploitations. He's got something on you, something you had to give in to.

HAL. No, no !

CORA. It's you and me, Hal. You ask silence of me because you didn't want to hurt me. It's you and me; you and me.

HAL. No, no !

CORA (*slowly*). Hal, it is that. Answer me, boy. It *is* that —isn't it ?

HAL (*admitting it, after a futile denial*). And I didn't want you to know.

CORA. He threatened to tell about our relations together if you testified against him?

HAL. Yes: the blackguard.

CORA (*moved*). And you love me more than —

HAL (*tenderly*). I only did what any man would. (*She lowers her head*) Dearest, don't take it so hard. I'm glad a chance came to show you how I loved you.

CORA. I knew without this proof, Hal; I knew. [*She sits with her face buried in her hands. He stands beside her.*

HAL. McQuinn met me to-night, on the street, alone. He said he knew about our three years — our summer abroad — this place — all. He said he hated to hit a woman, but he knew he was beaten and had to use any weapon he could find. All he asked of me was silence and he would give the same about us — or for me to forget a bit on the stand or muddle my testimony. Of course, I saw what it would mean to the case: but it was the only way to save you. (*He shrugs his shoulders*) He must have guessed I'd come straight to you. He has ways of finding out 'phone numbers. I suppose he wanted to frighten you and thus make sure I wouldn't change my mind.

CORA (*slowly*). Did he mention your wife?

HAL. Yes.

CORA (*desperately*). Did you tell him you and she had been separated before you met me? That she didn't love you, that she hated you, yet clung to your name because she knew you wanted freedom to marry me? Did you tell him she wouldn't give you that freedom, because of a few words mumbled over her by an official, and because she said she was "a good woman"?

HAL. I did not discuss the matter. It was my wife who told him about us.

CORA. Your wife!

HAL. Yes. That act describes her, doesn't it?

CORA (*bitterly*). And the law gives a woman like that the right to keep you — a woman whose body is dry and her love cold — and it discards me who — oh!

HAL (*sarcastically*). It was my wife's way of disentangling me. She thought I'd rather give you up than this case. She thought I'd sacrifice you. But she didn't know me: she never knew me.

CORA. And she knew me!

HAL. It's done. Now we must forget and go on.

CORA (*gazing dully before her*). What are you going to do now?

HAL. That's what we must think of.

CORA. It will mean you will have to leave the Monthly.

HAL. Yes. They're tired of the suit, anyway. Their advertising has fallen off. (*Putting his arm about her*) We have each other.

CORA (*ominously*). And always we'd fear McQuinn knocking at our door.

HAL (*trying to cheer her*). Nonsense, dear. He'll never bother to come up our stairs.

CORA. How we women hamper you men. (*He protests*) Yes, we do. Your wife's "respectability" — and my —

HAL. Hush, dear. It's not our fault.

CORA. That we love? No. But because we've spoken the whole language of love the world blames us. (*With growing emotion*) If I'd kept my love hidden, worn myself sapless, wasted without expression, then I'd have been "a good woman"! If I'd seen you casually, or if I'd let you come near me, with the flames smoldering, burning us both inside so that there was nothing in our thoughts but fire; nothing of comradeship and beauty that we now have — then I'd still have been "a good woman." But because I let you see my love, because I wasn't a contemptible tease, because I knew all things were equally important in love, because I gave myself to you, I'm *not* "a good woman"! [*She laughs ironically.*

HAL. We live in the world, dear.

CORA. And we must go on living. (*With a quick resolution*) But there is no need of our being cowards!

HAL. Cowards!

CORA. Yes. Up to now, Hal, as I see it, we have not been that. We did what we believed was right, no matter what others may say. But now you and I are thinking of doing what we *know* is wrong; and that is the test of our courage.

HAL. You mean?

CORA. That now we're asking somebody else to pay the price: the hundreds of women and children in this city whom McQuinn would still go on exploiting if you did not go on the stand and drive him out of power.

HAL (*losing momentary control*). It's true; it's true. But how could I ask that of *you?*

CORA. Why not?

HAL. No, no. We must think of ourselves now — ourselves.

CORA (*putting her hand on his arm*). You and I cannot do as many others. We've got to keep right, in each other's eyes, or the world will beat us.

HAL. I've done the hardest thing for you I could, Cora.

CORA. It's not always easy to be a coward, Hal. And that's what I'd also be if I accepted. Somebody else would be paying. Somebody else. That can never be right. (*She bows her head. There is a long pause. He rises, goes to the window, then paces up and down. The snow is heard freely beating against the pane. Her mind slowly gains control of her emotions and she looks up at him*) Hal?

HAL. Yes.

CORA. If you went on the stand to-morrow and told the truth about McQuinn, would your relations with me hurt your statement about him?

HAL (*bitterly*). No. It's only a *woman* whose sex morals can be taken that advantage of in our courts.

CORA (*with determination*). Then you must tell the truth.

HAL (*desperately*). And have you hurt? Never!

CORA. I would be hurt far worse if you did not love me enough to do what I ask.

HAL. Cora! (*Comes to her*) You don't realize what it means.

CORA (*calmly*). I realize that your public usefulness would be destroyed because you wished to protect my reputation. What people think of me matters little now.

HAL. What people think of you means everything to me.

CORA. You fear to have them think me a bad woman?

HAL. Cora!

CORA. Then what difference what they think so long as *we* understand each other?

HAL. They'd forgive a man. But you're a woman. They'd never forgive you — never.

CORA. Nothing will be harder than cowardice.

HAL (*going to her*). I can't do this — I can't. They'd think me a *cad* to sacrifice you like this.

CORA. That thought has made liars and cowards of many men!

HAL. We mustn't be foolish. There's nothing greater in life than what two people feel for each other.

CORA (*desperately*). That's why I am asking this of you. Don't make it harder for me — don't!

HAL. You are thinking of those out in the city; I am thinking only of you.

CORA. But you mustn't.

HAL. You're worth more to me than all of them.

CORA. But you must think of the people.

HAL. The people? That mob any fool can lead with a few catch phrases? That ignorant mass that cheers one day and crucifies the next? What do they really give anybody? I'll tell you. Nothing but ingratitude and scars while you live with immortelles and a monument when you're dead. Why should I sacrifice you for them?

CORA. Hal! You don't know them —

HAL. Oh, yes, I do. They can't sustain their moral attitudes. It's all a periodic fit with them. They shout a lot while the brass band plays and they cheer any fool in the red light. Then they settle back into their old self-righteousness while the McQuinns are always on the job.

CORA. You're unjust. You don't know what you're saying. It's because they *are* ignorant that strong leaders like you should go to them. (*He laughs*) You must not forget those others who are working with you against McQuinn.

HAL. The Reformers? Huh. I know them, too. I'm sick to death of political reforms and reformers who plant together but reap their fruits separately.

CORA (*trying to stop him*). They're human and —

HAL. Yes; that's it. Damn human! Why, even now they're squabbling over who shall run for Mayor once they put McQuinn out of power. They're fighting, just like the grafters, with all the same petty jealous personalities. Reformers! Would they put *you* on their visiting list even if they knew you sacrificed your reputation for them? With all their political morality do you think they'd dare go against public opinion on private morals? No! They couldn't run for office themselves if they did. They'd think you unclean —

CORA. No, no!

HAL. Yes: just as they think McQuinn unclean. They'd accept your sacrifice. But they'd use it as they use their causes: to ride into power themselves. Reformers! I sha'n't sacrifice you for them. What do they care for you and me?

CORA. But it's not a sacrifice to do what is right.

HAL. Others will try to do what I have failed in. There are always plenty of reformers. I don't want the glory. I've seen the graves of martyrs. No, no. I'll go through with what McQuinn demands just because it's you and me who matter — you and me.

CORA. With McQuinn always waiting at the door. (*The 'phone rings sharply again*) You see?

HAL. Damn him! Why doesn't he leave us alone?

CORA. We'll never be alone again.

HAL. I'll fix him.

CORA (*with calm strength*). He must be answered now as well as later.

HAL (*as she starts to the 'phone*). You sha'n't do this.

CORA. I'll not let your work be ruined by my cowardice.

HAL. I tell you I'm through with that work.

CORA. But you're not through with my love! It's my love speaking now for *our* love, which I must keep clean in my own eyes. Our love which the law punishes by denying it freedom to live in the open! Our love which keeps me from being "a good woman" — like your wife! (*She goes to the 'phone. Hal, seeing the futility of further words, sinks back into his chair overcome by what the future holds)* Yes. This is Cora Warren. . . . Who wishes to talk to Mr. Merrill? . . . Is this Mr. McQuinn talking? . . . Mr. McQuinn, I'm glad you rang up. . . . I'm fully acquainted with the particulars of the case. . . . Yes, of course, we're going to be sensible. . . . What are you going to do? . . . Thanks for putting it so clearly. I wanted you to say that to *me* also. We're not at all anxious to have this story come out. . . . No. But Mr. Merrill is going on the stand to-morrow to tell the truth. . . . Yes. . . . And . . . if the story is subsequently published . . . or if he is cross-examined by your lawyers about our relations, *I* shall go on the stand, produce a record that you 'phoned me twice, and corroborate his statement that you tried to blackmail him into silence. . . . You are quite sure you understand? . . . You're sorry for me? . . . Oh, that's all right, Mr. McQuinn. . . . What's that? *(Her voice trails off)* Yes, I know I'm "a hell of a fine woman." *(She hangs up the receiver and goes slowly to Hal)* You did what you thought best for me. I did what *is* best for you.

HAL *(holding her close as she kneels beside him)*. Poor dear, brave girl. He'll publish it. I know him. And then — oh!

CORA. Yes, dearest. But he didn't *laugh* this time! [*There is a triumphant smile upon her face.*

The curtain falls.

FUNICULI FUNICULA

RITA WELLMAN

MISS RITA WELLMAN was born in 1890 in Washington, D.C. She is a daughter of Walter Wellman, journalist and explorer. Miss Wellman's first story was published when she was seventeen, and since then she has been writing stories and plays continually. Her published plays are "Barbarians", "Funiculi Funicula", and "The Lady with the Mirror."

Her first play to be produced was a sketch for vaudeville. "Barbarians", given first by The Provincetown Players, has been produced by many of the Little Theatres in this country. All of her published plays have been produced, and in addition to the above, Miss Wellman has produced "The Rib-Person" and "The Gentile Wife."

FUNICULI FUNICULA

By RITA WELLMAN

Funiculi Funicula was originally produced by The Provincetown Players, 139 MacDougall Street, New York, December,
1918.

Original Cast

DOCTOR COLLINS	Ira Remsen
TADDEMA TANNER	James Light
ALMA WILLYS	Ida Rau

Produced under the direction of Nina Moise.

FUNICULI FUNICULA

SCENE: *Small Washington Square apartment. Has started out very gaily. Is now shabby and neglected. There is about the place an air of conquered attitude. Door right at back leads into an outer hall with stairs leading up. Door left on side wall leads into a back room. Bay window in center. This looks out into a court. Couch before the window with small table near by. Settee at right. Small table left with type-writer, etc. Bookcases right and left. New Art paintings on the wall. The couch is now covered with bed clothes and shows that some one has recently occupied it. The covers are thrown back at one end. A child's bathrobe lies on the bed, half falling from it. On the small table near the couch there are medicine bottles, a box of absorbent cotton and other medicinal things. A piece of blue paper torn from the cotton box is fixed with a hair pin to the lamp which stands on the table. The room is very untidy. There are toys scattered about, and many of the chairs are cluttered with clothing.*

It is about seven-thirty in the evening. Alma and Doctor Collins enter together from the bedroom. Alma is beautiful. Nevertheless, she is nervous and discontented — a failure. She wears a loose, brilliantly colored smock. Doctor Collins is what he calls himself — "a plain man." He feels an instinctive distrust for intellectual and artistic people. He agrees with Oscar Wilde that "Nature hates Mind." For this reason he is afraid of Alma and disapproves of her. He also thinks she is beautiful.

DOCTOR COLLINS (*as they enter*). I will write a prescription for you. Please have it filled at once.

ALMA. But I sent Mr. Tanner out with the other one — the one you gave me on Monday. Isn't it all right?

DOCTOR COLLINS (*writing*). No. I want her to have this now — every three hours.

ALMA. Is she worse, Doctor Collins?

DOCTOR COLLINS. She hasn't improved as I had hoped, Miss Willys.

ALMA (*walking about nervously, attempting listlessly to straighten the room*). I'm sure I've done everything you told me to. I'm sure I've tried to do everything for her.

DOCTOR COLLINS (*handing her the prescription*). Here — have this filled at once. You can continue with the tablets I gave you on Monday — those are for the fever. Her temperature is the most alarming thing. I don't see why we can't get it down. I wish you had called me before, Miss Willys. Why did you let it go so long? I told you on Monday that I wanted to see her again if there was any change.

ALMA. I don't know why I didn't call you. I hate getting excited over every little thing — I suppose that was the reason. She seemed all right. She was quite bright until yesterday morning. Then she began to droop and complain. It's very hard when you're all alone.

DOCTOR. Isn't Mr. Tanner here to help you?

ALMA. He's been busy. That is — he's been working at something, anyway — I don't know what it is — some club thing or other. He's always doing something of the kind — for charity. Doesn't it seem amusing that the people who never earn any money are always willing to do things for nothing?

DOCTOR. I should think that would work the other way about — that the people who are willing to work for nothing never make anything.

ALMA (*sitting*). You can get along very nicely without money — and that leaves you time to do all the pleasant things. And you never get paid for doing anything pleasant.

DOCTOR. I am too plebeian to understand you, I am afraid. I am a plain man, Miss Willys.

ALMA. That is almost a boast, Doctor Collins.

DOCTOR. Miss Willys, I am going to be frank with you, may I?

ALMA. By all means, Doctor Collins. Sit down, won't you? I am afraid it isn't very clean. I have a woman who comes in to clean, but she didn't come to-day. Her husband drinks. Not that that is any reason why she shouldn't come. (*As he picks up a chair filled with clothing*) Oh, I'm sorry. Just let them stay there. Here, take this chair.

DOCTOR (*removing the articles*). This will be all right, thank you.

[*Sits.*

ALMA. I suppose you are accustomed to having everything hygienic. I think all this modern excitement over the germ must have its bad effect, don't you? Think of the effect on the germ. I mean the psychological effect. There's something in that. But you doctors never realize these things. You're simply mathematicians.

DOCTOR. You are very clever, Miss Willys, and I am a very plain man.

ALMA (*annoyed*). Yes, so you told me.

DOCTOR. I want to speak to you seriously, Miss Willys. About — the little girl in there.

ALMA. I know. You are going to tell me what a bad mother I am. I know I am. I was never intended to be a mother. And now you are going to tell me that all women were intended to be mothers.

DOCTOR. No, I was not going to say that — just then. Miss Willys, is Mr. Tanner your husband or isn't he?

ALMA. We're not married — if that's what you mean.

DOCTOR. But he is the father of that little girl in there?

ALMA. Yes, he is Bambi's father.

DOCTOR (*who hesitates — because he feels ridiculous*). Just what — what is the idea?

ALMA. The idea? (*Smiles*) You mean — why aren't we properly married?

DOCTOR. Yes, exactly — why aren't you properly married?

ALMA (*serious*). I don't know why we didn't. We were afraid, I suppose.

DOCTOR. Afraid to be properly married?

ALMA. Yes. It seems strange to you, doesn't it? You see all people aren't alike. Some kinds of people are afraid to do what every one disapproves of — while our kind — we're afraid to do the things every one approves of. I suppose there were other reasons too at the time — I know it, in fact. But why should I discuss them with you? Being married or not married is a private matter, it seems to me. And what has my being married or not to do with my child's getting well?

DOCTOR. Everything.

ALMA. Oh, please don't be absurd, Doctor Collins.

DOCTOR. Miss Willys, this little girl you have brought into the world has never had proper care.

ALMA. Why, Doctor Collins!

DOCTOR. I mean it. You probably think because you have fed her and clothed her as well as you could that you have given her all that she needs. That is not enough. There is never enough that you can do for a small child struggling to live. It needs sunlight. It needs fresh air. It needs quiet and regularity. The most stupid person knows these things. You are a very brilliant young woman, but if you've ever known these things you've forgotten them — or you don't care.

ALMA. I don't *care!*

DOCTOR COLLINS. How long have you lived here in this place?

ALMA. Oh, I don't know — about three years.

DOCTOR. Ever since little Bambi was born.

ALMA. Yes — almost — think of it!

DOCTOR. Look at this place. Two little rooms on a court. Filled with the smell of tobacco smoke. The only sun

that ever comes in here is reflected from the wall opposite.
When you go out at night you take the child with you because there is no one to leave her with at home. She
goes to concerts and to the theatre. She has been taught
to dance and act. At three and a half years she is subjected
to all the excitements and nervous strain of an adult's
life.

ALMA. You seem to have been discovering many facts about
us, Doctor.

DOCTOR. It is my duty to know these things. They are
true, aren't they?

ALMA. Yes, of course. What would you have us do? We
have Bambi to take care of. We can't turn her over to
strangers. We haven't enough money to send her to
school. She must share our life — that's logical.

DOCTOR. Why shouldn't *you* share *hers*!

ALMA. We have our work to do. We can't give up our
work simply for Bambi? Why should we?

DOCTOR. Then your child's life isn't worth as much to you
as your — art — or whatever you call it?

ALMA (*coldly*). I call it my art — yes.

DOCTOR. You haven't answered my question.

ALMA. I never considered it that way. I never thought
about it at all. We have no set plan of life. That would
be stupid, and we couldn't live up to it if we had. We all
sort of live along somehow. Taddem goes his way, I go
mine. Bambi . . .

DOCTOR. Yes, Bambi . . .

ALMA. She will go hers in time, I suppose.

DOCTOR. So she is just to live along, too. A child cannot
just live along. A child must be guided and helped to
live. It cannot fight existence as a grown person can.
That is what parents are for. There is not a moment in
the twenty-four hours when your child is not in danger
from some cause. This applies to any child — and particularly to your child.

ALMA. To my child? Why?

DOCTOR. She has never been strong, I imagine, from birth. She is highly nervous and anæmic. Any infection which she might take in has twice as much power over her as it would have over a normal child leading a regular life. As soon as it is possible for you to do so I advise that you move away from here — into the country where she will get fresh air and a great deal of it.

ALMA. So you would make commuters out of Taddem and me. We would rather die first.

DOCTOR (*rising*). Miss Willys, in my work I have seen girls from the street — ignorant, brutal, the very dirt of life, you would say — I've seen such girls willing — and glad — to sacrifice themselves for their children.

ALMA. Sacrifice?

DOCTOR. You hadn't thought of that, had you?

ALMA. No. No, I hadn't. It is a dreadful word.

DOCTOR (*gets his bag — reaches out his hand to Alma to say good-by. He feels much more sure of himself now*). Good-night, Miss Willys. Will you let me know if there is any change? You know where you can get me? Greely 2340. Don't fail to call me. Have the prescription made out at once. I will be here first thing in the morning.

ALMA. But Doctor Collins — wait a minute. Those women — mothers — have they no rights at all? I remember right after Bambi was born — you doctors are so cruel to us mothers — you never think of us at all — everything is the child, the child — Have we no rights of our own at all? Is everything to be sacrificed to the children?

DOCTOR. Everything.

[*Goes out. Alma goes into the room and returns quickly. Taddema Tanner comes in. He is about twenty-eight years old, poetically beautiful. He has never been awake. His dreams are not great enough to carry him victoriously along, rather do they break over him and leave him floundering helplessly. A failure. He is defiantly shabby. There is even a flower in his buttonhole.*

TADDEMA. Hello. Here's your old prescription. Couldn't

get in earlier. I've been helping them upstairs. The room looks great, Alma. Gray, orange, and black. The Rebellious Rabelaisian Revel. How's that.

ALMA. Rather amusing. Whose idea was that?

TADDEMA. Don't know. Not particularly good, anyway. Any one could have thought of it. The main thing is to believe it. Want a cigarette?

ALMA. Thanks.

[*He lights a cigarette for her.*

TADDEMA. Where's the Bambi?

ALMA. The doctor took her into our room. He thought she would be more quiet.

TADDEMA. And where am I supposed to sleep then?

ALMA. I suppose you'll have to sleep here.

TADDEMA. With all that hellish racket going on upstairs at the dance? Bambi'd never notice it. She sleeps through any old kind of noise. Why did you let him do it, Alma? You might have thought of me. You know how noises get on my nerves. I won't be able to sleep the whole night. He takes a lot into his own hands, it seems to me.

ALMA. He's simply a doctor, Taddem.

TADDEMA. And the room's so messy you can't turn around in it. Clothes all over everything. Medicine bottles. And what's the decoration on the lamp for?

ALMA. I put it there last night to shade Bambi's eyes. Why don't you spend the night again at Hud's as you did last night?

TADDEMA. Because he doesn't want me. You know — that girl's come back — that little squint-eye illustrator — why don't you get Mrs. Farrell to come and clean up? I despise dirt.

ALMA (*sighing*). I don't know — oh, yes, her husband's drunk again. Although I don't know why we always accept that old excuse. But I feel sorry for her. Eight children. Imagine. (*Picking up things*) I'll see if I can't do something.

TADDEMA. Where's a broom? I'll help you.

ALMA. Oh, don't sweep. It always makes things worse. What costumes are they going to wear, Taddem?

TADDEMA. Oh, the usual old leopard skin, I suppose. You know, I'd like to go.

ALMA. Taddem! With Bambi sick!

TADDEMA. Oh, I suppose it wouldn't be right. I forgot, and Nina Cardell's come back.

ALMA. Oh, I see.

TADDEMA. You know she's grown to be really beautiful, Alma.

ALMA. I always told you she was, Taddem.

TADDEMA. Yes, probably that was the reason I didn't think so.

ALMA. Is she going? Of course she is. It's strange no one has told me anything of the dance. I never seem to be in anything any more. I wish we *could* go, Taddem.

TADDEMA. No, I suppose we shouldn't. It wouldn't do. How does she seem, anyway?

ALMA. Who — Bambi? Just about the same, that is, as far as I can see. The doctor seemed to think she wasn't getting on so well.

TADDEMA. Poor little brat. I brought her a toy. (*Reaching in his pocket*) A little mannikin — one of Hud's. It would amuse her. What in the name of . . . did I do with the thing? (*Pulls out a bunch of letters and clippings, but can't find the toy*) I must have lost it. Too bad. (*Goes to his work table — looks over papers*) Just saw Lee Hoyt. We had something to eat together. He's starting a new religion — very interesting. Sort of a Lily Cup Buddhism. The *Banner* did him out of his money just the way they did me. It's a shame. Looks fat enough. Fatter than ever. Some one must feed him.

ALMA. Did they take your poem?

TADDEMA. What poem? Oh, you mean that last one? No, they sent it back. Got it up at Hud's. I don't seem to be doing the stuff I used to. It's this everlasting . . .

ALMA (*quickly*). Everlasting what, Taddem?

TADDEMA. Never mind. We can't help it. No one can. We're nothing but worms. Worms under the foot. Even you, Alma, you're just a little writhing worm.

ALMA. I can't say I'm in any mood to be called a worm, Taddem, true as it may be. So they sent the poem back.

TADDEMA. Well, what difference does it make? I can write others. I have an idea now — a really great idea, Alma.

ALMA. I thought sure they'd take it — it's the worst thing you've done. Oh, Taddem, if you could only reason a little. We need money so dreadfully.

TADDEMA (*who has been thinking*). What'd you say, Alma?

ALMA. I said we need money. We need it terribly. I don't see what we're going to do. Oh, if you'd only *see*.

TADDEMA. I do see. I do see. I see everything. What can I do? What can we do? Just as I said — we are simply worms.

ALMA. But where is the money coming from?

TADDEMA. What makes you so uncomfortably practical all at once?

ALMA. Because we have to live. Because we have bills, hundreds of them. The doctor, the druggist — to mention the least of them.

TADDEMA. The doctor and the druggist have nothing to do with my immortal soul.

ALMA. No, perhaps not — but they have something to do with Bambi's.

TADDEMA. Oh, Bambi. Well, wait and see. We'll get money in some place. I'm going to get started soon and do something big. You'll see. And then there's your work. Who's that man — you know — he liked your drawings?

ALMA (*in disgust and despair*). Oh, my drawings!

TADDEMA. Well, what's wrong with them? They're good — awfully good. Some of them are awfully clever. Every one says so, Alma. I don't see what makes you always so pessimistic about your work.

ALMA.   Because I haven't the time to give to it.   I haven't
the time to think of it even.   And when I have I'm too
tired.   It's always Bambi first.   Bambi all day long.   Her
food, her bed, her toys, her this, her that, from morning
until night.   Even when she's well. . . . And when she's
sick I'm simply worked to death.   How can I do anything
else?   How can I have an art when I am a slave bound
hand and foot?

TADDEMA.   Funny how an idea comes to you.

ALMA (*who is worn out and nervous and on the point of losing
all control*).   Oh, I'm so tired.   I'm so tired.

TADDEMA (*who has been thinking his own thoughts and has not
listened*).   Hud is an awful fool.   He talks too much.
But he says so much he can't help being profound sometimes.   He said something last night that impressed me
very much.   "Elemental people fear death — intellectuals
fear life."   That's not a bad idea.   I could work it into a
sort of a play.   (*Starts to write*)   Damn the doctor and
the druggist.

[*Alma goes determinedly to a cupboard and gets out her
drawing board, etc.   She knows she isn't going to work, but she
needs the contact of these things she loves.*

ALMA (*turning toward door*).   They're beginning to go up to
the dance already.   (*After a pause in which he has paid no
attention to her*)   I haven't had any dinner, Taddem.

TADDEMA.   What did you say, Alma?

ALMA.   Nothing.

TADDEMA.   About dinner.   Haven't you had any?

ALMA.   No, how could I?   There's nothing here.

TADDEMA.   That's a shame.   You really ought to. . . .
[*And he gets engrossed in work again.*

ALMA.   I wonder who's going?   Probably' would be a bore,
anyway, don't you think, Taddem?

TADDEMA.   I wish you could keep quiet, Alma.

ALMA.   Excuse me.   I'm sorry.   (*After a minute*)   Do you
know any of the men who're going?   (*As he doesn't answer*)
I probably wouldn't know any one if we did go.   Still

there's sure to be some one of the old crowd. (*Putting away her things in disgust*) Oh, how rotten I am. Oh, how worthless I am!

TADDEMA. Oh, if you'd only keep quiet.

ALMA. If you'd only stop writing and pay some attention to me.

TADDEMA. Oh, if I could only have a little peace. [*Starts to go into room left.*

ALMA (*staying him*). You can't go in there, Taddem. The doctor said Bambi wasn't to be disturbed.

TADDEMA. Where am I to go then?

ALMA. You'll have to stay here and make the best of it — as I have to. Listen! Is she calling me?

TADDEMA. I didn't hear anything.

ALMA. My imagination. . . I'm always hearing her calling. Even in my sleep. Oh, if she'd only get well again. We'd have some peace.

TADDEMA. Well, at least you could keep quiet and let *me* work.

ALMA. Yes, let *you* work. That's just it. *You* can work. *You* can go on being yourself no matter what happens. But I must give up everything. I must be a mere protective animal. I must sacrifice everything. I'm to be nothing but a mother!

TADDEMA. Well, I'm sure you have yourself to blame for that. You insisted upon being a mother, didn't you?

ALMA (*sitting*). Yes, I did. It was a beautiful dream. Taddem — when we were in Rome all that time — was that real? Or is this? Or is nothing real?

TADDEMA (*interested — always ready to discuss them and their life*). Yes — when we were in Rome.

ALMA. I wonder why it is that all of our highest dreams always lead us to our worst miseries.

TADDEMA. Because we try to make our dreams realities.

ALMA. Poets joined in passion. That was your phrase, Taddem. And it was all so fine and high. Let us never do anything ugly, we vowed, let us never do anything

unworthy. And we married ourselves in the Browning
villa with these rings. They did it, we said, why shouldn't
we? And our dream of the Bambino. That was to prove
it. Oh, Taddem, can you forget? Do you remember how
eager I was? Never a painter, never a sculptor, planned
and moulded as I did.

TADDEMA. Do you remember the day we burned the candles
to the Virgin in the little church? There was an Italian
woman there and you knelt together. You both bent your
heads. I cried. But your eyes were shining, and you
looked so strong. You were a saint to me then.

ALMA. Oh, don't say that. It was all so wrong, so foolishly
wrong. We couldn't do it. We couldn't carry it through.
We've failed. The passion has gone. All the poetry and
splendor we drew from each other — that has all gone.
We've done what we vowed we would never do. We've
become ugly. We've become unworthy. We're petty and
commonplace. We're like all married people from here to
Harlem. We've a few pieces of furniture, a place to come
to and pay for, and a child — a child we both hate.

TADDEMA. Hate! Why, Alma!

ALMA. Oh, don't say that we don't hate her. We do. She's
in our way. She's always been in our way ever since she
was born. Ever since she became a reality she's annoyed
us. She's cost us money. She's kept us home when we
wanted to go out. She's cried when we wanted to work.
She's made our love ridiculous. She's made a family out
of us — something we can't stand. We've never forgiven
her for making us feel that all our passion was for her sake.

TADDEMA. That isn't true. Don't say such bitter, cruel
things.

ALMA. Oh, you know they're true.

TADDEMA. I'm fond of Bambi — awfully.

ALMA. Yes, when you're not at home, when you're away,
free to do what you please, when I'm here all alone, doing
my duty. My duty! How I despise my duty!

[*Just now the door bursts open and a young man and a young girl, both in costume, stumble backward into the room. The man has been chasing the girl upstairs and has just now caught her and is ardently trying to kiss her. The girl isn't really unwilling, but laughingly and temptingly pretends that she is. When they realize where they are, they laughingly run away.*

ALMA (*passionately*). I want to go up to the dance!

TADDEMA. We oughtn't to.

ALMA. If I could only go!

TADDEMA. Do you think we could? We could run up for an hour or so. We could come down from time to time.

ALMA. Oh, no, I should hate that. You don't want to think of medicine bottles when you're dancing. I'd rather not go at all then.

TADDEMA. We could ask one of the women to look down here every now and then. Lots of them like Bambi. Do you suppose we could, Alma? I'd love to go to-night.

ALMA. He gave her something to make her sleep. Oh, Taddem, I forgot the prescription. Well, we can have it filled in the morning. I'll go in and see how she is.

[*Starts to go to room left.*

TADDEMA. Yes, you go and see how she is. I'll get the costumes. Do you know where they are?

ALMA. I think they're in that box under the couch. (*Hesitating*) Do you think it's all right, Taddem?

TADDEMA. O, of course. It's just upstairs. (*Hesitating*) But if you don't . . .

ALMA. Get out that yellow thing I wore —

[*She goes out left. The orchestra is heard playing upstairs. It is very faint. It is playing Funiculi Funicula. Taddema gets out a Pierrot costume and puts it on, singing the words to the song.*

ALMA (*reëntering*). Taddem!

TADDEMA. What's wrong now? What's the matter, Alma?

ALMA. Taddem!

TADDEMA. What is it, Alma? What's wrong with you?

ALMA. Nothing. Nothing. Nothing's wrong. I was think-
ing . . . But why shouldn't we go? We must go.
I've got to go. Give me my domino. Where is it?
What did you do with my domino, Taddem?

TADDEMA. Here it is.

ALMA. It's all dusty. The moths have been in it. (*Laugh-
ing*) Moths in my gay little domino. Where's my hat,
Taddem. Get it for me. We must hurry. Oh, please
hurry. There it is — don't you see — in the paper — Give
it to me. Oh, my face — I have some powder here — Oh,
I look dreadful — (*She rouges and powders her face*)
Are you all dressed, Taddem? Powder your face. Pierrot
. . . Pierrot . . .

TADDEMA. If you think we shouldn't go, Alma . . .

ALMA. Keep quiet. Of course we're going. There, do I
look all right. Do I look pretty? I'm not an old woman,
am I? Am I, Taddem? (*Clinging to him*) Am I?
Answer me. Tell me something. Say something, say
something mad . . . Oh, Taddem, if I could only bring
you back to me. . . (*Pulling him to the door*) Be my
lover again — Come, be my lover — You are my lover,
aren't you? Aren't you? Tell me, tell me, tell me.

TADDEMA (*trying to resist*). But I don't understand . . .

ALMA (*pulling him to the door*). Understand, understand.
What is there to understand? You must understand that
I want to go to the dance. I want to dance and dance.
Don't pull back now. Come with me. Come with me.

TADDEMA. Alma, Bambi's worse. You're running away.

ALMA. Oh, please come. Hurry.

TADDEMA. She's all right then?

ALMA. Of course, of course. Oh, if you'd only hurry.

TADDEMA. I don't believe you. I am going to see for myself.
[*Starts left.*

ALMA (*staying him — frantically*). Don't. Don't do that.
You mustn't go in there. You mustn't go in there. Taddem, for God's sake, don't go in there now.

TADDEMA. What is it? Is she worse . . .

ALMA. Oh, come with me. Come away with me. (*Winding herself about him*) Dearest, come with me. You do love me. I know you do. Think only of me, and I will think only of you. Nothing else matters. Taddem, look at me. Look at me. Kiss me. Just once — kiss me.

TADDEMA (*fascinated*). Alma, I don't know you now.

ALMA (*breaking away as he is about to kiss her*). Oh, I can't. I can't.

[*She comes staggering back into the room.*

TADDEMA (*hoarsely*). Bambi . . .

ALMA. I went in . . . I couldn't hear anything — not a sound — then the curtain blew — I saw a light there — I went over — I went over — I touched her — her little face, Taddem — her little face — cold — cold, Taddem. (*She sees the little bathrobe and snatches it to her breast, sobbing*)

Oh, my baby. My baby. My little, little baby!

[*She staggers out left, weeping hysterically. Taddema follows her to the door and looks into the other room. Then he comes back. He walks over to the light and puts it out. He goes to the window where the light is streaming in and opens it. The music from upstairs is, of course, heard more plainly. He crouches a moment by the window. He is very young. He has loved his child in his own way. Now that she is dead he loves her more. He has real grief, but this was the night he wanted to be gay. He hates his grief. He is passionately angry that he is sad when others are gay. A man's voice is heard now singing the words to Funiculi Funicula, very gaily. A girl's voice chimes in. Taddema turns to his couch and with passionate anger bursts out "Damn! Damn!" Then he falls face down, bitterly weeping.*

CURTAIN

HUNGER

EUGENE PILLOT

MR. EUGENE PILLOT was born in Houston, Texas, and has studied at Culver Military Academy, the New York School of Fine and Applied Art, the University of Texas, Cornell University, and Harvard University.

He has written several plays, all of which have seen successful production. His "Simms — Vane Incident", a one-act play, was produced at the 47 Workshop of Harvard in 1917, and his "The Middle Window", a three-act play, at the same place in 1918. "The Glazing Globe", a one-act play, was produced at Houston, Texas, 1918. "Hunger" has been given by the Boston Community Players, and at recitals.

HUNGER

By EUGENE PILLOT

"Hunger" was originally produced by The Boston Community Players, Boston, Massachusetts, May 15 and 16, 1918.

Original Cast

THE BEGGAR	Robert Winternitz
THE POET	Frank Carson
THE GIRL	Beulah Auerbach
THE MAN	Reginald Coggeshawl
THE SATISFIED ONE	Eugene Pillot

Published originally in *The Stratford Journal.*
Application for the right of performing "Hunger" must be made to Mr. Eugene Pillot, 47 Workshop, Harvard University, Cambridge, Massachusetts.

HUNGER

SCENE. *A great gray tower, so tall that you cannot see its top,
is beside a gray road. A purple door, outlined with a latticed
band of gold, is in the center of the tower, and there are huge
light-green rocks on each side. In the distance are several
poplar trees and a rolling country.*

TIME. *A day before now.*

*When the curtain rises, the Beggar is asleep on the rock at the
left of tower. The mass of brown and yellow rags that cover
his fat body brings into bold relief his mop of shaggy red hair.
He sighs, sits up, yawns, rubs his eyes, and nods again sleepily.*

BEGGAR (*suddenly sitting erect, blinking*). Aw, tis a pity good,
sound sleep should ever end. (*Leans forward and looks up
at door*) So you're not open yet, old door, eh? (*Rises,
glances quickly to right, then to left, and limps up the three
stone steps to door, grabs door knob and feverishly tries to open
door, which remains immobile. Despondent, he slaps his
hand against the door*) Aw, ain't you going to *ever* open?
(*Pushes himself away from door and regards it contempla-
tively*) You might show just a crack of your inside anyhow. Stingy!

[*Slaps door. The sound of approaching footsteps from off
right causes him to scramble to his rock, where he sits with outstretched hand.*

*From right, enter the Poet, a thin, pale man with a thin, pale
voice. He is a curly-headed blond and wears loose-fitting
trousers of rather a dark blue; a long-waisted blouse of
light blue embroidered with gold; soft gold shoes, and carries
a long, light green quill. His head in the air, he walks along
dreamily until he sees the tower and hastens to its door.*

BEGGAR (*quickly*). Alms for a poor lame beggar! Alms for a poor lame beggar!

POET (*with a flourish of his hands*). Alms — I have none.

BEGGAR (*grabs his stomach with one hand, while the other remains outstretched*). Oh, but I ask for my hunger, sire! My hunger for bread!

POET. Bread? Forsooth, 'tis an earthly thing.

BEGGAR. Even so, my belly would feel the weight of it — so hungry am I, sire, so hungry!

POET. Yours is not the only hunger in the world. Alas, I have one of my own. (*Grabs door knob with both hands and tries to force open the door*) And I shall be fed! I shall! (*Appealingly, to door*) O Muses, Muses, let it open! Open the door — or I die of hunger. (*Sighs, drops his hands, and goes to rock at right of tower where he sits weeping, his face in his hands*) O-oh, oh, oh.

BEGGAR. Forsooth, you must have a long hunger, if it has brought you to dropping tears.

POET (*forlornly*). I have felt it since I was born.

BEGGAR. Aw, I've been hungry as an ox for longer than my belly will let me remember; but never could I afford to drop tears. Wastes too much salt. And my belly so needs salt for bread. (*Rocks himself*) Oh, how it needs the bread, too!

POET. Salt! The salt of desire!
[*Weeps.*

BEGGAR. Losing so much salt is what's made you so skinny, do you know it?

POET (*weeping*). Who knows! (*Weeps louder*) Who knows!

BEGGAR. Father of suffering pussy-cats! Stop wailing! Forsooth, you make me hungrier. (*Rocks himself*) Aw, stop it! Soon you'll be having me lose my own salt. Stop, I say, *stop!*

POET (*stops weeping and looks at him tearfully*). Ah, 'tis hard to stop, once you've begun. (*Sighs*) Seems to soothe like great waves rolling in from the sea.

BEGGAR. Huh, how you people with brains do fool yourselves. Just how long have you been hungry for bread, anyhow?

POET (*insulted*). I'm not hungry for *bread!*

BEGGAR. What! Not hungry for bread?

POET. Certainly not.

BEGGAR. Ye lolly-pop gods! How can you wail so, if your belly's not empty? In pretending you shame our best actor-men. You're a wonder of wonders! (*Rises*) What *do* you call yourself?

POET. A poet — a hungry poet.

BEGGAR. Indeed. (*Moves nearer, interested*) If not for bread, for what can a poet hunger?

POET. For love!

BEGGAR (*sarcastically*). For love? That puny thing that's always dying?

POET. It alone can make you live — really live!

BEGGAR (*scornfully, as he resumes his seat on the rock*). I breathe without it.

POET. But it warms the heart and makes of the world an Elysian field of rose-colored jasmines, where doves have the voices of angels and — (*Beggar is bowled over with hilarious laughter*) 'Tis no more of a jest to me' than your bread is to you.

BEGGAR. Bread! Ha, if I had it now, my teeth would bite into it and I'd jam it through my system till it was stuffed to the bursting.

POET. Alas, the hunger of the stomach is as nothing when compared to the hunger of the heart.

BEGGAR. Heart? Your grandmother's fiddlesticks!

POET (*his emotion causing him to spring from his rock*). But the heart-hunger makes you mad with desire! And love — only sweet love can still it. 'Tis the only food that satisfies an empty heart!

BEGGAR (*fretfully*). Bread's the only food. Eat some and you won't need this sweet love.

POET (*not heeding him*). The verses I write possess every charm but love. Ah, how I could write if I had it! Love!

LOVE!! So long have I hungered for you!

[*Weeps.*

BEGGAR. Stop, you weepy, poesy poet! My salt's ready to slip from me. Stop, I say, stop!

POET (*stops weeping, looks at Beggar*). All right, I'll stop — but I feel like starting all over again, when I think about what's on the other side of that door.

[*Points to purple door.*

BEGGAR (*eagerly*). What do you know about the other side of that door?

POET. That there is abundance of food there for all who hunger.

BEGGAR. So *you* know that too. (*Sits on steps before door*) Ain't it a wonderful thing to *think* about? In a great golden hall, yellow as the yolk of a healthy egg, is a table — piled higher than anybody can see — with every kind of food! Why, no matter what you're hungering for, your food's there on that table — and more of it than you could eat, if you lived till you were born again. A-ah, it must be a happy place.

[*Rises, moves toward right.*

POET (*rushing to door*). But I don't want to *think* about the food that's there! I want to *get* to it!

[*Fumbles with door knob.*

BEGGAR. Alas, getting through the door is the problem of the ages.

POET. But I don't see why I can't solve it! (*Jerks at door knob*) If I only knew the secret of your turn! If I only knew!

BEGGAR (*dryly*). Only one man knows that.

POET. Yes! Yes!

BEGGAR. Preserve your exclamations, for he won't tell.

POET. Who is he?

BEGGAR. The Satisfied One.

POET (*blandly*). I never heard of the Satisfied One.

BEGGAR. Well, he's the only one who's gone through that door and satisfied his hunger. That's doing enough to be talked about, let me tell you.

POET. But can't he be made to tell?

BEGGAR. No one's ever got the secret from him yet; but some day we shall, mark my word for that.

POET. How?

BEGGAR *(looking toward right)*. Quiet! Some one's coming.

POET. But I want to know how —?

BEGGAR. Hush! Take to your rock.

POET *(sits on his rock)*. Can you see who it is?

BEGGAR. No, the dust still flies in the road. *(Half-whisper, turning to Poet)* But it might be the Satisfied One — who knows?

POET. Why do you think so?

BEGGAR *(confidentially)*. Oh, I heard it spoken on the edge of a quiet corner — the Satisfied One might pass this way to-day. Ah, your ears get sharp when your belly's empty and hungry for bread.

POET. And I hungry for sweet love!

BEGGAR. Hist! He's here!

[*Quickly assumes a crouching position to left of door and extends his hand across the steps for alms.*

From the right, enter the Man — large and handsome, the orator type. Bare-limbed and sandalled, he wears a robe not unlike a Roman toga, light-green with a wide band of gold near the hem and across the chest. Bracelets of heavy gold. He walks straight to the door and is about to turn the knob, when the Beggar speaks.

BEGGAR. Alms for a poor, lame beggar! Alms for a *very* poor lame beggar!

MAN. Alms? Alms, fellow?

BEGGAR. For my hunger, sire! Give to a very, very poor lame beggar!

MAN. For your hunger?

BEGGAR. Yes, for all of it. 'Tis a long hunger, sire — a long one.

MAN *(stoutly)*. Fellow, I will give you all the bread in the kingdom —

BEGGAR (*licking his mouth in anticipation*). At last a man after mine own heart!

MAN. *If* you will tell me how to feed *my* hunger!

BEGGAR (*exploding*). Father of pussy-cats! Another one of us! Are all the hungries let loose to-day?

POET (*timidly*). Then you are not — the Satisfied One?

MAN. Satisfied? Indeed not! (*Oratorically*) My hunger runneth through the ages; and from the beginning of time to the Day of Judgment shall I seek its satisfaction. It is a thing eternal!

BEGGAR. Even eternal hunger is with us. (*Moans*) Unhappy day, unhappy day!

POET (*to Man*). My hunger for love — sweet love — is that great too. What food do you seek to appease your hunger?

BEGGAR (*moaning*). Hunger! Hunger!

MAN (*leans back against the door, glances at Poet, then at Beggar, who has crept to his rock*). Ah, what do either of you poor souls know of hunger? Wait until you feel mine — a hunger more than bread or love or any earthly thing!

BEGGAR. Forsooth, yours must give you the belly-ache.

POET. What is yours?

MAN. The only hunger that gives a hot, clear passion — fills you with a lust for life and power — thrills you with youth and love and wild desire!

BEGGAR. Name it quickly, Man, name it! Perhaps 'twill make ours seem sickly by comparison.

POET. Ah, yes. For what do you hunger?

MAN (*striking a dramatic pose*). For fame!

BEGGAR. What? Do my ears do their duty? For fame, you say?

MAN. Yes — glorious, glittering fame!

BEGGAR (*scornfully*). Huh, you rate your hunger high.

MAN (*facing door*). So high that the very stars will look down and give me strength to force this door that I may feed my lust for fame. (*Tries to force open door*) I've sacrificed every earthly joy to get through you. (*Tugs at knob*) And you shall open! You shall!

BEGGAR (*laughing*). Ha, ha, ha-h-a-a-!

MAN. Why do you laugh?

BEGGAR. Because you are as simple as a cow.

MAN. What?

BEGGAR. Butting a pasture never filled the cavity of a heifer. But do not take it so scowlingly. I will tell you something. Only the Satisfied One knows the way through the door and he's coming this way soon.

POET (*he has been looking toward right*). Some one's coming now! And in a hurry.

BEGGAR (*to Man*). Perhaps the Satisfied One! Quick, get your lowers under your uppers.

MAN. What?

BEGGAR. I mean — sit over there on the rock! Quick, before he gets here!

[*Beggar returns to his own rock.*

Man sits on rock at extreme right. From the right, enter the Girl, running. She is a wild, graceful creature, bare-armed, and clothed in lengths of many colored chiffons that hang from a band of gold at her shoulders. Seeing the door, she gives a gasp of joy and with outstretched arms rushes to it, gives the knob a quick turn, extracts a large gold hairpin from her flowing hair and wiggles it in the keyhole.

BEGGAR. A hairpin! Woman's refuge in all emergencies.

[*The hairpin is unsuccessful and the Girl goes to band that outlines the door, attempts to climb it. Interested, the others crowd round to see what she intends to do. She looks at band, contemplates its height. All are breathless as she makes an effort to climb up band. She slips back and all sigh, disappointed — except the Beggar, who laughs.*

GIRL (*faces them, angrily*). If any one of you can do it better, show me how. (*Embarrassed, they remain silent*) I thought not. Then get back! Get back! And let me do it my own way!

[*They move away from her. Reaching higher, she tries to climb, but slips back to the ground. The Beggar holds his sides with laughter. All are annoyed.*

MAN.   Don't laugh, you foolish Beggar.

POET.   No, don't; the Satisfied One may show us the way.

BEGGAR *(laughing louder than ever)*. Ho, ho, ho! That's — not — the — Satisfied One!

POET.   Are you sure it isn't?

BEGGAR.   Sure as a pig's egg that Easter comes on a Sunday.

MAN.   But it might be —

BEGGAR.   Might be an elephant's pig-tail! Why, look how she scrambles at the wall! She's as hungry as we are.

POET.   Surely, that's so. *(Then to Girl)* Sweet Girl, are you really hungry, too?

GIRL *(fiercely)*. Hungry? HUNGRY? I'm *starving!!*

BEGGAR.   Forsooth, this one has a rabid hunger!

MAN.   Then you aren't the Satisfied One either?

GIRL.   Satisfied? Huh, I've never had even one dress to satisfy me!

BEGGAR.   Dress? Dress? Father of pussy-cats, what kind of a hunger is this?

GIRL.   Oh, you'd hardly understand it — it's so much a woman's hunger.

BEGGAR.   Nevertheless, 'twould be a pleasure to know your hunger. *(Coaxing)* Come, tell us, won't you?

POET *(as all go nearer Girl)*   Oh, do tell, sweet one.

GIRL.   The world would call it — beauty. That's what it would call my hunger; but to me it means clothes! Soft, beautiful clothes!

BEGGAR.   Clothes! Such a hunger! *(Laughs)* Soft, beautiful clothes! ha, ha, ha!

[*He is bowled over with laughter.*

GIRL.   No man ever quite understands my hunger; but a woman would know what it is for your very soul to ache for a gown of golden-blue, shimmering with threads of green and gold that run through it like rivers of light! A-ah, that is a hunger indeed. And to throb and yearn for garments as sweeping as the singing winds over moon-lit fields, lavender and milk-white in the shifting shadows that make all the world into waves of silver-pearl and blurs of maddening blue!

MAN. But, child, in your own garments you have bits of all that you hunger for.

GIRL. Yes, bits, *bits* — like feathers from a last year's hat!

MAN. 'Tis something.

GIRL. Not to a woman, when she wants something new. Besides, these bits are but to keep me from forgetting what I want.

BEGGAR (*laughs*). Ha!

GIRL. Oh, you would not even smile, if you knew how hard it was to get them. This, for instance — (*holds up a length of blood-orange chiffon*) I stole from the sash of a gypsy man, because its flaming orange leaped at me!

BEGGAR. I don't see how a sash could leap at anybody.

GIRL. That's because you never passed shop windows in the springtime and had the clothes in them simply cry out for you to come and buy them.

BEGGAR. No, but maybe a bakery shop would.

GIRL. Well, this flaming orange leaped at me and cried out: "I am your soul from the sun-burned tropics! Take me, and know the delirium of the scorching sands at mid-day." I took it and paid for it with the laughter of my youth — a laughter as fresh and dewy as a summer's morn. And this — (*holds up a length of cold blue chiffon*) this I bought with my tears from a vendor of sorrows. But for this — (*holds up length of brilliant yellow chiffon*) I gave the highest price of all — the rapture of my betrothal kiss — for this thing of golden sunlight was in the robe of the man I loved — and loved — and loved —

MAN. But you hunger for a most vanishing thing. Clothes will wear out and then you will have nothing.

BEGGAR. Nothing but the holes.

GIRL. How little you understand a woman's hunger. Bread passes away, love dies, and fame vanishes overnight; but the memory of one beautiful, glorious dress is everlasting.

BEGGAR. Yes, no doubt it makes conversation for many a supper-time.

GIRL. Oh, I'd see it and feel it clinging to me always — even though the styles did change.

[*Turns to door.*

BEGGAR. Well, if you try to climb that door, you'll feel nothing but a hurt.

GIRL (*confidentially, to all*). You know, I thought if I could climb up this band, perhaps I could get to the top of the tower and slide down on the inside.

BEGGAR. It's not to be done. I tried that once already myself.

GIRL. And what happened?

BEGGAR. I got just as far as the middle up there — over the door and —

GIRL. Yes, go on!

BEGGAR. That was the pinch — couldn't go on. Nothing to step on.

GIRL. Nothing at all?

BEGGAR. Nothing but bare wall that keeps stretching up and up and up. The blame tower ain't got no top. Ol., I tried to slip up; that's how I fell down and got my limp. I tell you the only way's to go *through* the door.

GIRL (*despondently*). Then I'll never get there.

BEGGAR. Aw, buck up! Buck up! You got enough clothes to last you till we go through the door. We're waiting now for the Satisfied One. He knows how to get through.

GIRL. But will he tell?

BEGGAR. We ain't been starving for nothing. We'll make him tell, all of us together. Now go sit on that rock and keep the wait with us. (*Girl sits on rock that is between Man and Poet. Beggar sees some one coming down the road, right. Excitedly, to all*) See! He's coming! He's coming! [*All look eagerly.*

POET. Who — a sweet one?

BEGGAR. Naw, the Satisfied One. Now we'll get through the door!

MAN. It might be just another poor hunger.

BEGGAR. There ain't any more hungers in the world — except the little ones; and they don't count. Besides, this is an old man coming.

GIRL. Are you sure we're all the great hungers of the world?

BEGGAR. Sure. (*Pointing to each*) Clothes, love, fame — and bread, that's me. Only little fish would hunger for anything else.

GIRL. He's almost here. What shall we do to make him tell?

BEGGAR. We must hit upon a plan. Come nearer. (*All crowd round him*) Now what have you to suggest? You? You? (*All stare at him blankly*) Don't open your mouths without saying anything! Be quick! He's almost here! Quick! (*All "er" and "ah", but can think of nothing to suggest. Beggar is disgusted*) You don't deserve to get through the door. (*Ponders*) We must think of something. We must!

POET. I can think of nothing but that he shall not escape without telling us the secret.

BEGGAR. A mouthful of wisdom. That's the thing — he must not escape without telling us the secret.

ALL. No, not without telling!

BEGGAR. We may be stiff in our deaths when he comes again.

POET. It's our only chance.

BEGGAR. Hush! There he is!

[*From the right the Satisfied One enters slowly and stands watching them, sadly. He is a gray, weary old man in a trailing robe of silver-gray with a wide strip of scarlet down the back and front, full length. All smirk and smile before him. Then, abashed, each slinks to his rock and sits there, staring at the Satisfied One, who now sighs wearily and walks slowly across the stage.*

MAN. He did not even glance at the door. I shall walk that way when I have fame.

BEGGAR (*excited*). Bother the way you'll walk. He's getting away from us!

POET. He — he must not — because of my love!

BEGGAR. All of you sit there like bricks! (*Scrambles up and runs to Satisfied One, tugging at his robe*) Er — er — er would you please be so — so come-downish as to let us speak with you?

SATISFIED ONE (*facing beggar*). Assuredly. (*Beggar tries to find words for his thoughts, but fails. The others come forward and try, too, but with the same result*) Then you really have nothing to say to me, after all.

[*Turns to go. All become agitated.*

BEGGAR (*bowing*). Oh, yes, sire; but we — we have.

GIRL (*appealingly*). We would ask you something!

POET (*plaintively*). And you must answer — or we famish.

MAN (*grimly*). You must tell us.

SATISFIED ONE. My good people, what is it you wish me to tell you?

ALL. How to open the door! How to open the door!

SATISFIED ONE. And why do you wish to open the door?

BEGGAR (*whispers to Poet*). He's trying to get out of telling. He always asks questions like that. We must make him tell!

SATISFIED ONE. Well, you have not answered me.

GIRL. Because we are hungry — the same as you were!

SATISFIED ONE (*sadly*). The same as I *was* —

BEGGAR. Sure. Didn't you go through the door and get fed?

SATISFIED ONE. Yes, and like all who are fed there, I was gorged with food.

BEGGAR (*to the others*). You see, I told you. That's why he is the Satisfied One. That's why!

SATISFIED ONE. It is why I am the *Dis*-satisfied One.

BEGGAR. Nevertheless, we'll take the food. (*Tries to pull the Satisfied One to the door*) Come, show us how you opened the door.

SATISFIED ONE (*resisting, throws off Beggar*). No! I will not!

[*All rush to him and cling to his robe in angry appeal.*

POET. You really must tell us!

MAN. You must!

BEGGAR. You shall!

GIRL. Tell me, for I hunger!

SATISFIED ONE. Better, my child, to hunger than to know the disillusionment beyond that door.

BEGGAR. You can well say that. Your belly's been filled.

SATISFIED ONE. Yes, but I would save you from what I learned there.

GIRL. What did you learn?

SATISFIED ONE. That abundance of food never satisfies so much as just a little. (*Grunts of disapproval from the others*) Oh, I know what it is to hunger for a thing — and I know what it means to get it. You satiate yourself with the object of your desire, like an animal wallowing in the mire; and you cannot help it, especially when you have hungered long. So I say, better a great hunger, with a little food, than the dullness of satisfaction.

BEGGAR. Aw, I know the taste of bread. I'll take my chances.

GIRL. And a woman never could have too many clothes.

SATISFIED ONE. But the quantities of food in there will not satisfy so much as the hunger you have now. It is better just to have a little of the good things of life.

BEGGAR. Aw, that's turkey-dressing talk. How did you get through the door? That's what we want to know. (*Pulling on him*) How did you?

SATISFIED ONE. I will not tell you.

ALL. Oh, but you shall! You shall!

BEGGAR. Come, all of you! We'll make him show us! [*They grab him fiercely. He struggles to get away, but they are too many for him. They drag him to the door and hurl him against it.*

BEGGAR. Show us how to turn that knob!

SATISFIED ONE. No! I want to save you — not open the door to your destruction!

BEGGAR. Save us? Listen to the man!

ALL.   We will get in!   We will!

[*Like madmen, they pounce upon him, pressing him against the
door.*

BEGGAR (*suddenly*).   Oh, it's giving!   The door's giving!
All of us together are pushing it in!

POET (*pushing feebly*).   All together now!

BEGGAR.   I see a crack into the golden room!

GIRL.   It's opening!   We're opening the door!

[*The door swings inward, partly revealing a brilliant golden
room.*

SATISFIED ONE (*barring the doorway*).   Do not enter!   Oh, I
beg of you, do not!

BEGGAR.   Aw, I see bread — now for it!

[*Knocks Satisfied One aside, rushes through the door and off
left, followed pell-mell by the others, exclaiming as they go:*
"Oh, I see the clothes I want!" "Fame, Fame!" "Love,
I speak to you!"

BEGGAR (*within the tower, but not seen*).   Satisfied at last!

SATISFIED ONE.   Satisfied?   Ha!   (*Shakes a despairing hand
after the departed ones*)   Fools!   Stupid Fools!!

CURTAIN

IN THE ZONE

EUGENE G. O'NEILL

Mr. Eugene G. O'Neill was born October 16, 1888, in New York City. He spent one year at Princeton University (Class of 1910), after which he became secretary of a small mail-order concern in New York City. In 1909 he joined a gold prospecting expedition to Spanish Honduras. He found no gold, but plenty of fever. The latter part of the season of 1910 he worked as an assistant manager of a theatrical company on the road, playing in all "big" towns through the Middle West. In June of that year he made his first voyage as a sailor, Boston to Buenos Aires, on a Norwegian bark which took sixty-five days to make the trip. In the Argentine he found work first in the drafting department of the Westinghouse Electrical Company in Buenos Aires, and then in the Swift Packing Company's plant at La Plata. Later he worked for the Singer Sewing Machine Company in Buenos Aires. He made his second trip to sea on a British tramp, Buenos Aires to Durban, South Africa, and return. Finally he shipped on a British tramp steamer back to New York. He did not stay in New York long, however, but signed as an able seaman — he had been an ordinary seaman before — on the S.S. *New York* of the American Line. The *New York* was later laid up in Southampton for repairs and Mr. O'Neill was transferred to the *Philadelphia* of the same line, on which he made his return trip. This was his last experience as a sailor.

The following winter, Mr. O'Neill played a part in his father's tabloid version of "Monte Cristo" on the Orpheum vaudeville circuit in the Far West. The next summer and fall he worked as a reporter on the New London, Connecticut, *Telegraph*. Soon after, in 1914, he began to write. He studied the technique of the drama in Professor Baker's class at Harvard the next winter, and since then he has devoted himself exclusively to writing.

He has written seventeen short plays, of which eleven have been produced. The eleven are: "Thirst", "Bound East for Cardiff", "Before Breakfast", "Fog", "The Sniper" (1916–1917); "In the Zone", "The Long Voyage Home", "The Rope", "Ile" (1917–1918); "Where the Cross is Made" and "The Moon of the Caribbees" (1918–1919). All of these have been produced in New York, and many have been seen in Little Theatres throughout the country. Mr. O'Neill has published "The Moon of the Caribbees and Six Other Plays of the Sea", and "Fog and Other One-Act Plays." "In the Zone" is one of a cycle in which Mr. O'Neill has endeavored to portray different characteristic incidents of merchant-sailor life. He uses the same characters, members of the crew of a British tramp steamer, in each of the plays; and although each play is complete in itself and is in no way dependent on any of the others for its action or meaning, still there is a certain connection between them. The other plays of the cycle are: "Bound East for Cardiff", "Ile", "The Long Voyage Home", and "The Moon of the Caribbees."

IN THE ZONE

By EUGENE G. O'NEILL

"In the Zone" was originally produced by the Washington Square Players, October 31, 1917, at the Comedy Theatre, New York.

Original Cast

Seamen of the tramp steamer (British) *Glencairn*

SMITTY, the "Duke." Twenty-five — slender — his face is refined, and handsome in a weak way. He wears a short blond mustache . . . . . . Frederick Roland

DAVIS. Middle-aged — thin face with a black mustache. . . . . Robert Strange

OLSON. Middle-aged — short stocky Swede with a bushy blond mustache . . . . William Gillette

SCOTTY. Just past twenty — thin and wiry — sandy hair . . . . Eugene Lincoln

IVAN. In the thirties — hulking and awkward, with a broad, stupid, swarthy face . . . . Edward Balzerit

YANK. Twenty-eight — tall, well-built, dark, and rather good-looking in a tough sort of way . . . Gay Strong

DRISCOLL. Thirty — a powerfully-built Irishman with a battered, good-natured face . . . . . Arthur Hohl

COCKY. Fifty — a wizened runt of a man with a straggling wisp of gray mustache . . . . . Rienzi de Cordova

IN THE ZONE

SCENE. *The seamen's forecastle of the British tramp steamer Glencairn, an irregular-shaped compartment, the sides of which almost meet at the far end to form a triangle. Sleeping bunks about six feet long, ranged three deep, with a space of two feet separating the upper from the lower, are built against the sides. On the right, above the bunks, three or four portholes covered with black cloth can be seen. In front of the bunks, rough wooden benches. Over the bunks on the left, a lamp in a bracket. In the left foreground, a doorway. On the floor near it, a pail with a tin dipper. Oilskins are hanging from hooks near the doorway.*

The far side of the forecastle is so narrow that it contains only one series of bunks. In under the bunks a glimpse can be had of sea chests, suitcases, sea boots, etc., jammed in indiscriminately.

The lamp is not lit. A lantern in the middle of the floor, turned down very low, throws a dim light around the place. Five men — Scotty, Ivan, Olson, Smitty, and the Norwegian, Paul — are in their bunks, apparently asleep. There is no sound but the deep breathing of the sleepers and the rustling of the oilskins against each other as the ship rolls. It is about ten minutes of twelve in the night. The time is the spring of 1915.

Smitty turns slowly in his bunk, and, leaning out over the side, looks from one to another of the men as if he were assuring himself they were asleep. Then he climbs carefully out of his bunk and stands in the middle of the forecastle, fully dressed, but in his stocking feet, glancing around him suspiciously. Reassured, he leans down and cautiously pulls out a suitcase from under the bunks in front of him.

Just at that moment Davis appears in the doorway, carrying a large steaming coffee pot in his hand. He stops short when he sees Smitty. A puzzled expression comes over his face, followed by one of suspicion, and he retreats farther back in the alleyway, where he can watch Smitty without being seen.

All of the latter's movements indicate a fear of discovery. He takes out a small bunch of keys and unlocks the suitcase, making a slight noise as he does so. Scotty wakes up and peers at him over the side of his bunk. Smitty opens the suitcase and takes out a small black tin box. Scotty's eyes nearly pop out of his head with fright when he sees this, but he shuts them tight as Smitty turns around, and opens them again in time to see him place the black box carefully under his mattress. Smitty then climbs back into his bunk, taking great care to make no noise, closes his eyes, and commences to snore loudly.

Davis enters the forecastle, places the coffee pot beside the lantern, and goes from one to the other of the sleepers — with the exception of Paul, who is day man — and shakes them vigorously, saying to each in a low voice, "Near eight bells, Scotty. Arise and shine, Ollie. Eight bells, Ivan." He stops before Smitty's bunk and looks at him with a keen glance of mistrust which is both curious and timid. He reaches out his hand to grab Smitty's shoulder, hesitates, and finally ends up by saying gruffly: "Eight bells, Smitty." Upon which he sits down on a bench as far away from Smitty as the narrow forecastle will permit, glancing at him every moment out of the corner of his eye.

Smitty yawns loudly with a great pretence of having been dead asleep. All the rest of the men tumble out of their bunks, stretching and gaping, and commence to pull on their shoes. Except for these, they are fully dressed. Scotty betrays great inward uneasiness, staring suspiciously at Smitty whenever the latter's back is turned.

They go one by one to the cupboard which is near the open doorway, front, and take out their cups and spoons, put sugar in the cups, grab a couple of sea-biscuits, and sit down together on the benches. The coffee pot is passed around and placed back again beside the lantern. They munch their biscuits and sip their coffee in a dull silence.

DAVIS (*suddenly jumping to his feet — nervously*). Where's that air comin' from?

[*All are startled and look at him wonderingly.*

OLSON (*grumpily*). What air? I don't feel not'ing.

DAVIS (*excitedly*). I kin feel it — a draft. (*He stands on the bench and looks around — suddenly exploding*) Damn fool square-head! (*He leans over the upper bunk in which Paul is sleeping and slams the porthole shut*) I got a good notion to report him. Serve him bloody well right! What's the use o' blindin' the ports when that thick-head goes an' leaves 'em open?

OLSON (*yawning — too sleepy to be aroused by anything — carelessly*). Dey don't see what little light go out yust one port.

SCOTTY (*protestingly*). Dinna be a loon, Ollie! D'ye no ken the dangerr o' showin' a licht wi' a pack o' submarrines lyin' aboot?

IVAN (*shaking his shaggy ox-like head in an emphatic affirmative*). Dot's right, Scotty. I don' li-ike blow up, no, by devil!

SMITTY (*his manner slightly contemptuous*). I don't think there's much danger of meeting any of their submarines, not until we get into the war zone, at any rate.

DAVIS (*he and Scotty look at Smitty suspiciously — harshly*). You don't, eh? (*He lowers his voice and speaks slowly*) Well, we're in the war zone right this minit if you wants to know.

[*The effect of this speech is instantaneous. All sit bolt upright on their benches and stare at Davis.*

SMITTY. How do you know, Davis?

DAVIS (*angrily*). 'Cos Drisc heard the First send the Third below to wake the skipper when we fetched the zone — bout five bells, it was. Now whata y' got to say?

SMITTY (*conciliatingly*). Oh, I wasn't doubting your word, Davis; but you know they're not pasting up bulletins to let the crew know when the zone is reached — especially on ammunition ships like this.

IVAN (*decidedly*). I don' li-ike dees voyage. Next time I ship on windjammer Boston to River Plate, load with wood only so it float, by golly!

OLSON (*fretfully*). I hope British navy blow 'em to hell, those submarines, py damn!

SCOTTY (*looking at Smitty, who is staring at the doorway in a dream, his chin on his hands. Meaningly*). It's no the submarrines only we've to fear, I'm thinkin', Ollie.

DAVIS (*assenting eagerly*). That's no lie, Scotty.

OLSON. You mean the mines?

SCOTTY. I wasna thinkin' o' mines eitherr.

DAVIS. There's many a good ship blown up and at the bottom of the sea, Ollie, what never hit no mine or torpedo.

SCOTTY. Did ye neverr read of the Gerrman spies and the dirrty work they're doin' all the war?

[*He and Davis both glance at Smitty, who is deep in thought and is not listening to the conversation.*

DAVIS. An' the clever way they fool you!

OLSON. Sure; I read it in paper many time.

DAVIS. Well — (*He is about to speak, but hesitates and finishes lamely*) You got to watch out, that's all I says.

IVAN (*drinking the last of his coffee and slamming his fist on the bench — explosively*). I tell you dis rotten coffee give me belly-ache, yes!

[*They all look at him in amused disgust.*

SCOTTY (*sardonically*). Dinna fret aboot it, Ivan. If we blow up ye'll no be mindin' the pain in your middle.

[*Yank enters. He wears dungarees and a heavy jersey.*

YANK. Eight bells, fellers.

IVAN (*stupidly*). I don' hear bell ring.

YANK. No, and yuh won't hear any ring, yuh boob — (*lowering his voice unconsciously*) now we're in the war zone.

OLSON (*anxiously*). Is the boats all ready?

YANK. Sure; we can lower 'em in a second.

DAVIS. A lot o' good the boats'll do, with us loaded deep with all kinds o' dynamite and stuff the like o' that! If a torpedo hits this hooker we'll all be in hell b'fore you could wink your eye.

YANK. They ain't goin' to hit us, see? That's my dope. Whose wheel is it?

IVAN (*sullenly*). My wheel.

[*He lumbers out.*

YANK. And whose lookout?

OLSON. Mine, I tink.

[*He follows Ivan.*

YANK (*scornfully*). A hell of a lot of use keepin' a lookout! We couldn't run away or fight if we wanted to. (*To Scotty and Smitty*) Better look up the bo'sun or the Fourth, you two, and let 'em see you're awake. (*Scotty goes to the doorway and turns to wait for Smitty, who is still in the same position, head on hands, seemingly unconscious of every-thing. Yank slaps him roughly on the shoulder and he comes to with a start*) Aft and report, Duke! What's the matter with yuh — in a dope dream? (*Smitty goes out after Scotty without answering. Yank looks after him with a frown*) He's a queer guy. I can't figger him out.

DAVIS. Nor no one else. (*Lowering his voice — meaningly*) An' he's liable to turn out queerer than any of us think, if we ain't careful.

YANK (*suspiciously*). What d'yuh mean?

[*They are interrupted by the entrance of Driscoll and Cocky.*

COCKY (*protestingly*). Blimey if I don't fink I'll put in this 'ere watch ahtside on deck. (*He and Driscoll go over and get their cups*) I down't want to be caught in this 'ole if they 'its us.

[*He pours out coffee.*

DRISCOLL (*pouring his*). Divil a bit ut wud matther where ye arre. Ye'd be blown to smithereens b'fore ye cud say your name. (*He sits down, overturning as he does so the untouched cup of coffee which Smitty had forgotten and left on the bench. They all jump nervously as the tin cup hits the*

floor with a bang. Driscoll flies into an unreasoning rage)
Who's the dirty scut left this cup where a man 'ud sit on ut?

DAVIS. It's Smitty's.

DRISCOLL *(kicking the cup across the forecastle).* Does he think
he's too much av a bloody gentleman to put his own away
loike the rist av us? If he does, I'm the bye'll beat that
noshun out av his head.

COCKY. Be the airs 'e puts on you'd think 'e was the Prince
of Wales. Wot's 'e doin' on a ship, I arsks yer? 'E
ain't now good as a sailor, is 'e? — dawdlin' abaht on deck
like a chicken wiv 'is 'ead cut orf!

YANK *(good-naturedly).* Aw, the Duke's all right. S'posin'
he did ferget his cup — what's the dif? *(He picks up the
cup and puts it away — with a grin)* This war zone stuff's
got yer goat, Drisc — and yours too, Cocky — and I
ain't cheerin' much fur it myself neither.

COCKY *(with a sigh).* Blimey, it ain't no bleedin' joke, it
ain't, yer first trip, to know as there's a ship full of shells
li'ble to go 'orf in under your bloomin' feet, as you might
say, if we gets 'it be a torpedo or mine. *(With sudden
savagery)* Calls theyselves 'uman bein's, too! Blarsted
'Uns!

DRISCOLL *(gloomily).* 'Tis me last trip in the bloody Zone,
God help me. The divil take their twenty-foive per cent
bonus — and be drowned like a rat in a trap in the bargain, maybe.

DAVIS. Wouldn't be so bad if she wasn't carryin' ammunition.
Them's the kind the subs is layin' for.

DRISCOLL *(irritably).* Fur the love av hivin, don't be talkin'
about ut. I'm sick wid thinkin' and jumpin' at iviry bit
av a noise.

*[There is a pause during which they all stare gloomily at the
floor.*

YANK. Hey, Davis, what was you sayin' about Smitty when
they come in?

DAVIS *(with a great air of mystery).* I'll tell you in a minit.
I want to wait an' see if he's comin' back. *(Impressively)*

You won't be callin' him all right when you hears what
I seen with my own eyes. (*He adds with an air of satisfaction*) An' you won't be feelin' no safer, neither.

[*They all look at him with puzzled glances full of a vague
apprehension.*

DRISCOLL (*fiercely*). God blarst ut!

[*He fills his pipe and lights it. The others, with an air of
remembering something they had forgotten, do the same.
Scotty enters.*

SCOTTY (*in awed tones*). Mon, but it's clear ootside the
nicht! Like day.

DAVIS (*in low tones*). Where's Smitty, Scotty?

SCOTTY. Out on the hatch starin' at the moon like a
mon half-daft.

DAVIS. Kin you see him from the doorway?

DAVIS (*goes to doorway and carefully peeks out*). Aye; he's
still there.

DAVIS. Keep your eyes on him for a moment. I've got
something I wants to tell the boys and I don't want him
walkin' in in the middle of it. Give a shout if he starts
this way.

SCOTTY (*with suppressed excitement*). Aye, I'll watch him.
And I've somethin' myself to tell aboot his Lordship.

DRISCOLL (*impatiently*). Out wid ut! You're talkin' more
than a pair av auld women wud be, standin' in the road,
and gettin' no further along.

DAVIS. Listen! You 'member when I went to git the coffee,
Yank?

YANK. Sure, I do.

DAVIS. Well, I brings it down here same as usual and got as
far as the door there when I sees him.

YANK. Smitty?

DAVIS. Yes, Smitty! He was standin' in the middle of the
fo'c's'tle there (*pointing*) lookin' around sneakin'-like at
Ivan and Ollie and the rest, 'sif he wants to make certain
they're asleep.

[*He pauses significantly, looking from one to the other of his listeners. Scotty is nervously dividing his attention between Smitty on the hatch outside and Davis' story, fairly bursting to break in with his own revelations.*

YANK (*impatiently*). What of it?

DAVIS. Listen! He was standin' right there — (*pointing again*) in his stockin' feet — no shoes on, mind, so he wouldn't make no noise!

YANK (*spitting disgustedly*). Aw!

DAVIS (*not heeding the interruption*). I seen right away somethin' on the queer was up, so I slides back into the alleyway where I kin see him but he can't see me. After he makes sure they're all asleep he goes in under the bunks there — bein' careful not to raise a noise, mind! — an' takes out his bag there. (*By this time every one, Yank included, is listening breathlessly to his story*) Then he fishes in his pocket an' takes out a bunch o' keys an' kneels down beside the bag an' opens it.

SCOTTY (*unable to keep silent longer*). Mon, didn't I see him do that same thing wi' these two eyes. 'Twas just that moment I woke and spied him.

DAVIS (*surprised, and a bit nettled to have to share his story with any one*). Oh, you seen him too, eh? (*To the others*) Then Scotty kin tell you if I'm lyin' or not.

DRISCOLL. An' what did he do whin he'd the bag opened?

DAVIS. He bends down and reaches out his hand sort o' scared-like, like it was somethin' dang'rous he was after, an' feels round in under his duds — hidden in under his duds an' wrapped up in 'em, it was — an' he brings out a black iron box!

COCKY (*looking around him with a frightened glance*). Gawd blimey!

[*The others likewise betray their uneasiness, shuffling their feet nervously.*

DAVIS. Ain't that right, Scotty?

SCOTTY. Right as rain, I'm tellin' ye!

DAVIS (*to the others with an air of satisfaction*). There you are! (*Lowering his voice*) An' then what d'you suppose he did? Sneaks to his bunk an' slips the black box in under his mattress — in under his mattress, mind! —

YANK. And it's there now?

DAVIS. Corse it is!

[*Yank starts toward Smitty's bunk. Driscoll grabs him by the arm.*

DRISCOLL. Don't be touchin' ut, Yank!

YANK. Yuh needn't worry. I ain't goin' to touch it. (*He pulls up Smitty's mattress and looks down. The others stare at him, holding their breaths. He turns to them, trying hard to assume a careless tone*) It's there, aw right.

COCKY (*miserably upset*). I'm gointer 'op it aht on deck. (*He gets up, but Driscoll pulls him down again. Cocky protests*) It fair guvs me the trembles sittin' still in 'ere.

DRISCOLL (*scornfully*). Are ye frightened, ye toad? 'Tis a hell av a thing fur grown men to be shiverin' loike childer at a bit av a black box. (*Scratching his head in uneasy perplexity*) Still, ut's damn queer, the looks av ut.

DAVIS (*sarcastically*). A bit of a black box, eh? How big d'you think them — (*he hesitates*) — things has to be — big as this fo'c's'le?

YANK (*in a voice meant to be reassuring*). Aw, hell! I'll bet it ain't nothin' but some coin he's saved he's got locked up in there.

DAVIS (*scornfully*). That's likely, ain't it? Then why does he act so s'picious? He's been on ship near a year, ain't he? He knows damn well there ain't no thiefs in this fo'c's'le, don't he? An' you know 'swell 's I do he didn't have no money when he came on board an' he ain't saved none since. Don't you? (*Yank doesn't answer*) Listen! D'you know what he done after he put that thing in under his mattress? — an' Scotty'll tell you if I ain't speakin' truth. He looks round to see if any one's woke up.

SCOTTY. I clapped my eyes shut when he turned round.

DAVIS. An' then he crawls into his bunk an' shuts his eyes, an' starts in *snorin'*, *pretendin'* he was asleep, mind!

SCOTTY. Aye, I could hear him.

DAVIS. An' when I goes to call him I don't even shake him. I just says: "Eight bells, Smitty" in a'most a whisper-like, an' up he gets yawnin' an' stretchin' fit to kill hisself 'sif he'd been dead asleep.

COCKY. Gawd blimey!

DRISCOLL (*shaking his head*). Ut looks bad, divil a doubt av ut.

DAVIS (*excitedly*). An' now I come to think of it, there's the porthole. How'd it come to git open, tell me that? I know'd well Paul never opened it. Ain't he grumblin' about bein' cold all the time?

SCOTTY. The mon that opened it meant no good to this ship, whoever he was.

YANK (*sourly*). What porthole? What're yuh talkin' about?

DAVIS (*pointing over Paul's bunk*). There. It was open when I come in. I felt the cold air on my neck an' shut it. It would'a been clear's a lighthouse to any sub that was watchin' — an' we s'posed to have all the ports blinded! Who'd do a dirty trick like that? It wasn't none of us, nor Scotty here, nor Olson, nor Ivan. Who would it be, then?

COCKY (*angrily*). Must'a been 'is bloody Lordship.

DAVIS. For all's we know he might'a been signallin' with it. They does it like that by winkin' a light. Ain't you read how they gets caught doin' it in London an' on the coast?

COCKY (*firmly convinced now*). An' wots 'e doin' aht alone on the 'atch — keepin' 'isself clear of us like 'e was afraid?

DRISCOLL. Kape your eye on him, Scotty.

SCOTTY. There's no a move oot o' him.

YANK (*in irritated perplexity*). But, hell, ain't he an Englishman? What'd he want a —

DAVIS. English? How d'we know he's English? Cos he talks it? That ain't no proof. Ain't you read in the papers how all them German spies they been catchin' in England has been livin' there for ten, often as not twenty years, an' talks English as good's any one? An' look here,

ain't you noticed he don't talk natural? He talks it too
damn good, that's what I mean. He don't talk exactly
like a toff, does he, Cocky?

COCKY. Not like any toff as I ever met up wiv.

DAVIS. No; an' he don't talk it like us, that's certain.
An' he don't look English. An' what d'we know about
him when you come to look at it? Nothin'! He ain't
ever said where he comes from or why. All we knows is
he ships on here in London six months b'fore the war starts,
as an A.B. — stole his papers most lik'ly — when he don't
know how to box the compass, hardly. Ain't that queer
in itself? An' was he ever open with us like a good ship-
mate? No; he's always had that sly air about him 's if
he was hidin' somethin'.

DRISCOLL (slapping his thigh — angrily). Divil take me if
I don't think ye have the truth av ut, Davis.

COCKY (scornfully). Lettin' on be 'is silly airs, and all, 'e's
the son of a blarsted earl or somethink!

DAVIS. An' the name he calls hisself — Smith! I'd risk a
quid of my next pay day that his real name is Schmidt, if
the truth was known.

YANK (evidently fighting against his own conviction). Aw,
say, you guys give me a pain! What'd they want puttin'
a spy on this old tub for?

DAVIS (shaking his head sagely). They're deep ones, an'
there's a lot o' things a sailor'll see in the ports he puts in
ought to be useful to 'em. An' if he kin signal to 'em an'
they blows us up it's one ship less, ain't it? (Lowering
his voice and indicating Smitty's bunk) Or if he blows us
up hisself.

SCOTTY (in alarmed tones). Hush, mon! Here he comes!
[Scotty hurries over to a bench and sits down. A thick silence
settles over the forecastle. The men look from one to another
with uneasy glances. Smitty enters and sits down beside his
bunk. He is seemingly unaware of the dark glances of suspicion directed at him from all sides. He slides his hand back
stealthily over his mattress and his fingers move, evidently feel-

ing to make sure the box is still there. The others follow this movement carefully with quick looks out of the corners of their eyes. Their attitudes grow tense as if they were about to spring at him. Satisfied the box is safe, Smitty draws his hand away slowly and utters a sigh of relief.

SMITTY (*in a casual tone which to them sounds sinister*). It's a good light night for the subs if there's any about.

[*For a moment he sits staring in front of him. Finally he seems to sense the hostile atmosphere of the forecastle and looks from one to the other of the men in surprise. All of them avoid his eyes. He sighs with a puzzled expression and gets up and walks out of the doorway. There is silence for a moment after his departure and then a storm of excited talk breaks loose.*

DAVIS. Did you see him feelin' if it was there?

COCKY. 'E ain't arf a sly one wiv 'is talk of submarines, Gawd blind 'im!

SCOTTY. Did ye see the sneekin' looks he gave us?

DRISCOLL. If ivir I saw black shame on a man's face 'twas on his whin he sat there!

YANK (*thoroughly convinced at last*). He looked bad to me. He's a crook, aw right.

DAVIS (*excitedly*). What'll we do? We gotter do somethin' quick or —

[*He is interrupted by the sound of something hitting against the port side of the forecastle with a dull, heavy thud. The men start to their feet in wild-eyed terror and turn as if they were going to rush for the deck. They stand that way for a strained moment, scarcely breathing, and listening intently.*

YANK (*with a sickly smile*). Hell! It's on'y a piece of drift-wood or a floatin' log.

[*He sits down again.*

DAVIS (*sarcastically*). Or a mine that didn't go of — that time — or a piece o' wreckage from some ship they've sent to Davy Jones.

COCKY (*mopping his brow with a trembling hand*). Blimey!

[*He sinks back weakly on a bench.*

DRISCOLL (*furiously*). God blarst ut! No man at all cud be puttin' up wid the loike av this — an' I'm not wan to be fearin' anything or any man in the worrld'll stand up to me face to face; but this divil's thrickery in the darrk — (*he starts for Smitty's bunk*) I'll throw ut out wan av the portholes an' be done wid ut.

[*He reaches toward the mattress.*

SCOTTY (*grabbing his arm — wildly*). Arre ye daft, mon?

DAVIS. Don't monkey with it, Drisc. I knows what to do. Bring the bucket o' water here, Yank, will you? (*Yank gets it and brings it over to Davis*) An' you, Scotty, see if he's back on the hatch.

SCOTTY (*cautiously peering out*). Aye, he's sittin' there the noo.

DAVIS. Sing out if he makes a move. Lift up the mattress, Drisc, — careful now! (*Driscoll does so with infinite caution*) Take it out, Yank — careful — don't shake it now, for Christ's sake! Here — put it in the water — easy! There, that's fixed it! (*They all sit down with great sighs of relief*) The water'll git in and spoil it.

DRISCOLL (*slapping Davis on the back*). Good wurrk for ye, Davis, ye scut! (*He spits on his hands aggressively*) An' now what's to be done wid that blackhearted thraitor?

COCKY (*belligerently*). Guv 'im a shove in the marf and 'eave 'im over the side!

DAVIS. An' serve him right!

YANK. Aw say, give him a chance. Yuh can't prove nothin' till yuh find out what's in there.

DRISCOLL (*heatedly*). Is ut more proof ye'd be needin' afther what we've seen an' heard? Then listen to me — an' ut's Driscoll talkin' — if there's divilmint in that box an' we see plain 'twas his plan to murrdher his own shipmates that have served him fair — (*he raises his fist*) I'll choke his rotten hearrt out wid me own hands, an' over the side wid him, and one man missin' in the mornin'.

DAVIS. An' noone the wiser. He's the balmy kind what commits suicide.

COCKY. They 'angs spies ashore.

YANK (*resentfully*). If he's done what yuh think I'll croak him myself. Is that good enough for yuh?

DRISCOLL (*looking down at the box*). How'll we be openin' this, I wonder?

SCOTTY (*from the doorway — warningly*). He's standin' up.

DAVIS. We'll take his keys away from him when he comes in. Quick, Drisc! You an' Yank get beside the door and grab him. (*They get on either side of the door. Davis snatches a small coil of rope from one of the upper bunks*) This'll do for me an' Scotty to tie him.

SCOTTY. He's turrnin' this way — he's comin'!

[*He moves away from door.*

DAVIS. Stand by to lend a hand, Cocky.

COCKY. Righto.

[*As Smitty enters the forecastle he is seized roughly from both sides and his arms pinned behind him. At first he struggles fiercely, but seeing the uselessness of this, he finally stands calmly and allows Davis and Scotty to tie up his arms.*

SMITTY (*when they have finished — with cold contempt*). If this is your idea of a joke I'll have to confess it's a bit too thick for me to enjoy.

COCKY (*angrily*). Shut yer marf, 'ear!

DRISCOLL (*roughly*). Ye'll find ut's no joke, me bucko, b'fore we're done wid you. (*To Scotty*) Kape your eye peeled, Scotty, and sing out if any one's comin'.

[*Scotty resumes his post at the door.*

SMITTY (*with the same icy contempt*). If you'd be good enough to explain —

DRISCOLL (*furiously*). Explain, is ut? 'Tis you'll do the explainin' — an' damn quick, or we'll know the reason why. (*To Yank and Davis*) Bring him here, now. (*They push Smitty over to the bucket*) Look here, ye murrdherin' swab. D'you see ut?

[*Smitty looks down with an expression of amazement which rapidly changes to one of anguish.*

DAVIS (*with a sneer*). Look at him! S'prised, ain't you? If you wants to try your dirty spyin' tricks on us you've gotter git up earlier in the mornin'.

COCKY. Thorght yer weren't 'arf a fox, didn't yer?

SMITTY (*trying to restrain his growing rage*). What — what do you mean? That's only — How dare — What are you doing with my private belongings?

COCKY (*sarcastically*). Ho yus! Private b'longings!

DRISCOLL (*shouting*). What is ut, ye swine? Will you tell us to our faces? What's in ut?

SMITTY (*biting his lips — holding himself in check with a great effort*). Nothing but — That's my business. You'll please attend to your own.

DRISCOLL. Oho, ut is, is ut? (*Shaking his fist in Smitty's face*) Talk aisy now if ye know what's best for you. Your business, indade! Then we'll be makin' ut our's, I'm thinkin'. (*To Yank and Davis*) Take his keys away from him an' we'll see if there's one'll open ut, maybe. (*They start in searching Smitty, who tries to resist and kicks out at the bucket. Driscoll leaps forward and helps them push him away*) Try to kick ut over, wud ye? Did ye see him then? Tryin' to murrdher us all, the scut! Take that pail out av his way, Cocky.

[*Smitty struggles with all of his strength and keeps them busy for a few seconds. As Cocky grabs the pail Smitty makes a final effort and, lunging forward, kicks again at the bucket, but only succeeds in hitting Cocky on the shin. Cocky immediately sets down the pail with a bang and, clutching his knee in both hands, starts hopping around the forecastle, groaning and swearing.*

COCKY. Ooow! Gawd strike me pink! Kicked me, 'e did! Bloody, bleedin', rotten Dutch 'og! (*Approaching Smitty, who has given up the fight and is pushed back against the wall near the doorway with Yank and Davis holding him on either side — wrathfully, at the top of his lungs*) Kick me, will yer? I'll show yer what for, yer bleedin' sneak! [*He draws back his fist. Driscoll pushes him to one side.*

DRISCOLL.   Shut your mouth! D'you want to wake the whole ship?

[*Cocky grumbles and retires to a bench, nursing his sore shin.*

YANK (*taking a small bunch of keys from Smitty's pocket*). Here yuh are, Drisc.

DRISCOLL (*taking them*).   We'll soon be knowin'.

[*He takes the pail and sits down, placing it on the floor between his feet. Smitty again tries to break loose, but he is too tired and is easily held back against the wall.*

SMITTY (*breathing heavily and very pale*).   Cowards!

YANK (*with a growl*).   Nix on the rough talk, see! That don't git yuh nothin.'

DRISCOLL (*looking at the lock on the box in the water and then scrutinizing the keys in his hand*).   This'll be ut, I'm thinkin'.
[*He selects one and gingerly reaches his hand in the water.*

SMITTY (*his face grown livid — chokingly*).   Don't you open that box, Driscoll. If you do, so help me God, I'll kill you if I have to hang for it.

DRISCOLL (*pausing — his hand in the water*).   Whin I open this box I'll not be the wan to be kilt, me sonny bye! I'm no dirty spy.

SMITTY (*his voice trembling with rage. His eyes are fixed on Driscoll's hand*).   Spy? What are you talking about? I only put that box there so I could get it quick in case we were torpedoed. Are you all mad? Do you think I'm — (*chokingly*)   You stupid curs! You cowardly dolts!
[*Davis claps his hand over Smitty's mouth.*

DAVIS.   That'll be enough from you!

[*Driscoll takes the dripping box from the water and starts to fit in the key. Smitty springs forward furiously, almost escaping from their grasp, and drags them after him half-way across the forecastle.*

DRISCOLL.   Hold him, ye divils!

[*He puts the box back in the water and jumps to their aid. Cocky hovers on the outskirts of the battle, mindful of the kick he received.*

SMITTY (*raging*). Cowards! Damn you! Rotten curs! (*He is thrown to the floor and held there*) Cowards! Cowards!

DRISCOLL. I'll shut your dirty mouth for you. [*He goes to his bunk and pulls out a big wad of waste and comes back to Smitty.*

SMITTY. Cowards! Cowards!

DRISCOLL (*with no gentle hand slaps the waste over Smitty's mouth*). That'll teach you to be misnamin' a man, ye sneak. Have ye a handkerchief, Yank? (*Yank hands him one and he ties it tightly around Smitty's head over the waste*) That'll fix your gab. Stand him up, now, and tie his feet, too, so he'll not be movin'. (*They do so and leave him with his back against the wall near Scotty. Then they all sit down beside Driscoll, who again lifts the box out of the water and sets it carefully on his knees. He picks out the key, then hesitates, looking from one to the other uncertainly*) We'd best be takin' this to the skipper, d'you think, maybe?

YANK (*irritably*). To hell with the old man. This is our game and we c'n play it without no help.

COCKY. No bleedin' horficers, I says!

DAVIS. They'd only be takin' all the credit and makin' heroes of theyselves.

DRISCOLL (*boldly*). Here goes thin. (*He slowly turns the key in the lock. The others instinctively back away. He carefully pushes the cover back on its hinges and looks at what he sees inside with an expression of puzzled astonishment. The others crowd up close. Even Scotty leaves his post to take a look*) What is ut, Davis?

DAVIS (*mystified*). Looks funny, don't it? Somethin' square tied up in a rubber bag. Maybe it's dynamite — or somethin' — you can't never tell.

YANK. Aw, it ain't got no works, so it ain't no bomb, I'll bet.

DAVIS (*dubiously*). They makes them all kinds, they do.

YANK. Open it up, Drisc.

DAVIS. Careful now!

[*Driscoll takes a black rubber bag resembling a large tobacco pouch from the box and unties the string which is wound tightly around the top. He opens it and takes out a small packet of letters also tied up with string. He turns these over in his hands and looks at the others questioningly.*

YANK (*with a broad grin*). On'y letters! (*Slapping Davis on the back*) Yuh're a hell of a Sherlock Holmes, ain't yuh? Letters from his best girl too, I'll bet. Let's turn the Duke loose, what d'yuh say?

[*He starts to get up.*

DAVIS (*fixing him with a withering look*). Don't be so damned smart, Yank. Letters, you says, 's if there never was no harm in 'em. How d'you s'pose spies gets their orders and sends back what they finds out if it ain't by letters and such things? There's many a letter is worser'n any bomb.

COCKY. Righto! They ain't as innercent as they looks, I'll take me oath, when you read 'em. (*Pointing at Smitty*) Not 'is Lordship's letters; not be no means!

YANK (*sitting down again*). Well, read 'em and find out.

[*Driscoll commences untying the packet. There is a muffled groan of rage and protest from Smitty.*

DAVIS (*triumphantly*). There! Listen to him! Look at him tryin' to git loose! Ain't that proof enough? He knows well we're findin' him out. Listen to me! Love letters, you says, Yank, 's if they couldn't harm nothin'. Listen! I was readin' in some magazine in New York on'y two weeks back how some German spy in Paris was writin' love letters to some woman spy in Switzerland who sent 'em on to Berlin, Germany. To read 'em you wouldn't s'pect nothin' — just mush and all. (*Impressively*) But they had a way o' doin' it — a damn sneakin' way. They had a piece o' plain paper with pieces cut out of it an when they puts it on top o' the letter they sees on'y the words what tells them what they wants to know. An' the Frenchies gets beat in a fight all on account o' that letter.

COCKY (*awed*). Gawd blimey! They ain't 'arf smart bleeders!

DAVIS (*seeing his audience is again all with him*). An' even if these letters of his do sound all right they may have what they calls a code. You can't never tell. (*To Driscoll who has finished untying the packet*) Read one of 'em, Drisc. My eyes is weak.

DRISCOLL (*takes the first one out of its envelope and bends down to the lantern with it. He turns up the wick to give him a better light*). I'm no hand to be readin', but I'll try ut.

[*Again there is a muffled groan from Smitty as he strains at his bonds.*

DAVIS (*gloatingly*). Listen to him! He knows. Go ahead, Drisc!

DRISCOLL (*his brow furrowed with concentration*). Ut begins: "Dearest Man — (*His eyes travel down the page*) An' thin there's a lot av blarney tellin' him how much she misses him now she's gone away to singin' school — an' how she hopes he'll settle down to rale worrk an' not be skylarkin' around now that she's away, loike he used to before she met up wid him — and ut ends: "I love you bether than anythin' in the worrld. You know that, don't you, dear? But b'fore I can agree to live out my life wid you, you must prove to me that the black shadow — I won't menshun its hateful name, but you know what I mean — which might wreck both our lives, does not exist for you. You can do that, can't you, dear? Don't you see you must, for my sake?" (*He pauses for a moment — then adds gruffly*) Ut's signed: Edith.

[*At the sound of the name Smitty, who has stood tensely with his eyes shut as if he were undergoing torture during the reading, makes a muffled sound like a sob and half turns his face to the wall.*

YANK (*sympathetically*). Hell! What's the use of readin' that stuff even if —

DAVIS (*interrupting him sharply*). Wait! Where's that letter from, Drisc?

DRISCOLL.   There's no address on the top av ut.

DAVIS (*meaningly*).   What'd I tell you?   Look at the post-mark, Drisc, — on the envelope.

DRISCOLL.   The name that's written is Sidney Davidson, wan hunderd an' —

DAVIS.   Never mind that.   O' corse it's a false name.   Look at the postmark.

DRISCOLL.   There's a furrin' stamp on ut by the looks av ut. The mark's blurred so it's hard to read.   (*He spells it out laboriously*)   B-e-r-, the nixt is an l, I think, — i — an' an n.

DAVIS (*excitedly*).   Berlin!   What did I tell you?   I knew them letters was from Germany.

COCKY (*shaking his fist in Smitty's direction*).   Rotten 'ound! [*The others look at Smitty as if this last fact had utterly condemned him in their eyes.*]

DAVIS.   Give me the letter, Drisc.   Maybe I kin make somethin' out of it.   (*Driscoll hands the letter to him*)   You go through the others, Drisc, and sing out if you sees anythin' queer.

[*He bends over the first letter as if he were determined to figure out its secret meaning.   Yank, Cocky, and Scotty look over his shoulder with eager curiosity.   Driscoll takes out some of the other letters, running his eyes quickly down the pages.   He looks curiously over at Smitty from time to time, and sighs frequently with a puzzled frown.*]

DAVIS (*disappointedly*).   I gotter give it up.   It's too deep for me, but we'll turn 'em over to the perlice when we docks at Liverpool, to look through.   This one I got was written a year before the war started, anyway.   Find anythin' in yours, Drisc?

DRISCOLL.   They're all the same as the first — lovin' blarney, an' how her singin' is doin', an' the grreat things the Dutch teacher says about her voice, an' how glad she is that her Sidney bye is worrkin' harrd an' makin' a man av himself for her sake.

[*Smitty turns his face completely to the wall.*

DAVIS (*disgustedly*).   If we on'y had the code!

DRISCOLL (*taking up the bottom letter*). Hullo! Here's wan addressed to this ship — S.S. *Glencairn*, ut says — whin we was in Cape Town sivin months ago. (*Looking at the postmark*) Ut's from London.

DAVIS (*eagerly*). Read it!

[*There is another choking groan from Smitty.*

DRISCOLL (*reads slowly — his voice becomes lower and lower as he goes on*). Ut begins wid simply the name Sidney David-son — no dearest or swaetheart to this wan. "Ut is only from your chance meetin' wid Harry — whin you were drunk — that I happen to know where to reach you. So you have run away to sea loike the coward you are, be-cause you knew I had found out the truth — the truth you have covered over wid your mean little lies all the time I was away in Berlin and blindly trusted you. Very well, you have chosen. You have shown that your drunkenness means more to you than any love or faith av mine. I am sorry — for I loved you, Sidney Davidson — but this is the end. I lave you — the mem'ries; an' if ut is any satisfaction to you I lave you the real-i-zation that you have wrecked my loife as you have wrecked your own. My one remainin' hope is that nivir in God's worrld will I ivir see your face again. Good-by, Edith."

[*As he finishes there is a deep silence, broken only by Smitty's muffled sobbing. The men cannot look at each other. Driscoll holds the rubber bag limply in his hand and some small white object falls out of it and drops noiselessly on the floor. Mechanically Driscoll leans over and picks it up, and looks at it wonderingly.*

DAVIS (*in a dull voice*). What's that?

DRISCOLL (*slowly*). A bit av a dried-up flower, — a rose, maybe.

[*He drops it into the bag and gathers up the letters and puts them back. He replaces the bag in the box, and locks it and puts it back in under Smitty's mattress. The others follow him with their eyes. He steps softly over to Smitty and cuts the ropes about his arms and ankles with his sheath knife,*

*and unties the handkerchief over the gag. Smitty does not
turn around, but covers his face with his hands and leans his
head against the wall. His shoulders continue to heave
spasmodically, but he makes no further sound.*

DRISCOLL (*stalks back to the others — there is a moment of silence
in which each man is in agony with the hopelessness of finding
a word he can say — then Driscoll explodes*).   God stiffen us,
are we never goin' to turn in fur a wink av sleep?
[*They all start as if awakening from a bad dream and grate-
fully crawl into their bunks, shoes and all, turning their faces
to the wall, and pulling their blankets up over their shoulders.
Scotty tiptoes past Smitty out into the darkness. Driscoll
turns down the lights and crawls into his bunk as*

THE CURTAIN FALLS

THE BRINK OF SILENCE

ESTHER E. GALBRAITH

Miss Esther E. Galbraith was born July 20, 1893, in Washington, D. C. She graduated from George Washington University, where she received the degree of A.B. She has written for the newspapers, and editorially for various magazines. While in college she had some of her plays produced.

"The Brink of Silence" was written as an assignment to a playwriting group under the direction of The Drama League Players of Washington, each member of which was to develop the Enoch Arden situation in some new and original form. "The Brink of Silence" was chosen as the best of the group. It was produced later by The Drama League Players with great success.

THE BRINK OF SILENCE

By ESTHER E. GALBRAITH

"The Brink of Silence" was originally produced by The Drama League Players of Washington, D.C., at the Wilson Normal School, April 17, 1917.

Original Cast

COLE	G. A. Lyon
MACREADY	Frederic B. Wright
DARTON	Ralph Hayes
JOHNSON	Edwin Ludwig

Scene designed by Alice E. Edwards

THE BRINK OF SILENCE

SCENE. *The scene is inside a log house on a rocky island far down in the Antarctic. There is an outer door at the back; no windows; down right an inner door to another room. There is a bunk against the left wall; an oil stove burning, down left; a rough table at the center. There is one chair and a box which serves as one. The room is entirely bare of ornament; there are a few battered books and magazines piled on a packing box which has been improvised for a cupboard in the corner, up right. Cole is seated at the table playing solitaire in the light of an oil lamp. Macready is pacing slowly at the back of the room. Both men wear heavy sweaters and boots. Fur coats and gloves are hung on the wall. Neither speaks for a minute after the curtain rises.*

MACREADY. For God's sake, Cole — say something! Anything to break this damned quiet. — God, I'd like to go home this winter, wouldn't you!

COLE. England isn't home. — No, I'm here for a few more seasons in this nest of blizzards and I'll see it through.

MAC. It isn't too late for the boat to make another trip with supplies.

COLE. We've enough to last if she doesn't come before the force gets here next summer.

MAC. If she does come, I'm going back with her and so are you.

COLE. Nope.

MAC. Aw — nobody cares whether we spend the winter here or not. Nothing would be said one way or the other.

COLE. Well, you go ahead. There'll be that much more tobacco for me.

MAC. Go and leave you alone? Suppose you got sick here by yourself.

COLE. I haven't been sick in the past eight years.

MAC. But we need to get out. We need to see civilization again. We'll be a pair of savages soon.

COLE. We don't belong to a race that goes down-hill because the climate's hot or cold, nor from living six hundred miles from the nearest human. You know that as well as I do.

MAC. You couldn't stand the silence, Cole.

COLE. I don't mind it; I've stood it a long time.

MAC. I've had two years of it, and it's all I want. I want to see cities — and men and women and children. I've got two little nephews in Manchester. One's nine and the other's twelve. I'd give the world to see them to-night. You're a queer one — not wanting to go back.

COLE (*after a pause*). Mac, — I can't go back.

MAC (*staring at him*). I don't believe it.

COLE. Did you ever hear of the Darton expedition?

MAC. Think I did — Sir Gilbert Darton — about ten years ago. Seems to me — They never came back, did they?

COLE. The expedition never came back. I am Darton!

MAC. Sir Gilbert Darton?

COLE. Yes. — I lost my ship — that was the first of a series of disasters. Two injuries to men tied us up. Our small boats were useless because of ice conditions and our food was nearly gone before five of us were able to get off to try to reach help. We made progress for a few days and then a blizzard that would make ten of yesterday's storm struck us. We'd had little to eat and were too weak to handle the boat. It was simply dashed ashore on the rocky side of this island. — I got through alive; no one else did. — Lauter was here then and he found me. He didn't know who I was. It was six months before a whaler touched. I learned that the relief expedition had reached the men we were trying to save — too late. I went out with the whaler to Buenos Aires, to a hospital. Months later when I recovered, I learned that the Darton expedition had been given up as a total tragedy. — And I learned that my own place had closed up; that I was a living dead man.

MAC. What do you mean?

COLE. I read in a London paper that Lady Darton was to be married — married to a man named Carruthers.

MAC. And you didn't —?

COLE. No one ever knew. I took the name of Ernest Cole and came back here to stay.

MAC. So — that's it.

COLE. It seemed only justice. I had asked a beautiful, <u>wilful</u> woman to give up the best years of her life to waiting and loneliness, with an ugly fear always hovering over her heart. That's the portion of an explorer's wife. And I had no right to come back — a broken failure — and stand between her and happiness. — I made my decision, but I had to fight the impulse to claim my own.

MAC. Were there — any children?

COLE. A son. He was sixteen when I saw him last. I had planned to take him out with me on my next trip. I'd dreamed of months of comradeship that would make up for the years we'd spent apart. I thought perhaps he'd become an explorer and go on with my work. But his mother's happiness was at stake. I couldn't interfere. — God, how I wanted to see the boy!

MAC. And haven't you seen him since?

COLE. No. I couldn't go back. I might have been recognized. The fear of that drove me back — back here. Lauter was gone and I took his place at this station.

MAC. It's all wrong, Cole. You're too big a man to throw yourself away like this. You're wrong.

COLE. There was nothing else to do. I've left them a memory they can't be ashamed of. — I seldom think of England now. The distance, the stillness help me to forget. It's only the thought of my work — the work that was my life — that other men are carrying on. It gnaws and gnaws — God! It's worse than hunger!

MAC. Time makes a lot of difference. Things might be changed in England. You might find a way to go back. If not — it's a big world. You could go to America and perhaps take up your work.

COLE. I could never take up my work. Sooner or later I would come in contact with men who would recognize me.

MAC. I wish you'd get out of this with me.

COLE. Don't worry about me, Mac. What's the use! The only place I have now is here — in the frozen wilderness, with my dream of conquering it that I can never make real. — And some day I'll learn that Remensen or Courcelle has made the trip.

MAC. You ought to get out of this.

COLE (breaking out). I ought to have drowned out there with my men ten years ago.

MAC. There, you see. It's this damn silence makes you say things like that.

COLE. But the silence would always call me back.

[Macready can think of no more arguments. For a moment neither speaks. Mac gets a book, brings it down near the lamp and begins to read.

MAC. I think they'll send the whaler down. It isn't often she could make the trip this late. Been a queer season, hasn't it?

COLE. There hasn't been a season like it for years. I never saw one like it. We ought to have been frozen in tight two weeks ago.

MAC. It's pretty solid just south, I think. Yesterday's storm looked like winter, sure enough.

COLE. With a season like this I could have made it. The best summer I've ever seen. It's a big dream, Mac, crossing the end of the earth through that stark desolation — and this was the year the right man could have done it.

DARTON'S VOICE (some distance outside). Hallo! Hallo, there.

COLE. What's that! !

[*Both start to the door.*

MAC (*opening door*). Two men. One's hurt or frozen.

[*Darton and Johnson appear at the door. Both are under thirty. Darton's dress and equipment are in good condition and, in spite of the awkwardness of fur garments, he is fine looking. Johnson has his arm over Darton's shoulder and the latter is practically carrying him. There is a bleeding cut in his forehead and he is rather ragged.*

COLE. What's wrong.

DARTON (*coming in*). Nothing much, I guess. Bad landing over there. He was knocked down and got a nasty cut.

[*Mac steps to Johnson's side and they get him on the bunk.*

COLE (*hurrying into the other room*). We can fix him up.

[*Darton is taking off Johnson's hood. There is a short cry of pain.*

DARTON. Sorry, old man. Is that better?

MAC. Better leave your partner to Cole. He's quite a doctor.

COLE (*reënters, carrying a tin box and bandage*). I'll put on the bandage. Have something warm.

[*Darton takes off his gloves and Macready hands him a cup of steaming broth from the pot on the stove.*

DARTON (*takes it, smiles and impulsively extends his hand*). Thanks. This is great.

MAC (*shaking hands*). How'd you get here?

DARTON. I came down in the *Pathfinder* to bring out a party we left last year. Johnson was one of them. We located them but couldn't take the ship in, so ten of us went in boats. Got them all out, but yesterday's storm drove us away from the *Pathfinder*, and we landed on the other side of the island. Rest of our people are making camp until the ship picks us up.

COLE. This is Parker's Island.

DARTON. Yes. We located ourselves after landing. Didn't know there was a settlement. Saw your light and brought Johnson across. He was pretty badly done up before his accident. His party's had a hell of a time since last year.

We didn't reach them much too soon. — You here all alone?

MAC.   The company sends a force down during the season to get penguin and whale oil; the rest of the time we're alone.   No other ships touch here.

DARTON.   Been at it long?

MAC.   Cole's been at it eight years.   I've only been here two.

DARTON.   Isn't it pretty close to the edge?

MAC.   It is the edge!

DARTON (*half to himself*).   The brink of silence.

COLE (*coming toward him*).   That's my name for it — the great white silence.

DARTON.   A man can't forget the Antarctic.   The crude flaming color of the sunrise — the blue of the moon on the great white reaches in the long night, and the weird bright curtains of the Aurora — once he's seen them he never forgets.

COLE.   But it's the silence that brings him back.   There's none of the muddled, squirming turmoil of life out here. Just the infinite patience of nature, waiting in endless suspense — silent.   You seem always very close to the answer.

MAC.   The answer?   What are you talking about, Cole?

COLE (*to Darton*).   Macready's a Presbyterian.

MAC.   What's that got to do with it?

COLE.   Nothing whatever.

DARTON (*smiling, turns to the stove and throws off his hood*). (*To Cole*)

You've been further out?

[*As Cole hesitates, Johnson stirs and tries to sit up.*

JOHNSON.   Darton, are you there?   Darton!

[*Cole starts violently.   His expression is mingled amazement and fear, and he stands as if at bay, staring at them. Then as Darton steps to the bunk, he understands.*

DARTON.   Lie down, Johnson.   It's all right.

JOHNSON.   I thought for a minute I was back in the hut — that you hadn't come for us.

[*His voice is thick and he stammers a little.*

DARTON. Of course, it's me. Are you cold?

JOHNSON. Nearly frozen. Can't you give me something to eat now?

[*Macready fills a cup.*

DARTON. Yes, you can have a lot to eat now. Just had to be careful at first, you know.

[*He hands the cup to Johnson, who, instead of taking it, clutches his arm.*

JOHNSON. And you have come, Darton?

DARTON. Of course I have, you big fool. Drink some of this now.

[*Cole remains at the window, some distance from the light. When he speaks, it is in a strained voice which he tries to make natural.*

COLE. Were you trying to make the trip across?

DARTON. Yes. It's the fourth attempt.

MAC. Yours?

DARTON. No. My father made the first. You probably heard of the Darton expedition about ten years ago —

MAC (*quickly*). Yes, I heard of it.

DARTON. He didn't make it and he never got back. Two others have tried it since — Remensen and Courcelle.

COLE. And they —

DARTON. They had to turn back. We've had a good season, and luck, too, I guess. Anyhow, we did it.

COLE. Do you mean —?

DARTON. We came out at Ross Sea last month. We'd separated from Johnson's party on this side and hurried over to pick them up. Thought something might be wrong, and something was. Soon after we left they were caught in the nips, drifted for weeks, and finally their ship was crushed by the grinding.

COLE. You must have come out in fine shape to be here already.

DARTON. We did. Every man!

COLE. And who's your leader?

DARTON. I am —

COLE (*comes back to him and starts to put his hand on his shoulder, then stops*). That's wonderful!

DARTON. It's great of you to understand.

COLE. I do understand. You went through that bleak fury and came out safe. You made it! You won!

MAC. It's a queer thing.

DARTON. I suppose it is. The spirit of the men who have faced it and fought it and died in it seems to draw you on. I think that's why I finished my father's job. (*There is a sound of distant cheering*) Listen, that means they've sighted the *Pathfinder*. I'll have to get back. — I'm afraid Johnson can't travel yet —

MAC. Can't you leave him here for a while?

DARTON. Thanks. He needs to sleep. I'll be busy and I won't get back, but I'll send some one across in half an hour.

MAC. I'd like to see the party. Can't I come over with him?

COLE. And if the *Pathfinder* will take a passenger north —

DARTON. Yourself? Glad to.

COLE. No. Macready was planning to go back if the company's ship came down. I'm staying.

DARTON (*to Macready*). I'll expect you. (*To Cole*) Good-by, Mr. Cole.

COLE. Good-by, my boy.

[*Stands at the door looking after him.*

MAC. Your son!

COLE. Yes.

MAC. Are you going to let him go like that?

COLE. Yes. After all, my work is done — and my boy did it.

MAC. Aw — it's all wrong. Why —

[*But Cole does not hear him.*

COLE (*sits down at the table and slowly takes up the pack of cards*). Wasn't it funny, Mac. He called me — Mr. Cole!

CURTAIN

ALLISON'S LAD

BEULAH MARIE DIX

Miss Beulah Marie Dix graduated from Radcliffe, and there received her A.M. degree. Immediately after, she began to write novels, juveniles, stories, and a group of plays in collaboration with Evelyn Greenleaf Sutherland. This group was followed later by a collection of her own plays. Miss Dix (or Mrs. Flebbe, as she is known in private life) is now writing picture plays in California.

Her publications are many and various. Juveniles: "Hugh Gwyeth", "Soldier Rigdale", "A Little Captive Lad", "Merrylips", "Friends in the End", "Betty Bide at Home", "Blithe McBride", "Kay Danforth's Camp." Novels: "The Making of Christopher Ferringham", "The Beau's Comedy" (in collaboration with C. A. Harper), "Blount of Breckenhow", "The Fair Maid of Graystones", "The Gate of Horn", "Little God Ebisu", "The Fighting Blade", "Mother's Son", "Maid Melicent", "The Battle Months of George Daurella." Plays: "Allison's Lad", "Across the Border", "Moloch." In addition, Miss Dix has contributed various short stories to the magazines.

The plays written in collaboration with Evelyn Greenleaf Sutherland have had wide production. In "A Rose o' Plymouth Town" Miss Minnie Dupree starred during 1902–1903, with Guy Bates Post as her leading man and Douglas Fairbanks as the "juvenile." This was Mr. Fairbanks' introduction to Broadway. "The Breed of the Treshams" was first produced in England in 1903 by Mr. Martin Harvey. A

"second company" played it in the provinces for a time, and
it has been toured successfully in South Africa and Australia.
"Boy O'Carroll", first used by Mr. Harvey in 1906, was re-
vived by him this autumn.   Miss Dix's "The Road to Yesterday" was a great New York success.   In addition, Miss Dix
was a collaborator on "Matt of Merrymount", produced by
Fred Terry and Julia Neilson, 1907–1908, "The Lilac Room",
Miss Amelia Bingham's starring vehicle, 1906–1907, and
"Young Fernald", produced in this country by Henry Miller
and Margaret Anglin, 1906.

Of the plays of which she is the sole author, "Across the
Border" was produced by Holbrook Blinn at the Princess
Theater in the fall of 1914, and "Moloch" by Mr. Blinn and
Mr. George Tyler in 1915.

Her best-known one-act play is "Across the Border", but
it is a "freak" form (four short acts, playing nearly an hour)
and not a genuine specimen of the one-act type.   It was
very successful at the Princess Theater, and it has since
been reproduced at the Toy Theater in Boston, in San Francisco, and elsewhere.   Her "Legend of St. Nicholas", an
imitation of the old Miracle Play, was produced at the Toy
Theater in Boston in 1913 and has since been published in
Poet Lore.   Her first one-act play, "Ciceley's Cavalier",
was written while she was still an undergraduate and was
acted in the college theatre.   This play has since been published.   Miss Dix's other early one-act plays are: "Apples
of Eden" and "At the Sign of the Buff Bible."

ALLISON'S LAD

By BEULAH MARIE DIX

"Allison's Lad" was originally produced by the American Academy of Dramatic Arts at the Carnegie Lyceum, New York, on December 23, 1910.

Original Cast

COL. SIR WILLIAM STRICKLAND . . . Abner W. Cassidy
CAPTAIN GEORGE BOWYER . . . . James W. Mott
LIEUTENANT ROBERT GORING . . . Gerald Quina

Of the Cavalier Party

FRANCIS HOPTON . . . . Sidney K. Powell
TOM WINWOOD . . . . Donald Macdonald

Gentlemen Volunteers

COL. JOHN DRUMMOND of the Roundhead
Party . . . . LeRoy Clemens

Reprinted from "Allison's Lad and other Martial Interludes" by permission of, and special arrangement with, Beulah Marie Dix and Henry Holt and Company.

Application for the right of performing "Allison's Lad" must be made to Beulah Marie Dix, care of Henry Holt and Company.

ALLISON'S LAD

SCENE. *The village of Faringford, in the western midlands of England.*

PERIOD. *The close of the Second Civil War, autumn 1648.*
It is midnight of a cheerless autumn day, with a drizzle of slow rain. In an upper chamber of the village inn of Faringford, lit by guttering candles and a low fire that smolders on the hearth, are gathered five gentlemen of the Cavalier party, made prisoners that morning in a disastrous skirmish.

In a great arm-chair by the hearth, at stage left, sits their leader, Sir William Strickland. He is a tall, keen man of middle age, of the finest type of his party, a gallant officer and a high-souled gentleman. He has received a dangerous wound in the side, which has been but hastily dressed, and he now leans heavily in his chair, with eyes closed, almost oblivious of what goes on about him.

His captain, and friend of long standing, George Bowyer, a sanguine, stalwart gentleman of Strickland's own years, has planted himself in the center of the room, where he is philosophically smoking at a long pipe, while he watches the play at the rude table, which stands at the stage right.

Round the table, on rough stools, Goring, Hopton, and Winwood sit dicing and smoking, with a jug of ale between them for the cheering of their captivity. Goring is a swaggering young soldier of fortune; Hopton, a gentleman of the Temple, turned soldier, with something of the city fop still to be traced in his bearing. He has been wounded, and bears about his forehead a blood-flecked bandage. Winwood, the third gamester, is a mere lad of seventeen, smoothfaced, comely, with a gallant carriage.

It is to be noted that the men play but half-heartedly. Indeed, the cheerlessness of the midnight hour, in the dim chamber, with the rain tapping on the mullioned windows, may well bring home to them the dubiousness of their captive state and set them to anxious question of what the dawn may have in store. Goring, of the three the most hardened and professionally a soldier, is the first to speak, as he throws the dice.

GORING. Cinq and tray!

WINWOOD. The main is yours, Rob Goring.

GORING. That's a brace of angles you owe me, Frank Hopton.

HOPTON. Go ask them of the scurvy Roundhead had the stripping of my pockets.

BOWYER (*with the good-humored contempt of the professional for the amateur*). The more fool you to bear gold about you when you ride into a fight!

WINWOOD. A devil fly off with the money! The rebels have taken my horse — a plague rot them!

GORING. Faith, I'd care not, if the prick-eared brethren had not got me, and got me fast. 'Tis your throw, Tom Winwood.

[*Winwood takes the dice-box, but pauses, anxiously awaiting an answer to Hopton's next question.*

HOPTON. What think you, Captain Bowyer. Are they like to admit us speedily to ransom?

[*Bowyer shakes his head, smiling, half indifferent.*

GORING. You're swift to grumble, Frank. You've not been yet ten hours a prisoner. Throw, Tom, a wildfire burn you!

WINWOOD. There, then! And vengeance profitable gaming! We can't muster four farthings amongst us.

GORING. Curse it, man, we play for love and sport! I've never yet had enough of casting the dice. Look you, (*casts the dice*) I better you by three.

WINWOOD. On my life, no! I threw a tray and quatre.

GORING. Go to with your jesting! You mean a tray and deuce.

WINWOOD.   Tray and quatre I threw.

GORING (*starts to his feet, with his hand leaping to draw the sword which, as a prisoner, he no longer wears*).   Will you give me the lie in my teeth?

WINWOOD (*pluckily springs to his feet, with the same impulse*). Aye, if you say I threw —
[*At the sound of the angry voices and of the stools thrust back, Strickland opens his eyes and glances toward the brawlers.*

BOWYER (*laying a heavy hand upon a shoulder of each*).   Hold your tongues, you shuttle-headed fools!
[*Thrusts Goring down into his seat.*

HOPTON.   You'll rouse the Colonel, and he ill and wounded. Sit you down again!

WINWOOD (*dropping sullenly into his place*).   Yet 'twas a tray and quatre.

GORING.   Frank, you saw the cast.   A tray and deuce, and I will so maintain it.
[*The three at table talk heatedly in dumb-show, Hopton playing the peace-maker, until at last he wins the disputants to shake hands.   Meantime Bowyer has gone anxiously to Strickland's side.*

BOWYER.   How is it with you, Will, old lad?   Your wound is easier?

STRICKLAND.   My wound?   'Tis nothing, I tell you.

BOWYER.   Why, then, take heart!   Matters might well be worse.
[*He takes a candle from the chimneypiece, and relights his pipe.*

STRICKLAND.   Cold comfort, George!

BOWYER.   We are defeated, prisoners, yes, I grant you.   Yet we have fought our best.   And for the future — by this light, our enemies have used us handsomely so far!   No doubt they'll speedily accept of ransom.

STRICKLAND (*with eyes fixed on Winwood*).   From my heart I hope so!

BOWYER.   Aye, to be taken thus in his first fight, 'tis pity for little Tom Winwood.

STRICKLAND.   You say —

BOWYER.   'Tis of the lad yonder that you are thinking.

STRICKLAND.   Yes.   I was thinking of Allison's lad.

[*As the result of Hopton's persuasion, Winwood at that moment is most heartily drinking a health to Goring.*

BOWYER.   My cousin Allison's boy.   Look but upon him now!   A half minute agone he and Rob Goring were ready to fly at each other's throats and now they drink goodfellowship together.   Faith, by times young Tom is monstrous like unto his father.

STRICKLAND.   Your pardon!   Tom is his mother's son, Allison's lad, every inch of him — every thought of him. There's no taint of the father in the boy.

BOWYER.   Yes.   I wonder not that you speak thus of Jack Winwood.   'Twas a damnable trick he served you, when he won Allison from you with his false tales.

STRICKLAND.   Aye, and well-nigh broke her heart thereafter with his baseness.   You stood beside me, George, there at Edgehill, when we looked upon the death-wound — in his back!

BOWYER.   Poor wretch!   Gallant enough at the charge, but at two o'clock in the morning he'd no more courage than —

STRICKLAND.   He was a coward, and false from first to last.

For God's sake, George, never say that boy is like his father!   For his mother's sake —

BOWYER.   Aye, 'twould go near to killing Allison, should Tom prove craven.

STRICKLAND.   He'll never prove craven.   He's his mother's son.   Let be, George!   I'm in no mood for speech.

[*Bowyer goes back to the table, where Winwood, in the last minutes, has played with notable listlessness and indifference.*

HOPTON.   'Tis your cast, Tom.

WINWOOD.   Nay, but I'm done!

GORING.   Will you give over?

WINWOOD.   But for a moment.   My pipe is out.

[*Rises and goes to Strickland.*

HOPTON. Come, Captain! In good time! Bear a hand with us.

[*Bowyer sits in Winwood's place at table, and dices.*

WINWOOD. You called me, sir?

STRICKLAND. I did not call, but I was thinking of you. Sit you down!

(*Winwood sits on a stool at the opposite side of the hearth, and cleans and fills his pipe*)

I watched you to-day, Tom. You bore yourself fairly in the fight. I was blithe to see it.

WINWOOD. God willing, you'll see better in the next fight, sir.

STRICKLAND. Go to! You did all that might be asked of a youth for the first time under fire.

WINWOOD. Ah, but 'twas my second time under fire, sir.

STRICKLAND. Second time? How's that, my boy?

WINWOOD. Last June, faith, I was at Bletchingley when we held the house four hours against the rebels, my school fellow, Lord Bletchingley, and I, and the servants. I came by a nick in the arm there. I still have the scar to show.

[*Rises eagerly, and puts back his sleeve to show the scar.*

STRICKLAND (*lightly*). 'Twas right unfriendly of you, Tom, to keep me so in the dark, touching your exploits.

WINWOOD (*half embarrassed with the sense of having said too much, turns from Strickland and lights his pipe with the candle that he takes from the chimney-piece*). Truth sir, I was shamed to speak to you of Bletchingley.

STRICKLAND. Shamed? What do you talk of?

WINWOOD. Why, our fight at Bletchingley, it must seem mere child's play unto you, a tried soldier, my father's old comrade.

[*He speaks the word "father" with all the proper pride that a son should show.*

STRICKLAND. But your mother. She would have been proud to know that you had borne you well in the fight. You should have told her, Tom.

WINWOOD (*in swift alarm*). Told my mother? Why, sir, she — she would have been troubled. Perchance she would not have heard to my going out for the King with you, because of Bletchingley.

STRICKLAND. Why because of Bletchingley?

WINWOOD. Why? Well, you see, sir — sure, 'twas there I had this wound.

[*Reseats himself on the stool opposite Strickland.*

STRICKLAND. And for that you think she would have kept you from the field? Lad, you do not altogether know your mother.

[*Bowyer, at the end of a talk in dumb-show with Goring and Hopton, has risen, and now goes out at the single door, wide and heavy, that leads from the chamber center back to the outer corridor. At the sound of the closing of the door, Strickland starts.*

What was that?

GORING (*rises and salutes*). 'Twas Captain Bowyer, sir, went into the outer room to speak with the sentries.

[*Reseats himself.*

HOPTON. Heaven send he get them to talk! I'd fain know what's to become of us.

GORING (*stretching himself*). Go sleep, like a wise man, and cease your fretting!

[*He presently rests his head on his folded arms, which he places on the table, and goes to sleep.*

STRICKLAND. Sound advice, Tom! You were best take it.

WINWOOD (*smoking throughout*). Sleep? How can I, sir? I would it were day. I hate this odd and even time o' night. What think you will come of us?

STRICKLAND. What matters it, boy? We have fought our fight, and you bore yourself gallantly, Tom.

WINWOOD. Easy to do, sir, in the daylight, with your comrades about you, but this — this waiting in the dark! God! I would it were day. At two in the morning I've no more courage than —

STRICKLAND (*in sharp terror*). Tom! Hold your peace.

[*Bowyer comes again into the room. Hopton springs eagerly to his feet.*

HOPTON. What news, Captain?

BOWYER. Bad. They're quitting the village this same hour.

GORING. A retreat by night?

[*Rises and confers in dumb-show with Hopton.*

BOWYER. Your wound cannot endure this hasty moving, Will. In mere humanity they must let you rest here at the inn. You'll give them your parole.

STRICKLAND. You'll talk to our captors of paroles, after so many paroles have been broken by men that are a shame unto our party?

BOWYER. But you are known for a man of honor. And by happy chance the colonel in command of these rebels has come hither within the hour. He will listen to me. I knew him of old — one John Drummond.

WINWOOD. Drummond!

[*His hand clenches convulsively upon his pipe, which snaps sharply under the pressure.*

Colonel Drummond enters the room. He is a grave, stern gentleman of middle age, in military dress, with cuirass, and sword at side. Winwood, at his entrance, shifts his position so that his back is toward him, and sits thus, with head bent and hands tight clenched.

BOWYER. In good time, Colonel Drummond!

DRUMMOND (*throughout with the fine dignity of a soldier and a gentleman*). I fear not, Captain. There are three of you here in presence with whom I must have a word. (*Seats himself at table*) Lieutenant Goring!

GORING (*with some swagger*). Well, sir?

DRUMMOND. At Raglan Castle you gave your promise never again to bear arms against the Parliament. Now that you are taken with arms in your hands, have you aught to say in your defense?

GORING. Before I gave that promise to your damned usurping Parliament, I swore to serve the King. I keep the earlier oath.

DRUMMOND. And for that you will answer in this hour. Now you, Mr. Hopton!

BOWYER. Frank Hopton, too?

DRUMMOND. What defense is yours for your breach of parole?

HOPTON. It was forced from me. A forced promise, faith, 'tis void in the courts of law.

DRUMMOND. It well may be, but not in a court of war.

STRICKLAND. George! Did he say there were — three had broken faith?

DRUMMOND. And now for you, Thomas Winwood!

[*Winwood starts to his feet, but does not face Drummond.*

BOWYER. Tom! Not you!

DRUMMOND. Last June at Bletchingley, you, sir, gave to me personally your word of honor never again to take up arms —

STRICKLAND (*rising, for the moment unwounded, with all his strength*). Face that scoundrel! Face him and tell him that he lies!

WINWOOD (*unwillingly turns and faces Drummond, but stammers when he tries to speak*). I — I —

STRICKLAND. Speak out!

DRUMMOND. Well, Mr. Winwood?

STRICKLAND. Answer! The truth! The truth! Have you broken your parole?

WINWOOD (*desperately at bay, with his back to the wall, his comely young face for the moment the face of his coward and trickster father*). God's death! I've done no more than a hundred others have done. They've not kept faith with us, the cursed rebels. Why the fiend's name should we keep faith with them? It was a forced promise. And the King, I was fain to serve him, as my father served him, like my father —

STRICKLAND. Like your father! (*He staggers where he stands, a wounded man, a sick man — mortally sick at heart*) Allison's lad!

BOWYER (*catching Strickland as he staggers*). Will!

STRICKLAND (*masters himself and stands erect*). Let be! Colonel Drummond, I ask your pardon for my words, a moment since. I could not believe — I could not believe —

(*He sinks upon his chair*) He is his father's son, George! His father's son!

DRUMMOND. Come here, Winwood!

(*Heavily Winwood goes across the room and halts by the table, but throughout he keeps his dazed and miserable eyes on Strickland*)

You realize well, the three of you, that by the breaking of your paroles you have forfeited your lives unto the Parliament.

HOPTON. Our lives? You've no warrant —

DRUMMOND (*laying his hand upon the hilt of his sword*). I have good warrant — here. I was minded first to stand the three of you against the wall in the court below and have you shot, in the presence of your misguided followers.

BOWYER. Colonel Drummond, I do protest!

DRUMMOND. You waste your words, sir. This hour I purpose to give a lesson to all the promise-breakers of your party.

GORING. You purpose, then, to butcher us, all three?

DRUMMOND. Your pardon! Two of you I shall admit to mercy. The third —

HOPTON. Well! Which of us is to be the third?

DRUMMOND. You may choose by lot which one of you shall suffer. You have dice here. Throw, and he who throws lowest —

HOPTON (*with a burst of half hysterical laughter*). Heaven's light, Rob, for once ye'll have enough of casting the dice!

DRUMMOND. Winwood, you are the youngest. You shall throw first. Winwood!

[*Winwood stands as if dazed, his eyes still on Strickland.*

GORING. Are you gone deaf, Tom Winwood?

WINWOOD (*thrusts out a groping hand*). I — I — Give me the dice!

HOPTON (*putting the dice-box into Winwood's hand*). Here! Be quick!

[*A moment's pause, while Winwood, with twitching face, shakes the box and shakes again.*

GORING. For God's love, throw!

WINWOOD (*throws, uncovers dice, and averts his eyes*). What is it?

DRUMMOND. Seven is your cast. You, Hopton!

[*Feverishly Hopton snatches the box, shakes, and casts quickly.* Eleven!

HOPTON (*almost hysterically*). God be thanked for good luck! God be thanked!

GORING. Damn you! Hold your tongue!

[*Hopton snatches a cup from the table and drinks thirstily. Goring throws and holds dice for a moment covered.*

It's between us now, Tom!

WINWOOD (*wiping his forehead with his sleeve*). Yes.

[*Goring uncovers the dice.*

DRUMMOND. Eight!

GORING (*with a long breath of relief*). Ah!

DRUMMOND (*rising*). The lot has fallen upon you, Mr. Winwood.

WINWOOD. I am — at your disposal, sir.

DRUMMOND. You have ten minutes in which to make you ready.

GORING. Ten minutes!

[*Winwood sinks heavily into his old seat at table. Presently he draws to him the dice and box, and mechanically throws again and again.*

BOWYER (*intercepting Drummond, as he turns to leave the room*). You shall listen to me, Drummond. The boy's my kinsman. He —

DRUMMOND. Stand aside, George Bowyer!

[*He goes out of the room.*

BOWYER (*following Drummond out*). Yet you shall listen! Drummond! Listen to me!

HOPTON. But 'tis mere murder. 'Tis against all law.

GORING. Will you prattle of law to Cromwell's men? (*Comes to table and lays a hand on Winwood's shoulder*) Tom, lad, I would we could help you.

WINWOOD. I've thrown the double six — twice. 'Tis monstrous droll, eh, Rob? Before — I could throw no higher than seven — no higher than seven!

[*His voice rises higher and higher, and breaks into shrill laughter.*

GORING. Steady! Steady, lad!

[*Strickland looks up, as if rousing from a trance.*

HOPTON (*hastly fills a cup and offers it to Winwood*). Here, Tom, drink this down.

WINWOOD (*snatches the cup and starts to drink, but in the act looks up and reads in his comrades' faces the fear that is on them, that he is about to disgrace the colors that he wears. He sets down the cup*). You — you think — Will you — leave me — for these minutes? A' God's name, let me be!

[*Hopton and Goring draw away to the window and stand watching Winwood anxiously. He has taken up the dice-box, and again is mechanically casting the dice.*

HOPTON. How will he bear himself yonder?

GORING. You mean —

HOPTON. There in the courtyard, when they —

GORING. Speak lower!

STRICKLAND (*rises with effort, crosses, and lays his hand on Winwood's shoulder*). Tom!

WINWOOD (*starting up, furiously*). You're ashamed of me! You're ashamed! Don't pity me! Let me be! Curse you, let me be!

STRICKLAND (*sternly*). Tom! Look at me!

WINWOOD (*turns defiantly, meets Strickland's eyes, and desperately clings to him*). I can't! I can't! If they'll wait till it's light — but now — in the dark — Make them wait till morning! I can't bear it! I can't bear it!

STRICKLAND. Be still! You must face it, and face it gallantly.

WINWOOD (*stands erect, fighting hard for self-control*). Gallantly. Yes. My father — he died for the King. I mustn't disgrace him. I must bear myself as he would have done. I —

STRICKLAND. Don't speak of him! Think on your mother.

WINWOOD. Must you tell her — why they shot me? She would think of it — of that broken promise — as a woman might. God's life! Why will you judge me so? My father would have understood.

STRICKLAND. Yes. He would have understood you well.

WINWOOD. What do you mean? I'm a coward — a promise breaker. You think that. But my father — he died for the King. He —

(*In Strickland's face he reads that of which in all these years he has been kept in ignorance*)

How did my father die?

STRICKLAND. Not now, Tom!

[*Bowyer comes again into the room.*

WINWOOD (*almost beside himself*). Answer me! Answer me! Bowyer! You're my cousin. Tell me the truth! As God sees us! How did my father die? How did my father live? You won't answer? You've lied! You've lied! All of you — all these years! He was a coward. You don't deny it! A coward — a false coward — and I'm his son! I'm his son!

[*Sinks upon a stool, by the table, with face hidden, and breaks into rending sobs.*

BOWYER. Will! Will! You can bear no more.

STRICKLAND (*shakes off Bowyer's arm and goes to Winwood*). Stand up! Stand up! You are your mother's son as well as his!

WINWOOD (*rising blindly, as if Strickland's voice alone had power to lift him*). A coward! You see. Like him. And there in the courtyard — Ah, God! I'll break! I'll break!

STRICKLAND. You will not. For her sake — for her blood that is in you — Allison's lad!

WINWOOD (*with slow comprehension*). You — loved her!

STRICKLAND. Yes. And love that part of her that is in you. And know that you will bear you well unto the end.

WINWOOD. I'll — I'll — It's not the death. It's not that. It's the moment — before the bullet — God! If I fail — if I fail —

STRICKLAND. You will not fail.

WINWOOD. You believe that? You can believe that of me?

STRICKLAND. I believe that, Tom.

BOWYER. Will! The ten minutes are ended.

STRICKLAND. So soon! So soon!

BOWYER. Drummond will suffer me be with him to the last. Come, Tom, my lad!

[*Goes up, and from a chair beside the door takes a heavy military cloak — which shall thereafter serve as Winwood's shroud. He holds it throughout so that Winwood may not mark it.*

WINWOOD (*takes his hat, and turns to Goring and Hopton, with a pitiful effort at jauntiness*). God be wi' you, boys! (*Crosses, and holds out his hand to Strickland*) Sir William! I'll — try. But — can't you help me? Can't you help me when —

[*Clings to Strickland's hand.*

STRICKLAND. I can help you. You shall bear you as becomes her son.

WINWOOD. Aye, sir.

STRICKLAND. And I shall know it. God keep you!

WINWOOD (*faces about, to Bowyer*). I am ready, sir. (*Goes to door, and on the threshold wheels and stands at salute*) You shall have news of me, Sir William!

[*Winwood goes out, and Bowyer, with the cloak, follows after him.*

HOPTON. What did he mean?

GORING. He'll die bravely, poor lad, I'll swear to that!

[*Strickland sways slightly where he stands.*

Sir William! You're near to swooning. Sit you down, sir.

STRICKLAND. I pray you, gentlemen, for these moments do
not disturb me.

[*Stands upon the hearth, erect, steady, and very still.*

HOPTON. Truth, the man's made of stone. I thought he
had loved poor Winwood as his own son.

GORING. Quiet, will you?

[*Removes his hat.*

HOPTON. What —

GORING. Think on what's happening in the courtyard, man!

[*A moment's pause, and then from below, in the rainy courtyard, is heard the report of a muffled volley.*

HOPTON. Hark!

STRICKLAND (*in an altered, remote voice*). Well done!

GORING. Grant that he made a clean ending!

STRICKLAND (*turns slowly, with eyes fixed before him, and the
sudden smile of one who greets a friend*). Tom! Well done,
Allison's lad!

[*Pitches forward.*

GORING (*catching Strickland in his arms*). Sir William!
Help here, Frank!

[*They place Strickland in his chair. Goring starts to loosen
his neck gear. Hopton kneels and lays his hand on Strickland's heart. On the moment Bowyer comes swiftly into the
room.*

BOWYER. Will! Will! The lad died gallantly. He went
as if a strong arm were round him.

HOPTON (*lets fall the hand that he has laid on Strickland's
heart. Speaks in an awe-struck voice*). Perhaps there was!

GORING (*rises erect from bending over Strickland*). Captain!
Sir William —

[*Bowyer catches the note in Goring's voice, and removes his
hat, as he stands looking upon what he now knows to be the
dead body of his friend and leader.*

CURTAIN

MRS. PAT AND THE LAW

MARY ALDIS

Mrs. Arthur Aldis (Mary Aldis) was born in Chicago, Illinois, July 8, 1872, and was educated at St. Mary's School, Knoxville, Illinois. In 1892 she married Mr. Arthur Aldis.

She founded (1910) the Playhouse of Lake Forest, Illinois, a Little Theatre at her country home. This playhouse was one of the first of the typical Little Theatres which have developed so widely throughout the country. There Mrs. Aldis produced not only her own plays, but, in addition, many notable works of foreign and American playwrights.

Many of her one-act plays have been published in book form under the title of "Mrs. Pat and the Law, and Other Plays" (1915). She has also written "Florence Nightingale" (a pamphlet, 1914); "The Princess Jack", 1915; "Flash-lights", 1916; and "Drift", 1918.

The story of "Mrs. Pat and the Law" was taken directly from life. Mrs. Aldis has been greatly interested in district nursing for many years and heard the story of the plot from one of the Chicago nurses.

MRS. PAT AND THE LAW

By MARY ALDIS

"Mrs. Pat and the Law" was originally produced September 14, 1913, at the Aldis Playhouse, for the amusement of some visiting nurses.

Original Cast

PAT	Benjamin Carpenter
MRS. PAT	Mary Aldis
JIMMY, their son.	Polly Chase
MISS CARROLL	Isabel McBirney
JOHN BING	Charles Atkinson

Reprinted from "Plays for Small Stages" by permission of, and special arrangement with, Mrs. Arthur Aldis and Duffield and Company.

Application for the right of performing "Mrs. Pat and the Law" must be made to Mrs. Arthur Aldis, Lake Forest, Illinois.

MRS. PAT AND THE LAW

SCENE. *A small, poor room in a tenement flat. Cook-stove, back; shabby lounge, front; at left, kitchen table with a faded flower in a bottle; a wash-tub on bench, centre left, back near door. At left, door to bedroom. At right, door to hallway.*

When the curtain rises Nora O'Flaherty is discovered at the wash-tub. She is a large woman, with a worn, sweet face, across her forehead an ugly red cut. The room is untidy, and so is Nora. The stove is blazing hot. After stirring the clothes in the boiler Nora wipes her face with the back of her hand and sighs wearily as she puts a fresh lot into the tub of suds.

JIMMIE (*speaking from bedroom*). Maw, what time is it?

NORA. Most tin, Jimmie-boy.

JIMMIE. Whin'll Miss Carroll come?

NORA. Well, now, I shouldn't wonder if she'd be comin' along the shtreet and oup the shtairs and right in at that door about the time the clock gits 'round to half past tin, or maybe it's sooner she'll be. Do you think it's a flower she'll be bringin' to-day, Jimmie-boy?

JIMMIE. To-day's Tuesday, ain't it?

NORA. Shure!

JIMMIE. There's no tellin'. Sometimes she says there ain't enough to go 'round.

[*A pause.*

NORA (*sorting out clothes*). Sakes alive — the wash that's on me! I'll niver git through.

[*A short silence.*

JIMMIE. Maw, what time is it now?

NORA. Well, I couldn't rightly say, the steam bein' in me eyes like. Faith, ye must bear in mind there's many that's needin' her.   Maybe at this very minute it's a new-born baby just come into the world she's tendin', or an ould man just goin' out of it!   She'll be comin' soon now, I'll warrant ye.

JIMMIE.   But, Maw, me leg hurts, and Paw takes all the room in the bed, he's sleepin' so noisy!

NORA.   Och, Jimmie darlin', have a little patience!   Me name's not Nora O'Flaherty if Miss Carroll don't bring us a flower this day, or if there ain't enought to go 'round, shure it's the bright happy worrd or the little joke or plan she'll have in her mind for ye 'ull hearten the day as well as a flower.

[*Another pause.*

JIMMIE.   Maw!   Ain't it half past tin yit?

NORA.   Oh, laddie, an' I hadn't the great wash on me hands I'd dance a jig t' amuse ye!   Shure many's the song I've sung an' the jig I've danced whin I was a slip o' a gurrl back in the ould counthree, afore I had the four of yiz and yer Paw to look afther!   Now it's me arrms have need to move livelier than me legs, I'm thinkin'.   Listen, now, an' I'll see if I can call to mind a little song for ye.   (*Sings, keeping time with the wash-board*)

There was a lady lived at Rhin,
   A lady very stylish, man —
But she snapped her fingers at all her kin
   And — she fell in love wid an Irishman.
   A wild tremenjous Irishman,
   A rampin', stampin' Irishman,
A devil-may-take-'em — Bad as you make 'em —
   Fascinatin' Irishman!

Oh, wan o' his een was bottle green
   And the tother wan was out, me dear,
An' the calves o' his wicked twinklin' legs
   Were two feet 'round about, me dear.
   Oh — the slashin', dashin' Irishman —
   The blatherin', scatherin' Irishman,

> A whiskey, frisky, rummy, gummy,
>   Brandy, dandy Irishman!
>
> An' that was the lad the lady loved
>   Like all the gurrls o' quality.
> He'd smash all the skulls o' the men o' Rhin
>   Just by the way o' jollity.
> Oh, the rattlin', battlin' Irishman!
> The thumpin', bumpin' Irishman,
> The great he-rogue, wid his roarin' brogue!
>   The laughin', quaffin' Irishman![1]

There's a song fer ye now! Ha, Jimmie-boy, I'm thinkin'
that song 'u'd had more sense an' it told what she did
wid her rampin', roarin' Irishman wanst she got married
to him.

[*Knock on the hall door.*

JIMMIE. Ah, that's her!

NORA. There! Didn't I tell ye? (*Nora wipes her hands
and hurries to open the door, admitting Miss Carroll*). Ah!
Miss Carroll dear, it's welcome ye are this day. Jimmie's
been watchin' and wearyin' for ye since the daylight
dawned. How are ye?

[*She has turned away as Miss Carroll enters so as to conceal
her head, but Miss Carroll catches sight of it and, taking hold
of her arm, turns her around.*

MISS CARROLL. Why, Mrs. O'Flaherty, what an awful cut!
You look as if you had been hit with an axe!

NORA. Oh, git along with ye!

MISS CARROLL. How did it happen?

NORA. Shure, 'twas nothin' at all but his boot, and he that
unstiddy he couldn't aim shtraight! It's 'most well now.
[*She turns to tub.*

MISS CARROLL (*taking off her coat and opening her satchel*).
It isn't "'most well." It's a fresh wound and a bad, deep
cut. As I've told you before, I've no patience with you
for putting up with such treatment. Don't you know

[1] After Wm. McGinn.

the law would protect you? You ought to swear out a warrant for your husband's arrest on the grounds of personal violence. That might teach him a lesson. This is the third time now in a month he's struck you. It's outrageous! Has he got a job yet?

JIMMIE. Ain't you comin', Miss Carroll? Me leg hurts awful.

MISS CARROLL. Yes, Jimmie-boy, in a minute. (*She has been getting hot water from the stove, preparing cotton gauze, etc., for dressing. She stops a moment in her work and regards Mrs. O'Flaherty*) Has he got a job yet?

NORA. He had work last week.

MISS CARROLL. For how long?

NORA. For three days — an' a part o' four.

MISS CARROLL. And then he got drunk and got turned off, eh? And you gave him your wash money, too, I suppose, as usual.

NORA. No, no, Miss Carroll dear, I didn't do that at all. I only give him the half of it, and niver any of it would he have had but — well — knowin' it was in the house, it was coaxin' me mornin' and night he was with that wheedlin', soft way o' him, and the silly loverin' talk till the heart just ran melty within me. (*Miss Carroll regards her with her lips pursed*) I knows it's an ould fool you're thinkin' me, but jest let you be listenin' to his talk wanst and see what you'd do, and him tellin' stories to Jimmie the while so kind and lovely.

MISS CARROLL (*stopping at entrance to bedroom, basin in hand*). "Kind and lovely" indeed! When he takes your wages and hurts and abuses you, and Jimmie hasn't a decent place to live in because his father's a lazy — (*She stops in amazement on the threshold as she sees Pat asleep in the room within*) Well, I never! (*Comes back into the room*) Mrs. O'Flaherty, you must make Pat get up and get out of there while I take care of Jimmie.

[*Mrs. O'Flaherty looks injured, but wipes her hands and does as she is bid. Miss Carroll stands watching at the door.*

NORA (*within bedroom*). Pat! Pat! Wake up, will ye!
(*Pat groans*) My, but you're sleepin' hard! Pat! Miss
Carroll says ye're to git oup and git out o' here while she
takes care o' Jimmie. Come along, now! That's right,
Jimmie-boy, give him a good thump! Are ye oup on yer
legs now? Mind what yer doin'. There ye are!

PAT (*entering, yawning*). Wha' for Miss Carroll says git
oup and git out?
[*Miss Carroll glares at Pat. Pat, turning, catches her eye and
smiles sweetly ere she vanishes into the bedroom.*

NORA. Well, Pat O'Flaherty, I'm thinkin' Miss Carroll
ain't so awful admirin' o' your ways! Sometimes I'm
thinkin' she sees 'em clearer nor your lovin' wife does!
[*Pat picks up one of his shoes, sits down on the sofa and looks
around for the other; pays no heed to Nora's talk.*

PAT. Where's me other shoe? (*Gets down on hands and
knees and looks under the sofa*) Shure I had the two of 'em
on me feet yesterday. (*Laughs gaily*) Maybe I wore
wan on 'em out lookin' for that job that I didn't git!
[*Nora watches him a moment, then hands him the shoe she
has picked up near the stove.*

NORA. Here's your shoe.

PAT. Ah! That's the darlin'; thank ye kindly. I'd be
losin' me head some day if 'twern't for you, Nora gurrl.

NORA (*at tub while Pat slowly puts on shoes*). Oh, Pat, ye
will thry and git some worrk today, won't ye, man? Thry
hard. If they don't take ye on at the first place, go on
an' don't git discouraged. Ye know ye're the grand workman whin ye thry, and ye must git a stiddy job soon. Ye
really must, Pat. I'm shtrong; I don't mind the washin'
fer me own sake. I'd do anythin' fer you and the childer,
but whin Jimmie frets at me to play with him, an' the
others come rushin' in from school a-wantin' thur maw to
do this and that fer 'em, shure it comes harrd an' I dassn't
take me arrms from the suds to 'tend on 'em and comfort
'em and cook 'em thur meals nice like that visitin' house-
keepin' lady told me to.

[*Pat has not been listening very attentively, but has taken in* the drift of Nora's plea.

PAT (*pulling himself together and putting on hat and coat*).   Ah Nora gurrl, I'll be gettin' a good job today shure.   (*Suddenly catches sight of her forehead*)   Wha's that on your head?

NORA (*startled*).   Me head, is it?   Miss Carrol was sayin' just now it was "personal violence and breakin' the law." I was thinkin' afore that 'twas only the heel o' an ould boot walked around daytimes on Pat O'Flaherty, lookin' for a job.

[*Pat regards her uneasily, meditating speech, but appreciates he is too befuddled for argument, so begins to whistle as he gets himself out and down-stairs, leaving the door open.   Nora goes to shut it, and stands a moment reflecting, looking after Pat, then returns to the tub near the bedroom door, evidently thinking.   Short pause.*

JIMMIE (*within bedroom*).   Say, Miss Carroll, d'ye think I'll ever git it?

MISS CARROLL.   Christmas is coming, Jimmie-boy.

JIMMIE.   Huh!   So's Fourth o' July.

MISS CARROLL.   We'll see what we can do.

JIMMIE.   The other lady you told about me brung me a suit, but some cove lots bigger 'n me wore it all out first.   I don' like it.   Gee! but I wisht I had a bran'-new suit just wanst.

[*Nora makes a little yearning gesture towards the room.*

MISS CARROLL.   Now, Jimmie-boy, come along.   It won't hurt much.   When you're all fixed up on the lounge in there I've got something pretty for you.

JIMMIE.   Another flower?   What kind is it?

MISS CARROLL.   We'll see.   Now lean on me.

[*They enter.*

NORA.   That's the lad.   Are ye all fixed up now?   He's gettin' lots better, ain't he, Miss Carroll?

[*Jimmie is a pale, emaciated child with a wan little face of great sweetness of expression.   His clothes are much too large for him.   He holds up one bandaged leg and hobbles on*

*crutches. Miss Carroll helps him on to the lounge, produces
from a paper by her satchel two pink roses, holding them
up.*

JIMMIE. Gee! ain't they pretty! Can I keep 'em both?

MISS CARROLL. Both for you, Jimmie-boy, and we'll see
what can be done about the suit. Perhaps we can find
one somewhere that's bran' new. (*She gets a book from the
shelf*) See if you can learn all the new words on this page
before I come tomorrow, will you? That's a dear old
boy! Now, Mrs. O'Flaherty, let's see about that forehead.
Sit down here.

[*Miss Carroll places a chair, front stage.*

NORA (*washing*). Oh, what's the use botherin' about me
head? It'll git well of itself. It always does. Don't be
mindin' me.

MISS CARROLL. But, Mrs. O'Flaherty, you really must let
me see to it. It's a bad cut.

NORA (*wiping her hands*). Oh well, you're so good to Jimmie
I'll have to oblige you. I suppose you haven't had many
persons with holes in their heads made by boots to tind
to? But you're young, Miss Carroll dear, you're young
yit. (*She seats herself with a sigh*) I'm talkin' silly, Miss
Carroll, but there's no room for a joke in me heart this
day. I've been thinkin' — about what you said afore you
wint in to Jimmie.

MISS CARROLL (*binding up the injured head*). Yes?

NORA. You were tellin' me to git out a warrant 'gainst Pat.
Do you think it would keep him from drinkin' just for a
bit till we git caught up on the rint and the furniture? Do
you think it would?

MISS CARROLL. Mrs. O'Flaherty, you know it's a shame and
an outrage the way Pat's behaving. He's wearing you
out. He'll do you harm some day and then what will
become of Jimmie? He ought to be taught a good lesson.

NORA. Would they do any hurt to him, do you think, an'
they locked him up? Would they care for him kindly,
and he maybe helpless like?

MISS CARROLL. They certainly would care for him. Now, Mrs. O'Flaherty, you go over to the Maxwell Street Station and show them your forehead, and say you want Pat "took up" for a day or so just for a lesson, do you understand?

NORA. Yes, I understand. Oh, it seems an awful thing to be doin' to your own man, don't it? After all them things I said when we got married? No, no, I niver could do it, niver!

[*Goes back to tub.*

MISS CARROLL. Well, then, tell Pat you may do it, anyway. It will make him respect you. But you're such a softy, of course you'll do nothing. I must go now. Mrs. Flaherty, you must not let Pat sleep with Jimmie. It is not good for him.

NORA (*while Miss Carroll is packing satchel and getting on bonnet and coat*). Shure now, Miss Carroll, you're down on Pat for everythin'. He's a good, lovin' paw to Jimmie-boy he is — makin' him happy and pleasin' him like nobody else can. Everybody's kind to Jimmie and nobody's kind to Pat — and they're just alike — two childer they are — both on 'em foolish and lovin' and helpless like, and I love 'em both. Oh, I love 'em! If you'd hear 'em together an' you wid your eyes shut, it's hard set you'd be to say which was the man and which was the child. Sometimes I can't 'tind to me washin' fer listenin' to the funny talk o' the two o' them. Wan time they'll be settin' on the high moon for a throne, with the little shtars to wait on 'em and shootin'-shtars to run errands; another, they'll be swimmin' along through the deep green sea, a-passin' the time o' day an' makin' little jokes to the fishes. Ah, ye ought to hear 'em go on!

MISS CARROLL. Well, I'm glad he amuses Jimmie when he's at home, but he ought to be at work, a great strong man like him! He needs a good lesson, Pat does. Good-bye, Jimmie-boy. Be sure and have the new words learned.

[*She gives him a little pat, and with a wave of the hand goes out.* *Nora is unheeding Jimmie's call of "Maw."* *Jimmie has not listened to the conversation between Nora and Miss Carroll.*

JIMMIE (*raising himself and looking around*). Maw! She said she'd try and git me a bran'-new suit. Say, Maw, d'ye think she'll pay out her money fer it? I don't want her to do that. She just gets wages same as Paw. She told me how it was. Say, Maw, why don't Paw bring home no more wages?

NORA (*coming to him, then taking sudden decision*). Jimmie-boy, Maw's goin' out. (*Hastily gets out a very queer bonnet and mantle while she speaks and arrays herself, putting bonnet on crooked to partially conceal bandage*) You just lie quiet there like a good boy, an' a lamb's tail couldn't whisk itself three times till I'll be back again. I'm not goin' to be a fool softy no longer, and Paw'll bring home some more wages afther that lesson he's needin'. Are ye all right now? Ye won't be needin' anything?
[*Pats him on the head, then leans over and kisses him fiercely, protectingly.*

JIMMIE. Where you goin'?

NORA. I'm goin' to git the law to help us if it can. (*She goes out and bangs the door*)
[*Jimmie, left alone, is very bored and listless. He turns over the book, then lets it fall, twists himself wearily. Suddenly his whole face brightens happily at a step outside. Pat's gay whistle is heard coming up-stairs.*

PAT (*entering*). Hi, Jimmie-boy! There's the great lad for ye! All shtuffed full and a-runnin' over he is wid fine learnin' out of books. Did ye ever see the loike o' him? Sittin' up dressed like folks! Faith, it's the proud Pat I am this day! Let's see what great thing about the wide worrld is a-hidin' itself inside o' this yere.
[*Picks up book.*

JIMMIE. I'm tired o' that. Tell me a story.

PAT. A shtory, is it? An' me to be sittin' here tellin' a young lad shtories at the high noon of the day, and the

job takin' itself wings to fly off, I might be catchin' and
holdin' down and I to go afther it instid! (*Sitting down by
Jimmie*) Where's your Maw?

JIMMIE.   I dunno. She said she wasn't going to be no fool
softy no more, and then she went out quick like. What's
a fool softy?

[*Pat is very uneasy. He does not answer, then goes to the
door, looks out, comes back slowly.*

JIMMIE.   Paw, me leg hurts awful today. Tell me a story.

PAT.   All right, lad, I'll tell ye a story. (*Sits down near
sofa*) Did I ever tell you about the king of Ireland and
his siven sons? No? Once upon a time there was a great,
high-up, noble king reigned over Ireland with a golden
crown on his noble head an' a rulin' shtick in his hand —
Whin 'll your Maw be back?

JIMMIE.   I dunno. Go on with the story.

PAT.   Well, this grand king had siven sons, all fair and
beautiful they were in armour of silver and shteel, an' on
their heads helmets covered with precious stones dug up
out o' the earth that would make your eyes blink for the
shinin'. Bye-and-bye the siven lads grew up strong and
mighty, and whin the king saw that they were gettin' to
man's eshtate he got him together all of the workmen out of
a job there were in the kingdom of Ireland, and he sets
'em to buildin' siven great castles, each wan on a different
high-up mountain-top, so high that the peaks and shpires
of some of them made holes right through the blue sky,
do ye mind? Well, whin the castles were all grand and
ready he called his siven sons together, an' he stood 'em
all up in a glitterin' row and he said to 'em, "Now, me
byes, it's no end of a foine time ye've been havin' a-sky-
larkin' 'round me kingdom, but it's siven high castles I've
built for ye now and ye'd better be gettin' yourselves wives
and some bits of furniture on the installment plan, maybe,
and settlin' down. Go forth now through all the world and
find ye siven beautiful princesses, and the wan of ye that
gits the beautifullest shall have the biggest castle."

[*Nora enters, grim. Pat notes her demeanor, but concludes comment is unwise. She takes off her bonnet and shawl and goes to her tub, listening to Pat.*

JIMMIE. Go on, Paw, what did they do thin?

PAT (*keeping a weather eye on Nora*). What did they do thin? Well, they looked and looked fer a year and a day, ivery one o' them in a different counthry, but whiniver one of the siven would be findin' a princess who seemed handsome and likely, whin he looked again careful like, he'd be feared one of his brothers would be findin' a handsomer one, so he'd let her go and move on.

JIMMIE. An' all the beautiful princesses, weren't there any anywhere no more?

PAT (*slapping his leg in the joy of a sudden inspiration*). Faith, Jimmie-boy, it's just comin' into me head what was the throuble! Shure the siven grand princes must 'a' looked in the church window the day I married your Maw, and seein' her that wanst o' course no princess could plaze 'em afther. It was green-eyed envy filled their siven souls that day, I'm thinkin', for Pat O'Flaherty gettin' such a jewell and nobody left beautiful enough for them at all!

JIMMIE. Paw, quit yer jokin'! Git along with the story.

PAT. Jimmie darlin', it's not jokin' I am. Your Maw's a jewell, a rael beautiful jewell, and that's the truth. I don't deserve her, I don't.

[*Suddenly breaks down and sobs.*

JIMMIE. Aw, Paw, don't do that — don't.

[*He beings to whimper. Nora starts to comfort him when a knock is heard. Pat shakes himself together and opens the door, and John Bing, a policeman, enters.*

PAT (*to Nora*). A policeman!

JOHN BING (*glancing at paper in his hand*). Does Patrick O'Flaherty live here?

PAT. Faith, he does that, an' what would the majestic arm o' the law be wantin', if ye please, intrudin' in a peaceful man's house?

JOHN BING.   I've a warrant here for the arrest of Patrick O'Flaherty on the ground of repeated violence towards his wife.

PAT.   Howly Saints!   An' who shwore out that warrant?

JOHN BING (*glancing at paper*).   Nora O'Flaherty.   (*Looking at Nora*)   I guess it's true, all right.   Come along.

PAT.   Nora!   You niver did that to your own man?   (*Nora makes no reply but a sniffle*)   Nora!

JOHN BING.   Well, hurry up.   Better come quietly.

JIMMIE.   Paw, what's the matter?   What's he come for? Make him go 'way.

PAT (*taking Bing's coat lapel confidentially*).   Mr. Officer — you see the little lad there?   He's — well — well, he'll never walk no more.   Perhaps you got childer yourself? Would you mind just waitin' a bit of a minute, or maybe two, till I finish a shtory I was tellin' him?   He'll let me go aisier so.

JOHN BING (*looking at his watch*).   Five minutes, then.

PAT.   Thank ye kindly.   (*Returns to Jimmie, giving his lounge a little push so Jimmie will not see John Bing*)   Now, me lad, where were we in the shtory?

JIMMIE.   About the beautiful princesses.

PAT.   Shure, I'm thinkin' it's mortal weary them siven princes will be lookin' for their beautiful princesses all this time, when right here in this room with us two all so happy an' lovin'-like is your Maw, out o' their reach.   (*Jimmie suddenly laughs out merrily, the first time he has done more than smile wanly*)   So what do you think they did next?

JIMMIE.   I dunno.

PAT.   Guess.

[*Here Nora, who has been weeping and washing harder and harder, makes a dash and throws open the door to the hall, grabbing the warrant meanwhile out of the hand of John Bing.*

NORA.   Mr. Officer, you walk right out o' here and down them shtairs and don't you be waitin' no more for Patrick O'Flaherty.   He ain't goin' with you.   He's goin' to git a job stiddy and shtay here.

JOHN BING. You withdraw the charge? I'll have to report it at the station.

NORA. Charge nothin'! You git out o' here.

JOHN BING (*stopping to gaze at her a moment*). Well, what do you think of that? The next time one of them suffragist ladies asks me what I think, I'll tell her I think women is fools, that's what I'll tell her. Yep, all fools! (*He goes out*)

[*Pat has sat discreetly silent, twirling his thumbs rapidly and looking in front of him.*

JIMMIE. Paw! What's Maw talkin' about? What 'u'd he want?

PAT. Niver you mind, Jimmie-boy. It was just payin' the O'Flaherty family a call he was, nice and friendly like. Your Maw invited him, but when she saw how dishturbin' his august prisence was in our happy home, she invited him out again. Ain't that it, Nora darlin'?

[*He holds out his hand to Nora. Nora weakly approaches, sniffling, then falls on his neck.*

NORA. Oh, Pat, Pat! I niver meant to do that awful thing — I niver did. I dunno what made me. It was that nurse a-talkin' at me. She put a spell on me, she did. Oh Pat, oh Pat!

PAT (*patting her*). Niver mind, niver mind. I know ye didn't. It's all right. Niver mind, gurrl.

[*A knock at the door. Nora pulls herself free and opens the door to Miss Carroll.*

PAT (*retreating*). It's that dam' nurse! She'll be the death o' me yit.

MISS CARROLL (*coming quickly forward towards Jimmie*). I can't stop a second. I just ran in to tell Jimmie-boy I've been telephoning and it's all fixed. The bran'-new suit's going to happen next Saturday. It's my half-holiday and I'll come for you in a taxi and we'll go down-town and we'll buy it all bran' new to fit, made just for Jimmie.

JIMMIE. Aw! 'tain't so. You're kiddin' me!

MISS CARROLL. 'Tis so, honor bright! Cross my heart and hope to die. Well, I must run. (*Suddenly appreciating Nora's aspect*) Why, Mrs. O'Flaherty, what's the matter?

NORA. The matter is you're a wicked, interferin' woman, a-makin' me do them awful things to me pore man there! Look at him, so sweet and gentle like! Ain't ye 'shamed o' yourself, a-plottin' and workin' to put apart them as God 'as j'ined together in the howly estate of matrimony? It's a bad, wicked woman I am to be listenin' to your terrible talk. That there horrid big officer in his shiny buttons, lookin' so fat and so satisfied, waitin' there at the door to grab up me pore man hasn't a coat to his back hardly!

MISS CARROLL. What about the boot, Mrs. O'Flaherty?

NORA. The boot, is it? Shure it's the careless woman I am, happenin' in the way whin he was takin' 'em off and he with a bit of the creature in him made him excited like.

MISS CARROLL. All right, Mrs. O'Flaherty, I'm sorry. I won't give any more advice. It's against the rules. I shouldn't have said anything. (*She looks at Pat, who has been regarding her quizzically while Nora holds forth, and now, catching her eye, has the impertinence to wink. Miss Carroll struggles hard not to respond to his grin, but can't quite keep her gravity*) You see, I haven't any man of my own, so I suppose it's hard for me to understand married life. Good-bye till tomorrow. [*She waves her hand to Jimmie, accomplishes one severe look at Pat, and vanishes. Pat waves her off gaily.*

PAT. Goo'-bye, Miss Carroll, goo'-bye! Goo'-bye!
[*He gets his hat and coat, chuckling to himself.*

JIMMIE. Did ye hear that, Maw? A bran'-new suit made just for me. Nobody else never wore it at all, an' we'll go in a taxi to buy it on Saturday. Gee! Ain't it nice?

PAT (*sidling up to Nora at the tub*). Nora darlin', I'm thinkin' it's a foine job I'll be gettin' this day for the askin'; the heart's that big in me for gratitude, it'll shine right out through me two eyes and make me hopeful and stiddy-lookin', so that some boss'll think he's got a grand man to work for him. I'd better be startin' along now, I suppose, er some other chap'll git there before me. Say, Nora, it's only about twinty cints I do be needin' for carfare.

NORA. Pat, twinty cents is a lot. Where you goin'?

PAT. Well, maybe fifteen cints would do if I walk the wan way where there ain't no transfer. Shure it's hard on the poor when the shtreet-car companies git mad at each other. Say, Nora, I know a place where a good job is waitin' for Pat O'Flaherty, but the great city lies between us. Cruel long and wide it is, and hard stones all the way. It's too weary and sad like I'd look on arrivin', an' I couldn't ride on the cars to git there. Oh, come across with the fifteen cents!

[*Nora dubiously gets down an old china teapot from the shelf and takes out five cents, which she gives him gravely. She then gets five cents from another secret place.*

PAT (*as she is getting the money*). Faith, there's money all over the place.

[*Nora then gets five pennies from the depths of her pocket and slowly counts out the fifteen cents into his hand.*

PAT (*kissing her*). Oh! That's the shweetest wife ever blessed a bad, bad spalpeen of a husband. Good-bye, gurrl! 'Bye, Jimmie-boy. Be thinkin' what the siven princes could do, they havin' seen your Maw through the church window, and I'll finish the shtory tomorrow.

[*Pat exits, whistling, Nora watching him at the door.*

JIMMIE. Maw, what's a fool softy?

[*Nora wilts.*

CURTAIN

LIMA BEANS

ALFRED KREYMBORG

Mr. Alfred Kreymborg was born in New York City, December 10, 1883. He is the exponent of evolution in the form of music, prose, free verse, and the free verse play. He was the founder of *The Glebe* and edited it while it was in existence. During its life, it was the first publication to issue an imagist anthology (Ezra Pound's collection, 1914). He founded *Others, a Magazine of the New Verse*, July, 1915, and *The Other Players*, March, 1918, an organization devoted exclusively to American plays in poetic form. He is the author of "Mushrooms, a Book of Free Forms", "Erna Vitez, a Novel", and "Plays for Poem-Mimes", and has edited two anthologies of free verse: "Others for 1916", and "Others for 1917."

"Lima Beans" is the most popular of his plays and has been most frequently produced. It exemplifies Mr. Kreymborg's theory of "pantomime acting or dancing of folk or automatons to an accompaniment of rhythmic lines, in place of music."

Mr. Kreymborg's idea may be compared with that of Mr. Vachel Lindsay, who has conceived some of his own poems as a chant in lieu of music to accompany a dance. Where, in Mr. Lindsay's experiment, however, one person is needed for the dance and another for the chant, in Mr. Kreymborg's plays the dancer and the speaker are the same person. There is some difference also in the point of view: Mr. Lindsay uses the dance to aid interpretation of the poetry; Mr. Kreymborg is equally interested in both.

LIMA BEANS

A SCHERZO-PLAY

By ALFRED KREYMBORG

"Lima Beans" was originally produced by The Provincetown Players, autumn, 1916.

Original Cast

THE WIFE	Mina Loy
THE HUSBAND	William Carlos Williams
THE HUCKSTER	William Zorach

Set and costumes designed by William and Marguerite Zorach.

Reprinted from "Six Plays for Poem-Mimes" by permission of, and by special arrangement with, Mr. Alfred Kreymborg and The Other Press.

Application for the right of performing "Lima Beans" must be made to Mr. Alfred Kreymborg, The Other Press, 17 East 14th Street, New York City.

LIMA BEANS

A Scherzo-play

SCENE. *The characters are four : husband, wife, the voice of a huckster and — the curtain! Husband and wife might be two marionettes. The scene is a miniature dining room large enough to contain a small table, two chairs, a tiny sideboard, an open window, a closed door leading to the other rooms, and additional elbow space. Pantomime is modestly indulged by husband and wife, suggesting an inoffensive parody, unless the author errs, of the contours of certain ancient Burmese dances. The impedimenta of occasional rhymes are unpremeditated. If there must be a prelude of music, let it be nothing more consequential than one of the innocuous parlor rondos of Carl Maria von Weber. As a background color scheme, black and white might not prove amiss.*

As the curtain, which is painted in festoons of vegetables, rises gravely, the wife is disclosed setting the table for dinner. Aided by the sideboard, she has attended to her place, as witness the neat arrangement of plate, cup and saucer, and knife, fork and spoons at one side. Now, more consciously, she begins the performance of the important duty opposite. This question of concrete paraphernalia, and the action consequent thereupon, might of course be left entirely to the imagination of the beholder.

THE WIFE (*wistfully whimsical*). Put a knife here,
place a fork there —
marriage is greater than love.
Give him a large spoon,
give him a small —

you're sure of your man when you dine him.
A cup for his coffee,
a saucer for spillings,
a plate rimmed with roses
to hold his night's fillings —
roses for hearts, ah,
but food for the appetite!
Mammals are happiest home after dark!
(*The rite over, she stands off in critical admiration, her arms akimbo, her head bobbing from side to side.   Then, seriously, as she eyes the husband's dinner plate.*)
But what shall I give him to eat to-night?
It mustn't be limas,
we've always had limas —
one more lima would shatter his love!
[*An answer comes through the open window from the dulcet insinuatingly persuasive horn of the huckster.*
Oh, ah, ooh!

THE HUCKSTER (*singing mysteriously*).
I got toma*toes*,
I got pota*toes*,
I got new cabba*ges*,
I got *cauli*flower,
I got *red* beets,
I got *on*ions,
I got *li*ma beans —

THE WIFE (*who has stolen to the window, fascinated*).   Any fruit?

THE HUCKSTER.
I got oran*ges*,
I got pineap*ples*,
blackber*ries*,
*cur*rants,
*blue*berries,
I got ban*anas*,
I got —

THE WIFE.   Bring me some string beans!

THE HUCKSTER. Yes, mam!

[*His head bobs in at the window.*

The Wife takes some coins from the sideboard. A paper bag is flung into the room. The wife catches it and airily tosses the coins into the street. Presently, she takes a bowl from the sideboard, sits down, peeps into the bag, dramatically tears it open, and relapses into a gentle rocking as she strings the beans, to this invocation.

THE WIFE. String the crooked ones,
string the straight —
love needs a change every meal.
To-morrow, come kidney beans,
Wednesday, come white or black —
limas, return not too soon!
The string bean rules in the
vegetable kingdom,
gives far more calories, sooner digests —
love through with dinner is quicker to play!
Straight ones, crooked ones,
string beans are blessed!

[*Enter the husband briskly. In consternation, the wife tries to hide the bowl, but sets it on the table and hurries to greet him. He spreads his hands and bows.*

SHE. Good evening, sweet husband!

HE. Good evening, sweet wife!

SHE. You're back, I'm so happy —

HE. So am I — 'twas a day —

SHE. 'Twas a day?

HE. For a hot sweating donkey —

SHE. A donkey?

HE. A mule!

SHE. My poor, dear, poor spouse —

HE. No, no, my good mouse —

SHE. Rest your tired, weary arms —

HE. They're not tired, I'm not weary —
I'd perspire tears and blood drops
just to keep my mouse in cheese.

In a town or in the fields,
on the sea or in a balloon,
with a pickaxe or a fiddle,
with one's back a crooked wish-bone,
occupation, labor, work —
work's a man's best contribution.

SHE. Contribution?

HE. Yes, to Hymen!

SHE. Ah yes —

HE. But you haven't —

SHE. I haven't?

HE. You haven't —

SHE. I haven't?

HE. You have *not* —

SHE. Ah yes, yes indeed!

[*The wife embraces the husband and kisses him daintily six times.*

HE. Stop, queer little dear!
Why is a kiss?

SHE. I don't know.

HE. You don't?

SHE. No!

HE. Then why do you do it?

SHE. Love!

HE. Love?

SHE. Yes!

HE. And why is love?

SHE. I don't know.

HE. You don't?

SHE. No!

HE. And why don't you know?

SHE. Because!

HE. Because?

SHE. Yes!

HE. Come, queer little dear!

[*The husband embraces the wife and kisses her daintily six times.*

(*solemnly*).   And now!

SHE (*nervously*).   And now?

HE.   And now!

SHE.   And now?

HE.   And now I am hungry.

SHE.   And now you are hungry?

HE.   Of course I am hungry.

SHE.   To be sure you are hungry, but —

HE.   But?

SHE.   But!

HE.   But?

[*The wife tries to edge between the husband and the table. He gently elbows her aside. She comes back; he elbows her less gently, This pantomime is repeated several times; his elbowing is almost rough at the last. The husband reaches the table and ogles the bowl. His head twists from the bowl to the wife, back and forth. An ominous silence.*

String beans?

SHE.   String beans!

HE.   String beans?

SHE.   String beans!

[*A still more ominous silence. The husband's head begins fairly to bob, only to stop abruptly as he breaks forth.*

HE.   I perspire tears and blood drops
in a town or in the fields,
on the sea or in a balloon,
with my pickaxe or my fiddle,
just to come home
footsore, starving, doubled with appetite
to a meal of — string beans?
Where are my limas?

SHE.   We had —

HE.   We had?

SHE.   Lima beans yesterday — we had them —

HE.   We had them?

SHE.   Day before yesterday —

HE.   What of it?

SHE.   Last Friday, last Thursday —

HE.   I know it —

SHE.   Last Wednesday, last Tuesday —

HE.   What then, mam?

SHE.   We had them
    all the way since we were married —

HE.   Two weeks ago this very day —

SHE.   I thought you'd have to have a change —

HE.   A change —

SHE.   I thought you'd like to have a change —

HE.   A change?
    You thought?
    I'd like?
    A change?
    What!
    From the godliest of vegetables,
    my kingly bean,
    that soft, soothing,
    succulent, caressing,
    creamy, persuasively serene,
    my buttery entity?
    You would dethrone it?
    You would play renegade?
    You'd raise an usurper
    in the person of this
    elongated, cadaverous,
    throat-scratching, greenish
    caterpillar —
    you'd honor a parochial,
    menial pleb,
    an accursed legume,
    sans even the petty grandeur
    of cauliflower,
    radish, pea,
    onion, asparagus,
    potato, tomato —
    to the rank of household god?

Is this your marriage?
Is this your creed of love?
Is this your contribution?
Dear, dear,
was there some witch at the altar
who linked your hand with mine in troth
only to have it broken in a bowl?
Ah, dear, dear —

SHE.   Dear, dear!

HE.   You have listened to a temptress —

SHE.   I have listened to my love of you —

HE.   You, the pure, the angelic —

SHE.   Husband, dear —

HE.   Silence!

SHE.   Husband!

HE.   Silence!

(*The wife collapses into her chair.   The husband seizes the bowl to this malediction*)

Worms,
snakes,
reptiles,
caterpillars,
I do not know from whence ye came,
but I know whither ye shall go.
My love,
my troth,
my faith
shall deal with ye.
Avaunt,
vanish,
begone
from this domicile,
dedicated,
consecrated,
immortalized
in the name of Hymen!
Begone!

[*The husband throws the bowl and beans out of the window.
The customary crash of broken glass, off-stage, is heard.
A smothered sob escapes the wife. The husband strides
towards the door. The wife raises her head.*

SHE.   Husband.

HE.   Traitress!

SHE.   Love, sweet husband!

HE.   Traitress, traitress!

[*The husband glares at the wife, and slams the door behind
him. The wife collapses again. Her body rocks to and
fro. Silence. Then, still more mysteriously than the first
time, the horn and the voice of the huckster. The wife
stops rocking, raises her head and gets up. A woe-begone
expression vanishes before one of eagerness, of housewifely
shrewdness, of joy. She steals to the window.*

THE HUCKSTER.   I got oranges,

I got pineap*ples,*

I got blackberr*ies,*

I got *cur*rants,

I got *blue*berries,

I got ban*anas,*

I got —

THE WIFE.   Any vegetables?

THE HUCKSTER.   I got toma*toes,*

I got pota*toes,*

new cabba*ges,*

*cauli*flower,

red beets,

I got *string* beans,

I got —

THE WIFE.   Bring me some lima beans!

THE HUCKSTER.   I got onions,

I got —

THE WIFE.   Bring me some lima beans!

THE HUCKSTER.   Yes, mam!

[*His head appears again.
The performance of paper bag and coins is repeated. Ex-*

*citedly, the wife takes another bowl from the sideboard. She sits
down, tears open the bag, clicks her heels, and hastily, recklessly,
begins splitting the limas. One or two pop out and bound along
the floor. The wife stops. Pensively:*

THE WIFE. There you go,
hopping away,
just like bad sparrows —
no, no, more like him.
(*She smiles a little*)
Hopping away,
no, he's not a sparrow,
he's more like a
poor angry boy — and so soon!
(*She lets the beans slip through her fingers*)
Lima beans, string beans,
kidney beans, white or black —
you're all alike —
though not all alike to him.
(*She perks her head*)
It's alike to me.
what's alike to him —
(*She looks out of the window*)
though I'm sorry for you,
crooked strings, straight strings,
and so glad for you,
creamy ones, succulent —
what did he say of you?
(*She returns to splitting the limas; with crescendo animation*)
Heigho, it's all one to me,
so he loves what I do,
I'll do what he loves.
Angry boy? No, a man
quite young in the practice
of wedlock — and love!
Come, limas, to work now —
we'll serve him, heart, appetite,
whims, crosspatches and all —

though we boil for it later!
The dinner bell calls us,
ding, dong, ding, dell!

[*The husband opens the door and pokes in his head. The wife hears him and is silent. He edges into the room and then stops, humble, contrite, abject. Almost in a whisper*:

HE. Wife!

(*She does not heed him. He, louder*)

Sweet wife!

(*She does not answer. He, still louder*)

Beloved,
dear, dearest wife!

(*She does not answer. He approaches carefully, almost with reverence, watches her, takes the other chair and cautiously sets it down next to hers*)

Wife!

SHE. Yes?

HE. Will you —
I want to —
won't you —
may I sit next to you?

SHE. Yes.

HE. I want to —
will you —
won't you
forgive me — I'll
eat all the beans in the world!

[*The wife looks up at the husband roguishly. He drops down beside her with the evident intention of putting his arm about her, only to jump up as, inadvertently, he has looked into the bowl. He rubs his eyes, sits down slowly, looks again, only to jump up again. The third time he sits down with extreme caution, like a zoologist who has come upon a new specimen of insect. The wife seems oblivious of his emotion. He rises, looks from one side of her, then the other, warily. At last, rapturously.*

Lima beans?

[She looks up tenderly and invitingly, indicating his chair.

SHE. Lima beans!

[He sits down beside her. With greater awe and emphasis.

HE. Lima beans?

SHE. Lima beans!

[A moment of elfin silence.

HE. Sweet wife!

SHE. Sweet husband!

HE. Where —

  whence —

  how did it —

  how did it happen?

SHE. I don't know.

HE. You do —

  you do know —

SHE. I don't!

HE. Tiny miracle,

  you do —

  you're a woman,

  you're a wife,

  you're an imp —

  you do know!

SHE. Well —

HE. Well?

SHE. Er —

HE. Eh?

SHE. Somebody —

HE. Yes, yes?

SHE. Somebody —

  sent them —

HE. Sent them!

SHE. Brought them!

HE. Brought them?

SHE. Yes!

HE. Who?

SHE. Somebody!

HE. Somebody who?

SHE.   I can't tell —

HE.   You can.

SHE.   I — won't tell —

HE.   You will —

SHE.   I won't —

HE.   You will —

SHE.   Well!

HE.   Well?

SHE.   You ought to know!

HE.   I ought to?

SHE.   You ought to —

HE.   But I don't —

SHE.   Yes, you do!

HE.   I do not —

SHE.   You do!

[*The husband eyes the wife thoughtfully. She aids him with a gently mischievous smile. He smiles back in understanding.*

HE.   I know!

SHE.   You do not —

HE.   Yes, I do!

SHE.   Are you sure?

HE.   Sure enough —

SHE.   Who was it?

HE.   I won't tell —

SHE.   You will!

[*He points at the audience with warning, goes to the keyhole and listens, draws the window-shade and returns. She nods quickly and puts her head closer to his, her wide-open eyes on the audience. He puts his head to hers, his wide-open eyes on the audience, then turns quickly and whispers something in her ear. She nods with secret, uproarious delight.*

Yes!

HE.   Yes?

SHE.   Yes!

[*They embrace and click their heels with unrestrained enthusiasm. The wife holds out the bowl to the husband with mock solemnity. He grasps it and together they raise it above their heads, lower it to their knees, and then shell the beans with one accord.   They kiss each other daintily six times.   The curtain begins to quiver.   As before, but accelerando.*

HE.   Stop, queer little dear !
Why is a kiss ?

SHE.   I don't know.

HE.   You don't ?

SHE.   No !

HE.   Then why do you do it ?

SHE.   Love !

HE.   Love !

SHE.   Yes !

HE.   And why is —

[They are interrupted.   The curtain comes capering down ! The last we behold of the happy pair is their frantic signaling for the curtain to wait till they have finished.   But curtains cannot see — or understand ?

THE WONDER HAT

BEN HECHT

Perhaps the best conception of Mr. Ben Hecht can be secured from a short autobiography. During the war Mr. Hecht was the official Berlin correspondent of the *Chicago Daily News*. As he was dashing out on his way to the boat, Mr. Henry Blackman Sell, book editor of the *Chicago Daily News*, reminded him that the *News* had no facts concerning his life. Mr. Hecht sat down immediately and produced the following:

"I was born in New York City in 1893 and travelled extensively until the age of eight, when I located in Racine, Wisconsin. At seventeen, I was graduated from the Racine High School and arrived in Chicago a month thereafter. My original intention was to join the Thomas Orchestra as violinist. I secured a job on the staff of the *Chicago Journal* instead. I worked there for four years. I then joined the *Daily News* staff and have been more or less employed thereon since.

"I have, during eight and a half years of reporting, covered 221 fires, 9 hangings, 81 murder mysteries, interviewed 651 opera stars, 113 foreign diplomats, 99 domestic politicians, 1657 girls who have gone wrong; reported 56 murder trials, 901 divorce trials, and 59 trials on grand larceny charges.

"I have had 45 short stories published in *Munsey's, Smart Set, Black Cat, All Story, Parisienne, The Little Review*, and have had poetry printed in *Poetry — A Magazine of Verse*.

"I admire the domestic geranium. Lavender is my favorite color. I have no money in the bank. I am married and the father of one child, a girl.

"My favorite composers are Beethoven and Debussy. My favorite authors, Huysmans and Dostoyevsky. My favorite artist, Stanislaus Zulkalski.

"I have read the *Daily News* regularly for six years."

Mr. Ben Hecht is a collaborator with Kenneth Sawyer Goodman in "The Wonder Hat", "An Idyl of the Shops", and "The Hero of Santa Maria", and with Maxwell Bodenheim in "Mrs. Margaret Calhoun." He is sole author of a play entitled "Dregs."

KENNETH SAWYER GOODMAN

Lieutenant Kenneth Sawyer Goodman was born in 1883, and died very suddenly of pneumonia on November 29, 1918. At the time of his death he was chief aid to Captain Moffett at the Great Lakes Naval Station.

In coöperating with B. Iden Payne during the Chicago Theatre Society's season at the Fine Arts Theatre in 1913, he helped to give the city one of its most interesting repertory engagements. He was an officer of the Chicago Theatre Society during its three years of life, and contributed to the repertory of its Drama Players in 1911 a translation of Hervieu's "La Course en Flambeau", which was successfully acted at the Lyric Theatre (now the Great Northern) under the title of "The Passing of the Torch." By the study of playwriting (in which he showed marked talent), of stage decoration, and of theatre management, he was preparing himself for important work in dramatic art.

He is the author of: "Quick Curtains", which contains "Dust of the Road", "The Game of Chess", "Barbara", "Ephraim and the Winged Bear", "Back of the Yards", "Dancing Dolls", and "A Man Can Only Do His Best"; "An Idyl of the Shops", "The Hero of Santa Maria", and "The Wonder Hat" (in collaboration with Ben Hecht); "Holbein in Blackfriars", "Ryland", "Rainald and the Red Wolf", and "Masques of East and West" (in collaboration with Thomas Wood Stevens).

"Dust of the Road" was first acted by the Wisconsin Dramatic Society in 1911. "The Game of Chess" was first acted in the Fine Arts Theatre, Chicago, under the auspices of the Chicago Theatre Society, 1911, with Walter Hampden and Whitford Kane in the leading rôles. "Barbara" was first acted in the Fine Arts Theatre, Chicago, under the auspices of the Chicago Theatre Society, 1911, with Mona Limerick, Dallas Anderson, and B. Iden Payne in the cast. "Back of the Yards" was acted by the Players' Workshop of Chicago in 1917. "A Man Can Only Do His Best" was first acted at the Gaiety Theatre, Manchester, England, under the direction of B. Iden Payne, 1914.

THE WONDER HAT

A HARLEQUINADE

By BEN HECHT AND KENNETH SAWYER
GOODMAN

"The Wonder Hat" was originally produced at the Arts and Crafts Theatre, Detroit, Michigan, in 1916.

Original Cast

HARLEQUIN	Sam Hume
PIERROT	Charles E. Hilton
PUNCHINELLO	A. L. Weeks
COLUMBINE	Lento Fulwell
MARGOT	Betty Brooks

THE WONDER HAT

SCENE. *The scene is a park by moonlight. The stage setting is shallow. At the back center is a formal fountain, backed by a short wall about seven feet high and having urns at its two ends. At each side of the fountain are low groups of shrubbery. There is a clear space between the fountain and back drop so that the characters may pass round the shrubbery and the fountain. The back drop represents a night sky with an abnormally large yellow moon. A path crosses the stage parallel to the footlights.*

As the curtain rises, Harlequin and Pierrot saunter in from the left, arm in arm. They both have on long cloaks and are swinging light canes with an air of elegant ennui. They pause in the center of the stage.

HARLEQUIN (*indicating with a wave of his cane*). Dear fellow, this is a circular path. It runs quite around the outer edge of the park, a matter of a half mile or thereabouts. It delights me. I always spend my evenings here. One can walk for hours with the absolute certainty of never getting anywhere.

PIERROT (*removing his eyeglass*). Dear chap, in these days of suburban progress, I had not supposed such a place possible.

HARLEQUIN. There is another point in its favor. As you may have noticed, all the promenaders move continuously in the same direction. It is therefore only necessary to maintain an even pace in order to avoid making acquaintances.

PIERROT. One might retrace one's steps.

HARLEQUIN. It has been tried by certain elderly roués and ladies from the opera, but always with disastrous results. Our best people no longer attempt it.

PIERROT (*with a slight yawn*). How delightfully like life.

HARLEQUIN. In certain ways, yes. Those of a genial disposition may lag and allow others to catch up. The more adventurous may press on and possibly overtake somebody. But unlike life, one is never troubled by one's creditors.

PIERROT. How thoroughly charming. (*Takes pose at fountain*) Tell me, does Columbine ever come here?

HARLEQUIN (*becoming serious; takes pose other side of fountain*). That is the one drawback. She comes here very often.

PIERROT (*snappishly*). Humph! That is really annoying, deucedly, devilishly, foolishly annoying!

HARLEQUIN. You're very emphatic.

PIERROT (*still more snappishly*). I have never liked that woman, in spite of what the poets say about us.

HARLEQUIN. By keeping a sharp lookout, I have thus far managed to avoid her myself and yet keep her often in sight without her laying eyes on me.

PIERROT (*pleased*). I see that we are both confirmed bachelors, without a grain of sentiment in us. We agree perfectly.

HARLEQUIN. On the contrary, we don't agree at all. Because you dislike Columbine, you're too confoundedly polite to others. You make cynical love to all sorts of women and nobody likes you for it. On the other hand, I am immensely partial to the same young lady and detest all the rest of the sex. For that reason I am simply overwhelmed with dinner invitations.

PIERROT. If you're in love with Columbine, why don't you catch up with her some evening and have it out with her?

HARLEQUIN (*preening himself*). Gross materialist! For the sake of a few honeyed kisses would you have me risk the crumbling of an ideal? She would certainly fall in love with me like all the others.

PIERROT (*with equal self-satisfaction*). At least I should be spared the possibility of her falling in love with me.

HARLEQUIN. How selfish of you! (*Moves from the fountain*) But come, if you are quite rested, let us continue our walk.

PIERROT (*moves from fountain*). To be perfectly frank, dear chap, I find your conversation has made me extremely sleepy.

HARLEQUIN (*haughtily*). There is a beautiful stone bench just beyond that clump of lilacs.

PIERROT. Thanks. When we reach it, I shall sit down.

HARLEQUIN. By all means, dear fellow. I can then resume my stroll without the encumbrance of your society.

[*They saunter off, arm in arm. Punchinello enters, dressed in a long, ragged, green coat, carrying a large sack and a little bell. He wears long whiskers and a pair of bone-rimmed spectacles. He advances, tapping before him with a staff and ringing his little bell.*

PUNCHINELLO (*in a whining singsong*). New loves for old! New loves for old! New loves for old! I will buy broken ambitions, wasted lives, cork legs, rejected poems, unfinished plays, bottles, bootjacks, and worn-out religions. (*Drops pack*) Oyez! Oyez! Oyez! New loves for old! New loves for old! (*He wags his head, listening*) Nobody here. Damn it all, I've walked three times round this accursed park with never so much as a squirrel to nibble at my heels. I've seen moon-faced boys asleep on stone benches, stone tritons blowing water into the air, and a rabble of sick looking poets and silly looking girls, all walking in the same direction. But not a bona fide customer. I'll sit down. Yes, yes, I'll sit down, curse them, and ease this infernal crick in my back.

[*He unfolds a little camp stool, which he carries slung by a strap, and sits down. Columbine and Margot enter from the left and advance timidly to the center of the stage without noticing Punchinello.*

COLUMBINE. I'm sure, Margot, that I saw him here only a minute ago talking to that silly clown in the yellow suit.

MARGOT. Well, anyway, whether it was him or an hallucination he's gone now.

COLUMBINE. Oh, dear! I thought he might have stopped to let me catch up with him.

MARGOT. Do you want my honest opinion, Mistress Columbine?

COLUMBINE (*stamping her foot*). How can an opinion be anything but honest? An opinion is naturally and automatically honest.

MARGOT. Mine ain't, m'am. I always formulates my opinions to conform.

COLUMBINE. I don't want them. I'm miserable. I'm wretched.

MARGOT (*severely*). Then I won't give them to you. But if you'd act more like a lady and stop trapesing around in the damp of the night trying to scrape acquaintance with — with this Harlequin who, God knows, may have six or seven wives already —

COLUMBINE. I'm not trapesing after him!

PUNCHINELLO (*in his singsong voice*). New loves for old! New loves for old!

COLUMBINE (*frightened*). Oh, how you startled me!

MARGOT (*her hand on her heart*). Lord love us! I near swallowed my tongue with the jump he gave me.

PUNCHINELLO (*rubbing his hands*). Bargains! Cheap, wonderful bargains! What will the young lady buy? Something for her parlor? Something for her bedroom? Something for herself? Wall paper, eggbeaters, canary birds, salt shakers, oriental rugs, corset covers, diamonds, water bags, chums, potato peelers, hats, shoes, gas fixtures, new, old — bargains, lady, bargains.

COLUMBINE. No, no, no! I don't want to buy anything.

PUNCHINELLO (*kneeling and spreading out his wares*). I have cures to sell, and charms.

MARGOT. Can't you see she doesn't want any of your patent medicines?

COLUMBINE (*fascinated in spite of herself*). What — what charms have you?

PUNCHINELLO. Ho, ho! I have a charm to ward off evil spirits.

MARGOT (*in disgust*). Get along with you!

PUNCHINELLO. Against nightmares, then; against mice, toothaches, bunions, burglars, and broken legs.

COLUMBINE. I don't want them, any of them.

PUNCHINELLO (*wagging his head*). Ho, ho! Ha, ha! Then you're in love. You want a love charm.

COLUMBINE (*stamping her foot*). You're impudent! I tell you I'm not in love.

MARGOT (*beginning to be interested*). What makes you pipe her off as being in love?

PUNCHINELLO. A lady who isn't interested in mice, bunions, or burglars must be in love. There's no two ways about it.

MARGOT. What about the broken legs and toothaches?

PUNCHINELLO (*spreading his hands*). I just put that in for good measure.

COLUMBINE. Enough! I won't listen to you. I'm — not in love.

PUNCHINELLO. I can remedy that with a charm.

COLUMBINE (*almost in tears*). I don't want your charms. I don't want to be in love. I hate him! I hate him! I hate him!

PUNCHINELLO. Yes, yes, pretty lady. I know that sort of talk very well. But I have also a charm to attract love.

COLUMBINE (*brightening immediately*). You have a charm to attract love?

PUNCHINELLO. It will bring all men to you; little men, big men, pretty men, noble men, fat men —

COLUMBINE (*clasping her hands*). I want only one man — only Harlequin.

MARGOT (*interrupting*). If you want my opinion, m'am —

COLUMBINE. But I don't.

MARGOT. I'd leave this fellow's stuff alone, if I was you.

COLUMBINE. But I'm not you and I want the charm.

PUNCHINELLO (*searching through his wares*). It will bring Harlequin to you with the rest.

COLUMBINE (*on tiptoe with eagerness*). Oh, quick! Give it to me.

PUNCHINELLO (*taking an old slipper from his pocket*). Ho, ho! Here it is. An old slipper! Each stitch of it more effective than Sappho's complete works. Each thread more potent than the burning caresses of Dido. They say Cinderella wore a crystal slipper. It's a lie. This — this is what she wore. Ah, ha! Look at it!

COLUMBINE (*taken aback*). Do I have to wear *that*.

MARGOT (*scornfully*). Land's sake, it's all run down at the heel.

PUNCHINELLO. That's because it has been worn so often. Semiramis of Babylon, Lais of Corinth, and Thais of Alexandria all wore this boot.

MARGOT (*with a sniff*). Them names don't sound like respectable ladies to my way of thinking.

COLUMBINE (*dubiously*). It looks very old. Are you sure it has been fumigated?

PUNCHINELLO. It's no older than the light it will kindle in a thousand eyes when you wear it. But in its antiquity lies its chief charm. Cleopatra of Egypt abetted the lures of her person with this same ragged boot. Mary of Scotland and a hundred other beauties of history have inspired the enraptured supplications of their adorers with no more tangible asset then this homely boot. Put it on, pretty lady, and all the men will flock to your feet, especially to the foot that wears the slipper.

[*He hands Columbine the slipper.*

COLUMBINE. Ooh, ooh! How wonderful!

MARGOT (*with a superior air*). Take my word, miss, it'll be a nuisance to you.

COLUMBINE. I don't care. I'm going to teach Harlequin a lesson he won't forget in a hurry.

[*She takes off her own shoe, hopping on one foot and holding Margot's arm. She then puts on the magic slipper.*

MARGOT. Mind, I warned you.

COLUMBINE (*stamping her foot down*). There! It doesn't look so badly once I get it on. It fits perfectly.

PUNCHINELLO (*groveling on his knees*). Oh, most wonderful lady! Oh, most beautiful, most gracious, most divine lady!

MARGOT (*amazed at Punchinello's sudden fervor*). Lord love us! What's got into the old bag of bones?

PUNCHINELLO (*to Columbine*). You have melted the lump of ice in my old breast. I am young again. I can hear the birds singing and sweet waters falling.

MARGOT (*to Punchinello*). Get up this minute, before I burst a lung bawling for help.

COLUMBINE (*dancing up and down with delight*). Oh, oh, oh! Now I know it works. Don't you understand, Margot? It's the slipper, the magic slipper.

PUNCHINELLO. I love you! I love you! I love you!

MARGOT. Stop it, I tell you.

COLUMBINE (*gently*). That's very nice in you, of course, but get up, please, and tell me how much I owe you.

MARGOT. We can't stand here all night.

PUNCHINELLO (*still on his knees*) Oh, oh, oh!

COLUMBINE (*stamping her foot*). Don't you hear me? I say how much do I owe you for the magic slipper?

PUNCHINELLO (*still groveling*). Nothing! Nothing! You owe me nothing at all. I will give you everything in my sack, all my bargains, all my spells, all my charms.

MARGOT. She wouldn't touch them with the tip of a barge pole.

COLUMBINE (*to Margot*). I really think I ought to pay him.

MARGOT. If he won't take anything he won't. That's all there is to it.

PUNCHINELLO. Speak to me. My heart is bursting.

MARGOT. Let it burst then. Come, m'am. It's my advice to get away from here before he throws a fit and the police come for him.

COLUMBINE. Yes, yes. Let's run.

[*Columbine takes Margot by the hand and they run off right, laughing.*

PUNCHINELLO (*attempting to rise*). Wait, wait! You must listen to me. I love you. I — I — Oh, this stitch in my side!

[*As the girls' voices die away he struggles to his feet and rubs his head in a dazed sort of way.*

Gone! What have I done? By the seven witches of Beelzebub, by the long fanged mother of the great green spider, I have given my magic slipper away for nothing. (*He shakes his staff*) I've been tricked, cheated. Curses on her golden head. May she have nightmares and toothache! May — Old fool! A blight on my whiskers! I've given my darling slipper away for nothing.

(*He sits down again on his camp stool and rocks to and fro, muttering. Harlequin, having completed his circle of the park, enters from the left. He is smoking a cigarette and strolls along, wearing a gloomy and troubled expression. Punchinello sees him and resumes his whining chant*)

New loves for old. New loves for old. Bargains in cast-off sweethearts, old coats, umbrellas, glove buttoners, and household pets. Bargains sir. Cheap, wonderful bargains!

(*Harlequin passes and regards Punchinello with absolute indifference*)

I have pipes, swords, hosiery, snuff-boxes, underwear, wines, trinkets for beautiful ladies, furniture, spyglasses, motor cars, and bottle openers.

HARLEQUIN (*impatiently*). I want none of your bargains.

PUNCHINELLO. I have magic charms, sir. Spells and charms.

HARLEQUIN. Ah, more like it! You have charms, eh? What kind of charms?

PUNCHINELLO. I have charms against bunions, burglars, broken legs, nightmares, stomach-aches, and hangnails.

HARLEQUIN. Ordinary trash. I don't want them.

PUNCHINELLO (*looking furtively about*). I have a love charm.

HARLEQUIN (*in alarm*) God forbid!

PUNCHINELLO (*rubbing his hands*). Ho, ho! He, he!

HARLEQUIN. Have you, by any chance, a charm against love? Aye, more, have you some efficacious armour against womankind in general?

PUNCHINELLO. Ho, ho! A man after my own heart. A cautious man. A sensible man.

HARLEQUIN (*loftily*). Know you, antiquated pander, that in this day, a young man's lot is not a happy one. Everywhere I go, excepting only this park, women follow me. They stalk me. They covet me. They make my days miserable. They haunt my sleep. They simper about me, wink at me, rub against me like silken cats. (*With vexation*) Ah, I would almost end my life from very irritation with their wiles, their snaring pursuits, from the very annoyance of their cloying affection. And the worst part of it is that I know myself susceptible.

PUNCHINELLO (*slyly*). There is no charm in the world against falling in love, but I can sell you a powder which, tossed into the air, will bring destruction to women alone.

HARLEQUIN (*rubbing his chin doubifully*). No, that's too brutal. I couldn't kill them all even if I wanted to. And what use to destroy a hundred, a thousand, even a million women, and have one sneak up behind you and get you after all. It would be an effort wasted. Love is inevitable.

PUNCHINELLO. Wait. Ho, ho! I have it, the very thing. If one cannot remove the inevitable, at any rate one can hide from it. What doesn't see you, can't get you. Ha, ha! I can sell you a hat.

HARLEQUIN. I am not in the market for a hat.

PUNCHINELLO (*triumphantly*). But, a magic hat! A Wonder Hat! It will make you invisible.

HARLEQUIN (*incredulously*). Invisible!

PUNCHINELLO (*fishing in his bag*). When you put it on, you will be invisible to the world. You will exist only in your own mind. You will escape the pernicious sentimentality, the never-ending blandishments, the strategic coquetry of women. Ho, ho! Ha, ha!

HARLEQUIN (*eagerly*). Come, you millinery sorcerer. You have convinced me. Invisibility is the one thing I crave to make me sublimely happy. Splendid. They shall never simper at me again, never undulate before my tormented eyes. I will buy it.

PUNCHINELLO (*holding up the hat*). Is it not a creation?

HARLEQUIN (*looking at the hat with distaste*). God, what a thing to wear! I would not wear it, you may be sure, were it not invisible. Being invisible, I assure you, is its chief charm. Indeed, any man would prefer not to be seen in such a hat.

PUNCHINELLO. It may be unlovely in outline, coarse in texture, unrefined in color, but there is only one other such hat in the world. It belongs to the Grand Llamah of Thibet. Ha, ha! This one will cost you gold.

HARLEQUIN (*cautiously*). But, first I must see if it is really a wonder hat.

PUNCHINELLO. I will put it on.

[*He does so.*

HARLEQUIN (*delighted*). A miracle! Where are you?

PUNCHINELLO (*removing the hat with a flourish*). Now!

HARLEQUIN. What wonders I will do with that hat. I will walk the streets in comfort and security. But stay! What if the hat is only charmed for you? What if the charm does not apply to me?

PUNCHINELLO. You shall try it yourself. Put it on.

[*Harlequin takes the hat and puts it on.*

HARLEQUIN. Can you see me?

PUNCHINELLO. By St. Peter of Padua, not a speck of you! [*He gropes with his hands, then strikes out with his staff and strikes Harlequin on the shins.*

HARLEQUIN. Ooh! Ouch!

PUNCHINELLO. You see you are quite invisible.

HARLEQUIN. But not invulnerable.

[*He rubs his shin.*

PUNCHINELLO. How much will you give me for this Wonder Hat?

HARLEQUIN. Are you sure you can't see me?

PUNCHINELLO. You are one with the thin air and the fairies that inhabit it.

[*Rubbing his hands.*

HARLEQUIN. There's no uncanny trick by which Columbine can discover me?

PUNCHINELLO. None! None! I swear it. It's only by
your voice that I know where you are.

[*He swings out with his staff. Harlequin leaps nimbly aside.*

PUNCHINELLO. For years I have treasured this wonder hat.
A blind woman with seven teeth and one eye made it in
a haunted hut. It was cooked over a fire of serpents'
skins. (*As Punchinello speaks, Harlequin tiptoes away to
the right around the central group of shrubbery*) It is colored
with the dye of a magic root. It is older than the oldest
cloud and you can figure out for yourself how old that
would be. Ho, ho! There's no charm like it to be had
from one peak of the world to the other. (*He swings
out again with his staff*) Five bags of gold, sir. Cheap,
a bargain. Hey! (*He swings his staff*) Hey! Hey!
Where are you? Take off my hat so that I can see you.
Give me back my hat. (*He stands still and listens*)
Thief! Thief! He's gone. Oh, what a fool. First
my magic slipper, worth fifty pots of gold. What
a doddering idiot! I have lost my magic hat, my wonder
hat. I've been cheated, robbed. Oh, what a stitch in
my side. Oh, oh! (*He gathers up his pack hurriedly, then
stops and taps the side of his nose with his finger*) Ho, ho!
A thought! What a pair of lovers they will make! She
with her slipper. He with his hat. She said Harlequin.
He said Columbine. Yes, yes! I shall have my reward.
They are the fools, not I. As if love were not enough
magic of itself. Ho, ho, ho! I must follow her. She
went this way.

[*He moves off toward the right, leaving his camp stool. Harlequin appears round the left end of the shrubbery and advances cautiously to center of stage.*

HARLEQUIN (*looking after Punchinello*). I should have paid
him if he hadn't run away like that. I detest the idea of
cheating anybody. But of course, one can't be running
after tradespeople, pressing money upon them. It simply
isn't done. (*He looks in the other direction*) Columbine
should have made the round of the park by this time.

What's keeping her? Here I am waiting for her, as safe and invisible as the angels themselves. (*He sits down on the camp stool and holds his hand before his face*) No, I can't see it. I wonder if I have a hand or a leg, or a stomach, or a heart? If I don't take off my hat and look at myself I shall soon become a total stranger to myself. What a wonder hat! (*There is the sound of women's voices in the distance. He pricks up his ears*) Ah, her voice! Like the tinkling bells in a shrine of ivory. Like the patter of crystal rain in a pool of scarlet lilies. (*He slaps his leg*) Ah, ha! I'm in love. In love! To the tips of where my fingers ought to be. (*He becomes serious*) If I should take off my hat, I'd be lost. She would pounce on me, and, being in love, I should pounce back. My hat must stay on. I will tie it on. I will nail it on. Curse me if I take off my hat. (*He pulls his hat down to the tips of his ears, then clasps his hands*) Ah, to sit by her, safe and unseen! To bask in the splendor of her presence. To love and be loved only as a dream. To be free from all material entanglements and responsibilities. To touch her with invisible fingers and permit the stolen thrills to course up and down my invisible spine! (*He sings*)

Wandering Minstrel Air

A love-sick atom I,
A thing unseen and seeing,
For in my hat am I
A hypothetical being.

(*He suddenly has a new thought*) But what if, being unable to see me, she should fall in love with somebody else? That vapid ass, Pierrot, for instance? Oh, God, what if he should strike fire in her heart? But I will not take off my hat. Kind heaven, give me the strength to keep my hat on.
[*He pulls the hat still further over his ears, just as Columbine and Margot enter from the left.*

COLUMBINE. This is too much! Did you ever see such a rabble?

MARGOT. I shouldn't be so particular, miss, seeing as how you brought it on yourself.

COLUMBINE. They've risen from every bench to follow me. They've come from every corner of the park; burglars, doctors, poets, whiskered Don Juans, rumbling Romeos. Great Heavens, the idiots! If they hadn't fallen to fighting among themselves, we'd have been trampled to death. I — I hope they exterminate each other. I hope I never see them again. I — I —

[*Harlequin, seeing Columbine in such an angry mood, rises cautiously and in so doing upsets the camp stool. He stands trembling and holding on to his hat.*

MARGOT (*starting*). Bless me, what's that?

[*Both look around. Their eyes pass over Harlequin without seeing him.*

COLUMBINE. Nothing. There's nobody here.

[*Evidently much relieved, Harlequin tiptoes to the right end of the fountain.*

MARGOT. If you want my honest opinion, miss —

COLUMBINE (*stamping her foot*). How many times must I tell you —

MARGOT. Be careful with that magic boot, miss.

COLUMBINE. What's the good of it? It's brought me nothing but trouble.

MARGOT. Well, what did you expect?

COLUMBINE (*almost weeping*). It hasn't brought him. It hasn't brought Harlequin.

MARGOT. If you want my opinion, miss, honest or otherwise —

COLUMBINE (*stamping her foot again*). I don't!

MARGOT. Then I won't give it to you.

COLUMBINE. Oh, Margot, be gentle with me. I love him — and I'm dreadfully uncomfortable about it.

MARGOT. Well, there's worse discomfort. There's clergyman's sore throat, for instance, and housemaid's knee.

COLUMBINE (*clinching her hands*). Oh, if I could only see him now, the cold-hearted fish! I'd fix him! I'd melt his icy blood for him!

[*Harlequin holds tight to his hat.*

MARGOT (*soothingly*). Of course you would. Of course you would.

COLUMBINE (*sits on fountain*). But he can't escape. The magic slipper will draw him from the ends of the earth. I'll marry him. I'll have him for my own, locked under key in a house; a beautiful little house, all new and spick and span, with white trimmings and green shutters.

MARGOT. If I may put in a word for myself, miss, I hope you won't have a basement kitchen.

COLUMBINE. But I'll make him suffer first. I'll — I'll (*spitefully*) —

[*Harlequin jams his hat down tighter and disappears behind the fountain.*

MARGOT. If you must get het up and stamp, miss, I'd advise you to confine your stamping to the foot which ain't got the magic boot on.

COLUMBINE. Margot, were you ever in love?

MARGOT. You know very well, miss, I have three babies at home.

COLUMBINE. Tell me, did you love their father?

MARGOT. It's my honest opinion, miss, there were three fathers, and I loved them all very much.

COLUMBINE (*shocked*). Then you're a wicked woman.

MARGOT. There are opinions concerning that question, miss, honest and otherwise.

COLUMBINE. You are, I say.

MARGOT. Which I choose, begging your pardon, to consider as an otherwise opinion. Being a father to three babies puts an awful responsibility on a man, as you may find out for yourself some day. So I was careful to distribute the burden.

[*Pierrot enters dishevelled and breathless. He advances and flings himself on one knee before Columbine.*

PIERROT. At last, exquisite Columbine, ravishing vision, I have overcome my rivals. I have vanquished a legion of your adorers.

[*Harlequin peeps round the left side of the fountain.*

MARGOT. Lord love us, you look as though you'd been run through a threshing machine.

PIERROT. I have. I kicked Scaramouche in the stomach and pushed the Doctor of Bologna into a lily pond. Divine Circe, I have come to claim my reward.

[*He clutches at the edge of Columbine's dress.*

COLUMBINE. You're tearing the trimming off my petticoat.

PIERROT. Columbine, Columbine, I love you!

MARGOT (*taking his arm and pulling him to his feet*). Get up, you big baby.

[*Harlequin tiptoes across the stage and stands behind Margot and Pierrot.*

PIERROT (*clasping his hands*). I love you, Columbine. Listen to me.

COLUMBINE (*haughtily*). This is a very sudden change on your part, Mr. Pierrot. Yesterday you snubbed me quite openly.

PIERROT. Forgive me! I was blind! I was a dolt. I have only just now come to my senses.

MARGOT (*turning her shoulder to him and folding her arms*). You'll come to something worse presently.

PIERROT. I love you. I love you.

[*Harlequin reaches out and deftly extracts a long hat pin from the back of Margot's cap. Margot puts her hands to her head and turns fiercely on Pierrot.*

MARGOT. How dast you grab my hat?

PIERROT (*in astonishment*). I never touched your hat.

MARGOT. You did.

PIERROT (*turning on her*). I — I did nothing of the sort.

MARGOT. There's laws to cover this sort of thing — annoying women in a public park.

PIERROT. You're an impudent hussy.

MARGOT. You're nothing but a common, ordinary home wrecker.

[*Harlequin approaches Columbine and gently touches her hair. Pierrot and Margot glare at each other.*

COLUMBINE (*clasping her hands*). Margot, Margot, it's wonderful! It's divine. I feel as if the air were suddenly full of kisses.

[*Harlequin strikes an attitude of complete satisfaction.*

MARGOT. It's full of dampness and nasty language, that's what it is.

[*She gives Pierrot a venomous look.*

PIERROT (*again falling on his knees*). It's full of unspeakable ecstasy of my adoration.

COLUMBINE (*paying no attention to him*). It's full of marvelously shy caresses. They are like the wings of happy butterflies, brushing the white lilac blooms.

PIERROT. Ah, what did I tell you? The love I offer you is a gift, a treasure.

COLUMBINE (*her hands still clasped*). I can almost hear invisible lips sighing my name — his lips — Harlequin's lips.

PIERROT (*straightening himself up on his knees*). What's that you say about Harlequin?

COLUMBINE (*coming to herself*). It's none of your business.

PIERROT (*spitefully*). Good God! To think of intruding that fellow's name at a time like this. Why, the chap's positively a bounder. He has no taste, no education, no refinement. And his face — ugh! He'd frighten himself to death if he looked in a mirror before his barber got to him in the morning.

[*Harlequin steps behind Pierrot and prods him in the back with the hat pin.*

PIERROT. Ooh! Ouch! (*He springs to his feet and turns on Margot*) You — you did that. You — you know you did.

[*Shaking his finger in her face.*

MARGOT (*taken aback*). Did what?

PIERROT (*in a rage*). You — you stabbed me in the back and don't you deny it.

MARGOT. The man's stark, staring mad!

COLUMBINE (*to Pierrot in an icy tone*). Will you be good enough to explain what's the matter with you?

PIERROT (*his eyes still on Margot*). I've been attacked, lacerated.

MARGOT. If you don't behave yourself, I'll give you something to howl about.

PIERROT (*again falling at Columbine's feet*). But it's nothing, nothing to the torments I suffer from your heartlessness. Nothing to the —
(*Harlequin stabs again*)
Ouch! Wow! Hell's fire! Animals! I'm being bitten to death!
[*He clasps his hand to the spot.*

MARGOT. And a good riddance, too!

COLUMBINE. Come, Margot. I won't stay here. I won't be insulted.

PIERROT (*again grasping the hem of her gown*). No, no, I'll suffer everything. I'll suffer in silence. Only don't leave me. Speak to me. I love you. I —

COLUMBINE. Let go my dress or I'll scream for help.

MARGOT. If you really want help, miss, it's my advice take off the slipper.
[*Harlequin, who has been about to attack Pierrot, hesitates and looks puzzled.*

COLUMBINE. Yes, yes. Why didn't I think of it.
[*She whips off the magic slipper and holds it in her hand. The moment the slipper leaves her foot, Pierrot sits back on his haunches and lets go of the edge of Columbine's dress.*

PIERROT (*in a feeble voice*). I love you. I — (*He rubs his head*) By Jove, this is most extraordinary!

MARGOT (*clapping her hands*). Toss it to me, miss.
[*Columbine tosses the slipper to Margot.*

MARGOT (*examining the slipper*). What a rummy slipper! (*She takes off her shoe*) I wonder what's inside of it. Love? (*She puts it on her own foot*) Ooh! How it tickles!

[*Pierrot rises from his knees and looks helplessly from Columbine to Margot.*

COLUMBINE.   Well, Mr. Pierrot?

PIERROT (*completely puzzled*).   I am quite at a loss to explain my feelings.

[*He hesitates, then turns and kneels before Margot. Harlequin appears even more puzzled. He is also drawn toward Margot by the spell of the slipper, but his natural infatuation for Columbine seems to neutralize the charm. He is visibly perplexed.*

PIERROT.   Incomparable Margot! Queen among housemaids! Divine custodian of my deepest affections.

MARGOT.   You see, miss, the gentleman is now in love with me.

COLUMBINE.   Disgusting!

PIERROT.   I am drawn by some irresistible power of fascination.   I — belong to you utterly.

MARGOT.   You belong in jail, that's where you belong. You're nothing but a — a shameless affinity.

PIERROT (*clinging to the hem of Margot's skirt*).   I love you. I swear it. See, I kiss the hem of your gown. I throw myself on your mercy.

MARGOT (*weakening*).   Oh, la, la! Listen to the man talk!

COLUMBINE.   You're a brazen hussy to take advantage of your social superior.

MARGOT (*haughtily*).   My superior? Him?

COLUMBINE (*stamping her foot*).   You're forgetting your place.

PIERROT.   I love you.   I love you.

MARGOT (*slyly*).   Suppose, miss, I was to say I believe every word he says to me?

COLUMBINE.   I'd say you were an artful, designing minx. I'd discharge you without a shred of character.

MARGOT.   Well, you won't have to — because I ain't going to say it.

PIERROT (*making another grab at her skirt*).   You must listen to me.   You must.

[*Harlequin stabs him once more with the hat pin.*

Ouch! Wow! This is terrible.   I love you.

MARGOT.   Hey!   Get up.   A woman what works for a living can't afford to have her good nerves shattered for her. [*She tries to shake off Pierrot.*

COLUMBINE.   Give me back the slipper, this instant.

MARGOT.   You're welcome to it, I'm sure.
(*She snatches off the slipper and tosses it away from her. Columbine picks it up, but does not put it on*)
Now will you leave go of me?
[*To Pierrot.   He releases her in a dazed way.*

PIERROT.   I love you.   I —
[*He arises and again looks from one to the other.   Columbine holds the slipper in her hand.*

COLUMBINE.   Well, sir?

MARGOT.   Well?

PIERROT (*adjusting his collar and speaking quite calmly*).   I consider myself fortunate in having escaped you both.   I see now that there is something deadly about that slipper. To think that a man of my intellectual and artistic attainments should have been affected by such a slippery artifice.   In love with a boot!   How very trivial!

MARGOT.   Well, what are you going to do now?

PIERROT.   I don't know exactly.   Perhaps I shall drown myself in the fountain.
[*He turns his back on Margot and Columbine and assumes a pose of thoughtful indifference.   Harlequin again approaches Columbine.*

COLUMBINE.   Margot, Margot, what shall I do?   I'm faint. I'm intoxicated.   He hasn't come and yet I feel as if he were near me, almost touching me.   I feel all the exquisite uncertainty of love.   Yes, yes, I love him.   I love Harlequin and I know that he loves me in return.   I know it, and yet, and yet —

MARGOT.   Yes, miss, and yet —?

COLUMBINE (*wringing her hands*).   And yet I don't know what under heavens to do about it.
[*Harlequin clasps his hands in an ecstasy of complete satisfaction.   Margot and Columbine are now at one side and*

Margot speaks in a tone which Harlequin and Pierrot are not supposed to hear.

MARGOT. It's my advice, miss, put the slipper on again. What if it don't catch this here Harlequin? There's just as big perch in the puddle as ever came out of it. That's my motto. Besides, there is such a thing as making the right man jealous.

COLUMBINE (*brightening immediately*). I believe you're right. I'll put on the slipper. I'll have a desperate flirtation with Pierrot. I'll take him everywhere with me. I'll dangle him before Harlequin's eyes. It will serve them both right. (*She puts on the slipper and speaks archly*) Mr. Pierrot.

PIERROT (*turning*). Eh? I beg your pardon.

COLUMBINE. I — don't want you to be angry with me.

[*Pierrot looks puzzled for a moment, then succumbs to the spell of the slipper again and rushes toward her.*

PIERROT. I — I don't — (*He throws himself on his knees*) Columbine, Columbine, my angel, my flower, my enchantress!

COLUMBINE (*shaking her finger at him*). You were very rude to me a few moments ago.

[*Harlequin watches with puzzled interest.*

PIERROT. Forgive me! It was a dream. I love you!

COLUMBINE. You accused me of having ensnared your affections by means of a charm.

PIERROT. A charm? I don't know anything about a charm. I am charmed only by your eyes, your lips, the flow of your voice.

COLUMBINE. Do you know I think it's very sweet of you to say that, after all that's happened this evening.

PIERROT. I can say more, a thousand times more.

COLUMBINE. Perhaps I shall give you the chance.

HARLEQUIN (*aloud, completely overcome with jealousy*). Here's a fine kettle of fish!

PIERROT. You — you do love me then, after all?

COLUMBINE. I haven't said so.

HARLEQUIN. I shall put a stop to this. (*He seems to come to a tremendous resolution*) I — I shall take off my hat.

MARGOT. Lord have mercy, what is that?

COLUMBINE. Please give me your arm.

HARLEQUIN. Thousand devils, I can't get it off!

COLUMBINE. You may see me to my door.

HARLEQUIN (*frantically*). Wait! Stop! — If, — if I could only get my hat off!

MARGOT (*alarmed*). I want to get away from here.

COLUMBINE (*listening*). It's Harlequin's voice.

PIERROT. I don't see anybody.

[*They all look about them. Punchinello enters from the left with his pack on his back. They all see him.*

PUNCHINELLO. Ho, ho, ha ha! There you are, eh? There you are. I've been looking for you. Ho, ho! And now I've caught up with you.

[*Columbine hastily snatches off her slipper and hides it behind her. They all face Punchinello. Harlequin tiptoes to one side and watches curiously.*

COLUMBINE. What do you want?

PUNCHINELLO. What do I want, eh? You know very well what I want. I want my magic slipper, my magic slipper that you stole from me.

COLUMBINE. I didn't steal it. You gave it to me.

PUNCHINELLO. Ho, ho! That's a pretty story. I gave it to you, eh? Well, I changed my mind.

COLUMBINE. I — I'm perfectly willing to pay you for it.

MARGOT. Don't you give him a cent, the miserable oyster.

COLUMBINE. How much do you want for it?

PUNCHINELLO. I should think about ten bags of gold.

COLUMBINE. Ridiculous! There isn't so much money in the whole world.

PUNCHINELLO (*pointing to Pierrot*). Perhaps this nice gentleman would like to buy it for you?

PIERROT. I — (*He looks at Columbine*) I have only the most casual acquaintance with this lady.

HARLEQUIN (*in a rage, to Pierrot*). You infernal little cad! You —
[*He makes a movement toward Pierrot. All start away from his voice but Punchinello.*

PUNCHINELLO. Ho, ho! So you're here. Two birds with one stone. (*He rubs his hands*) My magic slipper and my beloved Wonder Hat. Well, well, well!
(*Harlequin, seeing he has betrayed his presence, stands as if undecided what to do. Punchinello strikes about him with his staff*)
Hey, where are you? Take off my hat.

MARGOT. For the love of heaven, what is he raving about now?

PUNCHINELLO. My hat, my Wonder Hat. I sold it to Harlequin for five bags of gold — six bags of gold.

COLUMBINE. You sold it to Harlequin?

PUNCHINELLO. Aye, the ruffian, the highwayman. He clapped it on his head and now he's invisible.

COLUMBINE (*in delighted wonder*). You really mean that Harlequin is here, near us? Oh, I knew it. I felt it.

PUNCHINELLO. Of course, he's here. Hey, you, take off my hat. (*He swings his staff and Harlequin dances out of the way*)
Take off my hat or give me my eight bags of gold. (*He swings his staff again*) Hey, thief!

HARLEQUIN. I'm not a thief. I'd have paid you for your hat if you hadn't run away in such a huff. Now, after the way you've acted, I shall take my own time about it.

COLUMBINE (*stamping her foot*). Harlequin.

HARLEQUIN (*in a dubious voice*). Ye — yes?

COLUMBINE. Take off that silly hat this minute!

HARLEQUIN. I — well, to tell the truth, I —

COLUMBINE. Don't you hear what I'm saying? Give it back this second.

HARLEQUIN. I would first like some sort of assurance, some guarantee of good faith, some —

COLUMBINE. I'm not making any promises this evening.

HARLEQUIN (*plaintively*). My dear Columbine, I have learned a good deal about my own feelings in the last half hour. I am perfectly willing to return this man's property and to submit to the ordinary and normal risks of society, but I positively insist that, before I reveal myself, you must also return to him all sundry charms, spells, et cetera, which might, if used either by accident or malice aforethought, affect my own future course of action.

COLUMBINE (*remaining absolutely firm*). I've told you once that I won't make any promises.

HARLEQUIN. Then, I remain invisible.

PUNCHINELLO. I tell you once more, give me back my hat.

HARLEQUIN (*folding his arms*). No.

PUNCHINELLO. Ah, ha! Then I shall have my revenge. Know, miserable butterfly, that you are trifling with magic beyond your own powers of control. There is a terrible clause in the incorporation of this hat. Listen. He who steals this Wonder Hat and places it upon his own head, cannot remove it again except in the presence and with the consent of its rightful owner. When I have left you, you will become for all time one with the interstellar atoms. You will never resume your mortal shape. You will haunt the cafés. You will moon among the boxes at the opera. You will sigh and pine in the wake of beautiful women, as futile and impalpable as a gust of summer wind. (*He picks up his pack*) Now, will you give me back my hat?

HARLEQUIN (*with evident effort at firmness*). No, not unless Columbine first returns the slipper.

PUNCHINELLO. Madam, I make my last appeal to you.

COLUMBINE (*folding her arms*). Not unless Harlequin first returns the hat.

[*Punchinello looks from one to the other.*

PUNCHINELLO. Come, ladies and gentlemen, I have urgent business elsewhere.

PIERROT. Might I suggest that the simplest way out of the dilemma would be for each of the principal parties to return the pilfered articles at the same exact time.

PUNCHINELLO. An excellent idea. *He goes center*

PIERROT. I shall count, and at the word "three" — is that satisfactory to everybody?

HARLEQUIN (*doubtfully*). Ye — yes.

COLUMBINE (*doubtfully*). Ye — yes.

PIERROT. Very well, then. One — (*Harlequin begins to loosen the hat*) Two —

MARGOT (*stepping forward*). Stop, everybody. You, Mistress Columbine, and you, invisible Mr. Harlequin. Because no matter what you do, somebody's bound to regret it. You, wherever you are, keep your lid on and your mouth shut. I want to put it up to the kind ladies and gentlemen that have been studying this performance and I asks them openly, what should be done at this point? Should Columbine give back the slipper or should she hang on to what she's got? Should Harlequin take off his hat? Personally, my honest opinion is that the question can't be answered to suit everybody so it's my advice that we ring down right here and allow every one to go home and fix up an ending to conform to the state of one's own digestion.

PIERROT. But you know, we're being paid to finish this thing.

HARLEQUIN. Paid? We're not working for money. We're working for love.

COLUMBINE. Love!

MARGOT. Aw, hell!

QUICK CURTAIN

SUPPRESSED DESIRES

GEORGE CRAM COOK

Mr. George Cram Cook was born in Davenport, Iowa, in 1873. He studied at the University of Iowa, Harvard, Heidelberg, and the University of Geneva. He was professor at the University of Iowa from 1895 to 1899, and at Leland Stanford University from 1902 to 1903. In 1911 he was Associate Literary Editor of the *Chicago Evening Post*.

He is the author of: "In Hampton Roads" (novel), "Roderick Taliaferro", "Evolution and the Superman", "The Chasm" (novel), "Battle Hymn of the Workers", "An American Hero", "The Third American Sex", "The W.C.T.U.", "The Breath of War" (play), and, in collaboration with Susan Glaspell, the two plays: "Suppressed Desires" and "Tickless Time."

He has been director of the Provincetown Players — of Provincetown, Massachusetts, in the summer, and of Greenwich Village, New York City, in the winter — since 1915. This organization has been one of the most ambitious of the Little Theatres of America, giving only original productions of new American plays. It has lived through the War, and has completed (1918–1919) its most substantial season, giving six different bills, each for an entire week.

SUSAN GLASPELL

Miss Susan Glaspell (Mrs. George Cram Cook) was born in Davenport, Iowa, in 1882. She studied at Drake University, Iowa, where she received the degree of Ph.B. After taking post-graduate work at the University of Chicago, she became State House and Legislative Reporter of *The News and the Capital*, Des Moines, Iowa.

She has contributed several stories to various magazines. Her novels are: "The Glory of the Conquered", "The Visioning", "Lifted Masks", and "Fidelity."

She has interested herself in the Little Theatre movement, and in the work of the Provincetown Players especially. All of her one-act plays have been produced in New York by this organization. They are: "Trifles", "Suppressed Desires" (in collaboration with George Cram Cook), "The People", "Close the Book", "The Outside", "Woman's Honor", and "Tickless Time" (in collaboration with George Cram Cook). She has written one three-act play, "Bernice", which has also been produced by the Provincetown Players.

SUPPRESSED DESIRES

SCENE I

The stage represents a studio, used as living and dining room in an upper story, Washington Square South. Through an immense north window in the back wall appear tree tops and the upper part of the Washington Arch. Beyond it you look up Fifth Avenue. There are rugs, bookcases, a divan. Near the window is a big table, loaded at one end with serious-looking books and austere scientific periodicals. At the other end are architect's drawings, blue prints, dividing compasses, square, ruler, etc. There is a door in each side wall. Near the one to the spectator's right stands a costumer with hats and coats, masculine and feminine. There is a breakfast table set for three, but only two seated at it — namely Henrietta and Stephen Brewster. As the curtains withdraw Steve pushes back his coffee cup and sits dejected.

HENRIETTA. It isn't the coffee, Steve dear. There's nothing the matter with the coffee. There's something the matter with *you.*

STEVE (*doggedly*). There may be something the matter with my stomach.

HENRIETTA (*scornfully*). Your stomach! The trouble is not with your stomach but in your subconscious mind.

STEVE. Subconscious piffle!

[*Takes morning paper and tries to read.*

HENRIETTA. Steve, you never used to be so disagreeable. You certainly have got some sort of a complex. You're all inhibited. You're no longer open to new ideas. You won't listen to a word about psychoanalysis.

STEVE. A word! I've listened to volumes!

HENRIETTA. You've ceased to be creative in architecture — your work isn't going well. You're not sleeping well —

STEVE. How can I sleep, Henrietta, when you're always waking me up in the night to find out what I'm dreaming?

HENRIETTA. But dreams are so important, Steve. If you'd tell yours to Dr. Russell he'd find out exactly what's wrong with you.

STEVE. There's nothing wrong with me.

HENRIETTA. You don't even talk as well as you used to.

STEVE. Talk? I can't say a thing without you looking at me in that dark fashion you have when you're on the trail of a complex.

HENRIETTA. This very irritability indicates that you're suffering from some suppressed desire.

STEVE. I'm suffering from a suppressed desire for a little peace.

HENRIETTA. Dr. Russell is doing simply wonderful things with nervous cases. Won't you go to him, Steve?

STEVE (*slamming down his newspaper*). No Henrietta, I won't!

HENRIETTA. But, Stephen — !

STEVE. Tst! I hear Mabel coming. Let's not be at each other's throats the first day of her visit.

[*He takes out cigarettes. Enter Mabel from door left, the side opposite Steve, so that he is facing her. She is wearing a rather fussy negligee and breakfast cap in contrast to Henrietta, who wears "radical" clothes. Mabel is what is called plump.*

MABEL. Good morning.

HENRIETTA. Oh, here you are, little sister.

STEVE. Good morning, Mabel. [*Mabel nods to him and turns, her face lighting up, to Henrietta.*

HENRIETTA (*giving Mabel a hug as she leans against her*). It's so good to have you here. I was going to let you sleep, thinking you'd be tired after the long trip. Sit down. There'll be fresh toast in a minute and (*rising from her chair*) will you have —

MABEL. Oh, I ought to have told you, Henrietta. Don't get anything for me. I'm not eating any breakfast.

HENRIETTA (*at first in mere surprise*). Not eating breakfast? [*She sits down, then leans toward Mabel and scrutinizes her.*

STEVE (*half to himself*). The psychoanalytical look!

HENRIETTA. Mabel, why are you not eating breakfast?

MABEL (*a little startled*). Why, no particular reason. I just don't care much for breakfast, and they say it keeps down — that is, it's a good thing to go without it.

HENRIETTA. Don't you sleep well? Did you sleep well last night?

MABEL. Oh, yes, I sleep all right. Yes, I slept fine last night, only (*laughing*) I did have the funniest dream!

STEVE. S — h! S — t!

HENRIETTA (*moving closer*). And what did you dream, Mabel?

STEVE. Look-a-here, Mabel, I feel it's my duty to put you on. Don't tell Henrietta your dreams. If you do she'll find out that you have an underground desire to kill your father and marry your mother —

HENRIETTA. Don't be absurd, Stephen Brewster. (*Sweetly to Mabel*) What was your dream, dear?

MABEL (*laughing*). Well, I dreamed I was a hen.

HENRIETTA. A hen?

MABEL. Yes; and I was pushing along through a crowd as fast as I could, but being a hen I couldn't walk very fast — it was like having a tight skirt, you know; and there was some sort of creature in a blue cap — you know how mixed up dreams are — and it kept shouting after me and saying, "Step, Hen! Step, Hen!" until I got all excited and just couldn't move at all.

HENRIETTA (*resting chin in palm and peering*). You say you became much excited?

MABLE (*laughing*). Oh, yes; I was in a terrible state.

HENRIETTA (*leaning back, murmurs*). This is significant.

STEVE. She dreams she's a hen. She is told to step lively. She becomes violently agitated. What can it mean?

HENRIETTA (*turning impatiently from him*). Mabel, do you know anything about psychoanalysis?

MABEL (*feebly*). Oh — not much. No — I — (*brightening*) It's something about the war, isn't it?

STEVE. Not that kind of war.

MABEL (*abashed*). I thought it might be the name of a new explosive.

STEVE. It *is*.

MABEL (*apologetically to Henrietta, who is frowning*). You see, Henrietta, I — we do not live in touch with intellectual things, as you do. Bob being a dentist — somehow — our friends —

STEVE (*softly*). Oh to be a dentist!
[*Goes to window and stands looking out.*

HENRIETTA. Don't you ever see anything more of that editorial writer — what was his name?

MABEL. Lyman Eggleston?

HENRIETTA. Yes, Eggleston. He was in touch with things. Don't you see him?

MABEL. Yes, I see him once in a while. Bob doesn't like him very well.

HENRIETTA. Your husband does not like Lyman Eggleston? (*Mysteriously*) Mabel, are you perfectly happy with your husband?

STEVE (*sharply*). Oh, come now, Henrietta — that's going a little strong!

HENRIETTA. Are you perfectly happy with him, Mabel?
[*Steve goes to work-table.*

MABEL. Why — yes — I guess so. Why — of course I am!

HENRIETTA. Are you happy? Or do you only think you are? Or do you only think you *ought* to be?

MABEL. Why, Henrietta, I don't know what you mean!

STEVE (*seizes stack of books and magazines and dumps them on the breakfast table*). This is what she means, Mabel. Psychoanalysis. My work-table groans with it. Books by Freud, the new Messiah; books by Jung, the new S

Paul; the Psycho-analytical Review — back numbers two-fifty per.

MABEL.   But what's it all about?

STEVE.   All about your sub-un-non-conscious mind and desires you know not of.   They may be doing you a great deal of harm.   You may go crazy with them.   Oh, yes! People are doing it right and left.   Your dreaming you're a hen —

[*Shakes his head darkly.*

HENRIETTA.   Any fool can ridicule anything.

MABEL (*hastily, to avert a quarrel*).   But what do you say it is, Henrietta?

STEVE (*looking at his watch*).   Oh, if Henrietta's going to start that!

[*He goes to his work-table, and during Henrietta's next speech settles himself and sharpens a lead pencil.*

HENRIETTA.   It's like this, Mabel.   You want something. You think you can't have it.   You think it's wrong.   So you try to think you don't want it.   Your mind protects you — avoids pain — by refusing to think the forbidden thing.   But it's there just the same.   It stays there shut up in your unconscious mind, and it festers.

STEVE.   Sort of an ingrowing mental toenail.

HENRIETTA.   Precisely.   The forbidden impulse is there full of energy which has simply got to do something.   It breaks into your consciousness in disguise, masks itself in dreams, makes all sorts of trouble.   In extreme cases it drives you insane.

MABEL (*with a gesture of horror*).   Oh!

HENRIETTA (*reassuringly*).   But psychoanalysis has found out how to save us from that.   It brings into consciousness the suppressed desire that was making all the trouble. Psychoanalysis is simply the latest scientific method of preventing and curing insanity.

STEVE (*from his table*).   It is also the latest scientific method of separating families.

HENRIETTA (*mildly*).   Families that ought to be separated.

STEVE. The Dwights, for instance. You must have met them, Mabel, when you were here before. Helen was living, apparently, in peace and happiness with good old Joe. Well — she went to this psychoanalyzer — she was "psyched", and biff! — bang! — home she comes with an unsuppressed desire to leave her husband.

[*He starts work, drawing lines on a drawing board with a T-square.*

MABEL. How terrible! Yes, I remember Helen Dwight. But — but did she have such a desire?

STEVE. First she'd known of it.

MABEL. And she *left* him?

HENRIETTA (*coolly*). Yes, she did.

MABEL. Wasn't he good to her?

HENRIETTA. Why yes, good enough.

MABEL. Wasn't he kind to her!

HENRIETTA. Oh, yes — kind to her.

MABEL. And she left her good kind husband — !

HENRIETTA. Oh, Mabel! 'Left her good, kind husband!' How naïve — forgive me, dear, but how bourgeoise you are! She came to know herself. And she had the courage!

MABEL. I may be very naïve and — bourgeoise — but I don't see the good of a new science that breaks up homes.

[*Steve clap hands, applauding.*

STEVE. In enlightening Mabel, we mustn't neglect to mention the case of Art Holden's private secretary, Mary Snow, who has just been informed of her suppressed desire for her employer.

MABEL. Why, I think it is terrible, Henrietta! It would be better if we didn't know such things about ourselves.

HENRIETTA. No, Mabel, that is the old way.

MABEL. But — but her employer? Is he married?

STEVE (*grunts*). Wife and four children.

MABEL. Well, then, what good does it do the girl to be told she has a desire for him? There's nothing that can be done about it.

HENRIETTA. Old institutions will have to be reshaped so
that something can be done in such cases. It happens,
Mabel, that this suppressed desire was on the point of
landing Mary Snow in the insane asylum. Are you so
tight-minded that you'd rather have her in the insane
asylum than break the conventions?

MABEL. But — but have people always had these awful
suppressed desires?

HENRIETTA. Always.

STEVE. But they've just been discovered.

HENRIETTA. The harm they do has just been discovered.
And free, sane people must face the fact that they have to
be dealt with.

MABEL (*stoutly*). I don't believe they have them in Chicago.

HENRIETTA (*business of giving Mabel up*). People "have
them" wherever the living Libido — the center of the
soul's energy — is in conflict with petrified moral codes.
That means everywhere in civilization. Psychoanalysis —

STEVE. Good God! I've got the roof in the cellar!

HENRIETTA. The roof in the cellar!

STEVE (*holding plan at arm's length*). That's what psychoanalysis does!

HENRIETTA. That's what psychoanalysis could *un*-do. Is
it any wonder I'm concerned about Steve? He dreamed
the other night that the walls of his room melted away
and he found himself alone in a forest. Don't you see how
significant it is for an architect to have *walls* slip away from
him? It symbolizes his loss of grip in his work. There's
some suppressed desire —

STEVE (*hurling his ruined plan viciously to the floor*). Suppressed hell!

HENRIETTA. You speak more truly than you know. It is
through suppressions that hells are formed in us.

MABEL (*looking at Steve, who is tearing his hair*). Don't you
think it would be a good thing, Henrietta, if we went somewhere else? (*They rise and begin to pick up the dishes.
Mabel drops a plate which breaks. Henrietta draws up short*

and looks at her — the psychoanalytic l   I'm sorry,
Henrietta.   One of the Spode plates, to   (*Surprised
and resentful as Henrietta continues to peer at her*)   Don't
take it so to heart, Henrietta.

HENRIETTA.   I can't help taking it to heart.

MABEL.   I'll get you another. (*Pause. More sharply as
Henrietta does not answer*)   I said I'll get you another plate,
Henrietta.

HENRIETTA.   It's not the plate.

MABEL.   For heaven's sake, what is it then?

HENRIETTA.   It's the significant little false movement that
made you drop it.

MABEL.   Well, I suppose every one makes a false movement
once in a while.

HENRIETTA.   Yes, Mabel, but these false movements all mean
something.

MABEL (*about to cry*).   I don't think that's very nice!   It
was just because I happened to think of that Mabel Snow
you were talking about —

HENRIETTA.   *Mabel* Snow!

MABEL.   Snow — Snow — well, what was her name, then?

HENRIETTA.   Her name is Mary.   You substituted *your own*
name for hers.

MABEL.   Well, *Mary* Snow, then; *Mary* Snow.   I never
heard her name but once.   I don't see anything to make
such a fuss about.

HENRIETTA (*gently*).   Mabel dear — mistakes like that in
names —

MABEL (*desperately*).   They don't mean something, too, do
they?

HENRIETTA (*gently*).   I am sorry, dear, but they do.

MABEL.   *But I am always doing that!*

HENRIETTA (*after a start of horror*).   My poor little sister,
tell me all about it.

MABEL.   About what?

HENRIETTA.   About your not being happy.   About your
longing for another sort of life.

MABEL. But I *don't.*

HENRIETTA. Ah, I understánd these things, dear. You feel
Bob is limiting you to a life which you do not feel free —

MABEL. Henrietta! When did I ever say such a thing?

HENRIETTA. You said you are not in touch with things intellectual. You showed your feeling that it is Bob's pro-
fession — that has engendered a resentment which has
colored your whole life with him.

MABEL. Why — Henrietta!

HENRIETTA. Don't be afraid of me, little sister. There's
nothing can shock me or turn me from you. I am not
like that. I wanted you to come for this visit because I
had a feeling that you needed more from life than you
were getting. No one of these things I have seen would
excite my suspicion. It's the combination. You don't
eat breakfast; you make false moves; you substitute your
own name for the name of another *whose love is misdirected.*
You're nervous; you look queer; in your eyes there's a
frightened look that is most unlike you. And this dream.
A *hen* — come with me this afternoon to Dr. Russell!
Your whole life may be at stake, Mabel.

MABEL (*gasping*). Henrietta, I — you — you always were
the smartest in the family, and all that, but — this is
terrible! I don't think we *ought* to think such things,
and (*brightening*) Why, I'll tell you why I dreamed I
was a hen. It was because last night, telling about that
time in Chicago, you said I was as mad as a wet hen.

HENRIETTA (*superior*). Did you dream you were a *wet* hen?

MABEL (*forced to admit it*). No.

HENRIETTA. No. You dreamed you were a *dry* hen. And
why, being a hen, were you urged to step?

MABEL. Maybe it's because when I am getting on a street
car it always irritates me to have them call "Step lively."

HENRIETTA. No, Mabel, that is only a child's view of it —
if you will forgive me. You see merely the elements used
in the dream. You do not see into the dream; you do
not see its meaning. This dream of the hen —

STEVE. Hen — hen — wet hen — dry hen — mad hen! (*Jumps up in a rage*) Let me out of this!

HENRIETTA (*hastily picking up dishes, speaks soothingly*). Just a minute, dear, and we'll have things so you can work in quiet. Mabel and I are going to sit in my room. [*She goes out with both hands full of dishes.*

STEVE (*seizing hat and coat from the costumer*). I'm going to be psychoanalyzed. I'm going now! I'm going straight to that infallible doctor of hers — that priest of this new religion. If he's got honesty enough to tell Henrietta there's nothing the matter with my unconscious mind, perhaps I can be let alone about it, and then I *will* be all right. (*From the door in a low voice*) Don't tell Henrietta I'm going. It might take weeks, and I couldn't stand all the talk.

[*Exit desperately. Enter Henrietta.*

HENRIETTA. Where's Steve? Gone? (*With hopeless gesture*) You see how impatient he is — how unlike himself! I tell you, Mabel, I am nearly distracted about Steve.

MABEL. I think he's a little distracted, too.

HENRIETTA. Well, if he's gone — you might as well stay here. I have a committee meeting at the book-shop, and will have to leave you to yourself for an hour or two. (*As she puts her hat on, her eye, lighting up almost carnivorously, falls on an enormous volume on the floor beside the work table. The book has been half hidden from the audience by the wastebasket. She picks it up and carries it around the table toward Mabel*) Here, dear, is one of the simplest statements of psychoanalysis. You just read this and then we can talk more intelligently. (*Mabel takes volume and staggers back under its weight to chair rear center. Henrietta goes to outer door, stops and asks abruptly*) How old is Lyman Eggleston?

MABLE (*promptly*). He isn't forty yet. Why, what made you ask that, Henrietta?

[*As she turns her head to look at Henrietta her hands move toward the upper corners of the book balanced on her knees.*

HENRIETTA.   Oh, nothing.   Au revoir.

(*Exit.*

*Mabel stares at the ceiling.   The book slides to the floor.
She starts; looks at the book, then at the broken plate on the
table*)   The plate! The book!   (*She lifts her eyes, leans
forward elbow on knee, chin on knuckles and plaintively queries*)
Am I unhappy?

CURTAIN

SCENE II

*The stage is set as in Scene I, except that the breakfast table
has been removed or set back against the wall.   During the first
few minutes the dusk of a winter afternoon deepens.   Out of
the darkness spring rows of double street-lights almost meeting
in the distance.   Henrietta is disclosed at the psychoanalytical
end of Steve's work-table.   Surrounded by open books and
periodicals she is writing.   Steve enters briskly.*

STEVE.   What are you doing, my dear?

HENRIETTA.   My paper for the Liberal Club.

STEVE.   Your paper on —?

HENRIETTA.   On a subject which does not have your sympathy.

STEVE.   Oh, I'm not sure I'm wholly out of sympathy with
psychoanalysis, Henrietta.   You worked it so hard.   I
couldn't even take a bath without its meaning something.

HENRIETTA (*loftily*).   I talked it because I knew you
needed it.

STEVE.   You haven't said much about it these last two
weeks.   Uh — your faith in it hasn't weakened any?

HENRIETTA.   Weakened?   It's grown stronger with each
new thing I've come to know.   And Mabel.   She is with
Dr. Russell now.   Dr. Russell is wonderful.   From what
Mabel tells me I believe his analysis is going to prove that
I was right.   To-day I discovered a remarkable confirma-
tion of my theory in the hen-dream.

STEVE.   What is your theory?

HENRIETTA.   Well, you know about Lyman Eggleston. I've
wondered about him. I've never seen him, but I know
he's less bourgeois than Mabel's other friends — more
intellectual — and (*significantly*) she doesn't see much of
him because Bob doesn't like him.

STEVE.   But what's the confirmation?

HENRIETTA.   To-day I noticed the first syllable of his name.

STEVE.   Ly?

HENRIETTA.   No—egg. (*Patiently*) Mabel dreamed she was
a *hen*. (*Steve laughs*) You wouldn't laugh if you knew how
important names are in interpreting dreams.   Freud is full
of just such cases in which a whole hidden complex is
revealed by a single significant syllable — like this egg.

STEVE.   Doesn't the traditional relation of hen and egg suggest rather a maternal feeling?

HENRIETTA.   There is something maternal in Mabel's love
of course, but that's only one element.

STEVE.   Well, suppose Mabel hasn't a suppressed desire to
be this gentleman's mother, but his beloved. What's to
be done about it? What about Bob? Don't you think
it's going to be a little rough on him?

HENRIETTA.   That can't be helped. Bob, like every one
else, must face the facts of life.   If Dr. Russell should
arrive independently at this same interpretation I shall
not hesitate to advise Mabel to leave her present husband.

STEVE.   Um — um! (*The lights go up on Fifth Avenue.
Steve goes to the window and looks out*)   How long is it we've
lived here, Henrietta?

HENRIETTA.   Why, this is the third year, Steve.

STEVE.   I — we — one would miss this view if one went
away, wouldn't one?

HENRIETTA.   How strangely you speak! Oh, Stephen, I
wish you'd go to Dr. Russell.   Don't think my fears have
abated because I've been able to restrain myself.   I had
to on account of Mabel.   But now, dear — won't you
go?

STEVE.   I — (*He breaks off, turns on the light, then comes and sits beside Henrietta*) How long have we been married, Henrietta?

HENRIETTA.   Stephen, I don't understand you! You must go to Dr. Russell.

STEVE.   I *have* gone.

HENRIETTA.   You — what?

STEVE (*jauntily*).   Yes, Henrietta, I've been psyched.

HENRIETTA.   You went to Dr. Russell?

STEVE.   The same.

HENRIETTA.   And what did he say?

STEVE.   He said — I — I was a little surprised by what he said, Henrietta.

HENRIETTA (*breathlessly*).   Of course — one can so seldom anticipate. But tell me — your dream, Stephen? It means — ?

STEVE.   It means — I was considerably surprised by what it means.

HENRIETTA.   *Don't* be so exasperating!

STEVE.   It means — you really want to know, Henrietta?

HENRIETTA.   Stephen, you'll drive me mad!

STEVE.   He said — of course he may be wrong in what he said.

HENRIETTA.   He *isn't* wrong. *Tell* me!

STEVE.   He said my dream of the walls receding and leaving me alone in a forest indicates a suppressed desire —

HENRIETTA.   Yes — yes!

STEVE.   To be freed from —

HENRIETTA.   Yes — freed from —?

STEVE.   Marriage.

HENRIETTA (*Crumples.   Stares*).   Marriage!

STEVE.   He — he may be mistaken, you know.

HENRIETTA.   *May* be mistaken!

STEVE.   I — well, of course, I hadn't taken any stock in it myself. It was only your great confidence —

HENRIETTA.   Stephen, are you telling me that Dr. Russell — Dr. A. E. Russell — told you this? (*Steve nods*) Told you you have a suppressed desire to separate from me?

STEVE.   That's what he said.

HENRIETTA.   Did he know who you were?

STEVE.   Yes.

HENRIETTA.   That you were married to me?

STEVE.   Yes, he knew that.

HENRIETTA.   And he told you to leave me?

STEVE.   It seems he must be wrong, Henrietta.

HENRIETTA (*rising*).   And I've sent him more patients — ! (*Catches herself and resumes coldly*)   What reason did he give for this analysis?

STEVE.   He says the confining walls are a symbol of my feeling about marriage and that their fading away is a wish-fulfillment.

HENRIETTA (*gulping*).   Well, is it?   Do you want our marriage to end?

STEVE.   Well, it was a great surprise to me that I did, Henrietta.   You see I hadn't known what was in my unconscious mind.

HENRIETTA (*flaming*).   What did you tell Dr. Russell about me to make him think you weren't happy?

STEVE.   I never told him a thing, Henrietta.   He got it all from his confounded clever inferences.   I — I tried to refute them, but he said that was only part of my self-protective lying.

HENRIETTA.   And that's why you were so — happy — when you came in just now!

STEVE.   Why, Henrietta, how can you say such a thing? I was *sad*.   Didn't I speak sadly of — of the view?   Didn't I ask how long we had been married?

HENRIETTA (*rising*).   Stephen Brewster, have you no sense of the seriousness of this?   Dr. Russell doesn't know what our marriage has been.   You do.   You should have laughed him down!   Confined — in life with me?   Did you tell him that I believe in freedom?

STEVE.   I very emphatically told him that his results were a great surprise to me.

HENRIETTA.   But you accepted them.

STEVE. Oh, not at all. I merely couldn't refute his arguments. I'm not a psychologist. I came home to talk it over with you. You being a disciple of psychoanalysis —

HENRIETTA. If you are going, I wish you would go to-night!

STEVE. Oh, my dear! I — surely I couldn't do that! Think of my feelings. And my laundry hasn't come home.

HENRIETTA. I ask you to go to-night. Some women would falter at this, Steve, but I am not such a woman. I leave you free. I do not repudiate psychoanalysis, I say again that it has done great things. It has also made mistakes, of course. But since you accept this analysis — (*She sits down and pretends to begin work*) I have to finish this paper. I wish you would leave me.

STEVE (*scratches his head, goes to the inner door*). I'm sorry, Henrietta, about my unconscious mind.

[*Exit. Henrietta's face betrays her outraged state of mind — disconcerted, resentful, trying to pull herself together. She attains an air of bravely bearing an outrageous thing. Mabel enters in great excitement.*

MABEL (*breathless*). Henrietta, I'm so glad you're here. And alone? (*Looks toward the inner door*) Are you alone, Henrietta?

HENRIETTA (*with reproving dignity*). Very much so.

MABEL (*rushing to her*). Henrietta, he's found it!

HENRIETTA (*aloof*). Who has found what?

MABEL. Who has found what? Dr. Russell has found my suppressed desire.

HENRIETTA. That is interesting.

MABEL. He finished with me to-day — he got hold of my complex — in the most amazing way! But, oh, Henrietta — it is so terrible!

HENRIETTA. Do calm yourself, Mabel. Surely there's no occasion for all this agitation.

MABEL. But there is! And when you think of the lives that are affected — the readjustments that must be made in order to bring the suppressed hell out of me and save me from the insane asylum — !

HENRIETTA. The insane asylum!

MABEL. You said that's where these complexes brought people?

HENRIETTA. What did the doctor tell you, Mabel?

MABEL. Oh, I don't know how I can tell you — it is so awful — so unbelievable.

HENRIETTA. I rather have my hand in at hearing the unbelievable.

MABEL. Henrietta, who would ever have thought it? How can it be true? But the doctor is perfectly certain that I have a suppressed desire for — [*Looks at Henrietta unable to go on.*

HENRIETTA. Oh, go on, Mabel. I'm not unprepared for what you have to say.

MABEL. Not unprepared? You mean you have suspected it?

HENRIETTA. From the first. It's been my theory all along.

MABEL. But, Henrietta, I didn't know myself that I had this secret desire for Stephen.

HENRIETTA (*jumps up*). Stephen!

MABEL. My brother-in-law! My own sister's husband!

HENRIETTA. *You* have a suppressed desire for *Stephen!*

MABEL. Oh, Henrietta, aren't these unconscious selves terrible? They seem so unlike us!

HENRIETTA. What insane thing are you driving at?

MABEL (*blubbering*). Henrietta, don't you use that word to me. I don't *want* to go to the insane asylum.

HENRIETTA. What did Dr. Russell say?

MABEL. Well, you see — oh, it's the strangest thing! But you know the voice in my dream that called "Step, Hen!" Dr. Russell found out to-day that when I was a little girl I had a story-book in words of one syllable and I read the name Stephen wrong. I used to read it S-t-e-p, step, h-e-n, hen. (*Dramatically*) Step Hen is Stephen. (*Enter Stephen, his head bent over a time-table*) Stephen is Step Hen!

STEVE. I? Step Hen!

MABEL (*triumphantly*). S-t-e-p, step, H-e-n, hen, Stephen!

HENRIETTA (*exploding*). Well, what if Stephen is Step Hen?
  (*Scornfully*) Step Hen! Step Hen! For that ridiculous
  coincidence —

MABEL. Coincidence! But it's childish to look at the
  mere elements of a dream. You have to look into it —
  you have to see what it means!

HENRIETTA. On account of that trivial, meaningless play
  on syllables — on that flimsy basis — you are ready —
  (*wails*) O-h!

STEVE. What on earth's the matter? What has happened? Suppose I *am* Step Hen? What about it?
  What does it mean?

MABEL (*crying*). It means — that — I — have a suppressed
  desire for *you!*

STEVE. For me! The deuce you have? (*Feebly*) What
  — er — makes you think so?

MABEL. Dr. Russell has worked it out scientifically.

HENRIETTA. Yes. Through the amazing discovery that
  Step Hen equals Stephen!

MABEL (*tearfully*). Oh, that isn't all — that isn't near all.
  Henrietta won't give me a chance to tell it. She'd rather
  I'd go to the insane asylum than be unconventional.

HENRIETTA. We'll all go there if you can't control yourself.
  We are still waiting for some rational report.

MABEL (*drying her eyes*). Oh, there's such a lot about names.
  (*With some pride*) I don't see how I ever did it. It all
  works in together. I dreamed I was a hen because that's
  the first syllable of *Hen*-rietta's name, and when I dreamed
  I was a hen, I was putting myself in Henrietta's place.

HENRIETTA. With Stephen?

MABEL. With Stephen.

HENRIETTA (*outraged*). Oh! (*Turns in rage upon Stephen,
  who is fanning himself with the time-table*) What are you
  doing with that time-table?

STEVE. Why — I thought — you were so keen to have me
  go to-night — I thought I'd just take a run up to Canada,
  and join Billy — a little shooting — but —

MABEL. But there's more about the names.

HENRIETTA. Mabel, have you thought of Bob — dear old Bob — your good, kind husband?

MABEL. Oh, Henrietta, "my good, kind husband!"

HENRIETTA. Think of him, Mabel, out there alone in Chicago, working his head off, fixing people's *teeth* for you!

MABEL. Yes, but think of the living Libido — in conflict with petrified moral codes! And think of the perfectly wonderful way the names all prove it. Dr. Russell said he's never seen anything more convicing. Just look at Stephen's last name — Brewster. I dream I'm a hen, and the name Brewster — you have to say its first letter by itself — and then the hen, that's me, she says to him: "Stephen, Be Rooster!"

[Henrietta and Stephen both collapse on chair and divan.

MABEL. I think it's perfectly wonderful! Why, if it wasn't for psychoanalysis you'd never find out how wonderful your own mind is!

STEVE (*begins to chuckle*). Be Rooster, Stephen, Be Rooster!

HENRIETTA. You think it's funny, do you?

STEVE. Well, what's to be done about it? Does Mabel have to go away with me?

HENRIETTA. Do you want Mabel to go away with you?

STEVE. Well, but Mabel herself — her complex — her suppressed desire — !

HENRIETTA. Mabel, are you going to insist on going away with Stephen?

MABEL. I'd rather go with Stephen than go to the insane asylum.

HENRIETTA. For Heaven's sake, Mabel, drop that insane asylum! If you *did* have a suppressed desire for Stephen hidden away in you — God knows it isn't hidden *now*. Dr. Russell has brought it into your consciousness — with a vengeance. That's all that's necessary to break up a complex. Psychoanalysis doesn't say you have to *gratify* every suppressed desire.

STEVE (*softly*). Unless it's for Lyman Eggleston.

HENRIETTA (*turning on him*). Well, if it comes to that, Stephen Brewster, I'd like to know why that interpretation of mine isn't as good as this one? Step, Hen!

STEVE. But Be Rooster! (*He pauses, chuckling to himself*) Step-Hen B-rooster. And *H*enrietta. Pshaw, my dear, Doc Russell's got you beat a mile! (*He turns away and chuckles*) Be rooster!

MABEL. What has Lyman Eggleston got to do with it?

STEVE. According to Henrietta, you, the hen, have a suppressed desire for *Egg*leston, the egg.

MABEL. Henrietta, I think that's indecent of you! He is bald as an egg and little and fat — the idea of you thinking such a thing of me!

HENRIETTA. Well, Bob isn't little and bald and fat! Why don't you stick to your own husband? (*Turns on Stephen*) What if Dr. Russell's interpretation has got mine "beat a mile"? (*Resentful look at him*) It would only mean that Mabel doesn't want Eggleston and does want you. Does that mean she has to have you?

MABEL. But you said Mabel Snow —

HENRIETTA. *Mary* Snow! You're not as much like her as you think — substituting your name for hers! The cases are entirely different. Oh, I wouldn't have believed this of you, Mabel. I brought you here for a pleasant visit — thought you needed brightening *up* — wanted to be nice to you — and now you — my husband — you insist — [*Begins to cry. Makes a movement which brushes to the floor some sheets from the psychoanalytical table.*

STEVE (*with solicitude*). Careful, dear. Your paper on psychoanalysis!
[*Gathers up sheets and offers them to her.*

HENRIETTA (*crying*). I don't want my paper on psychoanalysis! I'm sick of psychoanalysis!

STEVE (*eagerly*). Do you mean that, Henrietta?

HENRIETTA. Why shouldn't I mean it? Look at all I've done for psychoanalysis — and — what has psychoanalysis done for me?

STEVE.   Do you mean, Henrietta, that you're going to **stop**
talking psychoanalysis?

HENRIETTA.   Why shouldn't I stop talking it?   Haven't I
seen what it does to people?   Mabel has gone crazy about
psychoanalysis!

[*At the word "crazy" Mabel sinks with a moan into the arm-*
chair and buries her face in her hands.

STEVE (*solemnly*).   Do you swear never to wake me up in
the night to find out what I'm dreaming?

HENRIETTA.   Dream what you please — I don't care what
you're dreaming.

STEVE.   Will you clear off my work-table so the Journal of
Morbid Psychology doesn't stare me in the face when I'm
trying to plan a house?

HENRIETTA (*pushing a stack of periodicals off the table*).   I'll
burn the Journal of Morbid Psychology!

STEVE.   My dear Henrietta, if you're going to separate from
psychoanalysis, there's no reason why I should separate
from *you.*

[*They embrace ardently.   Mabel lifts her head and looks at*
them woefully.

MABEL (*jumping up and going toward them*).   But what about
me?   What am I to do with my suppressed desire?

STEVE (*with one arm still around Henrietta, gives Mabel a*
brotherly hug).   Mabel, you just keep right on suppress-
ing it.

CURTAIN

WHERE BUT IN AMERICA

OSCAR M. WOLFF

MR. OSCAR M. WOLFF was born July 13, 1876. He is a graduate of Cornell University and of Chicago Law School. During the war he was connected with the United States Food Administration at Washington. Although his main interest has been in law, which he has practised and taught, he has done a large amount of writing and editing. He has published a legal textbook and a number of articles on legal subjects, both in legal publications and in magazines of general interest. In addition, he has written one or two stories, and three plays: "Where But in America", "The Claim for Exemption", and "The Money Lenders."

WHERE BUT IN AMERICA

By OSCAR M. WOLFF

"Where But in America" was originally produced by the Players' Workshop of Chicago, on April 23, 1917.

Original Cast

MRS. ESPENHAYNE	Caroline Kohl
MR. ESPENHAYNE	George Francis Wolff
HILDA	Helen Cook

Printed originally in *Smart Set*.

Application for the right of performing "Where But in America" must be made to Mr. Oscar Wolff, 105 West Monroe Street, Chicago.

WHERE BUT IN AMERICA

SCENE. *The Espenhayne dining room.*

The curtain rises on the Espenhayne dining room. It is furnished with modest taste and refinement. There is a door, center, leading to the living room, and a swinging door, left, leading to the kitchen.

The table is set, and Robert and Mollie Espenhayne are discovered at their evening meal. They are educated, well-bred, young Americans. Robert is a pleasing, energetic business man of thirty; Mollie an attractive woman of twenty-five. The bouillon cups are before them as the curtain rises.

BOB. Mollie, I heard from the man who owns that house in Kenilworth. He wants to sell the house. He won't rent.

MOLLIE. I really don't care, Bob. That house was too far from the station and it had only one sleeping porch and you know I want white enamelled woodwork in the bedrooms. But, Bob, I've been terribly stupid!

BOB. How so, Mollie?

MOLLIE. You remember the Russells moved to Highland Park last spring?

BOB. Yes; Ed Russell rented a house that had just been built.

MOLLIE. A perfectly darling little house! And Fanny Russell once told me that the man who built it will put up a house for any one who will take a five year lease. And she says that the man is very competent and they are simply delighted with their place.

BOB. Why don't we get in touch with the man?

MOLLIE. Wasn't it stupid of me not to think about it? It just flashed into my mind this morning and I sat down at

once and sent a special delivery letter to Fanny Russell.
I asked her to tell me his name at once, and where we can
find him.

BOB.   Good! You ought to have an answer by to-morrow
or Thursday and we'll go up north and have a talk with
him on Saturday.

MOLLIE (*with enthusiasm*).   Wouldn't it be wonderful if he'd
build just what we want! Fanny Russell says every detail of their house is perfect. Even the garage; they use
it —

BOB (*interrupting*).   Mollie, that's the one thing I'm afraid
of about the North Shore plan. I've said repeatedly that
I don't want to buy a car for another year or two. But,
here you are, talking about a garage already.

MOLLIE.   But you didn't let me finish what I was saying.
The Russells have fitted up their garage as a playroom for
the children. If we had a garage we could do the same
thing.

BOB.   Well, let's keep temptation behind us and not even
talk to the man about a garage. If we move up north it
must be on an economy basis for a few years; just a half-
way step between the apartment and the house we used to
plan. You mustn't get your heart set on a car.

MOLLIE.   I haven't even thought of one, dear. (*Bob and
Mollie have now both finished the bouillon course and lay
down their spoons. Reaching out her hand to touch the
table button and at the same time leaning across the table
and speaking very impressively*). Bob, I'm about to ring
for Hilda!

BOB.   What of it?

MOLLIE (*decidedly and with a touch of impatience*).   You
know very well, what of it. I don't want Hilda to hear us
say *one* word about moving away from the South Side!

BOB (*protesting*).   But Mollie —

MOLLIE (*interrupting hurriedly and holding her finger to her
lips in warning*).   Psst!

(*The next instant Hilda enters, left. She is a tall, blond*

Swedish girl, about twenty-five years old. She is very pretty and carries herself well and looks particularly charming in a maid's dress, with white collars and cuffs and a dainty waitress's apron. Every detail of her dress is immaculate. (Speaking the instant that Hilda appears and talking very rapidly all the time that Hilda remains in the room. While she speaks Mollie watches Hilda rather than Robert, whom she pretends to be addressing) In the last game Gert Jones was my partner. It was frame apiece and I dealt and I bid one no trump. I had a very weak no trump. I'll admit that, but I didn't want them to win the rubber. Mrs. Stone bid two spades and Gert Jones doubled her. Mrs. Green passed and I simply couldn't go to three of anything. Mrs. Stone played two spades, doubled, and she made them. Of course, that put them out and gave them the rubber. I think that was a very foolish double of Gert Jones and then she said it was my fault, because I bid one no trump.

[As Mollie begins her flow of words Bob first looks at her in open-mouthed astonishment. Then as he gradually comprehends that Mollie is merely talking against time he too turns his eyes to Hilda and watches her closely in her movements around the table. Meanwhile Hilda moves quietly and quickly and pays no attention to anything except the work she has in hand. She carries a small serving tray and, as Mollie speaks, Hilda first takes the bouillon cups from the table, then brings the carving-knife and fork from the sideboard and places them before Robert and then, with the empty bouillon cups, exits left. Bob and Mollie are both watching Hilda as she goes out. The instant the door swings shut behind her, Mollie relaxes with a sigh and Robert leans across the table to speak.

BOB. Mollie, why not be sensible about this thing! Have a talk with Hilda and find out if she will move north with us.

MOLLIE. That's just like a man! Then we might not find a house to please us and Hilda would be dissatisfied and suspicious. She might even leave. *(Thoughtfully)* Of course, I must speak to her before we sign a lease, because I really don't know what I'd do if Hilda refuses to leave the South side. (*More cheerfully*) But there, we won't think about the disagreeable things until everything else is settled.

BOB. That's good American doctrine.

MOLLIE (*warningly and again touching her finger to her lips*). Psst!

(*Hilda enters, left, carrying the meat plates, with a heavy napkin under them. Immediately resuming her monologue*) I think my last year's hat will do very nicely. You know it rained all last summer and I really only wore the hat a half a dozen times. Perhaps not that often. I can make a few changes on it; put on some new ribbons you know, and it will do very nicely for another year. You remember that hat, don't you, dear? (*Bob starts to answer, but Mollie rushes right on*) Of course you do, you remember you said it was so becoming. That's another reason why I want to wear it this summer.

[*Hilda, meanwhile, puts the plates on the table in front of Bob and goes out, left. Mollie at once stops speaking.*

BOB (*holding his hands over the plates as over a fire and rubbing them together in genial warmth*). Ah, the good hot plates! She never forgets them. She *is* a gem, Mollie.

MOLLIE (*in great self-satisfaction*). If you are finally convinced of that, after three years, I wish you would be a little bit more careful what you say the next time Hilda comes in the room.

BOB (*in open-mouthed astonishment*). What!

MOLLIE. Well, I don't want Hilda to think we are making plans behind her back.

BOB (*reflectively*). "A man's home is his castle." (*Pauses*) It's very evident that the Englishman who first said that didn't keep any servants.

[*Telephone bell rings off stage.*

MOLLIE. Answer that, Bob.

BOB. Won't Hilda answer it?

MOLLIE (*standing up quickly and speaking impatiently*). Very well, I shall answer it myself. I can't ask Hilda to run to the telephone while she is serving the meal.

BOB (*sullenly, as he gets up*). All right! All right!

[*Bob exits, center. As he does so Hilda appears at the door, left, hurrying to answer the telephone.*

MOLLIE. Mr. Espenhayne will answer it, Hilda.

[*Hilda makes the slightest possible bow of acquiescence, withdraws left, and in a moment reappears with vegetable dishes and small side dishes which she puts before Mrs. Espenhayne. She is arranging these when Bob re-enters, center.*

BOB. Somebody for you, Hilda.

HILDA (*surprised*). For me? O! But I cannot answer eet now. Please ask the party to call later.

[*Hilda speaks excellent English but with some Swedish accent. The noticeable feature of her speech is the precision and great care with which she enunciates every syllable.*

MOLLIE. Just take the number yourself, Hilda, and tell the party you will call back after dinner.

HILDA. Thank you, Messes Aispenhayne.

[*Hilda exits, center. Bob stands watching Hilda, as she leaves the room, and then turns and looks at Mollie with a bewildered expression.*

BOB (*standing at his chair*). But, I thought Hilda couldn't be running to the telephone while she serves the dinner?

MOLLIE. But this call is for Hilda, herself. That's quite different, you see.

BOB (*slowly and thoughtfully*). O, yes! Of course; I see! (*Sits down in his chair*) That is — I don't quite see!

MOLLIE (*immediately leaning across the table and speaking in a cautious whisper*). Do you know who it is?

(*Bob closes his lips very tightly and nods yes in a very important manner. In the same whisper and very impatiently*) Who?

BOB (*looking around the room as if to see if anyone is in hiding and then putting his hand to his mouth and exaggerating the whisper*). The Terrible Swede.

MOLLIE (*in her ordinary tone and very much exasperated*). Robert, I've told you a hundred times that you shouldn't refer to — to — the man in that way.

BOB. And I've told you a hundred times to ask Hilda his name. If I knew his name I'd announce him with as much ceremony as if he were the Swedish Ambassador.

MOLLIE (*disgusted*). Oh, don't try to be funny! Suppose some day Hilda hears you speak of him in that manner?

BOB. You know that's mild compared to what you think of him. Suppose some day Hilda learns what you think of him?

MOLLIE. I think very well of him and you know it. Of course, I dread the time when she marries him, but I wouldn't for the world have her think that we speak disrespectfully of her or her friends.

BOB. "A man's home is his castle."

[*Mollie's only answer is a gesture of impatience. Mollie and Bob sit back in their chairs to await Hilda's return. Both sit with fingers interlaced, hands resting on the edge of the table in the attitude of school children at attention. A long pause. Mollie unclasps her hands and shifts uneasily. Robert does the same. Mollie, seeing this, hastily resumes her former attitude of quiet waiting. Robert, however, grows increasingly restless. His restlessness makes Mollie nervous and she watches Robert, and when he is not observing her, she darts quick, anxious glances at the door, center. Bob drains and refills his glass.*

MOLLIE (*she has been watching Robert and every time he shifts or moves she unconsciously does the same and finally she breaks out nervously*). I don't understand this at all! Isn't today Tuesday?

BOB. What of it?

MOLLIE. He usually calls up on Wednesdays and comes to see her on Saturdays.

BOB. And takes her to the theater on Thursdays and to dances on Sundays. He's merely extending his line of attack.

(*Another long pause, then Bob begins to experiment to learn whether the plates are still hot. He gingerly touches the edges of the upper plate in two or three places. It seems safe to handle. He takes hold of upper and lower plates boldly, muttering, as he does so, "*Cold as —*" Drops the plates with a clatter and a smothered oath. Shakes his fingers and blows on them. Meanwhile Mollie is sitting very rigid, regarding Bob with a fixed stare and beating a vigorous tattoo on the table cloth with her fingers. Bob catches her eye and cringes under her gaze. He drains and refills his glass. He studies the walls and the ceiling of the room, meanwhile still nursing his fingers. Bob steals a side-long glance at Mollie. She is still staring at him. He turns to his water goblet. Picks it up and holds it up to the light. He rolls the stem between his fingers, squinting at the light through the water. Reciting slowly as he continues to gaze at the light*) Starlight! Starbright! Will Hilda talk to him all night!

MOLLIE (*in utter disgust*). Oh, stop that singing.

[*Bob puts down his glass, then drinks the water and refills the glass. He then turns his attention to the silverware and cutlery before him. He examines it critically, then lays a teaspoon carefully on the cloth before him, and attempts the trick of picking it up with the first finger in the bowl and the thumb at the point of the handle. After one or two attempts the spoon shoots on the floor, far behind him. Mollie jumps at the noise. Bob turns slowly and looks at the spoon with an injured air, then turns back to Mollie with a silly, vacuous smile. He now lays all the remaining cutlery in a straight row before him.*

BOB (*slowly counting the cutlery and silver, back and forth*). Eeny, meeny, miney, mo. Catch a — (*Stops suddenly as an idea comes to him. Gazes thoughtfully at Mollie, for a moment, then begins to count over again*) Eeny, meeny, miney, mo; Hilda's talking to her beau. If we holler, she may go. Eeny, mee —

MOLLIE (*interrupting and exasperated to the verge of tears*). Bob, if you don't stop all that nonsense, I shall scream!

(*In a very tense tone*)   I believe I'm going to have one of my sick headaches!   (*Puts her hand to her forehead*)   I know it; I can feel it coming on!

BOB (*in a soothing tone*).   Hunger, my dear, hunger! When you have a good warm meal you'll feel better.

MOLLIE (*in despair*).   What do you suppose I ought to do?

BOB.   Go out in the kitchen and fry a couple of eggs.

MOLLIE.   O! be serious!   I'm at my wits end!   Hilda never did anything like this before.

BOB (*suddenly quite serious*).   What does that fellow do for a living, anyhow?

MOLLIE.   How should I know?

BOB.   Didn't you ever ask Hilda?

MOLLIE.   Certainly not.   Hilda doesn't ask me about your business, why should I pry into her affairs?

BOB (*taking out his cigarette case and lighting a cigarette*). Mollie, I see you're strong for the Constitution of the United States.

MOLLIE (*suspiciously*).   What do you mean by that?

BOB.   The Constitution says: "Whereas it is a self-evident truth that all men are born equal" — (*With a wave of the hand*) Hilda and you, and the Terrible Swede and I and —

MOLLIE (*interrupting*).   Bob, you're such a *heathen! That's not in the Constitution.*   That's in the Bible!

BOB.   Well, wherever it is, until this evening I never realized what a personage Hilda is.

MOLLIE.   You can make fun of me all you please, but I know what's right!   Your remarks don't influence me in the least — not in the least!

BOB (*murmurs thoughtfully and feelingly*).   How true! (*Abruptly*) Why don't they get married?   Do you know that?

MOLLIE.   All I know is that they are waiting until his business is entirely successful so that Hilda won't have to work.

BOB.   Well, the Swedes are pretty careful of their money. The chances are Hilda has a neat little nest egg laid by.

MOLLIE (*hesitating and doubtfully*). That's one thing that worries me a little. I think Hilda puts money — into — into — into the young man's business.

BOB (*indignantly*). Do you mean to tell me that this girl gives her money to that fellow and you don't try to find out a thing about him? Who he is or what he does? I suppose she supports the loafer.

MOLLIE (*with dignity*). He's not a loafer. I've seen him and I've talked with him and I know he's a gentleman.

BOB. Mollie, I'm getting tired of all that kind of drivel. I believe now-a-days women give a good deal more thought to pleasing their maids than they do to pleasing their husbands.

MOLLIE (*demurely*). Well, you know, Bob, your maid can leave you much easier than your husband can (*pauses thoughtfully*) and I'm sure she's much harder to replace.

BOB (*very angry, looking at his watch, throwing his napkin on the table and standing up*). Mollie, our dinner has been interrupted for fifteen minutes while Hilda entertains her (*with sarcasm*) gentleman friend. If you won't stop it, I will. [*Steps toward the door, center.*

MOLLIE (*sternly, pointing to Bob's chair*). Robert, sit down ! [*Bob pauses, momentarily, and at the instant Hilda enters, center, meeting Bob, face to face. Both are startled. Bob in a surly manner walks back to his place at the table. Hilda follows, excited and eager. Bob sits down and Hilda stands for a moment at the table, smiling from one to the other and evidently anxious to say something. Bob and Mollie are severe and unfriendly. They gaze at Hilda coldly. Slowly Hilda's enthusiasm cools and she becomes again the impassive servant.*

HILDA. Aixcuse me, Meeses Aispenhayne, I am very sorry. I bring the dinner right in.
[*Hilda exits left.*

BOB. It's all nonsense. (*Touches the plates again, but this time even more cautiously than before. This time he finds they are entirely safe to handle*) These plates are stone cold now.

[*Hilda enters, left, with meat platter. Places it before Bob
He serves the meat and Mollie starts to serve the vegetables
Hilda hands Mollie her meat plate.*

MOLLIE. Vegetables?

(*Bob is chewing on his meat and does not answer. Mollie
looks at him inquiringly. But his eyes are on his plate. Re
peating*) Vegetables?

(*Still no answer from Bob. Very softly under her breath*)
H'mm.

[*Mollie helps herself to vegetables and then dishes out a portion
which she hands to Hilda, who in turn places the dish beside
Bob. When both are served Hilda stands for a moment
back of the table. She clasps and unclasps her hands in a
nervous manner, seems about to speak, but as Bob and Mollie
pay no attention to her she slowly and reluctantly turns, and
exits left. Mollie takes one or two bites of the meat and then
gives a quick glance at Bob. He is busy chewing at his meat
and Mollie quietly lays down her knife and fork and turns to
the vegetables.*

BOB (*chewing desperately on his meat*). Tenderloin, I believe

MOLLIE (*sweetly*). Yes, dear.

BOB (*imitating Mollie a moment back*). H'mm! (*He takes
one or two more hard bites*) Mollie, I have an idea.

MOLLIE. I'm relieved.

BOB (*savagely*). Yes, you will be when you hear it. When we
get that builder's name from Fanny Russell, we'll tell him
that instead of a garage, which we don't need, he can
build a special telephone booth off the kitchen. Then
while Hilda serves the dinner —

[*Bob stops short, as Hilda bursts in abruptly, left, and comes
to the table.*

HILDA. Aixcuse me, Meeses Aispenhayne, I am so excited

MOLLIE (*anxiously*). Is anything wrong, Hilda?

HILDA (*explosively*). Meeses Aispenhayne, Meester Leend
quist he say you want to move to Highland Park.

[*Bob and Mollie simultaneously drop their knives and forks
and look at Hilda in astonishment and wonder.*

MOLLIE. What?

BOB. Who?

HILDA (*repeats very rapidly*). Meester Leendquist, he say you look for house on North Shore!

MOLLIE (*utterly overcome at Hilda's knowledge and at a loss for words of denial*). We move to the North Shore? How ridiculous! Hilda, where did you get such an idea? (*Turns to Robert*) Robert, did you ever hear anything so laughable? (*She forces a strained laugh*) Ha! Ha! Ha! (*Robert has been looking at Hilda in dumb wonder. At Mollie's question he turns to her in startled surprise. He starts to answer, gulps, swallows hard, and then coughs violently. Very sharply, after waiting a moment for Bob to answer*) Robert Espenhayne, will you stop that coughing and answer me!

BOB (*between coughs and drinking a glass of water*). Egh! Egh! Excuse me! Something, eh! egh! stuck in my throat.

MOLLIE (*turning to Hilda*). Some day we might want to move north, Hilda, but not now! Oh no, not now!

BOB. Who told you that, Hilda?

HILDA. Meester Leendquist.

MOLLIE (*puzzled*). Who is Mr. Lindquist?

HILDA (*surprised*). Meester Leendquist — (*pauses, a trifle embarrassed*) Meester Leendquist ees young man who just speak to me on telephone. He come to see me every Saturday.

BOB. Oh, Mr. Lindquist, the — the — Ter —

MOLLIE (*interrupting frantically, and waving her hands at Bob*).
Yes, yes, of course. You know — Mr. Lindquist! (*Bob catches himself just in time and Mollie settles back with a sigh of relief, then turns to Hilda with a puzzled air*) But where did Mr. Lindquist get such an idea?

HILDA. Mrs. Russell tell heem so.

MOLLIE (*now entirely bewildered*). What Mrs. Russell?

HILDA. Meeses Russell — your friend.

MOLLIE (*more and more at sea*). Mrs. Edwin Russell who comes to see me — every now and then?

HILDA. Yes.

MOLLIE. But how does Mrs. Russell know Mr. Lindquist and why should she tell Mr. Lindquist that we expected to move to the North Shore?

HILDA. Meester Leendquist, he build Meeses Russell's house. That ees hees business. He build houses on North Shore and he sell them and rent them.

[*Bob and Mollie look at each other and at Hilda in wonder and astonishment as the situation slowly filters into their brains. A long pause.*

BOB (*in awe and astonishment*). You mean that Mr. Lindquist, the young man who comes to see you every — every — every now and then — is the same man who put up the Russell house?

HILDA. Yes, Meester Aispenhayne.

BOB (*slowly*). And when Mrs. Espenhayne (*points to Mollie*) wrote to Mrs. Russell (*jerks his thumb to indicate the North*) Mrs. Russell told Mr. Lindquist (*jerks his thumb in opposite direction*) and Mr. Lindquist telephoned to you?

[*Points to Hilda.*

HILDA. Yes, Meester Aispenhayne.

[*Nodding.*

BOB (*very thoughtfully and slowly*). H'mm! (*Then slowly resuming his meal and speaking in mock seriousness, in subtle jest at Mollie, and imitating her tone of a moment or two back*) But of course, you understand, Hilda, we don't want to move to the North Shore now! Oh, no, not now!

HILDA (*somewhat crestfallen*). Yes, Meester Aispenhayne.

BOB (*reflectively*). But, of course, if Mr. Lindquist builds houses, we might look. Yes, we might look.

HILDA (*in growing confidence and enthusiasm*). Yes, Meester Aispenhayne, and he build such beautiful houses and so cheap. He do so much heemself. Hees father was carpenter and he work hees way through Uneeversity of Menresota and study architecture and then he go to

Uneeversity of Eelenois and study landscape gardening and now he been in business for heemself sex years. And oh, Meeses Aispenhayne, you must see hees own home! You will love eet, eet ees so beautiful. A little house, far back from the road. You can hardly see eet for the trees and the shrubs, and een the summer the roses grow all around eet. Eet is just like the picture book!

MOLLIE (*in the most perfunctory tone, utterly without interest or enthusiasm*). How charming! (*Pauses thoughtfully, then turns to Hilda, anxiously*) Then I suppose, Hilda, if we should decide to move up to the North Shore you would go with us?

HILDA (*hesitatingly*). Yes, Meeses Aispenhayne. (*Pauses*) But I theenk I must tell you thees spring Meester Leendquist and I aixpect to get married. Meester Leendquist's business ees very good. (*With a quick smile and a glance from one to the other*) You know, I am partner with heem. I put all my money een Meester Leendquist's business too. [*Mollie and Bob gaze at each other in complete resignation and surrender.*

BOB (*quite seriously after a long pause*). Hilda, I don't know whether we will move north or not, but the next time Mr. Lindquist comes here, I want you to introduce me to him. I'd like to know him. You ought to be very proud of a man like that.

HILDA (*radiant with pleasure*). Thank you, Meester Aispenhayne.

MOLLIE. Yes, indeed, Hilda, Mr. Espenhayne has often said what a fine young man Mr. Lindquist seems to be. We want to meet him, and Mr. Espenhayne and I will talk about the house and then we will speak to Mr. Lindquist. (*Then weakly*) Of course, we didn't expect to move north for a long time, but of course, if you expect to get married, and Mr. Lindquist builds houses — [*Her voice dies out. Long pause.*

HILDA. Thank you, Meeses Aispenhayne, I tell Mr. Leendquist.

[*Hilda stands at the table a moment longer, then slowly turns and moves toward door, left. Bob and Mollie watch her and as she moves away from the table Bob turns to Mollie. At this moment Hilda stops, turns suddenly and returns to the table.*

HILDA.   Oh, Meeses Aispenhayne, I forget one theeng!

MOLLIE.   What now, Hilda?

HILDA.   Meester Leendquist say eef you and Meester Aispenhayne want to look at property on North Shore, I shall let heem know and he meet you at station weeth hees automobile.

CURTAIN

A QUESTION OF MORALITY

PERCIVAL WILDE

MR. PERCIVAL WILDE was born March 1, 1887, and was graduated from Columbia University in 1906. After being in business for some years, he commenced writing, and in May, 1917, he enlisted in the navy. During the war he was an officer of the navy on active service.

He has published "The Line of No Resistance", 1913, "Dawn and Other One-Act Plays of To-day", 1915; "Confessional and Other American Plays", 1916; and "The Unseen Host and Other War Plays", 1917. He is co-author with Samuel Shipman of "Lambs are Lions", 1918.

Thirty-one of his plays have been produced and some have had many productions. They have been given in vaudeville and by various Little Theatres. Mr. Wilde wrote vaudeville one-acters exclusively from 1912 to 1914, but then effected a complete change in his writing and since 1915 has written with a more literary end in view. Mr. Wilde states that this has not prevented some of his recent plays from being reduced to a least common multiple, however, and being produced in vaudeville.

A QUESTION OF MORALITY

A COMEDY

By PERCIVAL WILDE

"A Question of Morality" was originally produced by the Brooklyn Repertory Theatre Company (affiliated with the People's Institute of Brooklyn) on Wednesday evening, March 7, 1917, at the People's Institute.

Original Cast

SHELTON . . . . Thomas Mitchell
CARRUTHERS . . . . Harmon Cheshire
DOROTHY SHELTON . . . . . . Beatrice Reinhardt

Printed originally in the *Century Magazine.* Reprinted in "Confessional and Other American Plays," and printed in this volume by permission of, and by special arrangement with, Mr. Percival Wilde and Henry Holt and Company.

Application for the right of performing " A Question of Morality " must be made to Mr. Percival Wilde, Society of American Authors, Candler Building, New York.

A QUESTION OF MORALITY

SCENE. *As the curtain rises, Shelton and Carruthers are discovered. Shelton, a not unattractive social butterfly of some thirty-five years of age, has inherited wealth, and having never had to concern himself with productive labor, has acquired a fine dilettantism: an ability to do many things badly, without doing any one of them so badly that it becomes evident he has neglected it. Carruthers, his friend, has even less claim to distinction. They would pass in a crowd — if the crowd were large enough, but no one, with the possible exception of a Society Editor, would give either of them a second glance. Were one to seek something visibly commendable about them, one might remark that they are groomed and tailored to an exquisite nicety — too exquisite, perhaps. They are in full dress, for they have just finished the evening meal, and as the assiduous butler lights their cigars, places the liqueur tray on the table, and discreetly effaces himself, they slowly push their chairs into more comfortable positions, and look at each other. There is something in that look: something unusual, and the shadow of a smile curls about the husband's lips as he raises his arm to consult a wrist-watch.*

CARRUTHERS. What time?

SHELTON. Twelve minutes of eight — no, ten minutes of. My watch is a little slow.

CARRUTHERS (*rather brilliantly after a pause*). Thought it was later than that.

SHELTON (*having weighed the pros and cons carefully*). So did I.

CARRUTHERS (*after another pause*). Thought it was at least quarter past.

SHELTON. So did I. (*Consulting the watch again*) It's eleven minutes of — that is to say, nine minutes of, now. (*He pauses and smiles reflectively*) Jerry!

CARRUTHERS. Yes?

SHELTON. I wonder what Cheever's saying to her now.

CARRUTHERS. I wonder?

SHELTON (*examining a time-table*). Their train pulls out at eight.

CARRUTHERS (*with a trace of animation*). I thought you said they were leaving this afternoon.

SHELTON. Eh?

CARRUTHERS. The six o'clock train, you said first.

SHELTON. Oh, yes. But she had to do some shopping. You can't get any decent clothes in Chicago, you know. (*He chuckles slowly*) I suppose she wanted the satisfaction of charging a final bill to me, eh, Jerry?

CARRUTHERS (*nodding sympathetically*). It's cost you a pretty penny, all in all.

SHELTON (*philosophically*). Well, your wife doesn't elope with some other chap every day, does she?

CARRUTHERS (*undecidedly*). Er, no.

SHELTON. This is a special occasion. If Dorothy feels she has a right to carte blanche on her last day as my wife, I don't know but what I ought to agree with her. It's sentimental, you know.

CARRUTHERS. But expensive.

SHELTON. Sentiment is always expensive. At any rate, I'm footing the bills. A little more or less doesn't matter. (*He rises, and produces a mass of papers from a convenient desk*) Just look at these.

CARRUTHERS. What are they?

SHELTON. The detectives' reports. (*He thumbs them over with a smile*) It's been like a continued-in-our-next story. I've been reading them for the last month.

CARRUTHERS (*surprised*). I didn't know you had detectives following her.

SHELTON (*confused*). Er, yes.

CARRUTHERS. Do you think that's cricket?

SHELTON (*hesitantly*). Well, I couldn't *ask* her if she **was** going to run away.

CARRUTHERS. Why not?

SHELTON. She's too good a woman to lie to me — and I didn't want to embarrass her. (*Carruthers smiles cynically. Shelton crushes him politely*) You wouldn't understand such things anyhow, Jerry. (*He bundles the reports together again*) The last installment reached me to-day. It took her a month to make up her mind. Cheever wanted her to elope long ago, but she wouldn't hear of it. She had scruples. And to-morrow!

CARRUTHERS (*thinking he is rising to the situation*). To-morrow's another day.

SHELTON (*with a faint frown*). No. To-morrow I'll be a free man — no wife, no responsibilities, no conscience. Rather clever of me, eh, Jerry? If I had told her I didn't mind, she never would have run off. Never!

CARRUTHERS. She's a moral woman, your wife.

SHELTON (*nodding emphatically*). Well, rather! (*Confidentially*) Do you know, I'm not sure that she isn't running off with Cheever because she wants to reform him? He's a bad lot, you know; gambles, and drinks, and a devil with the ladies.

CARRUTHERS (*slowly*). I'm not knocking anybody, but you used to travel around with him.

SHELTON (*not at all disturbed*). Yes: when I was single. Oh, I'm not making any bones about it: I was as bad as he — worse. (*With satisfaction*) Much worse. Cheever and I, well, we had reps! You know what they were like.

CARRUTHERS. I do.

SHELTON (*solemnly*). But that's all over with now. I'm a better man since I married Dorothy. She's reformed me. There was lots to reform, too. I was a bad 'un. But that didn't bother her: she enjoyed it. She used to talk to me, just like a mother, Jerry, and she got me to cut out cards, and the ponies — (*he pauses reflectively*) — I used to lose a bale of money on the races, Jerry. (*Carruthers does not answer. He finishes emphatically*) She's had an awfully good influence on me.

CARRUTHERS (*after a period of cogitation*). She's helped you?

SHELTON (*enthusiastically*). Helped me? I can't begin to tell you how many ways —

CARRUTHERS (*interrupting*). Then why are you letting her go?

SHELTON (*taken aback*). Eh?

CARRUTHERS. Why are you letting her run off with Cheever?

SHELTON (*nervously*). You don't keep on taking the medicine after you're cured, do you, Jerry? I'm cured, you know. And I don't want to be cured any more than I am. I'm a good man. I'm so good, Jerry, I'm so good sometimes, that I'm almost afraid of myself! (*He pauses, to continue candidly*) It's so different — and so strange. Before I married Dorothy I wasn't good: that was when I went around with Cheever. But it was so comfortable: I was so sure of myself. I never had any regrets. I wasn't afraid to drink, because even if I — well, even if I *did* take a drop too much I wouldn't make a fool of myself: I'd act just as if I were sober. (*He emphasizes his point with a clenched fist*) Jerry, I was *consistent* then! I was dependable. I never had anything to be ashamed of. Whatever I did, well, I stood back of it. I didn't have to worry. And now? I'm living on the brink of a volcano! I'm full of all kinds of impulses to do good things: things I don't want to do. I never know what's going to happen next, and Jerry, I don't like it! It's not fair to me. I'm like a man who has swallowed a stick of dynamite: he's expecting it to blow up any minute, but if it ever does blow up, there won't be enough of him left to be surprised at it. (*Carruthers, considerably beyond his depth, makes no reply*) A man should be true to himself. I don't know whom I'm true to, but it's not Billy Shelton! There's no Billy Shelton left: he's nine-tenths Dorothy, and one-tenth remnants!

CARRUTHERS (*shifting uneasily*). Isn't it time to go to a show?

SHELTON (*consulting his watch*). Eight o'clock. That is, two minutes after. Jerry, she's gone!

CARRUTHERS. All right. Let's get our coats on.

[*He rises.*

SHELTON. No. Wait a minute.

CARRUTHERS (*glancing at him curiously*). What's the matter with you?

SHELTON. It's too sudden. I can't realize it yet.

CARRUTHERS. You've been expecting it a month.

SHELTON. Yes.

CARRUTHERS. Waiting for it — counting the hours.

SHELTON. Yes. (*He throws his cigar away nervously*) Jerry, it's two years since I've been to a show without Dorothy.

CARRUTHERS. Well?

SHELTON. What are you going to do afterwards?

CARRUTHERS. Anything you like.

SHELTON. For instance?

CARRUTHERS. Stop in somewheres for a bite. Look in at the Club: there's always a game of stud.

SHELTON (*nodding thoughtfully*). I used to lose a lot of money at that, Jerry. (*He looks at him appealingly*) Jerry.

CARRUTHERS. Well?

SHELTON. Would you mind — if I stayed home to-night?

CARRUTHERS (*surprised*). What?

SHELTON. I mean it. I don't feel like going out so soon after —

CARRUTHERS. It's not a funeral, you know.

SHELTON. No. But —

CARRUTHERS. But what?

SHELTON. Dorothy wouldn't like it.

CARRUTHERS. Good Lord!

SHELTON (*nodding seriously*). I mean it. Anyhow, you want to see some musical comedy, don't you?

CARRUTHERS. Why not?

SHELTON. It would bore me to death. (*Rather shamefacedly*) I used to care for that sort of thing, but Dorothy taught me to enjoy the opera.

CARRUTHERS (*facing him resolutely*).   Answer me one question.

SHELTON.   Well?

CARRUTHERS.   *Is* Dorothy your wife, or *was* she your wife?

SHELTON (*hesitantly*).   I guess it's "is." You see, she's not more than ten miles away from New York now.

CARRUTHERS.   And you're afraid you may have to account to her?

SHELTON.   No. It's not that. She's left me, and I'm my own master. But the very day that she elopes, don't you think it would be a little (*he searches for a word*) — a little indecent if I were to start celebrating? I'm a gentleman, Jerry, and it wouldn't be quite respectful to Dorothy. She mighn't like it. (*He lights on a happy simile*) It's like reading the will while the corpse is still warm, isn't it? Come now, be honest, Jerry.

CARRUTHERS (*with warmth*).   Well, I'm thirty-three, and I'm a bachelor.

SHELTON.   What's the point?

CARRUTHERS.   I say if that's married life, I don't want to get married!

[*The door opens, and Dorothy, a tall, slim, rather attractive woman in her late twenties, stands on the threshold. She is quite excited, and she trembles a little. The men, thunderstruck at her sudden appearance, are unable to voice a greeting. Shelton, collapsed in his chair, gasps like a fish out of water, and Carruthers, petrified at the height of an oratorical gesture, is not much better.*

SHELTON (*at length*).   Good evening, Dorothy. (*Dorothy leaves the doorway, and staggers to a chair. Shelton, alarmed, hastens to her*)   Get some water, Jerry.

DOROTHY.   No, no. I want nothing.

[*Carruthers, carafe in hand, stands motionless. Shelton indicates the door. Carruthers nods, and goes.*

DOROTHY.   Is he gone?

SHELTON.   Yes. (*Genuinely anxious*) Is anything wrong with you, Dorothy?

DOROTHY.   No . . . (*She pauses*) Billy.

SHELTON.   Yes?

DOROTHY.   I've come back.   I've come home again.

SHELTON (*lamely*).   Yes.   So I notice.

DOROTHY.   You got my note?

SHELTON.   Your note?   What note?

DOROTHY.   I sent it with a messenger half an hour ago.

SHELTON.   I haven't seen it.

DOROTHY.   No?   (*She passes her hand over her forehead wearily*)   Billy, it was a farewell.

SHELTON (*with an affectation of surprise*).   What?

DOROTHY.   I was on the point of leaving you: of running off with another man.

SHELTON.   With Cheever?

DOROTHY.   You suspected?   (*Shelton nods.   She goes towards him with outstretched hands*)   Billy, at the last minute something stopped me.   Something made me come home to you.

[*For an instant Shelton is silent.   Then comes the amazing question.*

SHELTON.   Why?

DOROTHY (*staggered*).   What?

SHELTON (*insistently*).   You were on the point of running away.   You had planned everything carefully: people don't do such things on the spur of the moment.   What stopped you?

DOROTHY (*gasping at the shock*).   Don't you love me?

SHELTON (*not answering the question*).   Cheever is a rich man.   Of course, he hasn't got as much as I've got, but he has plenty to take care of you.   The scandal you must have been prepared for.   If you loved Cheever, what made you come back to me?

DOROTHY.   You don't love me, Billy?

SHELTON.   Would *that* have stopped you?

DOROTHY.   Would that have —?   (*She stops, thunderstruck at what she sees within herself*)   I don't know!   (*Breaking down and weeping*)   I don't know, Billy!   (*There is a pause.   Then she gathers herself together*)   Billy, look at me!

SHELTON. Well?

DOROTHY. Am I a good woman?

SHELTON (*hesitantly*). Well —

DOROTHY. Tell me the truth, Billy.

SHELTON. You *were* a good woman when you married me.

DOROTHY (*excitedly*). Yes! That's right! I was a good woman *then*. But am I a good woman *now?* (*He hesitates*) Answer me! Tell me!

SHELTON (*after a pause*). I don't know, Dorothy.

DOROTHY (*desperately*). Billy, neither do I! (*There is a pause*) No girl was ever brought up as I was. We were good: so good! All the people I met were so good! I don't believe any of them ever had a normal impulse. They were saints, Billy, saints! Then you were introduced to me — you remember?

SHELTON. Yes.

DOROTHY. I thought you were the worst man I had ever met. (*Shelton is a little upset, but Dorothy proceeds fluently*) I had heard the most awful stories about you, oh, the most unbelievable things! You and Cheever!

SHELTON (*nodding*). We were pals.

DOROTHY. Yes. I began to think. I knew that if I married a man as good as I was, I'd go mad: stark, staring mad! (*She pauses*) Billy, have you ever felt an impulse to do something outrageous?

SHELTON. Of course.

DOROTHY. What happened?

SHELTON. I did it.

DOROTHY. So did I! For the first time in my life! I married you!

SHELTON (*offended*). Thank you, Dorothy.

DOROTHY. Oh, I've had no regrets! It wasn't good for me, but I've enjoyed it! I've enjoyed it too much!

SHELTON. What do you mean?

DOROTHY. Billy, do you know you've had a great influence on me? (*He cannot answer*) Do you imagine a woman can live with you for two years, as I have lived with you, and remain a perfectly good woman?

SHELTON (*floundering*). Isn't that a little strong?

DOROTHY. The truth is always strong. I'm not blaming you, Billy. You've exerted an influence: it was the only influence you *could* exert.

SHELTON (*gasping*). A bad one?

DOROTHY. The best that was in you.

SHELTON. Which is to say, the worst?

DOROTHY. I suppose so.

SHELTON. And Cheever?

DOROTHY. Another impulse. (*She pauses*) Billy, I never knew until to-day how much bad there was in me. I didn't even know it when I began to go around with Cheever.

SHELTON (*bewildered*). Do you call him a *good* impulse?

DOROTHY. I don't know. I didn't know whether it was the bad in him calling to the bad in me, or that which was capable of being reformed in him calling to the good in me! Which was it? There's bad in me, and there must be some good left in me. But what am I? A good woman or a bad woman? I don't know.

SHELTON (*after a moment's reflection*). You made me stop gambling.

DOROTHY. Yes.

SHELTON. And drinking.

DOROTHY. Yes.

SHELTON. Why?

DOROTHY. I wasn't trying to reform you.

SHELTON. No?

DOROTHY. That came to me to-day. I used to talk to you about your bad habits because, well, because I *liked* to talk about such things. I liked to hear you tell about them.

SHELTON (*after a pause*). Anyhow, I'm reformed.

DOROTHY. Yes.

SHELTON. What are you going to do about it?

DOROTHY. What *can* I do about it? I can't influence you any more: there isn't any *me* left. I look into myself, and I see oceans of Billy Shelton, nothing but Billy Shelton, as far as the eye can reach, and here and there, tossed by the waves, a little wreckage, such pathetic wreckage, that used to be something better! Billy, to-day I am what you have made me.

SHELTON (*thunderstruck*). Which is to say that it was *I* who eloped with Cheever!

DOROTHY. That's what it amounts to.

SHELTON. Well then, what I want to know is, why didn't it go through?

DOROTHY. What do you mean?

SHELTON. If the me in you made you run off with Cheever, what brought you back?

DOROTHY (*after a pause*). Nothing brought me back.

SHELTON. No?

DOROTHY. Cheever *sent* me back. (*There is a long pause*) We had arranged to meet at the station. I met him. We were to send our trunks ahead to Chicago. Mine left yesterday. I was ready to go through with it to the bitter end, but he —

SHELTON. He?

DOROTHY. He changed his mind at the last minute.

SHELTON (*after deliberation*). Why?

DOROTHY. That's what I've been asking myself.

SHELTON. Did he give any reason?

DOROTHY. He didn't have to. Am I a good woman or a bad woman? Cheever knows. I'm not what he thought I was. That's why he didn't elope with me. He found out at the last minute.

SHELTON. That you were a good woman?

DOROTHY. Perhaps.

SHELTON. Or that you were a bad one?

DOROTHY. I'd give anything to know. Cheever knows.

SHELTON. And he won't tell.

DOROTHY. No.

SHELTON (*after a thoughtful pause*).   I like his nerve! (*Dorothy looks at him in mute inquiry*)   My wife not good enough for him to elope with! (*She does not answer*)   Aren't you pretty enough? (*She shrugs her shoulders*)   Or clever enough? (*He surveys her critically*)   Is that something new you're wearing?

DOROTHY.   Yes. I bought it to-day. Do you like it?

SHELTON (*nodding his approval*).   Yes. Looks well on you. (*There is a knock at the door*)   Come in.

THE BUTLER (*entering with a letter on a salver*).   Messenger just brought a note, sir.

DOROTHY.   Oh!

SHELTON (*glances at her. After an instant's hesitation, she nods her permission. He takes it, slowly opens the envelope, and reads the contents. The Butler waits. Shelton notices him*)   Well, why are you waiting?

THE BUTLER.   Is there an answer, sir?

SHELTON.   An answer? No.

[*The Butler goes. In the ensuing silence Shelton tears up the note.*

DOROTHY.   My farewell? (*He nods*)   Well?

SHELTON (*slowly, as if stating a mathematical problem*).   Whatever you are, good or bad, doesn't matter. You've re-formed me so thoroughly that you won't go far wrong in my company — and you're going to have lots of it.

DOROTHY (*submissively*).   Yes, Billy.

SHELTON.   You may make slips: I *expect* you to make slips, but while I'm here to watch you they won't be bad ones.

DOROTHY.   No, Billy.

SHELTON.   And before I forget it: if you have any more outrageous impulses, they will be in *my* direction. You understand? (*She nods. He folds her comfortably in his arms, and smiles happily*)   From now on, I'm prepared to enjoy life.

THE CURTAIN FALLS

MARTHA'S MOURNING

PHOEBE HOFFMAN

Miss Phoebe Hoffman is a resident of Philadelphia, where she was born in 1894 and was educated at Miss Irwin's School. She has published various poems in *Contemporary Verse*, *The Literary Digest*, *The Art World*, *Springfield Republican*, *Public Ledger*, and *Evening Ledger*. "Martha's Mourning" was produced by the Plays and Players of Philadelphia, under the auspices of the Browning Society.

MARTHA'S MOURNING

By PHOEBE HOFFMAN

"Martha's Mourning" was originally produced by the Plays and Players under the auspices of the Browning Society, at the Broad Street Theatre, Philadelphia, May, 1917.

Original Cast

AUNTY	Miss Balburney
MARTHA	Miss Welsh
NEIGHBOR	Mrs. Robert Geddes, Jr.

Printed originally in *Drama*.

Application for the right of performing "Martha's Mourning" must be made to Miss Phoebe Hoffman, 3805 Locust St., Philadelphia, Pa.

MARTHA'S MOURNING

SCENE. *A kitchen.*

An ill old woman lies on a sofa near the stove; close by is a table with some medicines and an oil lamp. In the corner stands a fine old secretary now used for china, and a handsome mahogany mirror hangs in full view of the sofa. The old woman's niece, Martha, sits by the stove. She is a timid girl with pretty hair mercilessly dragged back from her pale face, which is illumined by sad, gentle eyes. She is shabbily dressed and shivers between half-choked sobs. Glancing at the meager fire in the stove, she rises cautiously to fetch a log of wood.

AUNTY (*fearfully*). Stop, stop! (*Controlling herself*) Don't be wastin' the wood.

[*Martha drops the wood and slinks back to her seat.*

MARTHA (*apologetically*). It's so cold, Aunty.

AUNTY (*grimly*). It makes me think of what's comin' to me hereafter. (*Nervously*) Not that I'm afraid.

(*Martha sits down despondently, murmuring softly to herself.*

AUNTY (*sharply*) Don't be mumblin' any more prayers to yerself. I got through this world without askin' help from folk and I don't want others beggin' my pardon in the next. I'm not afraid to face the Lord myself.

MARTHA (*weeping*). But Aunty, that's agin all religion. Let me run and get the minister. He'll explain everything to ye.

AUNTY (*determinedly*). No, no, Martha. The last black-coated snivell came here when the man died. He couldn't change my notions now.

MARTHA. Aunty, let me help you up to bed.

AUNTY. You'll be the first of our folks to die in yer bed, they'll never say it of me.

[*Martha is silent and sits with her hands in her lap, looking vacantly into the stove. Once or twice she starts murmuring a prayer, but checks herself fearfully. Aunty lies rigid, suffering acute mental torture. Several times she raises her hands as if in prayer, but the unaccustomed words will not come to her lips. A clock strikes eight and Martha rises and .pours some medicine into a teaspoon.*

MARTHA (*holding the glass to Aunty's lips*). Here's your physic.

AUNTY (*snatching the spoon and throwing it across the room*). That stuff might make me die in my sleep.

[*Martha silently picks up the spoon.*

AUNTY. You might like that easy kind of an end, I suppose, but I've got red blood in my veins. I'm goin' to fight it out to the last.

[*Martha stands for a moment, the spoon in her hands. She is thinking and plucking up courage to say something unusually bold.*

MARTHA.   Aunty, it's pride, not bravery, that's makin' ye fight the Lord's will. Christ was the bravest man in the world, but He begged for God's mercy and yielded to His will. Ye've defied Him and every one else all yer life. But, Aunty, you mustn't die feelin' like that. (*Coming closer and patting her hand gently*) Aunty, yer half crazy with pain; take some physic and sleep a little, and when ye feel easier, throw yerself on the mercy of the Lord. It won't be too late to repent.

[*Aunty stares at her in astonishment. The truth of Martha's statement sinks deeply into her sin-laden conscience, but she is still too proud and obstinate to admit it to Martha, whom she has always despised for her meekness.*

AUNTY (*in somewhat softer tones*). I've got to settle with the Lord in my own way, Martha. (*More weakly*) I will take some physic, the pain's gnawin' at my shoulder agin. Though it's awful to think of good money bein' poured into a dyin' person at the end of a teaspoon.

[*Martha gives Aunty the medicine and watches her settle into a peaceful doze. Then she kneels in silent prayer shivering till the cold forces her to be active. She feels the windows and draws the rag-carpet against the outside door, then glancing apprehensively at Aunty, she steals out of the room. She returns in a few moments wearing a shabby old coat and carrying a black fur tippet. She sits down and starts mending the lining. As she turns it, the fur brushes against her cheek and she buries her face in it.*

MARTHA. How soft! (*Draws tippet over one shoulder*) I never had on fur before. How nice it feels.

[*Fastens tippet and stands up. Aunty wakens and watches her in amazement. She is about to speak, but changing her mind, closes her eyes as Martha suddenly remembers to look around.*

MARTHA. It must be real handsome. (*Cautiously picks up lamp and goes over to the mirror, peering at herself admiringly*) How stylish I look!

[*There is a rapping outside and Aunty chuckles as Martha, nearly dropping the lamp in her agitation, puts it on the secretary and opens the door. A neighbor enters.*

NEIGHBOR (*stumbling over the carpet*). I near fell.

[*She gives Martha a quick astonished look out of her sharp little eyes and glances inquisitively about the room. She carries a bundle.*

NEIGHBOR. How little ye've changed this place. How's yer Aunty, Martha?

MARTHA (*sadly*). She's low.

NEIGHBOR. The doctor told me she was goin', and I've come to help ye.

MARTHA (*still standing by the door*). Thank you.

[*Aunty is about to burst forth in a rage, but something in Martha's demeanor restrains her. Neighbor moves over to the secretary and puts down her bundle.*

NEIGHBOR. I just brought some things along as I knew ye'd want somebody in the house with ye.

[*Martha glances at Aunty, who feigns sleep.*

MARTHA (*firmly*). I'm afraid I can't ask ye to stay. Aunty

never did like folk about and I know she wouldn't want anybody here now.

NEIGHBOR. But I'll have to dress her out. I've helped with most all the folk that's died in the last twenty years. [*Aunty shudders.*

MARTHA. Thank you kindly, but I couldn't let any stranger touch Aunty.

NEIGHBOR. Surely, ye don't call me a stranger.

MARTHA. I've been so lonely that every one seems like a stranger to me except Aunty.

NEIGHBOR (*spitefully*). Ye're most dutiful to her memory, seein' how mean she treated ye.

[*Aunty shakes her fist in rage, but subsides hastily as Martha looks towards her.*

MARTHA (*hotly*). She never was mean. She always shared everything she had with me.

[*Aunty winces.*

NEIGHBOR (*seeing her chance to catch her up*). Even her tippet, I suppose. I saw ye prinkin' in front of the mirror while ye're Aunty was on her death-bed.

MARTHA (*struck with a sudden inspiration*). Yes, she was tellin' me to wear it at her funeral, and ye wouldn't have seen me if ye hadn't been peekin' through the key-hole.

[*Aunty gasps with astonishment.*

NEIGHBOR (*confused, but not yet downed*). Indeed, that's very generous. I was goin' to offer ye some mournin'.

MARTHA (*hesitating*). I haven't a black dress.

NEIGHBOR (*cheerfully*). I knew I could be of some use to ye. I'll lend ye my alpaca skirt and widder's hat and veil. They'd be grand with the tippet.

MARTHA. Thank you kindly.

NEIGHBOR (*going to secretary and picking up her bundle*). That's a grand piece, Martha, ye ought to sell it. I know a party that might buy it.

MARTHA. Aunty held on to it through thick and thin and I don't want to part with it either.

NEIGHBOR. It looks as if ye were goin' to be poor enough when yer Aunty's little annuity stops short. I should think ye'd be glad of the money.

MARTHA (*resignedly*). I know what's comin' to me.

NEIGHBOR (*turning at the door*). I'll bring the things to-morrer. But Martha, I'll have to charge ye damages if anything happens to my mournin'.

MARTHA (*opening the door, and thoroughly exasperated*). No-body asked for yer mournin'; and I'd rather come to Aunty's funeral in this old calico gown than touch it after that.

[*Shuts the door in the neighbor's face.*

AUNTY. Martha.

MARTHA. Yes. (*Suddenly realizing she still has on tippet and terrified at being caught, she sinks down beside the sofa, a quavering bundle of sobs*) Oh, Aunty, I never did it before.

AUNTY (*patting her hair and comforting her. Speaking tenderly*). Martha, Martha, how I've treated ye! I never knew what ye was like till I saw ye standin' up to that old pry-eyes that came peekin' in on yer trouble. Why ye used to slip round my finger like a piece of limp dough. The man always did favor ye, Martha, and say "Why don't ye send Martha to prayer-meetin' and sociables like other girls." I'd say, "Ah, she's a poor colorless thing with no feelin's." Oh, Martha, can you forgive me?

MARTHA (*weeping joyfully*). Aunty, I knew ye would soften at last, but its the Lord ye should ask for forgiveness. Let's ask Him together.

AUNTY (*stiffening up*). No, no, I can't pray. (*Fiercely*) Impudent old weazel, offerin' ye her shabby mournin'. Run up and fetch down my black silk and bonnet and widder's veil. You'll find 'em in the bottom burrer drawer.

[*While Martha is gone, Aunty raises herself slightly and gazes vacantly ahead, lost in deep thought. Suddenly, her face brightens as she conceives some brilliant idea and she sinks back relieved, with a softened and peaceful smile. Martha re-*

*turns in a few minutes, her arms full of clothes. She stands
awkwardly in front of Aunty, awaiting directions.*

MARTHA.   What shall I do with them?

AUNTY (*with business-like briskness*).   Give me the bonnet and
veil, and put the silk over there. (*Martha moves clumsily*)
Hurry, I haven't much time left. Now bring me the lamp
and the work basket.

MARTHA (*worried*).   Aunty, what are ye goin' to do?

AUNTY (*spryly*).   Trim ye a decent bit of mournin'!

MARTHA (*shocked*).   Aunty, ye should be turnin' yer thoughts
to the Lord.

AUNTY.   I'll relieve yer feelin's, Martha, by tellin' ye that
I had a sort of revelation from the Lord, while you was
upstairs, showin' me how I could make ye a kind of ret-
ribution.

MARTHA (*eagerly*).   A vision, Aunty? What was it?

AUNTY.   No, it was just an idea. I'll tell ye about it by and by.
But part of its trimmin' the mournin'. Now help me up.

MARTHA (*raising her*).   But this doesn't seem quite Christian.

AUNTY.   Christian, fiddle-sticks, I'm doin' as I was told.

MARTHA (*submissively*).   Well, Aunty, I suppose ye know
best. Ye always was one fer doin' yer own way.

[*Aunty groans as Martha arranges her.*

MARTHA (*soothingly*).   Now, what?

AUNTY (*still gasping a little for breath*).   Before I trim the
bonnet, I ought to tell ye there's a little loose board with
a pine knot in it back of the stove. Ye can pry it up with
a spoon handle, and ye'll find an old stockin' underneath.
(*Martha obeys her in blank astonishment*) Bring me the
stockin'. (*Feeling it*) There's a wad of bills in this.

MARTHA (*horrified*).   But haven't we always paid our debts?

AUNTY.   You fool! It's the money I've been savin' for the
last twenty years.

MARTHA (*with great innocence*).   Aunty, you mean ye've been
skimpin' and savin' out of yer little annuity all these
years just for me? (*Falls on her knees, kissing Aunty's
hand*) How generous of ye.

[*Aunty is too much taken aback by her misunderstanding to
explain it. She is confused and suffers Martha's caresses
till she can regain her self-control.*

AUNTY. When ye've paid for the funeral, Martha,—and
ye best give me a costly funeral, it shows filial piety, —
take the savin's to Deacon Wolcott and ask him to invest
it for ye. Ye'd best wear yer funeral rig; he's an awful
one for black. And promise me, Martha, ye'll never let
anybody else look after it, even if ye should marry. I
don't want some fool spendin' my good money.

MARTHA. Yes, Aunty, I promise.

[*Aunty pulls a piece of jet out of the stocking and begins pinning
it against the bonnet.*

AUNTY. Jet ain't regular mournin', but it'll spry ye up a bit.
Don't stand there like a lump of risin' dough, but get into
my black silk. I want to see it on ye.

MARTHA (*astonished*). But, Aunty, you was savin' it to be
laid out in.

AUNTY. But you can make me a real economical shroud.
Mind, I want no other women snivellin' around. I cursed
at 'em all when the man died and nobody's bothered me
since. It's profitable to be wicked.

MARTHA (*looking distressed, and carefully putting on the dress*).
But, ye been savin' it so long.

AUNTY. I won't have ye wearin' pry-eyes' shabby stuff,
and my good silk crumblin' away in the grave. Come
here, I want to try on the bonnet. (*Martha sets it awkwardly on the back of her head*) You make it look like a
hen goin' to roost. Kneel down.

(*Martha kneels and Aunty pinches and pulls at the bonnet
till it is quite becoming to Martha's gentle face. Loosening
Martha's hair*) Now, ye're less like a drowned mouse.
Stand off and let me see the dress.

[*Martha has already gained a new expression of self-confidence
and stands smiling gently.*

MARTHA. Don't it crackle grand?

AUNTY (*surveying it critically*). It'll do well enough under the tippet. Miss Flossy can alter it for ye afterwards. *~phatically)* Don't do it yerself. Ye have about a~ ~ch style as a canary. *(Gathering up the veil)* Now, come back, I want to hang this.

[Martha gives her the bonnet and sits down beside her.

MARTHA. Let me hold the pins, Aunty.

AUNTY. Now, Martha, when I'm dead and gone, don't hide away by yerself, but mingle with folk and go to prayer-meetin' and have the sewin'-circle here.

MARTHA *(with a smile)*. That's strange advice from you, Aunty.

AUNTY. Yes, and open the front parlor and give them some of my good old blackberry cordial to clacker over. If any of the men-folk join ye after meetin', ask 'em in, and be real sociable and give 'em some of yer good pie, but don't give away the receipts, Martha.

MARTHA. But why, Aunty?

AUNTY. It'll make the women talk about ye, and the men folk 'll soon catch on to what a good cook ye are. *(Draping the veil with great care)* It's beginning to look real stylish. There, I've left just a little jet peepin' through. Now, put it on and look at it.

[Martha takes the lamp and stands in front of the mirror. She hardly recognizes herself and beams with delight at her altered image.

MARTHA. Miss Flossy herself couldn't hang it more mournful.

AUNTY *(surveying her work with great satisfaction)*. The Lord ought to give me an awful lot of credit for trimmin' ye a smart bonnet, Martha.

MARTHA *(distressed)*. It's strange ideas ye've been gettin' from the Lord.

AUNTY. It ain't strange He should be rewardin' ye with a husband, is it?

MARTHA *(gasping, and putting down the lamp as her hand trembles)*. A husband, — now I begin to understand. Do you think any one would ever want to marry me?

AUNTY. Indeed, why else should I be expiatin' for my sins by tellin' ye now to catch some respectable, easy-goin' man.

MARTHA. And was that the revelation?

AUNTY. Certainly. The Lord sends strange messengers. It was pry-eyes set me on the road to salvation. (*Putting her hand into the stocking*) Here's my garnet pin.

MARTHA. Uncle's weddin' present!

AUNTY. Wear it to meetin' about a week after the funeral. It'll set the sewin'-circle agog and they'll argue the propriety of it back and forth, with the men on yer side — bein' born contrary. They'll be lookin' fer yer jewels by the next meetin'. Then, tell 'em at some sewin'-circle how yer poor dear Aunty asked ye always to wear her pin. Let me put it on. (*Martha stoops down while she pins it*) Now, put on the tippet and walk as if ye was comin' down the aisle. (*Martha adjusts the tippet and moves slowly and solemnly across the room, almost stately in her flowing draperies, with a new look of tender dignity*) That's it, that's it. Give me a glass of water, Martha.

(*Martha gives her a drink. She sips a little water and falls back wearily. Martha stoops over her anxiously. Feebly*) Pray for me, Martha.

(*Martha kneels in prayer. There is a rapping at the door, but no one heeds it. Presently, the neighbor pokes her head in and advances cautiously into the room, bearing a large box. She creeps up behind Martha, staring at her in astonishment. She studies the bonnet, feels the veil and fur, nodding her head approvingly. She notices the stocking and open jewel case on the sofa, and puts out her hand to take them. Aunty, who has been watching through half-closed eyes, suddenly sits up*) Get out, you old barn-cat! Martha don't want your mournin'. She's got silks of her own and money of her own.

[*She falls back. Martha gives the neighbor a look of contempt and continues kneeling beside the sofa. The neighbor slinks out.*

CURTAIN

RYLAND

A COMEDY

By THOMAS WOOD STEVENS AND KENNETH
SAWYER GOODMAN

"Ryland" was originally produced by The Stage Guild for the Chicago Society of Etchers, February 22, 1912, at the Art Institute, Chicago.

Original Cast

WILLIAM WYNNE RYLAND, Engraver	Frederick K. Cowley
THE GAOLER	Ralph Holmes
HENRY FIELDING, Ryland's Pupil	Roy S. Hambleton
HADDRILL, a print-seller . . .	Thomas Wood Stevens
SIR JOSHUA REYNOLDS . . .	Kenneth Sawyer Goodman
MARY RYLAND	Gertrude Spaller
ANGELICA KAUFFMAN . . .	Elaine Hyman

RYLAND

Scene. *Ryland's cell in Newgate. Right, window, with an engraving screen; a table and stool; engraving tools, etc.; on the wall a composition by Angelica Kauffman. Left, a bench and a barred door, leading to the corridor. Right Center, a small table with breakfast tray.*

Ryland and the Gaoler discovered.

THE GAOLER. Your breakfast, Mr. Ryland. Your last breakfast, God help us all! Many's the good man I've seen go out of here to Tyburn, housebreakers and murderers and thieves, but never a great artist, Mr. Ryland — never till you.

RYLAND. So I'm to be hanged to-morrow morning, eh?

GAOLER. Yes, sir. To-morrow at six.

RYLAND. Well . . . No more of this (*indicating the engraving*) and good-bye to that, eh?

[*With a gesture at the composition.*

GAOLER (*gloomily*). To-morrow at six, sir.

RYLAND. Buck up, man. It's I, not you. You will breakfast to-morrow.

GAOLER. It has been very pleasant, having you here, sir. And profitable, too.

RYLAND. I dare say.

GAOLER. Yes, Mr. Ryland, I've had a tidy bit from the gentlemen who have come in to see you. Some bacon, sir — I can recommend it — none of the prison fare, that. And you've been most comfortable to deal with. No howling, no shaking the bars, no cursing at night.

RYLAND. No, none of that, I hope.

GAOLER. It's because you've been busy with the plate, there. The picture-making has been a blessing to you. Then, you've never given up hope —

RYLAND. I find myself hungry. That's strange.

GAOLER. Not at all, sir. Many of them are so. (*Pause*) Mr. Ryland, might I make so bold as to say, it would be a great service to me, if you would get another reprieve; work a week longer on the plate. It can't be anything to you, sir, so near the end, or I wouldn't be asking it.

RYLAND. It would be a service to you, would it?

GAOLER. You could work at your engraving —

RYLAND. I've overworked it now.

GAOLER. Oh, I'm sorry to hear that, sir.

[*A knock outside. Enter Fielding outside the grating.*

FIELDING. May I speak with Mr. Ryland?

GAOLER. I don't know; it's against the rules. (*Fielding gives him money*) Who shall I say, sir?

FIELDING. Mr. Fielding. You've seen me often enough.

GAOLER. To be sure, Mr. Fielding, but I likes to observe the formalities. It'll be five shillings, sir.

FIELDING. Yesterday it was only two.

GAOLER. He'll be leaving me soon — I've got to make the best of him while he lasts, God help him.

[*He takes the money, unlocks the grating, and calls to Ryland.*

GAOLER. Mr. Fielding's compliments to Mr. Ryland.

[*Exit Gaoler.*

RYLAND. My dear Henry, this is kind of you.

FIELDING. Oh, Mr. Ryland, I came directly I could get word of Lord Wycombe's decision on your appeal —

RYLAND. Oh, the pardon?

FIELDING. Yes, sir —

RYLAND. You'll forgive me if I finish my breakfast. I can't offer you a chair —

FIELDING. Oh, Mr. Ryland!

RYLAND. Well — well?

FIELDING. I went to Lord Wycombe's secretary as soon as he was out of his bed. . . . Oh, Mr. Ryland!

RYLAND. Out with it! Am I pardoned, or only reprieved for another week?

FIELDING. Neither.

RYLAND. Come, come —

FIELDING. Neither, sir. Lord Wycombe denies both your appeals.

RYLAND. I've lost my appetite. . . .

FIELDING (*leaning over him; Ryland looking over his breakfast*). He said you had been three times reprieved, that you might finish this plate; that his lordship had been more than merciful, considering the nature of your crime —

RYLAND. I beg you not to mention it, Henry. I had committed no crime.

FIELDING. Never before, he said, had the statute in so grave a matter as forgery been stayed, and in your case only that your wife might not be left unprovided for.

RYLAND. I understand his lordship's mercy. . . .

FIELDING. And now, he says, if the plate is still unfinished, it must be carried on by another hand.

RYLAND. That will not be necessary

FIELDING. He said that your wife — Oh, Mr. Ryland! . . . where else shall I go? What other appeal is there?

RYLAND (*gets up and puts his hand on Fielding's shoulder*). My poor boy! You have been more than faithful. I can't be altogether worthless, to have you stick to me like this. Tell me — you will take care of her? You will be as devoted to her as you have been to me?

FIELDING. My life, Mr. Ryland, shall be spent in her service.

RYLAND. I dare say. (*Moving up stage*) Well, after all, there's a satisfaction in knowing the next day's work. It might have ended three week's ago. . . . The ride in the cart will be pleasant. The air, man! I've not had a full breath since — since the minions of the law broke in upon my seclusion. . . . But for these reprieves, I should have had it over and done with, and you and my wife would be already half comforted . . . shall I say? It's a miserable business, this shrinking back from the verge.

FIELDING. Oh, sir, you must see that we are on the verge —

RYLAND. I am on the verge, Fielding.

FIELDING. For God's sake, sir, drop this pretense. It's one thing to jest at death when you're safe at home. It's another when you're — . . . Until to-day I never dreamed that you . . . that you could not escape. We must make some last effort.

RYLAND. So you actually expect to see me kicking my heels at the end of a rope?

FIELDING. Oh, sir, you must see it, too. You must think. You must give me orders. If you sit and jest, I am helpless. It will all be over —

RYLAND. My dear boy, what is there you can do? You tell me to drop the pretense. . . . What have I left? I admit I never thought it would come to this. I still believed in my destiny. It's an ignominious end, it seems, . . . and I must meet it with what grace I may. In faith, it matters little : a wasted life gone out : a slender ghost of a talent strangled. . . . (*Moves over to the table where the plate is*) I'm not sorry I've had this respite, Fielding. I've made a good plate here, and in this have paid a last courtesy to Mistress Angelica. I hope she will like it . . . if she ever comes back to see it. She's a dem'd fine woman, Angelica Kauffman, and this is as good a thing as ever she painted. I hope she likes it. . . .

FIELDING. Could Mistress Kauffman do nothing to save you, sir?

RYLAND. She's a white moon, lad! She rides high on the winds of fame these days. It takes a long time for a cry of pain to mount that far, Fielding. . . .

FIELDING. But have you tried? Have you written?

RYLAND. I can be proud on occasion . . . even with a rope around my neck. Once she wasn't so far, so cold. . . . But that's another matter, a matter that's closed. To-morrow . . . tush, I'm content. I'm tired. I'm ready to step off.

FIELDING. But, sir, she might —

RYLAND. No. I had it from Sir Joshua at the trial. She's in Italy.

FIELDING. She's here in London! I saw her only this morning.

RYLAND. Say that again!

FIELDING. She's here in London.

RYLAND. You fool! Why didn't you tell me? You stand there and blither about Lord Wycombe's secretary, when Angelica Kauffman's in London. . . . In London! Why didn't I know it? I did know it. I felt it through these stifling walls. I was a dolt . . . I thought it was only Spring in the air, April in my blood. It was hope, it was life. A moment ago you had me seeing myself on Tyburn Hill! And all the time I knew it could never come to that.

FIELDING. What am I to do?

RYLAND. Bring her here. Hunt her from one end of the town to the other. Bring her here, lad; I must talk to her. She can twist the Queen around her little finger. Through the Queen she can get me a royal pardon.

FIELDING. The time is short.

RYLAND. Time enough if she still cares!

[*The Gaoler knocks at the door.*

GAOLER. A lady to see you, sir.

FIELDING. Ah!

RYLAND. Who is she?

GAOLER. Your wife, sir.

RYLAND. Show her in.

[*Fielding goes to the door and pays the Gaoler; Mary Ryland comes in, and runs across to Ryland.*

MARY RYLAND. William — . . .

RYLAND. Good morning, my dear.

MARY RYLAND. Aren't you glad to see me?

RYLAND. Why shouldn't I be glad to see you?

MARY RYLAND. You look disappointed. You haven't kissed me.

RYLAND. I beg your pardon! (*He kisses her hand, and turns to Fielding*) Well, why don't you go?

FIELDING. Where shall I look for her?

RYLAND. Her house is in Golden Street. If you fail there, go to Sir Joshua. Spend what you need, but lose no time.

MARY RYLAND. Has something happened? Where is he to go?

RYLAND. He is to bring Angelica Kauffman here. He has my orders.

MARY RYLAND. No, I say. I'll not have her here. I'll not have you see her. I'll not allow — . . .

RYLAND. Pardon me, my dear. He shall bring her.

MARY RYLAND (*weeping*). And I've come day after day, and you've treated me like a stranger . . . and now you're sending for her.

FIELDING (*taking a step toward her*). It's all as it should be, Mistress Ryland.

MARY RYLAND. You tell me that, Henry. Do you know? . . .

FIELDING. I know there is need for her.

MARY RYLAND. Then do as you think right.

FIELDING. It's not that, Mistress Ryland. It's necessary, now that Lord Wycombe —

RYLAND. Sst! Go. (*Fielding goes out*) My dear, I'm not flattered by your jealousy, I assure you. There is no need for you to question me — and Mistress Kauffman is a great artist. I must have her see this plate — to-day. That should be enough.

MARY RYLAND. But, William, you knew her before you ever saw me, and it hurts me to think — . . .

RYLAND. There, there, my dear.

[*The Gaoler knocks at the door.*

GAOLER. Mr. Haddrill, on important business with Mr. Ryland.

RYLAND. Ask Mr. Haddrill to sit down outside. You can squeeze an extra shilling out of him for a chair.

MARY RYLAND. But, William, you can't keep Mr. Haddrill waiting.

RYLAND. To-day it is my privilege to keep anybody waiting.

MARY RYLAND. But Mr. Haddrill's your publisher.

RYLAND. He's a tradesman to whom I'm doing a favor. A favor by which you are to profit, not I.

MARY RYLAND. Don't make it harder for me.

RYLAND. Mary, I want a few moments alone with you.

MARY RYLAND. I thought you'd rather be rid of me . . . that you'd rather —

RYLAND. My poor child. You seem to forget that my last plate, the thing I've let them stretch out my life, week by week, to finish — for your benefit; the only profitable thing I can leave you, in this world, is a copper mirror fashioned to reflect the genius of Angelica Kauffman.

MARY RYLAND. It's for her pleasure, her fame, you've been working, not for me. You've sent Fielding to fetch her. . . .

RYLAND. The plate's finished. It must have her approval before . . . I go.

MARY RYLAND. Don't! Don't speak of the end. . . . I can't bear it. I'm your wife.

RYLAND. Poor child. Poor little creature. I think you pity yourself more than you pity me.

MARY RYLAND. How can you? How can you?

RYLAND. Why all this snivelling about so simple a thing as death? A little jaunt from here to somewhere else . . . a step off into the empty air. My dear, it's I that take the step, not you.

MARY RYLAND. Oh! Oh, how can you go on about it this way?

RYLAND. Because I want to see you smile again. Because you're young. Because I've wasted a year of your life, and I'm sorry for it. . . . Because I want you to understand that if it happens I've come to the end of my lane, you are only turning into yours. . . and the hedgerows are white with hawthorn bloom. You'll see the green trees in the Mall, the red sun over the chimney pots, the silver river when you walk on the embankment at night.

MARY RYLAND. But the loneliness, the separation!

RYLAND (*losing patience a little*). Tush! Such separations are only terrible when two people love each other.

MARY RYLAND. But I love you.

RYLAND. No, I dazzled you. . . . And now I want to make it easy for you.

HADDRILL (*heard outside*). I won't wait any longer, Ryland. This business is urgent. (*He comes in, stops on seeing Mistress Ryland, and bows to her rather curtly*) Your servant, madam.

RYLAND. To what am I indebted, Mr. Haddrill?

HADDRILL. In Mistress Ryland's presence — . . .

MARY RYLAND. I pray you not to consider my feelings, Mr. Haddrill.

HADDRILL. Egad, madam, it's for you to say. (*Turns to Ryland*) Here you've put me in a fix! They say you've no more reprieve, no chance of pardon. That you hang at sunrise to-morrow. You should have considered my interest. You should have given me more time.

MARY RYLAND. No reprieve . . . no pardon!

HADDRILL (*paying no attention to her*). Is the plate done, signed, ready to print? Don't you see I've only the day for the edition, and the advertisement and all, or I'll miss the big sale at the stalls along the Tyburn road?

RYLAND. Ah, that would be a pity. It's ready, you see. [*Holds up plate.*

HADDRILL. Ready! . . . But the ink won't be dry before they have the halter on you. And I'd planned to make it a great day in the trade, — a great day, sir, for the art of England. It's a wonderful opportunity for a pushing man — the last plate and the artist hanged to-day . . . I had made some very striking preparations, Ryland.

RYLAND. Hadn't you forgotten something, Mr. Haddrill?

HADDRILL. Not a thing. . . . But you give me so little time. I plan to sell the prints at my shop, in Saint Paul's Churchyard, at Temple Bar, at stalls along the way to Tyburn; and I have six most lugubrious-looking fellows — picked them out for their woebegone faces — all with crepe on their hats, sir, to sell them at Tyburn. Then I've got out broadsides, sir; and I've had a ballad written to sell at the hanging — all about you and your crime, and the prints for sale at my shop. Here it is, sir — like to look at it? (*He hands Ryland a ballad*) And now there's so little chance to get 'em out. I take it very hard, Ryland.

RYLAND. This is miserable stuff.

HADDRILL. I'd have you know, sir, the same author wrote one last month for the celebrated highwayman, Jack Sparrow. It took the town by storm.

RYLAND. My name will go down in illustrious company. . . .

HADDRILL. Perhaps a little revision, with our help?

RYLAND. No, let it serve as it is. I've a bargain to strike with you, Haddrill.

HADDRILL. I thought you'd struck a pretty stiff bargain already, Ryland. I'm to pay your wife five shillings to the pound more than I'd give any living engraver. I've even advanced you ten pounds. I call it sharp practice — . . .

RYLAND. These are my final conditions, Mr. Haddrill. You offer five shillings. That won't do. You must double it.

HADDRILL. Double it!

RYLAND. All proofs must be numbered in the presence of Mr. Fielding.

HADDRILL. You mean you don't trust me, Ryland?

RYLAND. Remember, I shan't be here. I trust Fielding. You've advanced ten pounds. Before the plate leaves my hands she must have fifty.

HADDRILL. Egad, you're driving it altogether too hard.

RYLAND. No, Haddrill, but I understand my position. I'm a public figure to-day. London will stand tiptoe all night to see me hanged in the morning. Another condition. I must see the contract you sign with my relict widow, Mary Ryland here. I must see you sign it in the presence of Fielding and Sir Joshua. They'll hold you to it.

HADDRILL. Look you, Mr. Ryland, I agree to the double royalty. But this goes too far, too dem'd far! I'm a man of my word, sir. I'll not be treated like a shuffling huckster, like a cheating fishmonger, like a dem'd criminal. I'm a communicant of the Church of England, sir! I won't be bound hand and foot.

RYLAND. I thought not.

HADDRILL. Deuce take you, sir! Blast your eyes, sir! What do you mean by that, sir?

RYLAND. Only this. You promise quickly enough, but I mean to see that you perform.

HADDRILL (*taking up his hat*). Very well, sir. Very well. I'm sorry you're so headstrong.

RYLAND. You know how many printsellers there are in London. . . . All waiting for this chance.

HADDRILL. You won't abate your conditions?

RYLAND. Not a penny.

HADDRILL. I'm sorry I can't take you. . . . And I had it all planned.

RYLAND. You had it planned! A clumsy, niggardly plan you had. I know what the town will think. I know how the town will buy. Six hang-dog hucksters with crepe on their hats! That's like you, Haddrill; no taste whatever. Twelve young gentlemen, dressed in the height of fashion — veritable macaronis, — that's what you should have, and them selling the prints like mad, and all for the sake of charity to a pretty widow. . . . Flowers! My cart to be loaded with violets when it stops at St. Sepulchre's. It's an occasion, sir, when the King's Engraver rides to Tyburn! At Holborn Bar you will have them fetch me a flagon of old port —

HADDRILL. But think of the expense, man, the expense!

RYLAND. Will you stick at a few pounds at a time like this? I wouldn't deal in sixpences on a great day for the art of England.

HADDRILL. You dealt in thousands, and see where it brought you. Think of me.

RYLAND. Why should I think of you! I'm the one to be hanged, Haddrill, not you. Broadsides, and a ballad! I can make a speech from the scaffold that'll ring through the town until this plate's worn thin as paper. Where will your ballad and your broadsides be then?

HADDRILL. You'll make a speech?

RYLAND. Aye, that I will. But it depends on you, Haddrill, what sort of speech.

HADDRILL. You're a genius, Ryland.

RYLAND. The speech will cost you twenty pounds extra to Mistress Ryland — mentioned in the contract.

HADDRILL (*writing*). Mentioned in the contract. Violets at Saint Sepulchre's; a flagon of port at Holborn Bar: twenty pounds extra for a speech on the scaffold; twelve young gentlemen — no crepe on their hats. You're a genius, Ryland — but you bargain like a Jew.

RYLAND. I must protect Mistress Ryland's interests.

MARY RYLAND. Oh, oh!

HADDRILL. You'll give me the plate immediately?

RYLAND. When you bring me the contract.

HADDRILL. I give you my oath I'll treat your wife handsomely. I had something else in mind. . . . A very pretty idea, and quite genteel, too; quite up to your tone. If Mistress Ryland would sit in my shop for a week after the hanging and sell the prints herself — . . .

MARY RYLAND. Oh! the shame of it.

RYLAND. How much will you pay her?

MARY RYLAND. William, William, how can you? . . .

RYLAND. Hush, my dear. Mr. Haddrill will think you are over-sensitive. This is a matter of business.

HADDRILL. It would have a great effect. You might mention it in your speech. . . .

MARY RYLAND. This is monstrous. . . . This is terrible. I'll have nothing to do with it. I won't listen. I —

RYLAND. You see, Haddrill, there is still some delicacy of feeling left in England.

HADDRILL. I thought it most genteel, most suitable. Very — well, touching. But it's for Mistress Ryland to say.

RYLAND. She appears to object.

HADDRILL. At least she'll be at Tyburn . . . dressed in black, when the young gentlemen sell the prints. She'll be where the crowd can see her? It would help amazingly.

RYLAND. Surely, my dear, you can't refuse him that much. It's only what any dutiful wife would be expected to do, under the circumstances. . . . You'll have everyone's sympathy.

HADDRILL. Very fitting, very proper, I'm sure. Have you a black dress, Mistress Ryland?

MARY RYLAND. William, this is a nightmare. . . . Tell me I'm not awake, William.

RYLAND. There, there, child! Go with Mr. Haddrill. He'll take you to a draper's. Be sure you get a becoming frock — he has no taste.

MARY RYLAND. No, no!

HADDRILL. Come, madam. I'll bring you back when I fetch the contract.

RYLAND. Yes, child, go. I'm expecting other visitors. . . . Go on with your preparations, Mr. Haddrill.

[*Haddrill and Mistress Ryland start to go out; as they turn away, Ryland laughs aloud, and Haddrill faces about.*

RYLAND. But what if I shouldn't be hanged?

HADDRILL. Good Lord!

RYLAND. Do you think there's a reasonable doubt?

HADDRILL (*thinking it over and smiling grimly*). No, Ryland, I don't. . . . But I confess you gave me a turn.

RYLAND. Au revoir, Mr. Haddrill.

[*Haddrill again turns toward the door, finds it barred, the Gaoler with his hand on the lock. Haddrill steps toward the door, but the Gaoler makes no move to open it.*

HADDRILL. Den of thieves.

[*He pays the Gaoler and goes out. Ryland hums a line of song, and moves about the table, putting his proofs and materials in order. Fielding's voice is heard outside the door.*

FIELDING. Mr. Ryland, Mr. Ryland. I've seen her. . . .

RYLAND. She's coming?

FIELDING. Yes.

RYLAND. Alone?

FIELDING. No. . . . She's bringing Sir Joshua.

RYLAND. The devil!

GAOLER. I don't call this fair to me, Mr. Ryland.

RYLAND. My dear man, you've spoken yourself of the generous treatment you've had from me and my friends. Let this pass, don't be grasping. . . . Besides, there's a lady coming — and a gentleman. They'll pay handsomely. In fact, it would be worth your while to bring in another chair.

GAOLER. I've no wish to be hard with you, Mr. Ryland, but there are rules.

RYLAND. I know. You make them yourself.

FIELDING (*outside*). Am I to come in, Mr. Ryland?

RYLAND (*putting on his coat*). No. You've done your share. Wait and see that this . . . butler welcomes them properly.
[*The Gaoler brings in the chair, and goes out. Ryland moves the chair so that Angelica and Sir Joshua must sit far apart, and hums the song again. The door opens.*

GAOLER. Sir Joshua Reynolds. Mistress Angelica Kauffman.
[*The Gaoler goes out, smiling broadly, as the visitors have been generous.*

SIR JOSHUA REYNOLDS. I trust you'll pardon my intrusion, Mr. Ryland. But ladies of fashion . . . gentleman's apartment . . . you understand. Even in so irreproachable a place as Newgate.

ANGELICA KAUFFMAN (*crossing Sir Joshua*). It grieves me deeply, Mr. Ryland — . . .

RYLAND (*to Angelica*). Couldn't you have trusted me enough to come alone?

SIR JOSHUA (*adjusting his ear trumpet*). Eh, what's that?

ANGELICA. Mr. Ryland spoke of his sense of the honour you do him in coming, Sir Joshua.

SIR JOSHUA. Ah, did he say that? Well, well, where's the plate? We came to see the plate you've engraved from Mistress Kauffman's picture.

[*Ryland holds up the plate, bows Sir Joshua to the chair, extreme right, and goes over to Angelica, handing her the plate.*

RYLAND (*to Angelica*).   It was more, much more than the plate. . . .

SIR JOSHUA.   Eh, what's that?   A little more distinctly, sir.

RYLAND (*to Angelica*).   Confound your dragon. (*To Sir Joshua*)   I wish to consult Mistress Kauffman about the drawing of the arm.

SIR JOSHUA.   Eh?   Oh. . . .   Ah, the drawing.   I shouldn't examine it.   Better let it pass.

ANGELICA.   Oh, lud, sir, I scarcely know how to take you.

SIR JOSHUA.   Always said, dear lady, your art . . . transcends mere drawing.

ANGELICA.   Ah, the kind lies he tosses to the vanity of his friends.   Dear Sir Joshua.

SIR JOSHUA.   Well, sir, have you nothing to show?   No trial proofs?   Let me see the work, sir, and I'll toss you no kind lies.   I've an engagement.

RYLAND.   Give it to him, madam, and for God's sake grant me a moment's speech with you apart.

SIR JOSHUA.   If you desire my criticism, Mr. Ryland, you must speak more distinctly.

ANGELICA (*hands a proof to Sir Joshua*).   Do me the honor, sir.   (*Referring to the plate*) This is all my intention in the cartoon, Mr. Ryland.   You have a wonderful gift of patience.

RYLAND.   Not patience, Mistress, but an exquisite pleasure. . . . to follow your fancy, your sentiment. . . .

SIR JOSHUA.   It does you credit, sir — and the lady as well. Admirable. . . .   Though I see nothing in it to stay the course of justice.

RYLAND (*with lofty resignation*).   So you believe it to be justice, sir?

SIR JOSHUA.   My belief has no weight, Ryland. . . .   But now that this is done, and the legal pother over with, what are you going to do with it?

RYLAND. If it has Mistress Kauffman's approval, what do I care — what they do with it?

SIR JOSHUA. You take it too lightly. The plate must be worth money, and your obligations to your —

RYLAND (*glancing toward Angelica*). Spare me that, Sir Joshua, I beg you. What is money, to a man who lodges here for the last night?

SIR JOSHUA. Rubbish! Your affairs should be left in order. . . . That is the least you can do for —

RYLAND. Do you not understand, sir, that this pains me deeply. Money has been the shadow, the strain of discord, the flaw in the metal. . . . Money has been my ruin . . . and you ask me to spend my last hours haggling —

SIR JOSHUA. Calm yourself, sir. Haddrill, I suppose, brings it out. I'll look to this for you.

RYLAND. That is more than I have a right to ask of you, Sir Joshua.

SIR JOSHUA. Tush, tush. I'm not speaking of your rights, but in the interest of your —

RYLAND. Haddrill will attend to everything. He's bringing me a contract. He's a very generous fellow, Haddrill. I shall sign it, Sir Joshua, without reading.

SIR JOSHUA. Not without *my* reading. . . . Must take care of you, even if you choose to hang yourself.

ANGELICA (*protesting at the word*). Oh, Sir Joshua.

RYLAND. I thank you for that, Mistress.

GAOLER (*at the door*). Mr. Haddrill is back. Says he's forgotten something. Shall I admit him, Mr. Ryland?

SIR JOSHUA. Very fortunate. . . . Show him in. I'll arrange this matter now . . . take care of all the quibbles before they come up.

RYLAND. Sir Joshua, I beg you not to afflict me. I have only a few hours . . . and this is torture. If you are inflexible in your kindness toward me, go to Haddrill and do what you can in my behalf. It's more than I ought to ask . . . and I hope you will not find I have been too heedless.

SIR JOSHUA. It should be done in your presence, but you're so dem'd improvident.

RYLAND. I am not so improvident as to be ungrateful, sir. (*He bows Sir Joshua out and turns to face Angelica*) You at least have a sympathy for me, Mistress; you who understand so well the delicacy of my feelings in an hour like this.

ANGELICA. I hardly know. This is all so shocking, so terrible. I am . . .

RYLAND. Dear lady, I have been a brute to drag you here, you, who live in the glow and the music . . . to see a man in this hopeless gloomy cell, a poor devil who is about to die —

ANGELICA. Please don't . . . . I shall faint.

RYLAND. I beg you not to faint. I will speak of other days, and you shall listen — out of charity. It doesn't so much matter to me now; I've done with it all. But it was hard to face the end without seeing you again. Now I can go. . . . I'm not unready.

ANGELICA. What difference can seeing me make?

RYLAND. What difference? . . . I ride to Tyburn with a vision of you in my eyes, the sound of your voice in my ears, the touch of your pity on my defeated heart. . . . What difference? . . . If you had not come, I should have gone out of here with the gallows swinging before me, and my misspent years blowing in my face.

ANGELICA. This is very sentimental, Ryland. I hardly imagined that you . . . that I —

RYLAND. That it meant so much to me, when you last refused me?

ANGELICA. There, there, Ryland. You knew it was impossible.

RYLAND. I know. . . . You thought you loved —

ANGELICA. I beg you not to speak of him. He was unworthy, and he is gone . . . out of my life.

RYLAND (*suddenly hilarious*). And out of England! Egad, why shouldn't I speak of him. The town talked on nothing else : The distinguished Count de Horn shows an interest in the incomparable Mistress Kauffman; he is accepted; he isn't; he is. . . . They are married; they are not; they are. . . . He is an impostor; he is a prince in disguise; he is the son of his father's cook! and then . . . pouf! He's gone.

ANGELICA. You can not imagine, sir, this is pleasant to me.

RYLAND. Nor was it pleasant to me. The Count de Horn . . . the son of his father's cook . . . and a bigamist! Mistress Kauffman will prosecute; she will not; she will. . . . He was a criminal. He had imposed upon your faith, your heart, your honour. You could have let him hang. . . . But instead of that you gave him his freedom and five hundred pounds.

ANGELICA. Three hundred.

RYLAND. Generous soul!

ANGELICA. I will not remain here, sir, to be taunted with my past misfortunes.

RYLAND. Nothing was further from my intention.

ANGELICA. Then why do you recall this?

RYLAND. I'm sure I don't know. . . . It's my whim to marvel, just for the moment, at the charity which gives a scoundrel, who had wronged you, his freedom and three hundred pounds, while you see a man who has devoted his life to the spreading of your fame, a man who has loved you, and who still loves you, go to the gallows without the compliment of a tear.

ANGELICA. This is most unjust. You have given me neither time nor proper occasion for weeping, Ryland.

RYLAND (*coming close to her*). And it does not occur to you, now that you see me again? . . .

ANGELICA (*she backs toward the door*). Nothing occurs to me; I'm all upset by your impudence.

RYLAND. Unkind, unkind! When this is my last living day, and you could, if you chose . . .

ANGELICA. If you come a step nearer, I shall call Sir Joshua.

RYLAND (*stops and looks at her, his eyes filled with admiration*). The winter in Italy has agreed with you. . . . I've never seen you look so . . . dangerous, Angelica.

ANGELICA. You mustn't call me that. . . . My name —

RYLAND. That was what I called you when we danced together at Tunbridge, the night you laughed with me over Fuseli's proposal; Angelica I called you when we sat together on Richmond Hill, and watched the moon trace out the Thames with silver fingers; Angelica I called you that divine day in Windsor Forest, — the day I first told you I loved you; — Angelica —

ANGELICA. You play upon the word, Ryland, as though it were a refrain.

RYLAND. The refrain of a living love, dearest . . . in the song of a dead life.

ANGELICA. Is it a dead life, William? . . .

RYLAND. It dies at sunrise . . . and all for a few pounds unwisely borrowed, a few creditors inhumanly clamorous, and the lies of a paper-maker who hated me.

ANGELICA. What is it they accuse you of?

RYLAND. Forgery.

ANGELICA. And you are not guilty.

RYLAND. Guilty? . . . I have borrowed unwisely, I tell you. I was hungry for the sight of . . . Italy. Is that guilt? There was a matter of a note — an India company note. Thirty men had signed it, and not one of them at the trial could say the hand was not his own. (*She makes a gesture of inquiry*) This paper-maker . . . he swore he had made the paper on which it was written a year after the date of the note. Guilty? . . . That would have been criminally stupid, and of stupidity no one has ever accused me. . . . For all that, the court passed sentence.

ANGELICA. And is there no appeal?

RYLAND. What need of appeal, if it no longer touches you?

ANGELICA. But if it does touch me?

RYLAND. We have tried what we could. . . . I have been three times reprieved, to finish this plate. It is done. His Majesty is inexorable. But with you in England, with the lure of you —

ANGELICA. Don't tell me you would not make the effort except as I inspired it.

RYLAND. Why?

ANGELICA. I could not believe you.

RYLAND. The truth, then: you can reach the Queen. Through her, King George. Till you came, I had no voice to reach him. You can have what you ask. Let it be . . . my life.

ANGELICA. You want me to go to the Queen?

RYLAND. Yes!

ANGELICA. This would compromise me more deeply than you can imagine.

RYLAND (*sardonically*). You have not imagined how high it will hang me . . . if you refuse.

ANGELICA. And if I fail?

RYLAND. I shall not murmur. . . . But I do not believe you can fail.

ANGELICA. Willliam. William. . . . No, don't come near me. I will go. This must be secret —

RYLAND. You can trust me.

ANGELICA. And there must be no more talk of love . . . no notes, messages, flowers, tokens. You are to be merely a man — an artist — in whose work I take a great interest . . . an innocent man whom I endeavor to deliver from an unjust death —

RYLAND. Stop. I agree to the secrecy, but I do not pledge myself not to love you.

ANGELICA. You must.

RYLAND. I will not take life on these terms. Secrecy — discretion — yes. . . . You can not require that I forget you.

ANGELICA. It cuts me . . . you have been faithful to a memory so long. Perhaps, when this is over, I may permit you to remember again.

RYLAND (*seizing her hand and kissing it*).   Better to blot out
my life than the memories of Richmond Hill!

ANGELICA.   You must keep them deep hidden, William. . . .
These are perilous things, these memories.

RYLAND.   They have been my stay, my comfort, since these
ungentle days came upon me.   A faith like mine, Angelica,
a love that endures unshaken . . . it must be something,
even to you.   Tell me you go to the Queen because you
too remember —

ANGELICA.   It is enough that I go.

RYLAND.   No. . . .   That you go out of love for me.

ANGELICA.   You must content yourself, William. . . .   For
you I go to the Queen.

[*She starts toward the bars, when the Gaoler opens them quietly
and Mary Ryland comes in.   Mistress Ryland pauses,
glances at Angelica, and goes over to Ryland, who waves her
away and sinks back against the table.   Mary comes down,
Left, hesitates a moment, then comes down above Angelica,
Left Center, and falls on her knees, clasping Angelica's
hand.*

MARY RYLAND.   Oh madam, madam!

ANGELICA.   What's this? . . . Let go my hand, girl.

RYLAND.   What brings you back? . . .

MARY RYLAND.   Mr. Haddrill says . . . Oh, Madam, you
could do something, you could help us —

ANGELICA.   Help us?   Who are you, child?

MARY RYLAND.   I'm the unhappiest woman . . . I've been a
jealous fool . . .   But I know he's too proud, too hon-
ourable.   He would die rather than be too heavily beholden
to you.   But I have no pride: I can beg you to plead for
him; I can beseech you on my knees.   If you are not moved
to do your utmost for him, at least you must look with
pity on me. . . .

ANGELICA.   Is this lady your wife, Mr. Ryland?

RYLAND.   Yes.

ANGELICA (*with menace*).   I regret that you omitted to
mention her.

[*Mary Ryland moves away from her, and Ryland sinks back in despair.*

SIR JOSHUA (*heard outside*). Well, I must say, Haddrill, he's driven a sharp bargain with you.

HADDRILL. Sharp bargain! Dem'd close to robbery, I call it.

[*Enter Sir Joshua and Haddrill, Fielding following them.*

ANGELICA (*to Sir Joshua*). So *you've* not found him so simple?

SIR JOSHUA. Simple! He has bound this poor fellow to support *his* wife for the rest of her days.

HADDRILL. I'm a man of my word, Ryland. If you're satisfied, I'll trouble you for the plate. (*Ryland hands over the plate, bowing*) I shall live up to my part of the contract.

RYLAND. You may rest assured as to my part of it.

SIR JOSHUA. I'm sorry, Ryland. I tell you frankly, I wished to think well of you. But this contract . . . a man capable of such a document, sir — I spare you my opinion, in your wife's presence.

ANGELICA (*joining Haddrill and Sir Joshua*). Your presumption, sir; your lack of candour — . . .

RYLAND. My best friends . . . it grieves me exceedingly that the confidence of one's best friends should be turned aside by a man's natural efforts to save his neck and to provide for his family.

MARY RYLAND (*to Angelica*). Madam, is there nothing you can do?

ANGELICA. Nothing I care to do.

FIELDING. Oh, Mr. Ryland, if you would only —

RYLAND. Let me alone. You won't grieve long. You'll get your reward.

MARY RYLAND. Oh, William, William!

RYLAND. Tush, child, go with Fielding. He'll take care of you. You've done enough . . . for me.

ANGELICA. For shame, Ryland! (*She gathers Mary Ryland under her arm*) When you need to see her, Mr. Haddrill, come to me.

HADDRILL (*from the door, where he and Sir Joshua are about to go out*). Your servant, madam.

SIR JOSHUA. Come, Mistress Angelica. Remember, Ryland, I wished to think well of you.

RYLAND. I have not long to remember. Sir, your very humble servant.

[*Exeunt Sir Joshua, Haddrill, and Fielding. Angelica stops at the door and turns back, Mary Ryland with her.*

ANGELICA. She goes under my protection, Ryland.

[*Mistress Ryland leaves Angelica for a moment, and goes slowly over to Ryland, who kisses her forehead and leads her back to Angelica.*

RYLAND. I am filled with gratitude, Mistress. Mary, you will find it most pleasant I am sure. . . . A gay household, Mary — you'll like that.

ANGELICA. Not so gay as it has been, Ryland. You see, I have my husband to consider.

[*Ryland draws himself up, swiftly.*

RYLAND. Your husband? . . . I'm sorry you omitted to mention him. My compliments, madam. (*Exeunt Angelica and Mistress Ryland. Ryland speaks to the Gaoler, who is about to close the door*) It won't be necessary to admit any more visitors.

GAOLER. No, sir. But there's the chaplain to see you, sir.

RYLAND. What's that?

GAOLER. The chaplain of the prison, Mr. Ryland, to see you.

RYLAND (*rising and fumbling with his cravat*). The chaplain.
. . . Oh, God, yes! . . . Yes, yes, yes! I suppose I shall have to see the chaplain.

CURTAIN

THE LAST STRAW

BOSWORTH CROCKER

Mr. Bosworth Crocker was born in Surrey, England, on March 2, 1882, and was brought to the United States in childhood.   He has published "The Last Straw", 1917, "Pawns of War", 1918, and some poems, short stories, criticism, and feature articles, which have appeared in magazines and newspapers, over other signatures.

"The Last Straw" was produced by The Washington Square Players.   "The Dog", "The First Time", "The Cost of a Hat", "The Hour Before", "The Baby Carriage", and "Stone Walls" (a play in three acts), have been successfully given at amateur performances.

THE LAST STRAW

By BOSWORTH CROCKER

"The Last Straw" was originally produced by The Washington Square Players at the Comedy Theatre, New York City, February 12, 1917.

Original Cast

FRIEDRICH BAUER, janitor of the Bryn Mawr	Arthur E. Hohle
MIENE, his wife	Marjorie Vonnegut
KARL, elder son, aged ten	Nick Long
FRITZI, younger son, aged seven . .	Frank Longacre
JIM LANE, a grocer boy	Glenn Hunter

THE LAST STRAW

Time. *The present day.*

Scene. *The basement of a large apartment house in New York City.*

Scene. *The kitchen of the Bauer flat in the basement of the Bryn Mawr. A window at the side gives on an area and shows the walk above and the houses across the street. Opposite the windows is a door to an inner room. Through the outer door, in the centre of the back wall, a dumb-waiter and whistles to tenants can be seen. A broken milk bottle lies in a puddle of milk on the cement floor in front of the dumb-waiter. To the right of the outer door, a telephone; gas-range on which there are flatirons heating and vegetables cooking. To the left of the outer door is an old sideboard; over it hangs a picture of Schiller. Near the centre of the room, a little to the right, stands a kitchen table with four chairs around it. Ironing board is placed between the kitchen table and the sink, a basket of dampened clothes under it. A large calendar on the wall. An alarm-clock on the window-sill. Time: a little before noon. The telephone rings, Mrs. Bauer leaves her ironing and goes to answer it.*

MRS. BAUER. No, Mr. Bauer's out yet. (*She listens through the transmitter*) Thank you, Mrs. Mohler. (*Another pause*) I'll tell him just so soon he comes in — yes ma'am.

[*Mrs. Bauer goes back to her ironing. Grocer boy rushes into basement, whistling; he puts down his basket, goes up to Mrs. Bauer's door and looks in.*

LANE. Say — where's the boss?

MRS. BAUER. He'll be home soon, I — hope — Jim. What you want?

[*He stands looking at her with growing sympathy.*

LANE. Nothin'. Got a rag 'round here? Dumb-waiter's all wet. . . . Lot of groceries for Sawyers.

MRS. BAUER (*without lifting her eyes, mechanically hands him a mop which hangs beside the door*). Here.

LANE. What's the matter?

MRS. BAUER (*dully*). Huh?

LANE (*significantly*). Oh, I know.

MRS. BAUER. What you know?

LANE. About the boss. (*Mrs. Bauer looks distressed*) Heard your friends across the street talkin'.

MRS BAUER (*bitterly*). Friends!

LANE. Rotten trick to play on the boss, all right, puttin' that old maid up to get him pinched.

MRS. BAUER (*absently*). Was she an old maid?

LANE. The cruelty to animals woman over there (*waves his hand*) — regular old crank. Nies * put her up to it all right.

MRS. BAUER. I guess it was his old woman. Nies ain't so bad. She's the one. Because my two boys dress up a little on Sunday, she don't like it.

LANE. Yes, she's sore because the boys told her the boss kicks their dog.

MRS. BAUER. He don't do nothin' of the sort — jus' drives it 'way from the garbage pails — that's all. We coulda had that dog took up long ago — they ain't got no license. But Fritz — he's so easy — he jus' takes it out chasin' the dog and hollerin'.

LANE. That ain't no way. He ought to make the dog holler — good and hard — once; then it'd keep out of here.

MRS. BAUER. Don't you go to talkin' like that 'round my man. Look at all this trouble we're in on account of a stray cat.

LANE. I better get busy. They'll be callin' up the store in a minute. That woman's the limit. . . . Send up the groceries in that slop, she'd send them down again. High-toned people like her ought to keep maids.

* Pronounced *niece*.

[*He mops out the lower shelf of the dumb-waiter, then looks at the broken bottle and the puddle of milk inquiringly.*

MRS. BAUER (*taking the mop away from him*). I'll clean that up. I forgot — in all this trouble.

LANE. Whose milk?

MRS. BAUER. The Mohlers'. — That's how it all happened. Somebody upset their milk on the dumb-waiter and the cat was on the shelf lickin' it up; my man, not noticin', starts the waiter up and the cat tries to jump out; the bottle rolls off and breaks. The cat was hurt awful — caught in the shaft. I don't see how it coulda run after that, but it did — right into the street, right into that woman — Fritz after it. Then it fell over. "You did that?" she says to Fritz. "Yes", he says, "I did that." He didn't say no more, jus' went off and then after a while they came for him and —

[*She begins to cry softly.*

LANE. Brace up; they ain't goin' to do anything to him. . . . (*Comes into kitchen. Hesitatingly*) Say! . . . He didn't kick the cat — did he?

MRS. BAUER. Who said so?

LANE. Mrs. Nies — says she saw him from her window.

MRS. BAUER (*as though to herself*). I dunno. (*Excitedly*) Of course he didn't kick that cat. (*Again as though to herself*) Fritz is so quick-tempered he mighta kicked it 'fore he knew what he was about. No one'd ever know how good Fritz is unless they lived with him. He never hurt no one and nothing except himself.

LANE. Oh, I'm on to the boss. I never mind his hollerin'.

MRS. BAUER. If you get a chance, bring me some butter for dinner — a pound.

LANE. All right. I'll run over with it in ten or fifteen minutes, soon as I get rid of these orders out here in the wagon.

MRS. BAUER. That'll do.

[*She moves about apathetically, lays the cloth on the kitchen table and begins to set it. Lane goes to the dumb-waiter, whistles up the tube, puts the basket of groceries on the shelf of the dumb-waiter, pulls rope and sends waiter up. Mrs. Bauer continues to set the table. Boys from the street suddenly swoop into the basement and yell.*

CHORUS OF BOYS' VOICES. Who killed the cat! Who killed the cat!

LANE (*letting the rope go and making a dive for the boys*). I'll show you, you —

[*They rush out, Mrs. Bauer stands despairingly in the doorway shaking her clasped hands.*

MRS. BAUER. Those are Nies's boys.

LANE. Regular toughs! Call the cop and have 'em pinched if they don't stop it.

MRS. BAUER. If my man hears them — you know — there'll be more trouble.

LANE. The boss ought to make it hot for them.

MRS. BAUER. Such trouble!

LANE (*starts to go*) Well, — luck to the boss.

MRS. BAUER. There ain't no such thing as luck for us.

LANE. Aw, come on. . . .

MRS. BAUER. Everything's against us. First Fritz's mother dies. We named the baby after her — Trude. . . . Then we lost Trude. That finished Fritz After that he began this hollerin' business And now this here trouble — just when things was goin' half ways decent for the first time.

[*She pushes past him and goes to her ironing.*

LANE (*shakes his head sympathetically and takes up his basket*). A pound you said?

MRS. BAUER. Yes.

LANE. All right. (*He starts off and then rushes back*) Here's the boss comin', Mrs. Bauer.

[*Rushes off again.*

LANE'S VOICE (*cheerfully*). Hello, there!

BAUER'S VOICE (*dull and strained*). Hello!

[*Bauer comes in. His naturally bright blue eyes are tired*

and lustreless; his strong frame seems to have lost all vigor and alertness; there is a look of utter despondency on his face.

MRS. BAUER (*closing the door after him*). They let you off?

BAUER (*with a hard little laugh*). Yes, they let me off — they let me off with a fine all right.

MRS. BAUER (*aghast*). They think you did it then.

BAUER (*harshly*). The judge fined me, I tell you.

MRS. BAUER (*unable to express her poignant sympathy*). Fined you!. . . O Fritz!
[*She lays her hand on his shoulder.*

BAUER (*roughly, to keep himself from going to pieces*). That slop out there ain't cleaned up yet.

MRS. BAUER. I've been so worried.

BAUER (*with sudden desperation*). I can't stand it, I tell you.

MRS. BAUER. Well, it's all over now, Fritz.

BAUER. Yes, it's all over . . . it's all up with me.

MRS. BAUER Fritz!

BAUER. That's one sure thing.

MRS. BAUER. You oughtn't to give up like this.

BAUER (*pounding on the table*). I tell you I can't hold up my head again.

MRS. BAUER. Why, Fritz?

BAUER. They've made me out guilty. The judge fined me. Fined me, Miene! How is that? Can a man stand for that? The woman said I told her myself — right out — that I did it.

MRS. BAUER. The woman that had you — (*He winces as she hesitates*) took?

BAUER. Damned —

MRS. BAUER (*putting her hand over his mouth*). Hush, Fritz.

BAUER. Why will I hush, Miene? She said I was proud of the job. (*Passionately raising his voice*) The damned interferin' —

MRS. BAUER. Don't holler, Fritz. It's your hollerin' that's made all this trouble.

BAUER (*penetrated by her words more and more*). My hollerin'! . . . .

[*The telephone rings; she answers it.*

MRS. BAUER. Yes, Mrs. Mohler, he's come in now. — Yes. — Won't after dinner do? — All right. — Thank you, Mrs. Mohler. (*She hangs up the receiver*) Mrs. Mohler wants you to fix her sink right after dinner.

BAUER. I'm not goin' to do any more fixin' around here.

MRS. BAUER. You hold on to yourself, Fritz; that's no way to talk; Mrs. Mohler's a nice woman.

BAUER. I don't want to see no more nice women. (*After a pause*) Hollerin'! — that's what's the matter with me — hollerin', eh? Well, I've took it all out in hollerin'.

MRS. BAUER. They hear you and they think you've got no feelings.

BAUER (*in utter amazement at the irony of the situation*). And I was goin' after the damned cat to take care of it.

MRS. BAUER. Why didn't you tell the judge all about it?

BAUER. They got me rattled among them. The lady was so soft and pleasant — "He must be made to understand, your Honor," she said to the judge, "that dumb animals has feelin's, too, just as well as human beings" — *Me*, Meine, — made to understand that! I couldn't say nothin'. My voice just stuck in my throat.

MRS. BAUER. What's the matter with you! You oughta spoke up and told the judge just how it all happened.

BAUER. I said to myself: I'll go home and put a bullet through my head — that's the best thing for me now.

MRS. BAUER (*with impatient unbelief*). *Ach*, Fritz, Fritz!
[*Clatter of feet.*

CHORUS OF VOICES (*at the outer door*). Who killed the cat! Who killed the cat!

[*Bauer jumps up, pale and shaken with strange rage; she pushes him gently back into his chair, opens the door, steps out for a moment, then comes in and leaves the door open behind her.*

BAUER. You see? . . . Even the kids . . . I'm disgraced all over the place.

MRS. BAUER. So long as you didn't hurt the cat —

BAUER. What's the difference? Everybody believes it.

MRS. BAUER. No, they don't, Fritz.

BAUER. You can't fool me, Miene. I see it in their eyes. They looked away from me when I was comin' 'round the corner. Some of them kinder smiled like — (*Passes his hand over his head*) Even the cop says to me on the way over, yesterday: "Don't you put your foot in it any more'n you have to." You see? He thought I did it all right. Everybody believes it.

MRS. BAUER (*putting towels away*). Well, then *let* them believe it. . . . The agent don't believe it.

BAUER. I dunno. He'da paid my fine anyhow.

MRS. BAUER. He gave you a good name.

BAUER (*with indignant derision*). He gave me a good name! . . . Haven't I always kept this place all right since we been here? Afterwards he said to me: "I'm surprised at this business, Bauer, very much surprised." That shows what he thinks. I told him it ain't true, I didn't mean to hurt it. I saw by his eyes he didn't believe me.

MRS. BAUER. Well, don't you worry any more now.

BAUER (*to himself*). Hollerin'!

MRS. BAUER (*shuts the door*). Well now holler a little if it does you good.

BAUER. Nothin's goin' to do me good.

MRS. BAUER. You just put it out of your mind. (*The telephone rings. She answers it*) Yes, but he can't come now, Mrs. McAllister. He'll be up this afternoon. [*She hangs up the receiver.*

BAUER. And I ain't goin' this afternoon — nowhere.

MRS. BAUER. It's Mrs. McAllister. Somethin's wrong with her refrigerator — the water won't run off, she says.

BAUER. They can clean out their own drain pipes.

MRS. BAUER. You go to work and get your mind off this here business.

BAUER (*staring staight ahead of him*). I ain't goin' 'round among the people in this house . . . to have them lookin' at me . . . disgraced like this.

MRS. BAUER. You want to hold up your head and act as if nothin's happened.

BAUER. Nobody spoke to me at the dumb-waiter when I took off the garbage and paper this morning. Mrs. Mohler always says something pleasant.

MRS. BAUER. You just think that because you're all upset. (*The telephone rings; she goes to it and listens*) Yes, ma'am, I'll see. Fritz, have you any fine wire? Mrs. McAllister thinks she might try and fix the drain with it — till you come up.

BAUER. I got no wire.

MRS. BAUER. Mr. Bauer'll fix it — right after dinner, Mrs. McAllister. (*Impatiently*) He can't find the wire this minute — soon's he eats his dinner.

BAUER (*doggedly*). You'll see. . . .

MRS. BAUER (*soothingly*). Come now, Fritz, give me your hat.

[*She takes his hat from him.*

VOICES IN THE STREET (*receding from the front area*). Who killed the cat! Who killed the cat!

[*Bauer rushes toward the window in a fury of excitement.*

BAUER (*shouting at the top of his voice*) *Verdammte* loafers! *Schweine!*

MRS. BAUER (*goes up to him*). Fritz! Fritz!

BAUER (*collapses and drops into chair*). You hear 'em.

MRS. BAUER. Don't pay no attention, then they'll get tired.

BAUER. Miene, we must go away. I can't stand it here no longer.

MRS. BAUER. But there's not such another good place, Fritz — And the movin' . . .

BAUER. I say I can't stand it.

MRS. BAUER (*desperately*). It . . . it would be just the same any other place.

BAUER. Just the same?

MRS. BAUER.   Yes, something'd go wrong anyhow.

BAUER.   You think I'm a regular Jonah.

[*He shakes his head repeatedly in the affirmative as though wholly embracing her point of view.*

MRS. BAUER.   Folks don't get to know you. They hear you hollerin' 'round and they think you beat the children and kick the dogs and cats.

BAUER.   Do I ever lick the children when they don't need it?

MRS. BAUER.   Not Fritzi.

BAUER.   You want to spoil Karl. I just touch him with the strap once, a little — like this (*illustrates with a gesture*) to scare him and he howls like hell.

MRS. BAUER.   Yes, and then he don't mind you no more because he knows you don't mean it.

BAUER (*to himself*).   That's the way it goes . . . a man's own wife and children . . .

MRS. BAUER (*attending to the dinner. Irritably*).   Fritz, if you would clean that up out there — and Mrs. Carroll wants her waste-basket. You musta forgot to send it up again.

BAUER.   All right.

[*He goes out and leaves the door open. She stands her flat-iron on the ledge of the range to cool and puts her ironing-board away, watching him at the dumb-waiter while he picks up the glass and cleans up the milk on the cement floor. He disappears for a moment, then he comes in again, goes to a drawer and takes out rags and a bottle of polish.*

MRS. BAUER (*pushing the clothes-basket out of the way*).   This ain't cleanin' day, Fritz.

BAUER (*dully, putting the polish back into the drawer*).   That's so.

MRS. BAUER (*comforting him*).   You've got to eat a good dinner and then go upstairs and fix that sink for Mrs. Mohler and the drain for Mrs. McAllister.

BAUER (*in a tense voice*).   I tell you I can't stand it. . . . I tell you, Miene. . . .

MRS. BAUER.   What now, Fritz?

BAUER.   People laugh in my face.   (*Nods in the direction of the street*)   Frazer's boy standin' on the stoop calls his dog away when it runs up to me like it always does.

MRS. BAUER.   Dogs know better'n men who's good to them.

BAUER.   He acted like he thought I'd kick it.

MRS. BAUER.   You've got all kinds of foolishness in your head now . . . .   You sent up Carroll's basket?

BAUER.   No.

MRS. BAUER.   Well —

[*She checks herself.*

BAUER.   All right.

[*He gets up.*

MRS. BAUER.   It's settin' right beside the other dumb-waiter. (*He goes out*)   O Gott! — O Gott! — O Gott!

[*Enter Karl and Fritzi.   Fritzi is crying.*

MRS. BAUER (*running to them*).   What's the matter?

[*She hushes them and carefully closes the door.*

KARL.   The boys make fun of us; they mock us.

FRITZI.   They mock us — "Miau! Miau!" they cry, and then they go like this —

[*Fritzi imitates kicking and breaks out crying afresh.*

MRS. BAUER.   Hush, Fritzi, you mustn't let your father hear.

FRITZI.   He'd make them shut up.

KARL.   I don't want to go to school this afternoon.

[*He doubles his fists.*

MRS. BAUER (*turning on him fiercely*).   Why not?   (*In an undertone*)   You talk that way before your little brother. — Have you no sense?

FRITZI (*beginning to whimper*).   I d-d-d-on't want to go to school this afternoon.

MRS. BAUER.   You just go 'long to school and mind your own business.

KARL AND FRITZI (*together*).   But the boys. . . .

MRS. BAUER.   They ain't a goin' to keep it up forever.   Don't you answer them.   Just go 'long together and pay no attention.

KARL.   Then they get fresher and fresher.

FRITZI (*echoing Karl*).   Yes, then they get fresher and fresher.
[*Mrs. Bauer begins to take up the dinner. The sound of footfalls just outside the door is heard.*

MRS. BAUER.   Go on now, hang up your caps and get ready for your dinners.

FRITZI.   I'm going to tell my papa.
[*Goes to inner door.*

MRS. BAUER.   For God's sake, Fritzi, shut up.   You mustn't tell no one.   Papa'd be disgraced all over.

KARL (*coming up to her*)   Disgraced?

MRS. BAUER.   Hush!

KARL.   Why disgraced?

MRS. BAUER.   Because there's liars, low-down snoopin' liars in the world.

KARL.   Who's lied, Mamma?

MRS. BAUER.   The janitress across the street.

KARL.   Mrs. Nies?

FRITZI (*calling out*).   Henny Nies is a tough.

MRS. BAUER (*looking toward the outer door anxiously and shaking her head threateningly at Fritzi*).   I give you somethin', if you don't stop hollerin' out like that.

KARL.   Who'd she lie to?

MRS. BAUER.   Never mind.   Go 'long now.   It's time you begin to eat.

KARL.   What'd she lie about?

MRS. BAUER (*warningly*).   S-s-sh!   Papa'll be comin' in now in a minute.

KARL.   It was Henny Nies set the gang on to us.   I coulda licked them all if I hadn't had to take care of Fritzi.

MRS. BAUER.   You'll get a lickin' all right if you don't keep away from Henny Nies.

KARL.   Well — if they call me names — and say *my* father's been to the station-house for killing a cat . . . ?

FRITZI.   Miau! Miau! Miau!

MRS. BAUER.   Hold your mouth.

FRITZI (*swaggering*).   My father never was in jail — was he, Mamma?

KARL. Course not.

MRS. BAUER (*to Fritzi*). Go, wash your hands, Fritzi.

[*She steers him to the door of the inner room, he exits.*

MRS. BAUER (*distressed*). Karl . . .

KARL (*turning to his mother*). Was he, Mamma?

MRS. BAUER. Papa don't act like he used to. Sometimes I wonder what's come over him. Of course it's enough to ruin any man's temper, all the trouble we've had.

CHORUS OF VOICES (*from the area by the window*). Who killed the cat! Who killed the cat!

[*Sound of feet clattering up the area steps. Fritzi rushes in, flourishing a revolver.*

FRITZI. I shoot them, Mamma.

MRS. BAUER (*grabbing the revolver*). *Mein Gott!* Fritzi! Papa's pistol! (*She examines it carefully*) You ever touch that again and I'll . . . .

[*She menaces him.*

FRITZI (*sulkily*). I'll save up my money and buy me one.

MRS. BAUER (*smiling a little to herself*). I see you buyin' one.

[*Carries revolver into inner room.*

FRITZI (*in a loud voice and as though shooting at Karl*). Bang! Bang! Bang!

[*Karl strikes at Fritzi; Fritzi dodges.*

KARL (*to his mother as she re-enters*). Trouble with Fritzi is he don't mind me any more.

MRS. BAUER. You wash your dirty hands and face this minute — d'you hear me, Fritzi!

FRITZI (*looking at his hands*). That's ink stains. I got the highest mark in spelling today. Capital H-e-n-n-y, capital N-i-e-s — Henny Nies, a bum.

[*Mrs. Bauer makes a rush at him and he runs back into the inner room.*

KARL (*sitting down beside the table*). Do we have to go to school this afternoon?

MRS. BAUER. You have to do what you always do.

KARL. Can't we stay home. . . .

MRS. BAUER (*fiercely*). Why? Why?

KARL (*sheepishly*) I ain't feelin' well.

MRS. BAUER. Karlchen! . . . *sham dich!*

KARL. Till the boys forget. . . .

MRS. BAUER. Papa'd know somethin' was wrong right away. That'd be the end. You mustn't act as if anything was different from always.

KARL (*indignantly*). Sayin' *my* father's been to jail!

MRS. BAUER. Karl. . . .

KARL. Papa'd make them stop.

MRS. BAUER (*panic-stricken*). Karl, don't you tell Papa nothing.

KARL. Not tell Papa?

MRS. BAUER. No.

KARL. Why not tell Papa?

MRS. BAUER. Because —

KARL. Yes, Mamma?

MRS. BAUER. Because he *was* arrested yesterday.

KARL (*shocked*). What for, Mamma? Why was he —

MRS. BAUER. For nothing. . . . It was all a lie.

KARL. Well — what was it, Mamma?

MRS. BAUER. The cat got hurt in the dumb-waiter — Papa didn't mean to — then they saw Papa chasin' it — then it died.

KARL. Why did Papa chase it?

MRS. BAUER. To see how it hurt itself.

KARL. Whose cat?

MRS. BAUER. The stray cat.

KARL. The little black cat? Is Blacky dead?

MRS. BAUER. Yes, he died on the sidewalk.

KARL. Where was we?

MRS. BAUER. You was at school.

KARL. Papa didn't want us to keep Blacky.

MRS. BAUER. So many cats and dogs around. . . .

FRITZI (*wailing at the door*). Blacky was my cat.

MRS. BAUER. S-s-h! What do you know about Blacky?

FRITZI. I was listening. Why did Papa kill Blacky?

MRS. BAUER. Hush!

FRITZI. Why was Papa took to jail?

MRS. BAUER. Fritzi! If Papa was to hear. . . .
[*Mrs. Bauer goes out.*

FRITZI (*sidling up to Karl*). Miau! Miau!

KARL. You shut up that. Didn't Mamma tell you.

FRITZI. When I'm a man I'm going to get arrested. I'll shoot Henny Nies.

KARL (*contemptuously*). Yes, you'll do a lot of shooting.
[*Fritzi punches Karl in back.*

KARL (*striking at Fritzi*). You're as big a tough as Henny Nies.

FRITZI (*proud of this alleged likeness*). I'm going to be a man just like my father; I'll holler and make them stand around.

KARL (*with conviction*). What you need is a good licking.
[*Telephone rings; Karl goes to it.*

KARL. No, Ma'am, we're just going to eat now.

FRITZI (*sits down beside the table*). Blacky was a nice cat; she purred just like a steam engine.

KARL. Mamma told you not to bring her in.

FRITZI. Papa said I could.
[*There is the sound of footfalls. Bauer and his wife come in and close the door behind them.*

MRS. BAUER (*putting the dinner on the table*). Come, children. (*To Bauer*) Sit down, Fritz.
[*She serves the dinner. Karl pulls Fritzi out of his father's chair and pushes him into his own; then he takes his place next to his mother.*

MRS. BAUER (*to Bauer, who sits looking at his food*). Eat somethin', Friedrich.
[*She sits down.*

BAUER. I can't eat nothin'. I'm full up to here.
[*He touches his throat.*

MRS. BAUER. If you haven't done nothin' wrong why do you let it worry you so?
[*Children are absorbed in eating.*

FRITZI (*suddenly*). Gee, didn't Blacky like liver!

[*Mrs. Bauer and Karl look at him warningly.*

MRS. BAUER (*fiercely*). You eat your dinner.

BAUER (*affectionately, laying his hand on Fritzi's arm*).
Fritzi.

FRITZI (*points toward the inner room*). I'm going to have a
gun, too, when I'm a man.

[*Bauer follows Fritzi's gesture and falls to musing. There
is a look of brooding misery on his face. Karl nudges
Fritzi warningly and watches his father furtively. Bauer
sits motionless, staring straight ahead of him.*

MRS. BAUER (*to Bauer*). Now drink your coffee.

BAUER. Don't you see, Miene, don't you see? . . . Nothing makes it right now; no one believes me — no one
believes me — no one.

MRS. BAUER. What do you care, if you didn't do it.

BAUER. I care like hell.

MRS. BAUER (*with a searching look at her husband*). Fritzi,
when you go on like this, people won't believe you didn't
do it. You ought to act like you don't care . . . (*She
fixes him with a beseeching glance*) if you *didn't* do it.

[*Bauer looks at his wife as though a hidden meaning to her
words had suddenly bitten into his mind.*

BAUER (*as though to himself*). A man can't stand that.
I've gone hungry . . . I've been in the hospital . . . I've
worked when I couldn't stand up hardly. . . .

MRS. BAUER (*coaxingly*). Drink your coffee, drink it now,
Fritz, while it's hot.

[*He tries to swallow a little coffee and then puts down the cup.*

BAUER. I've never asked favors of no man.

MRS. BAUER. Well, an' if you did . . .

BAUER. I've always kept my good name. . . .

MRS. BAUER. If a man hasn't done nothin' wrong it don't
matter. Just go ahead like always — if —

BAUER (*muttering*). If — if —

MRS. BAUER (*to the boys*). Get your caps now, it's time to
go to school.

[*Karl gets up, passes behind his father and beckons to Fritzi to follow him.*

FRITZI (*keeping his seat*). Do we have to go to school?

BAUER (*suddenly alert*). Why, what's the matter?

FRITZI. The boys —

MRS. BAUER (*breaking in*). Fritzi!

(*The boys go into the inner room. Bauer collapses again. Mrs. Bauer, looking at him strangely*) Fritzi — if you didn't —

BAUER. I can't prove nothing — and no one believes me. (*A pause. She is silent under his gaze*) No one! (*He waits for her to speak. She sits with averted face. He sinks into a dull misery. The expression in his eyes changes from beseeching to despair as her silence continues, and he cries out hoarsely*) No one! Even if you kill a cat — what's a cat against a man's life!

MRS. BAUER (*tensely, her eyes fastened on his*). But you didn't kill it?

[*A pause.*

MRS. BAUER (*in a low appealing voice*). Did you, Fritz? DID you? (*Bauer gets up slowly. He stands very still and stares at his wife. Karl's voice.* "Mamma, Fritzi's fooling with Papa's gun.")

[*Both children rush into the room.*

KARL. You oughta lock it up.

MRS. BAUER (*to Fritzi*). Bad boy! (*To Karl*) Fritzi wants to kill himself — that's what. Go on to school.

[*Boys run past area.*

VOICES. Who killed the cat! Who killed the cat!

[*At the sound of the voices the boys start back. Instinctively Mrs. Bauer lays a protecting hand on each. She looks around at her husband with a sudden anxiety which she tries to conceal from the children, who whisper together. Bauer rises heavily to his feet and walks staggeringly toward the inner room.*

MRS. BAUER (*in a worried tone as she pushes the children out*). Go on to school.

[*At the threshold of the inner room, Bauer stops, half turns back with distorted features, and then hurries in.   The door slams behind him.   Mrs. Bauer closes the outer door, turns, takes a step as though to follow Bauer, hesitates, then crosses to the kitchen table and starts to clear up the dishes.   The report of a revolver sounds from the inner room.   Terror-stricken, Mrs. Bauer rushes in.*

MRS. BAUER'S VOICE.   Fritz!   Fritz!   Speak to me!   Look at me, Fritz!   You didn't do it, Fritz!   I know you didn't do it!

[*Sound of low sobbing . . .   After a few seconds the telephone bell . . . It rings continuously while the* CURTAIN *slowly falls.*

HATTIE

ELVA DE PUE MATTHEWS

MRS. ELVA DE PUE MATTHEWS (Mrs. Warren Shepard Matthews) was born in California, April 23, 1889. She has studied at Dana Hall, Massachusetts, The University of California, Columbia University, and in Europe. In June, 1918, she married Warren Shepard Matthews. She has written several articles for magazines, but "Hattie" is her only play.

HATTIE

A DRAMA

By ELVA DE PUE

"Hattie" was originally produced by The Morningside Players, April 22, 1917, at the Comedy Theatre, New York.

Original Cast

HATTIE	Sophie Wilds
MINA	Clarice McCauley
MRS. SCROGGINS	Mildred Hamburger
TIM	Robert A. Pines
HEINRICH	Roger Wheeler

Printed originally in "Morningside Plays."
Application for the right of performing "Hattie" must be made to Mrs. Warren Shepard Matthews, 2226 Sacramento Street, San Francisco, California.

HATTIE

TIME: *The Present.*

SCENE: *Room in a New York tenement. At the back of the stage a cot in left corner, and next it a mattress made up as a bed. On the right a cupboard and a table. On the left an old bureau. A door at the back leads into the next room; a door at the right into the hall. Across the hall from it are supposed to be the outside door to the street and a window. A woman comes in hurriedly from the hall. She is a small, bright German, whose hair at first appears to be gray, but turns out to be flaxen. When excited, she has an accent. She goes hastily to the door in the back of the stage.*

MINA (*calls*). Mrs. Scroggins! Oh, Mrs. Scroggins!

[*A tall woman opens the door and gestures to silence Mina. She has a long neck that stretches forward, near-sighted eyes with which she is always examining what is nearest, and a parrot nose. She has in her hand a brown blanket.*

MRS. SCROGGINS. Sh . . . ! He's asleep. You don't want him hollering all evening, do you?

MINA. I'll just take a look at him.

[*She slips past Mrs. Scroggins into the other room.*

MRS. SCROGGINS (*tossing the blanket on the mattress*). Aw, shucks! He's all right . . . if you'd let him alone.

[*Mina reappears smiling, closing door carefully.*

MRS. SCROGGINS. Well, I ain't hurt him, have I? Where's Hattie? I want to talk to her . . . I thought you two worked in the same laundry.

MINA. She stayed behind for something to-night. She wouldn't tell me. . . . You know how quiet she is. I just had to run ahead and see if my baby was all right.

[*She takes off her cape and battered hat and hangs them on hooks over the mattress.*

MRS. SCROGGINS (*huffily*). All right! I ain't going to eat him. . . . Here's your blanket. But now let me tell you something . . . if you expect to stay right along here as a steady thing, Hattie's got to pay me more for this room. You said when you come you was going to stay *a few days*. A few days! It's been *some* few! Nearly three weeks.

MINA (*blinking rapidly*). Ah, Mrs. Scroggins, you ain't goin' to put up the rent on her! Every day I think I hear dot my Heinrich has got a job. Sure I thought it was goin' to be a few days!

MRS. SCROGGINS. You Germans, you think you just about own the country! Here I been takin' care of your squallin' kid for only fifty . . .

MINA (*pleadingly*). I'll pay you a little more for that . . . lemme see . . . only I don't want to get Hattie into trouble. Mrs. Scroggins, please don't say nothin' to her . . . she's been so good to me. I wasn't used to workin' right along at one job . . . them irons seemed so heavy to me . . . You see, little Heinie ain't only six months old, and I give out, the first day . . . Hattie, she was the only one was sorry for me . . . she brought me here to stay so's I could be pretty near to my work.

MRS. SCROGGINS. Yes, you and her's been as thick as thieves. . . . (*Suddenly*) . . . What'd you go and turn her against my son Tim, for? Hey? That's what I'd like to know! [*The door opens and Hattie comes in. She is a big, raw-boned girl, seemingly gruff. She has had few friends and seems shy and suspicious. She looks defiantly at Mrs. Scroggins. She is carrying three packages, which she lays down. Mrs. Scroggins approaches them, peering curiously.*

MRS. SCROGGINS (*in a conciliatory tone*). Well, here you are! Been shoppin'?

HATTIE (*shortly*). Where's the baby?

MINA. Oh, he's in there sleepin' just fine. . . . I thought I wouldn't wake him up.

[*Hattie goes into the next room. Mina has thrown herself on the cot in an attitude of exhaustion. Mrs. Scroggins wanders about aimlessly, Hattie comes back. She notices Mrs. Scroggins eyeing the packages and removes her things deliberately. Finally she undoes one bundle, a loaf of bread. She starts to put it in the cupboard, then puts it out on the table instead. With it she sets out some sausage.*

MRS. SCROGGINS (*no longer able to contain herself, pokes the large bundle*). What you got here, Hattie?

HATTIE (*sheepishly*). Nothin'.

MRS. SCROGGINS (*with withering sarcasm*). Seems to take a terrible lot o' good paper to do up nothin' in!

[*Hattie looks at her sullenly. There is nothing left to do but to open the package. It is a baby's tin bath tub. Mina gives an exclamation of pleasure. While Mrs. Scroggins is examining the tub, bottom side up, Hattie slips the third package in the bureau drawer.*

MRS. SCROGGINS. For the land's sakes! The way you do for that child . . . you'd think he was your first born, 'stead of another girl's . . . .

MINA (*sitting up, much enlivened by the good fortune of acquiring a tub*). Ach, I must go to phone to the grosmutter . . .

MRS. SCROGGINS. To who?

MINA. She's . . . Why, my husband's mutter. . . . She's been takin' care of my other children ever since. . . .

MRS. SCROGGINS. Your other children?

MINA (*proudly*). Sure! I got two nice girls . . . one can't see so very good, but she's getting better . . . and one more boy. . . . Say, Hattie, you got two nickels for this dime?

[*Hattie gets them from her coat pocket.*

MRS. SCROGGINS. For the love o' Gawd! And you so little and sick like. . . .

MINA. Oh, I ain't really sick!

[*She puts on her dingy cape, but no hat, and goes out.*

MRS. SCROGGINS (*spitefully*). You see here, Hattie. . . . You're throwin' money around on other people's brats, when you ought to be havin' some of your own. (*Hattie, putting coffee on the stove to heat, turns suddenly and stares at the other woman)* And you can up and pay me a dollar more for this here room; understand? You make good wages . . . . I heard tell you was one of the best workers they got, doin' that fancy ironin'. (*She pauses for breath. Hattie looks at her steadily without answering. Annoyed at not feeling justified in her demands, Mrs. Scroggins tries to work herself up into a fit of indignation)* What on earth did you get yourself all mixed up with her for, anyhow?

HATTIE (*muttering*). The work was too hard for her.

MRS. SCROGGINS. Well, you fool, you can't afford to start a hospital for all the laundry girls that ain't feelin' like workin', can you? (*Hattie makes no reply, which irritates Mrs. Scroggins, who cannot understand any one not liking to talk)* What on earth's the matter with you lately, anyhow? You go around with your jaw hangin' . . . like this . . . (*Makes a face denoting dejection)* Why can't she help you pay for the room . . . . She makes good money at that laundry, too, I bet.

HATTIE (*drily*). Good money!

MRS. SCROGGINS (*stamping her foot*). You drive me crazy just repeating what I says! Why don't she pony up, I'm askin'?

HATTIE (*in a low tone*). Sends it to the other kids. Husband's lost his job.

MRS. SCROGGINS. Oh, yes. That's what she's tellin' you, I know. I guess, maybe, there ain't no more husband than there is a job! Ha! Ha!

HATTIE (*hotly*). There is too!

[*As they talk Hattie unconsciously draws near the door, for there is a noise of thumping outside, going along the hall. Hattie, drawn up tensely, keeps looking toward the door. The thumping passes without stopping. Her shoulders droop forward dejectedly.*

MRS. SCROGGINS You seen him yourself?

HATTIE (*with a start*). Seen him? Seen who?

MRS. SCROGGINS (*with exasperation*). There you go again! Why don't you listen to what I'm sayin'? Seen her husband, of course.

HATTIE (*sullenly*). Naw! When he come, I was out with Tim.

MRS. SCROGGINS. Now you take my word for it, I've seen the world. . . . I know these here soft-spoken little chits. . . .

VOICE OUTSIDE. Say, Maw!

HATTIE (*jumping*). That's Tim, ain't it? Why don't he . . . s-stop in here any more?

MRS. SCROGGINS. I guess you know that as well as me.

HATTIE. What do you mean?

MRS. SCROGGINS. You know all right . . . I can tell by the look on your face. What d'ye tell him you wasn't goin' with him no more unless he quit sellin' papers? D'ye think a sperrited feller like Tim is goin' to stand for that kind o' talk? He was doin' all right at it, too. You kep' at him till he nearly went an' tuk a job as bartend in O'Shaunessy's saloon down here at the corner . . . (*With a sneer*) . . . You're so high and mighty . . . too good for him, eh?

HATTIE (*tensely, with clenched fists*). No, no. That wasn't it at all. I wanted him to get a better job, something that would get him on . . . so as . . . so as . . . I didn't want him to be a bartend, though.

MRS. SCROGGINS. Yes, so as to have money to throw around on you.

HATTIE. No, no . . . so as we could . . . get married . . . sometime.

MRS. SCROGGINS. He works hard enough. He was willing to marry you on what he's getting.

HATTIE. That's not enough! You know that's not enough! Why look at Mina . . . she says . . .

MRS. SCROGGINS (*furiously*). That Mina! I knowed it was her turned you against him!

HATTIE (*slowly*). I saw . . . from her . . . you got to be careful.

MRS. SCROGGINS. Careful? Tim would make any girl a good husband! There's plenty as thinks so too.

HATTIE (*on the verge of breaking down*). I didn't go to make him mad. I just spoke of the delicatessen shop . . . they need a clerk there. Tim's so smart . . . he could . . . he could . . . I hate to have him have to borrow money off of me.

MRS. SCROGGINS (*hotly*). See here! Don't you come a-complainin' of Tim to me! I've always humored him with his lameness and all . . . I ain't goin' to have no abusin' of him. You're too old for him anyways . . . . He's got another girl now.

HATTIE (*with effort*). Who do you mean?

MRS. SCROGGINS. That Sadie Horst . . . .

HATTIE (*shrilly*). That . . . that little . . . she . . . she makes eyes at every feller . . . .

MRS. SCROGGINS. Shut up your insults. She ain't makin' eyes at Tim. . . . She means business.

VOICE (*from back*). Say, Maw, what about supper? Do I get it or don't I?

MRS. SCROGGINS (*annoyed*). I'm *comin'*, if you'll wait a second. [*She goes out, reopens the door and sets a clothes basket on the mattress with a bump. Hattie stares at the door a moment, then runs to the basket, takes out the baby, holds him close, hiding her face. Through the window comes the glow of a street lamp. Pause. Mina opens the door and enters.*

MINA. Hattie! Ach, there you are! Why don't you light the gas?
[*Mina finds a match, lights the gas in center of the room. She hangs up her cape and holds out her arms for the baby.*

HATTIE (*in a husky voice*). Say, Mina, can't I . . . fix him and give him a bath to-night? It kind o' takes my mind off of . . .

MINA (*solicitously*). Why, Hattie, what's been happening? Mrs. Scroggins . . . did she . . . did she stay long after I went out? (*Indignantly*) Did she sass you about the rent or anything? (*Hattie bends over the baby, but does not answer. Putting an arm over Hattie's shoulder*) That Tim . . . Has he been bothering you again?

HATTIE (*throwing off Mina's arm; in a tearful voice*). Botherin'? Not likely he'll bother me no more! He's got another girl.

MINA. Another girl! How do you know? Did he tell you?

HATTIE. No, Mrs. Scroggins did. (*Suddenly*) You never did like Tim! I wish I'd never listened to you.

MINA. Mrs. Scroggins! Ach, she just tries to make you jealous! Don't you pay no attention to that.

HATTIE (*wistfully, wanting to be convinced*). Do you think that's it?

MINA (*heartily*). Sure! Don't you see? She wants that Tim to get you. She wants him to have an easy time . . . to live off of you instead of off of her. She was as sweet as honey cakes to you till you had that fight with him . . . now she's a little grouchy.

HATTIE (*her spirits rising somewhat*). We'd ought to be a-givin' him his bath.

[*Mina gets the tub and fills it in the hall. She kneels on the other side of it from Hattie.*

MINA. Tim, he yust waitin' for you to make up with him.

HATTIE (*undressing the baby*). Don't you be too sure. Fellers here ain't so faithful as they are . . . some places.

MINA. Well, if you want to make up with him, you stick to what I told you. . . . You tell him you won't marry him without enough to bring up a family on. . . . You better give him to me, your hand is shaky. (*Hattie hands her the child, cooing to him*). . . Look, he's getting fat . . . just since I come here to you.

HATTIE (*in a dull voice*). Aw, you needn't worry about me and Tim. We ain't goin' to make up.

MINA (*to the baby*). Ach, you was a little kicker! Yust see him kick . . . Hattie, you're awful touchy. I noticed it with the girls at the laundry. You seemed like you was scared of Tim.

HATTIE (*shamefacedly*). Always think people ain't goin' to like me . . . I feel so kind o' awkward and ugly.

[*She gets a towel for Mina.*

MINA. Ach, no, you ain't so bad.

[*She blinks at her friend in embarrassment.*

HATTIE. Now you, you're friendly to all of 'em, and you make me feel right to home with you.

MINA. Anyway, you got the best heart of 'em all. When I was so sick, it was you who took me home. The others said they was sorry, but they shied off, I noticed . . . (*Wiping the child*) . . . He was pretty weak when he was born, but I think he's gaining all right now.

HATTIE (*hesitatingly*). The other ones, are they strong?

MINA (*after a moment*). The two oldest, they are. I had a little girl that died, and then little Elsa, I had an awful time with her . . . poor little thing . . . I used to wish I could feel the pains for her.

HATTIE (*with her face buried, shuddering*). Yes, it don't seem fair for them to start out without a chance . . . ain't it funny? Those that have 'em don't want 'em, always . . . and there's other people, that hasn't anybody of their own . . .

MINA (*reflectively*). It's mighty different here from on a farm in the old country. Here you haf to like a feller pretty much before you want to take a chance on all the trouble . . . (*In a more cheerful voice*) . . . Now my Heinrich, he's so different to most of the Americans. I don't mind the trouble . . . if we . . . if we could only stay together.

[*She puts the baby in the basket and takes the tub away to empty it.*

HATTIE. Do you think he will find something soon?

MINA. Oh, yes, I know he will. He tries so hard . . . I yust know how crazy he is for to get us all together again.

[*Her face lights up and she looks much younger.*

HATTIE (*wistfully*). It must be fine to be so sure of anybody. You don't mind the hard work, if you think it's getting

you anywheres. (*Suddenly*) Now what am *I* workin'
for, I'd like to know? What am I livin' for?

MINA (*alarmed by Hattie's unusual violence*). Ach, Hattie,
you'll get somebody of your own. . . . You'll feel better
to-morrow, maybe.

HATTIE. Somebody! You can't understand why I like
Tim. . . . His shiftlessness just makes me like him all the
more. I kind o' want to look out for him. It ain't his
fault his mother spoiled him. And the way he grins, kind
of to one side, and his blue eyes shinin', and all . . . I guess
I'm a fool.

[*She breaks down, sobbing hard.*

MINA (*patting her on the shoulder*). Say, he'll be comin' out
from his supper pretty soon. (*She goes to the bureau and
pokes about in the drawer. She holds up a little white dress,
which she has taken out of the paper in which it was wrapped.
To divert Hattie's mind*) Did you do this, Hattie? When
did you iron it? (*Hattie nods, wiping her eyes*) When
did you? It's just swell!

HATTIE (*with an occasional sob*). After you left to-day. The
boss let me use the fluter.

MINA. It's lovely. I put it on him the first time my Heinrich is to see him.

[*She hunts further in the drawer and finally brings out a
piece of bright green ribbon, which she takes to Hattie.*

MINA. I don't wear this now, try it on.

[*Hattie shakes her head. A thumping is heard in the hall.
Hattie suddenly rouses herself, gets up and takes the ribbon.
She ties it nervously around her neck, glancing now and then
furtively in the little cracked mirror over the bureau. She
wipes her eyes. The thumping goes into the hall. Mina
opens the door, and motions Hattie towards it. Hattie,
trembling, does not move, but shrinks back. Mina pulls her
with all her might. They almost struggle. Hattie finally
stands in the door, pressed against the casing. She breathes
hard with a rigid face. Mina slips back and busies herself
about the food.*

HATTIE (*faintly*).   Hello, Tim!

VOICE (*outside, carelessly*).   Hello, Hat!
[*He does not stop.*

HATTIE (*with visible effort as he is passing*).   Say, Tim, can't
you come in . . . just a minute?
[*Tim limps into the room, standing just inside the door.   He
is slightly shorter than Hattie, with reddish hair, blue eyes,
and a thin face, with a sarcastic smile which has an indefin-
able charm for girls, in spite of his infirmity.   A short
pause ensues, agonizing for Hattie, boring to Tim, and
unnoticed by Mina, who is scanning Tim carefully.*

HATTIE (*choking a little*).   Make you acquainted with my
friend, Mrs. Kleber.
[*Tim murmurs an inarticulate salutation, looking at the door.*

MINA.   Can't you set down, Mr. Scroggins?

TIM.   Naw, I can't. . . . Got to see somebody . . . outside.
[*He turns.*

HATTIE (*with a gasp*).   Right . . . right away?

MINA (*seeing how disturbed Hattie is*).   Ach, stay awhile and
eat somethin' . . . or have a cup of coffee.

TIM (*looking uncomfortably toward the door*).   Naw, I can't,
sure . . . I just eat.   I got a date . . . .
[*With a faint smile.*

HATTIE (*throwing her pride to the winds*).   You don't ever. . .
make dates with . . . with me, no more, Tim.

TIM.   Whose fault's that?

HATTIE.   Oh, Tim!   I never meant to throw you down.
I only wanted you to get another job . . . for your own
good. . . .

TIM.   Yes, for my own good.   Say, I can picture myself in
the delicatessen joint there among the pickles and cheeses
and sauerkraut!   Nobody ever goes in there but fat old
Dutch women.   I'm off the Germans, I tell you.   (*Hattie
looks ready to faint*)   'Stead of being outside with the fellers that sells for me, goin' where I please, seein' all that
goes on, talkin' to all kinds of folks . . . that's my job, and
it's as good or better than any . . . it's good enough for me.

MINA. But you don't get ahead.

TIM (*resenting Mina's interference and her knowledge of his having been repulsed*). Well, there's others as ain't so fussy about my gettin' ahead.

HATTIE (*taking a sharp breath and moving toward him*). Tim, forget what I said. I don't care what you do . . . I . . .

[*Tim, showing off before the other woman, holds up his hand humorously to ward off Hattie. He smiles crookedly, not unkindly.*

TIM. It's pretty late to come honeyin' round me now. How d'ye know I ain't goin' to get married . . . maybe this afternoon? There's somebody outside.

HATTIE. Tim . . . you're not. . . .

TIM (*loftily*). Well, maybe I'll put it off a day or two . . . but I'm goin' to get hitched, all right. . . . So long.

[*He limps out with unusual speed. Hattie waits a moment, then runs after him. She calls him once, but it is muffled in the bang of the door. She looks out the window in the hall and Mina hears her give a sharp ejaculation. Then she reënters the room, staggering a little, and tears the ribbon from her neck, dropping it and treading on it. She throws herself face downward on the mattress. For a moment Mina watches her with clasped hands and an agonized expression, not daring to speak.*

MINA. Hattie. . . .

HATTIE (*frantically*). What did you make me see him for? What did you push me for? I'm so ashamed. . . . Oh, I'm so ashamed.

MINA (*in a small voice*). I . . . I knew you wanted to talk to him. . . . Did you see who was outside?

[*She blinks apprehensively at Hattie.*

HATTIE (*smothering her sobs in the bed*). That Sadie . . . that girl with the black eyes. . . . Oh, oh! I always knew he would like somebody else.

MINA (*trying to soothe her*). Never mind, Hattie, he wasn't good enough for you anyway!

HATTIE (*bursting forth vehemently*). Not good enough! Not good enough! (*With a laugh like a scream*) . . . Who's good enough then? Who's good enough? Who's ever goin' to look at me? He's the only feller I ever had. It's better to have one like him than nobody at all. . . .

MINA. Ach, poor Hattie, I'm so sorry. . . .

HATTIE. You, . . . you spoiled my last chance. You told me not to marry him . . . I was a coward . . . I was afraid . . . I can just see that Sadie's black eyes. . . .

MINA (*feeling that she has brought disaster, and sobbing more than Hattie*). Ach, Hattie, an' you bin so good to me too. . . . [*She creeps up to Hattie and takes her hand. Seeing that Hattie does not resent it, she puts her arm about her and they cry together.*

MINA (*sitting up, trying to divert Hattie*). Say, we ain't ate our supper. . . . (*Hattie makes no answer. She takes the coffee from the stove and pours out a cupful*) Come on, Hattie, you better have a bite . . . (*Hattie shakes her head*) . . . A cup of this kaffee will do you good.

HATTIE (*drags herself up and leans over the basket*). He ain't had his . . . (*sobs*) . . . milk. (*Mina gets the baby's bottle, but Hattie takes it from her. She pours milk into a saucepan to heat. She goes into the hall to rinse the bottle, then tries to fill it from the pan. Turning suddenly to Mina*) How old are you?

MINA (*surprised*). I . . . guess I'm twenty-six.

HATTIE (*tonelessly*). You got four children, ain't you?. . . (*She lets the milk drip on the floor*) And I'm thirty-seven . . . thirty-seven years old, and . . .

MINA (*changing the subject*). Look out, Hattie, all the milk is spilling. Leave a little in the pan, we can feed him again in the night . . . the way you did last night. Ach, Gott! How tired I was last night. Anyway, Hattie, you got your strength!

HATTIE (*bitterly*). What good's that?

MINA. Last night when you was so good to get up and feed him, I thought for a minute I had my good Heinrich

back. You bin so awful good, I'd like to help you sometime. . . . I'd like to do something nice for you.

[*Hattie gives the baby his bottle and stands watching him.
Mina is putting away the food.*

HATTIE. Lemme take care of him, then.

[*There is a knock at the door. Hattie starts violently, runs
toward it, then stops to get her breath.*

HATTIE (*in a loud whisper*). Did you hear anybody . . .
come up . . . did you, Mina? We was talkin' and maybe
didn't hear. . . .

MINA (*also agitated*). Open the door, quick.

[*The knock is repeated and Hattie opens the door, so that Mina
does not at first see who it is. From Hattie's attitude Mina
knows it is not Tim.*

VOICE (*outside*). Say, my wife Mina . . . she bin here?

[*Mina runs to the door and pulls in a big man with clean
skin and a shock of blond hair, his clothes those of a workman. Hattie draws back. The couple stand looking joyfully
into each other's eyes, then Mina with a little cry throws her
arms about his neck. Hattie turns away, bends over the
basket, and seeing they do not notice her, picks up the baby.
The two whisper, and Heinrich's voice rises as he says
something in German. He kisses his wife below the ear, and
Mina smiles.*

MINA (*remembering they are not alone*). Say, Hattie, what do
you think? He's bin and got a job in Brooklyn, driving
a wagon for a big grocer. He's took a room already in
Brooklyn, and he's got the wagon downstairs, right now
to take us over in. He wanted to surprise me.

HEINRICH. Where's the little one? Ach, so, here he is.

[*He takes the baby from Hattie clumsily.*

MINA (*delightedly*). Ain't he got fat, Heinrich?

HEINRICH (*beaming and laying the baby in the basket*). Oh,
Mina, I brought some boxes that you can put your things
in. You don't have to carry them in the shawl. I better
go get them while you get ready.

[*He goes out.*

MINA (*excitedly*). He thinks of every single thing. Ain't he a fine man? And so good. He says he got a job where they let him drive horses. (*She spreads her shawl and piles a few things in*) You see he lost his job before 'cause they changed the horses to having autos . . . he likes so much better to drive horses . . . he likes them.

[*She sees Hattie is not listening.*

HATTIE (*in a high unnatural voice*). You goin' to take . . . the baby . . . away?

MINA. What you say?

HATTIE. You goin' to take . . . .

[*Pointing to the basket.*

MINA (*in amazement*). Take my little Heinie? Why, what you think I do?

HATTIE. Couldn't you leave him . . . just a few days . . . till I got used to bein' alone?

MINA. Leave him here? How could I leave him here?

HATTIE (*desperately*) You said . . . maybe you'd do something for me . . . I'll be all alone, and . . .

MINA (*after a pause, much concerned*). Yes, that's right . . . I been so happy, I forgot all about that.

HATTIE. You got all the others, and your husband . . .

MINA (*very doubtfully*). But I'm afraid . . . supposin' he gets sick, or . . .

HATTIE. I'll let you know right away. I know how to take good care of him. Oh, please, Mina.

MINA (*uncertainly, not knowing how to refuse*). Well, I'd like to do it for you, sure I would, Hattie, but I got to see what Heinrich says.

HATTIE. He won't let me . . . you beg him . . . can't you make him?

[*She holds Mina's arm in a frantic grip. Heinrich enters with two large boxes. Hattie drops Mina's arm.*

HEINRICH. Whew! I run up all them steps. Here's your trunks, Mina.

[*Mina piles her belongings into the box, glances at her husband, but says nothing. She looks around the room to see if she has left anything. Hattie hands her a saucepan. Heinrich looks around, too, finds an empty baby's bottle and puts that in. Hattie stares at it, looking from it to Mina. Mina sees the tin bath tub, which she does not take.*

HEINRICH (*pleasantly unconscious of anything*). Well, you don't need so many trunks, eh?

MINA (*slowly*). Heinrich, Hattie, she been awful good to me.

HEINRICH. Much obliged to you, Miss, I'm sure. It was fine for you and Mina to be company for one another. I'd like to pay you for half your room. How much do you give for it? (*Hattie shakes her head and mumbles*) Yes, yes, go ahead, I can afford to pay you.

[*He sets the empty box on end by the door. Hattie looks at him appealingly.*

MINA (*not knowing how to begin*). Heinrich, she don't want the money, but . . .

HEINRICH. Well, if she won't have it . . . much obliged, Miss, I'm sure. . . . Come on, Mina, you bring Heinie, and I'll take this.

[*He starts to take up the full box.*

MINA (*trying to gain time*). Maybe can't we stay here a little while longer?

HEINRICH (*straightening up*). Stay here? It's getting late and we got a long way to go.

MINA. Well, you see, Hattie, she's goin' to be awful lonesome. Maybe we could leave . . . little Heinie . . . with her.

HEINRICH. That's a good joke . . . leave little Heinie, eh? His father ain't seen him for some time.

MINA. No, but really, Hattie, she would like to keep him . . . just a little while; she can feed him fine now.

HEINRICH. You giving away your baby? You're crazy, Mina?

MINA. Hattie, she goin' to be awful lonesome.

HEINRICH. What's the matter with you, Mina? You ain't never complained about takin' care of the children before.

How can she look out for him like his mother? (*More sternly*) You and she been havin' too easy a time, yes?

MINA (*reproachfully*). Ach, Heinrich.

HEINRICH. Now come on, no more nonsense!

MINA (*more and more faintly*). But I promised her I would do something for . . .

HEINRICH (*used to being obeyed and getting angry*). Sure you can do something for her, but not give her your child, Gott im Himmel!

MINA (*breathing fast*). Not for one night?

HEINRICH. Why don't she get an orphan, if she don't want a family of her own? (*Mina tries to stop him, but he raises his voice*) There's too many unmarried women in this country. All they want is an easy time . . . no responsibility.

[*Hattie has drawn further back in the room. Heinrich takes the child summarily and the box under the other arm and stalks out of the room. Mina, with alarm, goes toward Hattie, who stares at her fixedly. Mina murmurs "Good bye, Hattie, good bye, I . . . I'll come and see you." Hattie does not answer and Mina slips out. The baby cries, Hattie listens and takes a few steps toward the door. She turns and looks about the room, sees the green ribbon on the floor, picks it up, and starts across the room, stumbles over the bathtub, picks it up, stands holding it for a moment, and then lets it fall with a clatter and throws herself across the mattress.*]

CURTAIN

DREGS

FRANCES PEMBERTON SPENCER

MRS. FRANCES PEMBERTON SPENCER is a resident of Los Angeles, California, where she is at present turning out eighteen and more synopses of scenarios a week, besides doing a great amount of critic work and revising. In addition to this, however, she has found time to write a few plays, all of which have been successfully produced and one of which, "Dregs", received a first prize from the Plays and Players of Philadelphia.

Mrs. Spencer states that "Dregs" was not a sudden inspiration, but on the contrary, was written in order to keep her from being bored by life in a sanatorium where she was trying to recuperate from a case of shattered nerves. The play began as a collaboration, but the partnership dissolved almost immediately when it was found that the two authors disagreed entirely upon the kind of person who leads a crook's life. Mrs. Spencer maintained that the fashionable, charming person, who is so very often seen as a crook upon the stage, is not true to life, for when he is so charming he is not under the necessity of leading a crook's life, but may be a president, a moving picture actor, or anything else he pleases. With this theory, Mrs. Spencer began her own creation of the plot. When it was presented by the Plays and Players it was a great success, and won by a big majority over the two other plays which were chosen for the contest.

Mrs. Spencer's other plays are: "In That Darkest Hour", "Patriotism", and "The Eternal Triangle."

DREGS

By FRANCES PEMBERTON SPENCER

"Dregs" was originally produced by the Plays and Players, at the Little Theatre, Philadelphia, on May 8, 1916.

Original Cast

JIM . . . . Mr. Henry C. Sheppard
NANCE . . . . Mrs. Frances Pemberton Dade
THE BOY . . . . Miss Emma Fegley Mearns
THE DETECTIVE . . . . Mr. Vinton Freedley
POLICEMAN . . . . Mr. Howard F. Brinton

Director — Mrs. C. Yarnall Abbott

DREGS

A MELODRAMA IN ONE ACT

TIME.   *The Present.*

SCENE.   *A room distinctly sordid in appearance, the furnishings unhappily combining the kitchen, dining, parlor, and bedroom all in one.   Up stage to the right, an unvarnished wooden table with an oilcloth covering.   Above this two shelves hold some battered-looking dishes, one tin and one china cup.   Door at center back.   Up stage to the left, a dilapidated folding bed, down stage left, an old-fashioned stove built into the wall with shelf above.   A kitchen chair is facing it.   A depressing remnant of upholstery and satin, falsely posing as an "easy-chair", holds the center of the stage.   To the right of this a musty looking lounge decorated with an equally musty looking pillow and an untidy scattering of woman's clothes.*

As the curtain rises Nance is discovered sitting hunched up close to stove.   That the coals are not "burning brightly" is quite evident, since her hands are almost touching them and her contracted position suggests anything but warmth.   She looks about the room vaguely until her eyes light on a cigarette box that rests upon the center chair.   She crosses stage and opens it eagerly.   It is empty.   She throws it impatiently upon floor and returns to former position at stove.   Discovers a cigarette stump under it; lights it from matches on shelf, inhales a long puff and sinks back into smoky meditation.

The door opens and Jim enters.   He is breathing quickly and rather heavily, partly from excitement, partly from the weight of the child that he carries in his arms.

Nance goes forward with something of the adoration of a dog for its master showing in her eyes.

NANCE. Hello, Jim. (*Then, seeing the child she stops*) Why! What in Hell? A child!

JIM (*peremptorily*). Lock the door.

[*She obeys quickly.*

NANCE. Where'd ye get him? — What are ye goin' to do with him? Why did you bring him here?

JIM (*moving toward couch*). Move those things.

[*She obeys and the clothes are dropped upon the floor. He lets the child slide with rough carelessness from his arms to the couch.*

NANCE (*suppressed exclamation of dismay*). Yer cruel rough handlin' a kid.

JIM (*laughing sardonically*). He ain't likely to object at the present time.

NANCE. Ye don't mean — he ain't —

JIM. Yep — doped, — that's what he is.

NANCE. Jim! Jim! hadn't I better try to rouse him? He looks fearful strange. Hadn't I better wake him? Hadn't I, Jim?

[*She leans over the boy.*

JIM. And have him rouse the whole police force with his yells? Damn ye. He's all right. It's only one-sixteenth grain of morphine. Here's the rest of it. (*Takes small box from pocket. Grimly*) I'm saving it; if things don't pan out right he'll need a bigger dose next time.

[*Puts drug back in pocket, removes coat and throws it over chair, center.*

NANCE (*with a little moan, covering her face with her hands*). Gawd, ye *have* kidnapped him then?

JIM. Did ye think I was hired as his wet nurse? (*Nance moans again*) Here, brace up. No hysterics. This is going to be the biggest thing we ever pulled — if ye keep yer wits about ye.

NANCE (*with an effort at control*). Whose child is he?

JIM. Did ye ever hear of Judge Freeman?

NANCE (*with wide, awe-stricken eyes*). Freeman, the millionaire?

JIM (*with emphasis*). The multi-millionaire.

NANCE. Jim! This ain't the kid Freeman has jest adopted, that the papers is all talkin' about and showin' pictures of and all that.

JIM. Yes, it's his legally adopted son all right. Of course the free advertisin' they give him does add to the danger, but if we win — we'll get at least twenty thousand *each*.

NANCE (*in a low tone*). And if we lose, at least twenty years is comin' to us both.

JIM. Oh, ye white-faced snivellin' female! Can't ye do anything but croak?

NANCE (*swallowing the insult submissively*). Are ye goin' to tell me how ye swiped him, Jim?

JIM (*eyeing her suspiciously*). No, I ain't, nor how I'm goin' to get rid of him again. Taxi Louis is in this game with me and I guess we'll play our hands without yer help. Ye can get out if ye want to; there ain't no ties between us that need hold ye here.

NANCE (*wincing*). Don't, Jim. I'd rather ye beat me than talk to me like that — Is it my fault a minister ain't said words above our heads? — Could a wife be faithfuler? — Love ye more? — Don't I obey ye absolute?

JIM. Then what in Hell is wrong?

NANCE. This deal is, Jim, — so wrong it scares me. I never balked before — ye know that. I've stole fer ye, lied, done any crooked thing ye told me to.

JIM. Cut it. Ye was crooked when we met. I plucked ye off the prison steps.

NANCE (*eagerly*). That's just it. That's what I'm sayin'. I've always been a bad un. We're just two seeds, Jim, you and me, two seeds that was planted in the mud. Gawd hisself must find excuse for us; don't his own flowers stretch up towards the sun?

JIM. Ah, what are ye drivin' at?

NANCE. Don't ye see? Oh, don't ye understand? We gotta live, and so we pick pockets, play any con games that we can — but kidnappin', stealin' a helpless little child and sellin' him for gold — that's different. Horrible! It'll bring its punishment.

JIM. Rot, it don't hurt the kid if they take him back again.

NANCE. But suppose they don't take him back. Suppose the Judge decides a kid out of a charity home ain't worth payin' twenty thousand for, what then?

JIM. Do ye think me a fool? Do ye suppose I haven't looked into all that? He'll pay $20,000, double that if I choose to ask it; he's dippy over the kid. Would he made it heir to all his millions if he wasn't? What's twenty or forty or eighty thousand dollars to a man like him? He'll pay. He'll pay just what I choose to bleed him for (*savagely*) or by God I'll —

NANCE (*down on her knees beside his chair*). No! No! Jim! Don't say it, don't swear no oath like that. Yer queer hard-set when once ye've said a thing. Don't yer see what yer doin'? Boltin' the jail door from the inside, buildin' your own scaffold. Look at all the kidnappin' cases that ye know. How many gets away with it? The whole world's yer detective, even the crooks; yer own kind'll despise you.

(*He rises, throwing off her hands which clutch in frantic entreaty. Crosses left*) Take the child back. Just this once do what I ask, do it, Jim. Ye can cook up a story about findin' him wanderin' along the street. Ye gotta do what I ask ye. Take him back.

[*Her voice rises hysterically.*

JIM (*shaking her savagely and putting his hand across her mouth*). Swallow that or I'll put ye both to sleep.

NANCE. Ye-es, I'm tryin' to. (*She slips her arms about his neck*) No, don't shove me away. Don't ye want me close like this?

JIM. I don't want no coward woman.

NANCE. Do ye think I wouldn't go through Hell if ye could face it with me? It ain't the fear of prison, Jim, it's the separatin'. Twenty years they'd send us up for, twenty years apart! When we met again perhaps ye wouldn't be so different; yer a man, but I'd be a bent, wrinkled, yellow thing, jest a *thing* that ye'd spit at fer darin' to look ye in the face. What's twenty or forty thousand, Jim, against the strength of yer arms, the softness of me, the bein' young together? Why, even when you've beat me the pain's a kind of hurtin' joy. Twenty thousand. Why, Jim, there's things that Mr. Rockefeller, with all his millions, couldn't buy.

JIM (*with an effort shaking off the influence of her appeal*). It ain't no use, Nance.

[*He passes left, picking up his hat and starting towards the door.*

NANCE. *Jim*, where are ye goin'?

JIM. A woman always runs to fear and pity. I don't trust ye. I'm goin' to 'phone Louis to bring his taxi here and take the kid away.

NANCE. Jim, for Gawd's sake, there ain't nothing in this world ye could ask of me, I wouldn't do for ye. Just this one — for Gawd's sake —

JIM. Cut it. (*Nance stares at him a moment, throws herself face downward into chair on which his coat is lying. It is an acknowledgment of defeat. She sobs, Jim opens door, but closes it again. He stands looking down at her and then sinks into chair at left. He covers his face with his hands, remaining motionless until her sobs have quieted, then slowly, and evidently with an effort, he speaks*) I tell ye it ain't no use, Nance. It's mebbe all true, what ye've been sayin', I dunno — it makes no difference. If I'm jailed for all time, if I've got to *swing* for it, *I'm goin' to see this through.* If ye want to listen — I'll try to make ye understand.

I'll begin where ye spoke of us bein' two seeds that was planted in the mud. Life didn't start me that way. Oh, I hadn't any fancy riches, but my people was — respectable and I was straight enough, until I run to seed. I guess it's an ordinary happenin' — go to any ten-cent movie and ye'll see it on the screen. Young man falls in love, marries.

Love! I thought Gawd proved hisself by creatin' her.
He comes home from work one night, finds a letter; she's
gone off with another man. At the end of a few months
the man tires of her, taunts her with desertin' of her child
and husband, she comes back home, dies.

I guess the movie actors has got more strength than I had.
The boy had heart trouble, a leakin' valve the Doctor called
it. There was the Hell o' death behind me, and it looked
as though the future was a-holdin' it again. I paid a
woman half my wages to look after the boy, but he kept
gettin' worse. I took to drinkin'; it seemed to ease somethin' inside of me that burned. The boss warned me, but
I wouldn't stop; then one day he fired me. There was a
row; I beat him up. After that there wasn't no chance of
gettin' other work.

If it hadn't been for the boy, I would have ended it all,
cashed in; but the woman had gone when I couldn't pay
her. There was just him and me to face things — it seemed
to bring us closer. I couldn't chuck him — my little pal.
I quit drinkin', tried — My God, how I did try to get work,
but luck all played against me — I suppose I was a pretty
rough-lookin' customer, all my clothes was hocked except
the suit I wore; in the scrap with the foreman he'd managed to plant his fist inside my eye — it didn't want to heal.
There was a discouragin' afternoon when I come in and the
boy didn't shout and run to meet me, but just lay a smilin'
little heap upon the floor. That night I held up a man —
successful. The swag lasted for a week. But I was too
green to know the ropes, and the third time that I crooked
they caught me in a pawnshop with the goods on.

I was "sent up" fer a year. I knew I deserved the medicine, so I didn't howl against the dose, but kept on "good
behavior" the whole term.

When they let me out o' jail, I went straight to the charity
that had my boy in charge. I'd learned my lesson, and I
meant to live straight and decent when I got my boy again.
I could hardly wait to hold him in my arms. I couldn't

understand when they wouldn't let me see him. (*Intensely bitter*) I didn't know what charity meant then. (*With the resentment and despair of that morning in his voice*) They wouldn't even tell me where he was. All Hell let loose in me. I dunno just what happened. Even now it's all kind of dim and misty. I didn't realize nothin' until I found myself arrested and back in jail again.

I wouldn't have no lawyer when the case come up in court. I thought if I stood up man to man and told the judge my story he'd understand. I told it bad, I guess. I was still pretty young and the sobs kept chokin' in my throat and my hands was twistin' around my cap to keep them still. I told him why I'd done the things I done and how I meant to be different. I thought he *did* understand, I thought so. He seemed to hesitate a minute, and then I heard the sentence — two more years for me, and the boy give to charities for keeps. (*He rises*) That's all, except, the man who sentenced me was Judge Freeman. (*Bringing his hand down on table*) Damn him — damn him to Hell. [*Exit*.

NANCE (*raises hand, stares vacantly in a state of dazed despair. In a half whisper*). He don't know what he's doin'. He's crazy hatin' so. They'll take him away from me. Oh, Gawd! Oh, Gawd! Ain't love stronger'n hate? Ain't there somethin' I can do? (*Looks at child*) Poor little kid. If I could, I'd steal ye away from him and take ye back myself. (*Drops head on back of chair, sobbing*) Gawd! [*Quick indrawn breath. Her face has pressed against the morphine inside Jim's coat. She draws it out, rises, goes to door, locks it, takes down cups from shelf, gets whiskey bottle back of folding bed. She is breathing quickly. Jim is heard at the door.*

JIM. Open the door! D'ye hear, open, I say.

NANCE. Comin' right away, Jim. (*She empties contents of box into cup and pours out drinks. Jim shakes door angrily and kicks it with feet while this is going on. She opens door*) Gee, yer in a hurry.

JIM (*enters — looks about suspiciously*).   What did ye do that fer?

NANCE (*whose manner is now transformed to affected gaiety*). Why, I — I didn't want to chance some one walkin' in on me. (*He still looks suspicious; she laughs up in his face*) Not with twenty thousand lyin' there dozin' on the couch.

JIM.   All right — I've phoned to Louis.   He'll be here pretty soon to take the boy in charge.

NANCE (*laughing excitedly, with a touch of hysteria*).   I've been thinkin' over what ye told me, and I've changed my mind. The drinks is on me, Jim.   See, I've already poured 'em out. (*He starts to help himself*) No, ye take the cup, it holds more liquor.   To success, Jim!   And damn the Judge. (*They drink*) Gee, ye looks all in.   Sit down here by the fire while yer waitin' for Louis and I'll stir up some grub.

JIM.   It's a good thing ye come to yer senses.   I am pretty nearly all in.

[*Jim, after pouring himself another drink, flings himself into a chair.*

NANCE (*leaning over back of his chair*).   Close yer eyes and rest.   Ye needn't never be afraid to trust me, Jim; I wouldn't never do nothin' that wasn't fer yer good.

(*Nance moves softly about the room, sets table, interrupting the silence by low humming sounds; she glances frequently at Jim, waiting for the drug to take effect.   He begins to drowse almost at once, rouses himself as though startled at his own intense languor, and then falls into a heavy sleep. Nance gets shawl from hook, goes to child and shakes it gently. Child does not stir*).

Wake up, kid, wake up. (*Whispering*) I'm goin' to take ye back to yer governesses and ribboned nusses, to yer Jedges and satin canopies.   Wake up! Wake up! Ye lazy little lubber, ye don't expect me to carry ye that distance?   Gawd, there ain't much time!   Wake up! [*Glances uneasily at Jim, attempts to lift child.   Something about the limp form startles her.   She puts hand upon his face, draws back, her own face blanching, forces herself to feel his heart. She utters a piercing scream; it reaches Jim's drugged senses and he struggles to throw off the effect of the drug. He rises, staggering, collects his blurred senses.*

JIM. What is it? What is the matter with my head? I'm drunk. (*Looks at Nance who is standing in frozen attitude, staring at the child*) No, I'm not, drink never made me feel like this. What is it? I feel as if I'm drugged. [*He takes in the fact she is wearing outdoor clothes, and understands. Lunges at her in frenzied rage, his hands at her throat in strangling hold.*

JIM. Ye done this. Ye drugged me. You've got your street things on. Ye meant to steal the boy, ye she devil, ye female stool pidgeon — ye was going to double-cross me.

NANCE (*choking inarticulate*). Jim! Jim! the boy. [*Points with hand. He releases his hand so roughly that she is thrown upon the floor. He is about to turn and look at the boy when there is a pounding on the door. Enter officer and detective.*

JIM (*whipping out pistol from his pocket, insolent, defiant, snarling like an animal at bay*). All right, ye found me. Now take me.

DETECTIVE (*easily*). Oh, I guess not this time, Jim. Just give us the boy. The Judge has a sentimental prejudice against arresting a father for stealing his own child. [*Jim's figure crumples as the truth dawns upon him. He drops upon his knees beside the child, lifts the small body that is now hanging head downward, draws it into his arms, holding him close and hungrily, staring down into the white face. Suddenly his face presses against the child's, he sobs convulsive, racking sobs, that tell the audience the boy is dead. Nance drags herself like some faithful dog across to him until her head rests upon his foot.*

The curtain slowly falls.

BIBLIOGRAPHIES

1. THE LITTLE THEATRE MOVEMENT

IN AMERICA

Burleigh, Louise. "The Community Theatre." Little, Brown & Company, Boston, 1917.

Cheney, Sheldon. "The Art Theatre." Alfred A. Knopf, New York, 1917.

Dickinson, Thomas H. "The Insurgent Theatre." B. W. Huebsch, New York, 1917.

Mackay, Constance D'Arcy. "The Little Theatre in the United States." Henry Holt & Co., New York, 1917.

ABROAD

Bakshy, Alexander. "The Path of the Modern Russian Stage." Palmer & Hayward, London, 1916.

Boyd, E. A. "Contemporary Drama of Ireland." Little, Brown & Company, Boston, 1917.

Carter, Huntley. "The Theatre of Max Reinhardt." F. & C. Palmer, London, 1914.

Clark, Barrett H. "Four Plays of the Free Theatre" (Introduction). Stewart & Kidd, Cincinnati, 1915.

Dickinson, Thomas H. "Contemporary Drama of England." Little, Brown & Company, Boston, 1917.

Filon, Augustin. "De Dumas à Rostand." A. Colin, Paris, 1911.

Jullien, Jean. "Le Théâtre Vivant." G. Charpentier & E. Fasquele, Paris, 1892.

Long, R. E. C. "The People's Theatre in Russia." *Nineteenth Century*, Vol. 52, p. 775.

Mackay, Constance D'Arcy. "The Little Theatre in the United States" (Introduction). Henry Holt & Co., New York, 1917.

Thalasso, A. "Le Théâtre Libre." Mercure de France, Paris, 1909.

2. THE ONE–ACT PLAY

Corbin, John. "The One-Act Play." *New York Times*, May, 1918, § IV, p. 8, col. 1.

Eaton, Walter P. "Washington Square Plays" (Introduction). Doubleday, Page & Co., Garden City, 1916.

Gibbs, Clayton E. "The One-Act Play." *Theatre*, Vol. 23, 143, 156, March, 1916.

Goodman, Edward. "Why the One-Act Play." *Theatre*, Vol. 25, 327, June, 1917.

Hamilton, Clayton. "The One-Act Play in America." *Bookman*, April, 1913: "Studies in Stagecraft." Henry Holt & Co., New York, 1914.

Lewis, B. Roland. "The Technique of the One-Act Play." John W. Luce & Co., Boston, 1918.

Loving, Pierre. Introduction to "Comedies of Words", by Arthur Schnitzler. Stewart & Kidd, Cincinnati, 1917.

Middleton, George. "The Neglected One-Act Play." *Dramatic Mirror*, January 31, 1913, pp. 13–14, New York.

Moses, Montrose J. "The American Dramatist." Comment on the one-act play. Little, Brown & Company, Boston, 1917.

Underhill, John Garrett. "The One-Act Play in Spain." *Drama*, February, 1917.

3. BIBLIOGRAPHIES OF ONE–ACT PLAYS

Actable One-Act Plays. Chicago Public Library, 1916.

Cheney, Sheldon. "The Art Theatre." (Appendix: Plays produced at the Arts and Crafts Theatre, Detroit.) Alfred A. Knopf, New York, 1917.

Clapp, John Mantel. "Plays for Amateurs." Drama League of America, Chicago, 1915.

Clark, Barrett H. "How to Produce Amateur Plays." Little, Brown & Company, 1917.

Dickinson, Thomas H. "The Insurgent Theatre." (Appendix: List of plays produced by Little Theatres.) B. W. Huebsch, New York, 1917.

Drummond, A. M. "Fifty One-Act Plays." *Quarterly Journal of Public Speaking*, Vol. 1, p. 234. 1915.

Drummond, A. M. "One-Act Plays for Schools and Colleges." *Education*, Vol. 4, p. 372. 1918.

Mackay, Constance D'Arcy. "The Little Theatre in the United States." (Appendix: List of plays produced by Little Theatres.) Henry Holt & Co., New York, 1917.

Riley, Alice C. D. "The One-Act Play — Study Course." *Drama League Monthly*, February–April, 1918, Washington, D.C.

Selective List of Christmas Plays. *Drama League Calendar*, November 15, 1918. New York.

Selected List of Patriotic Plays and Pageants Suitable for Amateurs. *Drama League Calendar*, October 1, 1918. New York.

Selective List of Plays for Amateurs. Drama League, Boston, 1915.

4. SELECTIVE LIST OF AVAILABLE ONE–ACT PLAYS BY AMERICAN AUTHORS

Titles designated by † are collections.

Akins, Zoë. "Did It Really Happen?" Sophisticated drama. *Smart Set*, Vol. 52, 343. New York, 1917.

"The Magical City." Drama in free verse. *Forum*, Vol. 55, 507. New York, May, 1916.

"Such a Charming Young Man." Sophisticated comedy. *Smart Set*, Vol. 48, 67. New York, 1916.

Aldis, Mary. "Mrs. Pat and the Law" (included in this volume).

"The Drama Class of Tankaha, Nevada." Satirical comedy.

"Extreme Unction." Serious play on spiritism.

"The Letter." Play of ideas in which real and false love are demonstrated.

"Temperament." Humorous play on the subject of artistic temperaments.

(In "Plays for Small Stages." † Duffield, New York, 1915.)

Andrews, Kenneth. "America Passes By." Humorous sketch. Walter Baker & Co., Boston, 1918; (In "Plays of the Harvard Dramatic Club." † Brentano, New York, 1918.)

Bates, W. O. "Polly of Pogue's Run." Play of Civil War times in Indiana. Frank Shay, New York, 1917.

Beach, Lewis. "The Clod." Character drama. (In "Washington Square Plays." † Doubleday, Page & Co., Garden City, 1916.)

Belasco, David. "Madame Butterfly." Drama in the life of a Japanese. (In "Representative American Plays", † edited by A. H. Quinn, p. 649. The Century Co., New York, 1917.)

Block, Bertram. "The Maiden Over the Wall." Fantasy. *Drama*, Vol. 8, 436. Chicago, 1918.

Bodenheim, Maxwell. "The Master Poisoner" (in collaboration with Ben Hecht). A poetic play in which the woman is the master poisoner.

"Poet's Heart." An idyll of the poet's heart.

(In "Minna and Myself," † Pagan Publishing Co., New York, 1918.)

Bottomley, Gordon. "Laodice and Danaë." A poetic play, laid in Smyrna, 246 B.C. Four Seas Publishing Co., Boston, 1916.

Boyce, Neith. "The Two Sons." Drama. Frank Shay, New York, 1916.

"A Winter's Night." Drama. *Trend*, Vol. 7, 524–530. New York, 1914.

Briggs, Caroline. "One a Day." Comedy. (In "Morningside Plays." †
Frank Shay, New York, 1917.)

Brock, Howard. "The Bank Account." Serious play of money and
marriage.
(In "Plays of the Harvard Dramatic Club." † Brentano,
New York, 1918.)

Brown, Alice. "Dr. Auntie." Serious.
"Joint Owners in Spain." Comedy.
"The Loving Cup." Play of mingled pathos and humor.
"Melia's Tramp." Play of mingled pathos and humor.
"Milly Dear." Serious.
"The Web." Serious. Norman Lee Swartout, Summit,
N. J.

Browne, Maurice. "King of the Jews." Passion play. *Drama*, Vol. 6,
496. Chicago, 1916.

Bryant, Louise. "The Game." Morality. Frank Shay, New York, 1916.

Bynner, Witter. "The Little King." Story of the French Revolution.
Forum, Vol. 51, 605. New York, April, 1914; Mitchell Kennerley, New York, 1914.
"Tiger." Drama of the underworld. *Forum*, Vol. 49,
522. New York, May, 1913.

Cowan, Sada. "In the Morgue." Sordid drama. *Forum*, Vol. 55, 339.
New York, April, 1916.
"Sintram of Skagerrak" (included in this volume).
"The State Forbids." Serious presentation of the theme of
birth control. Mitchell Kennerley, New York, 1915.

Cronyn, George W. "The Sandbar Queen." Crass melodrama. E.
Arens, New York, 1918.

Dargan, O. T. "Woods of Ida." Masque of forty years before the Fall of
Troy. *Century*, Vol. 74, 590–604, August, 1907.

Davies, Mary Caroline. "The Slave with Two Faces." Morality. E.
Arens, New York, 1918.

Davis, R. H., and Sheehan, P. P. "Efficiency." Drama of the War.
George H. Doran, New York, 1917.

Dell, Floyd. "The Angel Intrudes." In which a man is saved by his
guardian angel from running away with a flirt. E.
Arens, New York, 1918.
"King Arthur's Socks." Sophisticated farce. Frank Shay,
New York, 1916.
"A Long Time Ago." Fantasy. *Forum*, Vol. 51, 261.
New York, February, 1914.

Dickinson, Thomas H. "In Hospital." Serious study. (In "Wisconsin
Plays," † Vol. I. B. W. Huebsch, New York, 1914.)

Dix, Beulah. "Allison's Lad" (included in this volume).

"The Hundredth Trick." Drama at the time of the reign of Elizabeth.

"The Weakest Link." Laid in Brittany during the Hundred Years' War.

"The Snare and the Fowler." Drama during the early days of the French Republic.

"The Dark of the Dawn." Drama of the Thirty Years' War.

(In "Allison's Lad and Other Martial Interludes." † Henry Holt & Co., New York, 1910.)

"Clemency." Serious play on the theme of war.

"The Enemy." Serious play of war.

"The Glorious Game." Serious play of war. American School Peace League, Boston, 1916.

"A Legend of St. Nicholas." Poetic drama for children. *Poet Lore*, Vol. 25, 473. Boston, 1914.

Dreiser, Theodore. "The Dream." Play of the natural and supernatural. *Seven Arts*, Vol. 2, 319. New York, 1917.

"The Girl in the Coffin." Naturalistic play of ideas.

"The Blue Sphere." Play of ideas upon the natural and the supernatural.

"Laughing Gas." Play of ideas upon the natural and the supernatural.

"In the Dark." Play of ideas upon the natural and the supernatural.

"The Spring Recital." Supernatural play on the power of music.

"The Light in the Window." Thoughtful presentation of the action which passes before a house in the city.

"Old Rag-Picker." Serious play.

(In "Plays of the Natural and Supernatural." † John Lane Co., New York, 1916.)

Field, Rachel L. "Rise up, Jennie Smith." Liberty Loan propaganda. Samuel French, New York, 1918.

"Three Pills in a Bottle." Moral fantasy in which real souls appear. (In "47 Workshop Plays."† Brentano, New York, 1918.)

Fillmore, J. E. "War." Melodrama. *Poet Lore*, Vol. 25, 523. Boston, 1914.

Flexner, Hortense. "Voices" (included in this volume).

"47 Workshop, Plays of the" † :

Field, Rachel L. "Three Pills in a Bottle."

Osborne, Hubert. "The Good Men Do."

Pillot, Eugene. "Two Crooks and a Lady."

Prosser, William L. "Free Speech." (See Authors for descriptions of plays.) Brentano, New York, 1918.

Frank, Florence Kiper. "Jael." Poetic drama of the Jewish life. Chicago Little Theatre, 1914.

Freybe, C. E. "In Garrison." Drama of garrison life at Christmas time. *Poet Lore*, Vol. 26, 499. Boston, 1915.

Froome, John Redhead, Jr. "Listening." Play built about a tense situation. *Poet Lore*, Vol. 28, 422. Boston, 1917.

Galbraith, Esther. "The Brink of Silence" (included in this volume).

Gale, Zona. "Neighbors." Comedy of rural life. (In "Wisconsin Plays," † Vol. 1. B. W. Huebsch, New York, 1914.)

Garland, Robert. "At Night All Cats Are Gray." Melodrama. *Smart Set*, Vol. 48, 247. New York, 1916.

"Double Miracle." Mystical drama of love and religion in Sicily. *Forum*, Vol. 53, 511. New York, April, 1915.

Gerstenberg, Alice. "Beyond" (included in this volume).

"Overtones." Unusual play involving the actors and their subconscious selves. (In "Washington Square Plays." † Doubleday, Page & Co., Garden City, 1916.)

Gilman, Thornton. "We Live Again." Serious play about religion. (In "Wisconsin Plays", † Vol. 2, B. W. Huebsch, 1918.)

Glaspell, Susan. "Close the Book." Farce.

"The People." In which "the banner of the ideal" is flown in a magazine office. Frank Shay, New York, 1918.

"Trifles." Drama inherent in trifles. Frank Shay, New York, 1916.

Glaspell, Susan, and Cook, George Cram. "Suppressed Desires" (included in this volume).

Goodman, Edward. "Eugenically Speaking." Farce. (In "Washington Square Plays." † Doubleday, Page & Co., Garden City, 1916.)

Goodman, Kenneth Sawyer. "Dust of the Road." Serious play with religious theme.

"The Game of Chess." Serious play set in Russia.

"Barbara." Satirical farce.

"Ephraim and the Winged Bear." Fantasy.

"Back of the Yards." Serious play of Chicago.

"Dancing Dolls." Dolls in their off-stage moments.

"A Man Can Only Do His Best." Farce.
    (In "Quick Curtains." † Stage Guild, Chicago, 1915.)

Goodman, Kenneth Sawyer, and Ben Hecht. "The Hero of Santa Maria."
    Farce of a country town. Stage Guild, Chicago, 1916.

Goodman, Kenneth Sawyer, and Thomas Wood Stevens. "Holbein in
    Blackfriars." Comedy of the sixteenth century in
    England. Stage Guild, Chicago, 1913.

Gould, Felix. "The Marsh Maiden," "The Stranger," "In the Marshes."
    Plays of mood and symbol.
    (In "The Marsh Maiden and Other Plays," † Four Seas
    Publishing Co., Boston, 1918.)

Halman, Doris. "Will o' the Wisp" (included in this volume).

"Harvard Dramatic Club, Plays of the ": †
    Hawkridge, Winifred. "The Florist Shop."
    Brock, Howard. "The Bank Account."
    Smith, Rita C. "The Rescue."
    Andrews, Kenneth. "America Passes By." (See Authors
    for descriptions of plays.) Brentano, New York,
    1918.

Hawkridge, Winifred. "The Florist Shop." Humorous play of life as
    seen in a florist shop. (In "Plays of the Harvard
    Dramatic Club." † Brentano, New York, 1918.)

Hecht, Ben, and Kenneth Sawyer Goodman. "The Wonder Hat" (in-
    cluded in this volume).

Helburn, Theresa. "Enter the Hero." Farce, but embodying a psycho-
    logical truth. E. Arens, New York, 1918.

Hoffman, Phoebe. "Martha's Mourning" (included in this volume).

Ilsley, S. Marshall. "The Feast of the Holy Innocents." Comedy of
    rural life. (In "Wisconsin Plays", † Vol. 2. B. W.
    Huebsch, New York, 1918.)

Jex, John. "Violet Souls." A satire upon the affinity theme.
    "The Nest." A serious play in which the Doctor censures
    the husband's immorality.
    "Mr. Willoughly Calls." A serious play in which opportu-
    nity to marry the man she loves does not come to the
    woman a second time.
    "The Unnecessary Atom." A tragedy in which a man's
    hopes, ambitions, and achievements collapse with the
    disintegration of his home life.
    (In "Passion Playlets", † Cornhill Company, Detroit, 1918.)

Jones, Howard Mumford. "The Shadow." Arabesque. (In "Wisconsin
    Plays", † Vol. 2. B. W. Huebsch, New York, 1918.)

Kallen, Horace M. "Book of Job." Tragedy of the Book of Job. Moffatt,
    Yard & Co., New York, 1918.

Kemp, Harry. "The Prodigal Son." Comedy of the prodigal son. *Smart Set*, Vol. 52, 83. New York, 1917.

Kennedy, Charles Rann. "The Terrible Meek." Religious drama. Harper & Bros., New York, 1912.

       "The Necessary Evil." Sentimental melodrama. Harper & Bros., New York, 1913.

King, Pendleton. "Cocaine." Sordid melodrama. Frank Shay, New York, 1918.

Kinkead, Cleves. "The Fourflushers." Farce of New York life. Norman Lee Swartout, Summit, N. J., 1918.

Kreymborg, Alfred. "When the Willow Nods." Dance-play.

       "Jack's House." Cubic-play.

       "Lima Beans" (included in this volume).

       "Blue and Green." Shadow-play.

       "Manikin and Minikin." Bisque-play.

       "People Who Die." Dream-play.

       (In "Plays for Poem Mimes." † The Other Press, New York, 1918.)

Langner, Lawrence. "Another Way Out." Sophisticated farce. Frank Shay, New York, 1916.

       "Wedded." Serious study. *Little Review*, Vol. 1, No. 8, p. 8. Chicago, 1914.

       "The Broken Image." Wherein the image of Christ is broken by Von Ludendorf. Egmont Arens, New York, 1918.

Leland, Robert DeCamp. "Purple Youth." Satire in which two artist-lovers trap the "Puritan." Four Seas Co., Boston, 1918.

Leonard, William Ellery. "Glory of the Morning." Play of Indian life. (In "Wisconsin Plays," † Vol. 1. B. W. Huebsch, New York, 1914.)

Levinger, Elmer. "The Burden." Serious play of Jewish life. Walter Baker & Co., Boston, 1918.

Macdonald, Zillah. "Light Along the Rails." Drama of the New York subway. *Touchstone*, Vol. 3, 229. New York, 1918.

       "Markheim." Dramatization. (In "Morningside Plays." † Frank Shay, New York, 1917.)

Mackay, Constance D'Arcy. "Festival of Pomona." Story of the Greek myth of Pomona and Vertumnus. *Drama*, Vol. 5, 161. Chicago, 1915.

       "The Gift of Time." Masque for the New Year.

       "A Masque of Conservation." Of forests and of rivers.

       "The Masque of Pomona." Masque for spring or autumn.

       "The Sun Goddess." Masque of Old Japan.

(In "The Forest Princess and Other Masques." † Henry
Holt & Co., New York, 1916.)

"The Beau of Bath"; "The Silver Lining"; "Ashes of
Roses"; "Gretna Green"; "Counsel Retained";
"The Prince of Court Painters." One-act plays of
18th-century life.
(In "The Beau of Bath and Other One-Act Plays." †
Henry Holt & Co., New York, 1915.)

"The Pioneers"; "The Fountain of Youth"; "May Day";
"The Vanishing Race"; "The Passing of Hiawatha";
"Dame Greel o' Portland Town." Historical pageant
plays. (In "Plays of the Pioneers." † Harper &
Bros., New York, 1915.)

MacKaye, Percy. "Chuck." Orchard fantasy.
"Gettysburg." Woodshed commentary.
"The Antick." Wayside sketch.
"The Cat-Boat." Fantasy for music.
"Sam Average" (included in this volume).
(In "Yankee Fantasies." † Duffield & Co., New York,
1912.)

Mapes, Victor. "Flower of Yeddo." Noh of old Japan. Samuel French,
New York, 1906.

Marks, Jeannette A. "The Merry, Merry Cuckoo" (included in this
volume).
"The Deacon's Hat." Play of peasant religion in Wales.
"Welsh Honeymoon." Play of Welsh superstition on
Allhallows' Eve.
(In "Three Welsh Plays." † Little, Brown & Company,
Boston, 1917.)

Matthews, Elva DePue. "Hattie" (included in this volume).

McFadden, Elizabeth. "Why the Chimes Rang." Poetic story of Christmas and the Christ Child. Samuel French, New
York, 1915.

Middleton, George. "Back of the Ballot." Woman suffrage farce
Samuel French, New York, 1915.
"Criminals." Play about marriage. B. W. Huebsch,
New York, 1915.

"Embers"; "The Failures"; "The Gargoyle"; "In His
House"; "Madonna"; "The Man Masterful."
Serious plays of contemporary life.
(In "Embers and Other One-Act Plays." † Henry
Holt & Co., New York, 1911.)

"The Groove"; "The Unborn"; "Circles"; "A Good Woman" (included in this volume); "The Black Tie." Serious plays of contemporary life.

(In "Possession and Other One-Act Plays." † Henry Holt & Co., New York, 1915.)

"The Reason." Serious play. *Smart Set*, Vol. 53, 89. New York, 1917.

"Tradition"; "On Bail"; "Their Wife"; "Waiting"; "The Cheat of Pity"; "Mothers." Serious plays of contemporary life.

(In "Tradition and Other One-Act Plays." † Henry Holt & Co., New York, 1913.)

Moeller, Philip. "Helena's Husband"; "A Roadhouse in Arden"; "Sisters of Susannah"; "The Little Supper"; "Pokey." Burlesques.

(In "Five Somewhat Historical Plays." † Alfred A. Knopf, New York, 1918.)

"Two Blind Beggars and One Less Blind." Symbolic play. E. Arens, New York, 1918.

"Morningside Plays" † :

DePue, Elva. "Hattie."

Briggs, C. "One a Day."

Macdonald, Zellah. "Markheim."

Reizenstein, Elmer L. "The Home of the Free." (See Authors for descriptions of plays.) Frank Shay, New York, 1917.

Mosher, John Chapin. "Sauce for the Emperor." Burlesque. Frank Shay, New York, 1916.

O'Neill, Eugene G. "Before Breakfast." Tragedy. Frank Shay, New York, 1916.

"Bound East for Cardiff." Tale of the sea. Frank Shay, New York, 1916.

"In the Zone" (included in this volume).

"The Long Voyage Home." Serious play of seamen on land. *Smart Set*, Vol. 53, 83. New York, 1917.

"The Moon of the Caribbees." Seamen in the forecastle. *Smart Set*, Vol. 55, 73. New York, 1918.

"Thirst." Impressionistic drama on the theme of thirst.

"The Web." Melodramatic episode of sordid life.

"Warnings." Dramatic episodes of the sea.

"Fog." Symbolic play of a life-boat in the open sea.

"Recklessness." A drama of love and marriage. (In

"Thirst and Other One-Act Plays." † Gorham Press, Boston, 1914.)

Oppenheim, James. "Night." Thoughtful, poetic play in free verse. E. Arens, New York, 1918.

"Prelude." (To Creation.) Mystical and pictorial play in verse. *Seven Arts*, Vol. 1, 240, 1917.

Osborne, Hubert. "The Good Men Do." In which Shakespeare's plays are interred with his bones. (In "47 Workshop Plays." † Brentano, New York, 1918.)

O'Shea, Monica Barrie. "The Rushlight." Drama laid in Ireland during the Rebellion. *Drama*, Vol. 7, 602. Chicago, 1917.

Peabody, Josephine Preston. "Fortune and Men's Eyes." A tale of Shakespeare. Samuel French, New York, 1917.

"The Wings." Poetic drama of Northumberland in 700 A.D. *Harper*, Vol. 110, 947. New York, 1905; *Poet Lore*, Vol. 25, 352. Boston, 1914.

Pillot, Eugene. "Hunger" (included in this volume).

"Two Crooks and a Lady." Unusual presentation of crook melodrama. (In "47 Workshop Plays." † Brentano, New York, 1918.)

Prosser, William L. "Free Speech." Farce on law and order in Russia. (In "47 Workshop Plays." † Brentano, New York, 1918.)

Provincetown Plays, Series 1 †:

O'Neill, Eugene G. "Bound East for Cardiff."

Bryant, Louise. "The Game."

Dell, Floyd. "King Arthur's Socks."

Series 2. Glaspell, Susan, and George Cram Cook. "Suppressed Desires."

Series 3.

Boyce, Neith. "The Two Sons."

Kreymborg, Alfred. "Lima Beans."

O'Neill, Eugene G. "Before Breakfast."

(See Authors for descriptions of plays.) Frank Shay, New York.

Reizenstein, Elmer L. "The Home of the Free." Sophisticated comedy. (In "Morningside Plays." † Frank Shay, New York, 1917.)

Rice, Cale Young. "Giorgione." Drama of love in Italy.

"Arduin." Drama of love in Egypt.

"O-Umè's Gods." Love drama of Japan.

"The Immortal Lure." Love drama in India.

(In "The Immortal Lure and Other Poetic Dramas." † Doubleday, Page & Co., Garden City, 1911.)

"A Night in Avignon." Poetic drama of love and marriage.
(In "Collected Plays and Poems." † Doubleday, Page & Co., Garden City, 1915.)

Rice, Wallace, and Thomas Wood Stevens. "Chaplet of Pan." Masque of a May Day in the 15th century. Stage Guild, Chicago, 1912.

Rogers, Robert Emmons. "Behind a Watteau Picture." Fantasy. Norman Lee Swartout, Summit, N. J.

Sherry, Laura. "On the Pier." Serious play. (In "Wisconsin Plays",† Vol. 2. B. W. Huebsch, New York, 1918.)

Smith, Rita C. "The Rescue." Serious play in which mind rules matter. (In "Plays of the Harvard Dramatic Club." † Brentano, New York, 1918.)

Spencer, Frances Pemberton. "Dregs" (included in this volume).

Stevens, Thomas Wood, and Kenneth Sawyer Goodman. "The Daimio's Head." Masque of old Japan.
"The Masque of Montezuma."
"Caesar's Gods." Byzantine masque.
"Rainald and the Red Wolf." Mediæval masque of the Shrovetide miracle.
"The Masque of Quetzal's Bowl."
(In "Masques of East and West." † Vaughan and Gomme, New York, 1914.)

Stevens, Thomas Wood, and Kenneth Sawyer Goodman. "Ryland" (included in this volume).

Stratton, Clarence. "The Coda." Serious play. *Drama*, Vol. 8, 215. Chicago, 1918.

Tarkington, Booth. "Beauty and the Jacobin." Interlude of the French Revolution. *Harper*, Vol. 125, 390. New York, 1912; Harper & Bros., New York, 1912.

Torrence, Ridgely, "The Rider of Dreams." Poetic drama of negro life.
"Granny Maumee." Poetic tragedy of negro life.
"Simon the Cyrenian." Biblical play.
(In "The Rider of Dreams, and Other One-Act Plays." † Macmillan, New York, 1917.)

Walker, Stuart. "The Trimplet"; "Nevertheless"; "The Medicine Show"; "Six Who Pass While the Lentils Boil" (included in this volume). Fantasies.
(In "Portmanteau Plays." † Stewart & Kidd, Cincinnati, 1917.)

"Washington Square Plays" † :
Beach, Lewis. "The Clod."
Goodman, Edward. "Eugenically Speaking."

Gerstenberg, Alice. "Overtones."

Moeller, Philip. "Helena's Husband." (See Authors for descriptions of plays.) Doubleday, Page & Co., Garden City, 1918.

Wellman, Rita. "Funiculi Funicula" (included in this volume).

"The Lady with the Mirror." Allegory. *Drama*, Vol. 8, 299. Chicago, 1918.

Wentworth, Marion Craig. "War Brides." Play of the War. The Century Co., New York, 1915.

Wilde, Percival. "Confessional." Serious play.

"The Villain in the Piece." Dramatic situation

"According to Darwin." Naturalistic play of sordid life.

"A Question of Morality" (included in this volume).

"The Beautiful Story." Thoughtful play.

(In "Confessional and Other American Plays." † Henry Holt & Co., New York, 1916.)

"Dawn." Drama of the dawn after death.

"The Noble Lord." Artificial comedy.

"The Traitors." Surprise drama.

"A House of Cards." Surprise play.

"Playing with Fire." Comedy.

"The Finger of God." Serious.

(In "Dawn and Other One-Act Plays." † Henry Holt & Co., New York, 1915.)

"Mothers of Men"; "Pawns"; "In the Ravine"; "Valkyrie." Plays giving different viewpoints on the War.

(In "The Unseen Host, and Other War Plays." † Little, Brown & Company, Boston, 1917.)

"Wisconsin Plays." † Series 1:

Gale, Zona. "Neighbors."

Dickinson, Thomas H. "In Hospital."

Leonard, W. E. "Glory of the Morning." (See Authors for descriptions of plays.) B. W. Huebsch, New York, 1914.

Series 2:

Ilsley, Marshall. "The Feast of the Holy Innocents."

Sherry, Laura. "On the Pier."

Jones, Howard Mumford. "The Shadow."

Gilman, Thornton. "We Live Again." (See Authors for descriptions of plays.) B. W. Huebsch, New York, 1918.

Wolff, Oscar M. "Where But in America" (included in this volume).